XeLaTeX Secrets

Hunter C. Johnson

ISBN: 978-1-998557-00-4
Imprint: Telephasic Workshop
Copyright © 2024 Hunter C. Johnson.
All Rights Reserved.

Contents

Introduction to XeLaTeX

What is XeLaTeX?

History of XeLaTeX

XeLaTeX, also known as XeTeX, is a powerful typesetting system that is widely used for creating high-quality documents. It is an extension of the LaTeX typesetting system, which was developed by Leslie Lamport in the early 1980s. LaTeX quickly became popular among scientists, researchers, and academics for its ability to produce well-formatted documents with mathematical equations and complex structures.

In the early years of LaTeX, the system primarily supported the Computer Modern font family, which was created by Donald Knuth for use with his TeX typesetting system. However, as more users began to adopt LaTeX for different purposes, the need for additional font options and support for non-Latin scripts became apparent.

XeLaTeX was born out of the desire to address these limitations. It was developed by Jonathan Kew in the early 2000s as an extension of the original TeX typesetting system. XeLaTeX introduced several key features that made it a preferred choice for many users:

- **Unicode Support:** Unlike traditional TeX engines, which had limitations in handling characters from different scripts, XeLaTeX fully embraced Unicode. This meant that users could easily typeset documents in multiple languages, including those with non-Latin scripts, without the need for workarounds or complex font configurations.

- **Font Flexibility:** XeLaTeX allowed users to seamlessly integrate system fonts into their documents. This meant that instead of being limited to the Computer Modern font family, users could choose from a wide range of fonts available on their operating system, including TrueType, OpenType, and PostScript fonts. This greatly expanded the design possibilities and improved the overall aesthetic of the documents.

- **Advanced Typography:** With XeLaTeX, users gained access to advanced typographic features, such as ligatures, kerning, and special characters. These features allowed for more refined and visually appealing typesetting, making XeLaTeX a preferred choice for professionals in the publishing, design, and typography industries.

- **Simplified Font Handling:** XeLaTeX introduced a straightforward method for font loading and usage. Users could easily specify fonts using their names or file paths directly in the LaTeX document, eliminating the need for complex font installation procedures or configuration files.

The development of XeLaTeX opened new possibilities in typesetting and document design. Its ability to handle a wide range of fonts, support multiple languages, and produce high-quality output made it a valuable tool for various applications, including scientific papers, technical documentation, and even artistic typography.

Today, XeLaTeX continues to be actively maintained and updated by a dedicated community of developers. It has gained widespread adoption in different fields and is often the tool of choice for professionals and academics who require precise control over document layout, advanced typography, and support for multilingual content.

As with any software, the evolution of XeLaTeX has been driven by the needs and feedback of its users. The development team continues to refine and improve the system, ensuring that it remains a reliable and efficient tool for typesetting complex documents.

In the next section, we will explore the key differences between XeLaTeX and the original LaTeX system, highlighting the advantages and disadvantages of using XeLaTeX for various typesetting tasks.

Differences between XeLaTeX and LaTeX

In this section, we will explore the key differences between XeLaTeX and LaTeX, which are two popular document preparation systems based on the TeX typesetting language. Although they share some similarities, there are some fundamental differences that set them apart. Understanding these differences will help you decide which system is better suited to your needs.

Character Encoding

One major difference between XeLaTeX and LaTeX lies in their approach to character encoding. LaTeX uses the ASCII character set by default and has limited support for non-English characters and scripts. On the other hand, XeLaTeX fully supports the Unicode standard, which means that it can handle a vast range of characters from different writing systems, including non-Latin scripts like Cyrillic, Chinese, Japanese, and more.

The ability of XeLaTeX to support Unicode simplifies the handling of multilingual and multicultural documents. It allows you to seamlessly incorporate text from different languages into your document without needing to resort to complicated workarounds.

Font Support

Another key difference between XeLaTeX and LaTeX is their handling of fonts. LaTeX relies on the original TeX font system, which can be quite complex and limited in terms of font selection. It requires the use of specialized font packages and font metrics to make fonts available for use in documents.

In contrast, XeLaTeX takes advantage of modern font technologies and provides native support for TrueType and OpenType fonts. This means that you can use any font installed on your system directly in your XeLaTeX document. The ability to choose from a wide range of high-quality fonts makes XeLaTeX particularly appealing for designers and users working on visually rich or typography-driven publications.

Language Support

XeLaTeX showcases significant improvements in language support compared to LaTeX. While LaTeX provides various language-specific packages for typesetting multilingual documents, it often requires additional setup and can be cumbersome to work with.

XeLaTeX, with its built-in Unicode support, makes it easier to typeset documents in different languages. It allows you to use different scripts and provides better support for complex scripts, such as Arabic or Devanagari, which include features like bidirectional text and ligatures. Additionally, XeLaTeX also supports OpenType features, allowing for advanced typographic control in various languages.

Graphics and Multimedia

When it comes to including graphics and multimedia in documents, XeLaTeX offers more flexibility and capabilities compared to LaTeX. LaTeX relies on the EPS (Encapsulated PostScript) format for graphics inclusion, which can be restrictive and sometimes require additional conversion steps.

XeLaTeX, on the other hand, supports a wide range of image formats, including PDF, PNG, and JPG, making it much more versatile when it comes to including graphics in your documents. Additionally, XeLaTeX also provides support for multimedia elements, such as audio and video, allowing you to create interactive and engaging documents.

System Integration

One of the advantages of XeLaTeX is its seamless integration with modern operating systems. XeLaTeX can directly access system fonts, making it easier to work with and manage fonts within your document. It also supports advanced features like system-installed language environments, allowing for better integration with system libraries and tools.

In contrast, LaTeX, being an older system, may require additional configuration and workarounds to access system resources or use modern features. This makes XeLaTeX a more user-friendly and convenient choice for many users.

Compatibility with Legacy LaTeX

Despite the differences mentioned, XeLaTeX remains highly compatible with LaTeX. Most LaTeX documents can be compiled successfully with XeLaTeX without many modifications. The majority of LaTeX packages and functionality are also compatible with XeLaTeX, ensuring that the transition from LaTeX to XeLaTeX is relatively smooth.

However, it is worth noting that some complex LaTeX documents or packages that rely heavily on specific LaTeX features may require adjustments or modifications to work correctly with XeLaTeX. It is always a good practice to thoroughly test your documents when transitioning from LaTeX to XeLaTeX.

In summary, XeLaTeX offers several advantages over LaTeX, such as native Unicode support, enhanced font handling, better language support, improved graphics and multimedia capabilities, and seamless system integration. These features make XeLaTeX a compelling choice for users who require advanced typographic control, support for non-Latin scripts, or integration with modern operating systems. However, it is crucial to assess your specific requirements and consider compatibility issues when deciding between XeLaTeX and LaTeX for your projects.

For more information and guidance on transitioning from LaTeX to XeLaTeX, we recommend consulting the official documentation and online resources available.

Advantages of using XeLaTeX

XeLaTeX, a powerful typesetting system based on LaTeX, offers several advantages over traditional LaTeX and other document processing tools. In this section, we explore the unique benefits of using XeLaTeX for creating professional documents, from enhanced typography to multilingual support.

Enhanced Typography

One of the key advantages of using XeLaTeX is its exceptional support for modern typography. XeLaTeX provides extensive font handling capabilities, allowing you to use any TrueType or OpenType font directly in your documents. This means you can take advantage of a wide range of high-quality fonts available on your system, including custom and non-Latin scripts fonts.

Moreover, XeLaTeX includes robust features for fine-tuning letter-spacing, kerning, and tracking, enabling precise control over the spacing between characters. This results in visually appealing and professional-looking documents. You can also enrich your typography by using ligatures and special characters supported by the fonts you select.

Additionally, XeLaTeX provides advanced typesetting techniques such as hyphenation and justification, ensuring improved readability and aesthetics. With its comprehensive support for complex scripts and writing systems, including bidirectional typesetting, XeLaTeX is an ideal choice for multilingual documents with diverse typography requirements.

Unicode Support and Multilingual Typesetting

One of the major advantages of XeLaTeX over LaTeX is its native Unicode support. XeLaTeX fully embraces Unicode, making it easier to typeset documents in multiple languages. In LaTeX, you often need to rely on external tools and packages to handle non-Latin characters, which can be complex and cumbersome. XeLaTeX, on the other hand, handles Unicode characters seamlessly, eliminating the need for workarounds.

With XeLaTeX, you can easily typeset documents in languages with non-Latin scripts such as Chinese, Arabic, and Devanagari. It provides comprehensive support for complex scripts, including bidirectional typesetting for languages such as Hebrew and Arabic. XeLaTeX also allows you to customize language-specific typographic rules, enabling accurate formatting for various languages.

Moreover, XeLaTeX simplifies the process of incorporating multilingual content into your documents. You can seamlessly switch between different languages within a single document, applying language-specific features such as hyphenation patterns and quotation styles. This makes XeLaTeX an excellent choice for international collaborations, academic papers with multilingual abstracts, or documents requiring translations.

Integration with External Tools and APIs

XeLaTeX offers seamless integration with external tools and APIs, increasing its flexibility and enhancing workflow automation. Through the use of packages and custom scripts, you can easily include data from external sources, automate repetitive tasks, and generate dynamic content directly within your documents.

For example, you can use the `biblatex` package to incorporate bibliographic databases into your XeLaTeX documents, making it easy to manage and update references. You can also leverage the power of external tools like Git and GitHub for version control, Overleaf for collaborative editing, and content management systems for seamless integration with web publishing workflows.

Furthermore, XeLaTeX enables you to interact with APIs to dynamically fetch data, generate charts and graphs, or incorporate real-time information into your documents. This makes it possible to create dynamic reports, visualize data, and automate the generation of documents with up-to-date information.

Tight Integration with LaTeX Ecosystem

Another advantage of using XeLaTeX is its seamless compatibility with the vast LaTeX ecosystem. XeLaTeX can directly use LaTeX packages and libraries, allowing you to leverage the extensive collection of tools, templates, and resources available in the LaTeX community.

By harnessing the power of well-established LaTeX packages, you can easily implement complex mathematical equations, create tables and figures, manage bibliographies, and generate professional-looking documents. Whether you are writing scientific papers, technical reports, or academic theses, XeLaTeX provides a wide range of resources and support for various document types and formats.

Furthermore, XeLaTeX's compatibility with existing LaTeX code ensures a smooth transition for users already familiar with LaTeX. You can reuse your existing LaTeX documents and templates, minimizing the effort required to migrate to XeLaTeX while taking advantage of its enhanced capabilities.

Extensive Customization and Styling

XeLaTeX empowers you with extensive customization options, enabling you to create unique and visually appealing documents tailored to your specific needs. You can customize document styles, define macros and custom commands, and create and manage your own document classes and packages.

Moreover, XeLaTeX enables you to create and incorporate custom fonts and font families, allowing for unparalleled flexibility in document design. From selecting the perfect font to applying advanced typographic features, XeLaTeX puts you in complete control of the visual elements of your document.

In addition to font customization, XeLaTeX provides fine-grained control over page layout, including margins, headers, and footers. You can also insert figures, create tables, add annotations, and customize cross-referencing within your documents. This level of customization ensures that your document not only conveys information effectively but also reflects your personal style and preferences.

Community Support and Extendability

XeLaTeX benefits from the strong LaTeX community support and the vast collection of packages and resources available. The LaTeX community actively maintains and develops new packages, ensuring continuous enhancements and updates to the LaTeX ecosystem. XeLaTeX users can tap into this extensive knowledge base, accessing a wealth of tutorials, examples, and expert advice.

Furthermore, XeLaTeX's extendability makes it possible to add new features and functionalities tailored to specific requirements. You can create and share your own packages and document classes, contributing to the community and enriching the LaTeX ecosystem.

With its active community and vibrant ecosystem, XeLaTeX offers continuous support, advancements, and solutions to users, making it an excellent choice for professional document preparation.

Summary

In this section, we have explored the advantages of using XeLaTeX for professional document preparation. We have seen how XeLaTeX provides enhanced typography features, including extensive font handling and advanced typesetting techniques. Its native Unicode support enables seamless multilingual typesetting, making it easier to create documents with diverse languages and scripts.

XeLaTeX's integration with external tools and APIs enhances its flexibility and automation capabilities. Its tight compatibility with the LaTeX ecosystem further extends its functionality and offers a wide range of resources and support. XeLaTeX also allows extensive customization and styling options, empowering users to create visually appealing and unique documents.

With its active community and rich ecosystem, XeLaTeX ensures continuous advancements and robust solutions to meet the diverse needs of professional document preparation. With its numerous advantages, XeLaTeX proves to be an excellent choice for a wide range of document types, from scientific papers to multilingual publications.

Disadvantages of using XeLaTeX

XeLaTeX is a powerful typesetting system that offers many advantages over traditional LaTeX. However, it also has a few disadvantages that users should be aware of. In this section, we will explore some of the limitations and challenges that you may encounter when using XeLaTeX.

Limited package compatibility

One of the main disadvantages of XeLaTeX is its limited compatibility with packages designed for LaTeX. While XeLaTeX boasts an extensive range of packages and libraries, it may not be compatible with all the packages that were originally created for LaTeX. This can be especially problematic if you heavily rely on specific packages that are not supported by XeLaTeX.

To mitigate this issue, you can search for alternative packages that are specifically designed for XeLaTeX or try to adapt existing LaTeX packages for use with XeLaTeX. However, this requires some effort and may not always be possible.

Lack of backward compatibility

XeLaTeX is known for its great font and Unicode support, but this comes at the cost of limited backward compatibility with older LaTeX documents. XeLaTeX expects documents to be written in UTF-8 encoding, which can cause issues if you try to compile documents that were originally written in a different encoding.

Additionally, certain commands and macros that work in regular LaTeX may not be supported in XeLaTeX or may behave differently. Consequently, you may need to modify your existing LaTeX documents to make them compatible with XeLaTeX, which can be time-consuming, especially for large projects.

Slower compilation times

Compared to regular LaTeX, XeLaTeX has longer compilation times, particularly for complex documents. This is primarily due to the additional processing required for its advanced font handling and Unicode support. The more complex the document, the more time it will take to compile.

To mitigate this issue, you can try to optimize your document by removing unnecessary code, reducing the number of included packages, and simplifying the use of fonts. Additionally, you can make use of tools like incremental compilation to only compile the parts of the document that have been modified, rather than the entire document.

Limited community support

While XeLaTeX has gained popularity in recent years, it still has a smaller user base compared to regular LaTeX. As a result, the community support and available resources for XeLaTeX may be more limited. Finding answers to specific questions or troubleshooting issues may be more challenging, especially for niche or specialized topics.

To overcome this limitation, it is advisable to seek help from forums, mailing lists, or online communities that specifically focus on XeLaTeX. By engaging with other XeLaTeX users, you can share knowledge, discuss problems, and find solutions to common issues.

Lesser control over microtypography

Microtypography refers to the finer typographic adjustments that can enhance the appearance of documents. Unfortunately, XeLaTeX provides less control over microtypography compared to some other modern typesetting systems.

For instance, certain microtypographic features like hanging punctuation, optical margin alignment, and font expansion are not fully supported by default in XeLaTeX. While there are workarounds and packages available to partially address these issues, the level of control and finesse may still be limited.

In conclusion, while XeLaTeX offers many benefits, such as advanced font support, Unicode compatibility, and extended language support, it also comes with a few drawbacks. These include limited package compatibility, challenges with backward compatibility, slower compilation times, limited community support, and lesser control over microtypography. However, with careful consideration and workarounds, these limitations can often be overcome, allowing you to leverage the unique features and advantages of XeLaTeX for your projects.

Common use cases for XeLaTeX

XeLaTeX is a powerful tool that offers various advantages over traditional LaTeX. It is widely used in many different scenarios, catering to diverse needs across different fields. In this section, we will explore some of the common use cases for XeLaTeX.

Academic Writing

One of the primary use cases for XeLaTeX is academic writing. XeLaTeX provides excellent support for mathematical equations and scientific notations, making it an ideal choice for writing research papers, theses, dissertations, and technical reports.

With its Unicode support, XeLaTeX allows you to typeset documents in multiple languages, including those with non-Latin scripts or complex writing systems. This makes it suitable for multilingual academic writing, where you may need to incorporate various languages or include translations.

Moreover, XeLaTeX offers extensive customization options for formatting and typesetting scientific and technical content. It provides robust support for mathematical equations and expressions, allowing you to create complex formulas with ease. Additionally, XeLaTeX's font selection capabilities enable you to choose from a wide range of professional fonts, ensuring a polished and professional look for your academic documents.

Book Publishing

XeLaTeX is an excellent tool for book publishing, allowing you to create professional-quality documents with sophisticated typography and layout. Its extensive font support enables you to choose from a vast collection of fonts, including system fonts and custom fonts, that can greatly enhance the visual appeal of your book.

With XeLaTeX, you can easily create and format various elements of a book, such as title pages, chapter headings, section numbers, table of contents, and indices. The fine-tuning options available in XeLaTeX allow you to adjust letter-spacing, kerning, and tracking, resulting in visually pleasing and aesthetically consistent typography throughout the book.

Additionally, XeLaTeX provides features for advanced layout techniques, such as implementing grid systems and modular design, which can be particularly useful for designing complex book layouts. You can create visually appealing magazine and newspaper layouts, implement advanced typesetting effects, and design brochures and promotional materials.

Presentation Slides

XeLaTeX is not limited to traditional print media; it can also be used for creating professional presentation slides. With its capabilities for precise typesetting and advanced typography, XeLaTeX offers an alternative to popular presentation software, allowing you to design visually appealing and content-rich slides.

One of the advantages of using XeLaTeX for presentations is its support for LaTeX packages and libraries. These packages provide additional functionality, such as creating complex mathematical equations, including graphics and multimedia, and customizing the presentation layout. XeLaTeX's font selection capabilities also enable you to utilize a wide range of professional fonts to enhance the visual appeal of your slides.

Moreover, XeLaTeX allows you to create interactive presentations with JavaScript, incorporating interactive elements and animations. This can be particularly useful for delivering engaging and dynamic presentations that go beyond the limitations of traditional slide-based presentations.

Web Publishing

In the era of digital content, XeLaTeX can be a powerful tool for web publishing. With its ability to generate PDF output, XeLaTeX allows you to publish high-quality documents on the web that retain the professional typesetting and layout of print media.

XeLaTeX provides features for creating responsive designs for web and mobile, ensuring that your documents look great on different devices and screen sizes. Additionally, XeLaTeX supports the inclusion of interactive and multimedia elements, allowing you to create engaging and interactive web content.

Furthermore, XeLaTeX offers options for optimizing documents for web and mobile performance, such as minimizing file size and improving rendering speed. It also provides features for creating accessible documents, ensuring that your content is available to a wide range of users, including those with disabilities.

Creative Writing

While XeLaTeX is commonly associated with technical and academic writing, it can also be a valuable tool for creative writing. With its extensive font support and advanced typography features, XeLaTeX allows you to create visually stunning documents that reflect your creative vision.

Whether you are writing a novel, a collection of poems, or a graphic novel, XeLaTeX offers customization options for formatting and typesetting that can enhance the visual appeal of your work. You can experiment with different fonts, layouts, and typesetting effects to create a unique and visually captivating document.

Additionally, XeLaTeX's support for non-Latin scripts and complex writing systems enables you to incorporate various languages and writing styles in your creative writing. This can be particularly useful if you are writing multilingual or culturally diverse works.

In conclusion, XeLaTeX is a versatile typesetting system with a wide range of applications. From academic writing to book publishing, presentation slides to web publishing, and even creative writing, XeLaTeX offers powerful features and customization options that cater to diverse use cases. Its ability to handle complex equations, support multiple languages, and provide fine-tuned typography make it a go-to choice for many professionals in different fields. Whether you are a scientist, researcher, author, or designer, XeLaTeX can help you produce visually stunning and professionally typeset documents.

Setting up XeLaTeX environment

Setting up the XeLaTeX environment is the first step towards creating beautiful and professional documents with XeLaTeX. In this section, we will walk through the process of setting up XeLaTeX on different platforms and discuss some useful tools and packages for a seamless workflow.

Installing XeLaTeX

Before we start, we need to install XeLaTeX on our system. XeLaTeX is available for Windows, macOS, and Linux distributions.

Windows: To install XeLaTeX on Windows, we recommend using the MikTeX distribution. You can download the MikTeX installer from the MikTeX website (https://miktex.org/download), run the installer, and follow the on-screen instructions to complete the installation. MikTeX provides a user-friendly interface for managing LaTeX packages and updates.

macOS: On macOS, we can install XeLaTeX using the MacTeX distribution. Visit the MacTeX website (https://www.tug.org/mactex/) and download the MacTeX installer. After downloading, run the installer and follow the instructions to install XeLaTeX and related packages. MacTeX also includes several useful tools such as TeXShop, a LaTeX editor for macOS.

Linux: Linux distributions often provide TeX Live, a comprehensive LaTeX distribution that includes XeLaTeX. Depending on your Linux distribution, you can use the package manager to install TeX Live. For example, on Ubuntu or Debian-based systems, you can open the terminal and run the following command:

```
sudo\index{sudo} apt-get\index{get} install\index{install} texlive
```

This command will install the complete TeX Live distribution, including XeLaTeX and all the required packages.

Integrated Development Environments

An Integrated Development Environment (IDE) can greatly enhance the XeLaTeX workflow by providing features such as syntax highlighting, code completion, and compilation tools. Here are some popular choices for XeLaTeX IDEs:

TeXstudio: TeXstudio is a feature-rich LaTeX editor that supports XeLaTeX. It provides a clean and intuitive interface, with powerful features like syntax highlighting, auto-completion, and PDF preview. TeXstudio is available for Windows, macOS, and Linux.

Overleaf: Overleaf is an online LaTeX editor that allows collaborative editing and real-time compilation. It supports XeLaTeX and provides a wide range of templates and tools for different document types. Overleaf is accessible from any web browser, making it a convenient choice for collaborative writing and editing.

Visual Studio Code: Visual Studio Code (VS Code) is a popular code editor with extensive LaTeX support. It offers various plugins, such as LaTeX Workshop, that enable XeLaTeX compilation and provide rich features like IntelliSense and linting. VS Code runs on Windows, macOS, and Linux.

Basic XeLaTeX Structure

Let's now explore the basic structure of a XeLaTeX document. A XeLaTeX document begins with the document class declaration and ends with . In between, we can add content such as sections, paragraphs, equations, and figures. Here is a minimal XeLaTeX document:

```
\section{Introduction}
```

```
This is my first XeLaTeX document\index{document}.
```

In this example, we use the `article` document class, which is suitable for basic documents. Other document classes like `book` and `report` offer more features for longer documents.

Compiling XeLaTeX Documents

To compile a XeLaTeX document, we need to run the XeLaTeX compiler on our document file. The compilation process generates a PDF output that reflects any changes or updates made to the document.

In most IDEs, there are dedicated buttons or menu options to compile XeLaTeX documents. Alternatively, we can use command-line tools to compile from the terminal. For example, to compile a document named `mydocument.tex` using XeLaTeX, we can run the following command:

```
xelatex\index{xelatex}\index{xelatex} mydocument.tex\index{tex}
```

The XeLaTeX compiler will process the document and generate the PDF output. If there are any errors or warnings during compilation, they will be displayed in the terminal or IDE.

Common Issues and Troubleshooting

While working with XeLaTeX, we may encounter some common issues. Here are a few troubleshooting tips to help address these problems:

Missing Packages or Fonts: If XeLaTeX gives an error about missing packages or fonts, ensure that the necessary packages and fonts are installed. Use the package manager of your TeX distribution to install missing packages. For fonts, make sure they are installed and accessible to XeLaTeX.

Compilation Errors: If XeLaTeX encounters an error during compilation, carefully review the error message and check for any syntax or formatting issues. Often, a missing or misplaced command can cause compilation errors.

Incorrect Output or Formatting: If the generated PDF output does not match your expectations in terms of formatting or layout, double-check your document's structure and formatting commands. Make sure you are using the correct syntax and commands for achieving the desired layout.

Further Resources

XeLaTeX offers a vast range of possibilities for document creation and typesetting. To further explore and enhance your XeLaTeX skills, here are some recommended resources:

1. *The XeTeX Companion* by Michel Goossens and Johannes Braams: This comprehensive guide provides in-depth coverage of XeLaTeX and its features, along with useful tips and tricks for typesetting various document types.

2. *The LaTeX Wikibook*: The LaTeX Wikibook is an extensive online resource that covers all aspects of LaTeX, including XeLaTeX. It provides detailed explanations, examples, and tutorials for beginners and advanced users alike.

3. Online LaTeX communities and forums such as *TeX Stack Exchange* (https://tex.stackexchange.com/) are excellent places to seek help, share knowledge, and engage with the LaTeX community.

By following the steps discussed in this section, we can set up the XeLaTeX environment, create our first XeLaTeX document, and compile it successfully. In the next section, we will delve into the basics of XeLaTeX, including packages, fonts, and typography. Let's continue our journey of mastering XeLaTeX!

Getting started with XeLaTeX

XeLaTeX is a powerful and versatile typesetting system that allows you to create high-quality documents with ease. In this section, we will cover the basics of getting started with XeLaTeX, including setting up the environment, creating a basic document structure, and compiling XeLaTeX documents.

Setting up XeLaTeX environment

Before you can start using XeLaTeX, you need to set up the necessary software and tools. Here are the steps to get started:

1. Install TeX distribution: XeLaTeX is part of the TeX Live distribution, which is available for various operating systems. You can download and install TeX

Live from the official website (https://www.tug.org/texlive/) or use a package manager specific to your operating system.

2. Choose an integrated development environment (IDE): While you can write XeLaTeX code in any text editor, using an IDE designed for LaTeX makes the process much more efficient. Some popular choices include TeXstudio, TeXmaker, and Overleaf.

3. Install required fonts: XeLaTeX allows you to use system fonts directly in your documents. You can install additional fonts from trusted sources or use the fonts that come with your operating system.

Creating a basic document structure

Now that you have set up the environment, let's create a basic document structure in XeLaTeX. Open your preferred IDE and follow these steps:

1. Start with a document class declaration: Begin your document by declaring the document class. For example, you can use the "article" class by including the following line at the beginning of your document:

2. Define the document metadata: Next, provide the necessary metadata for your document, such as the title, author, date, and any other relevant information. Use the " ", " ", and " " commands to define these fields.

3. Begin the document environment: After the metadata, you need to start the document environment using the "" command.

4. Write your content: Now you can start writing the content of your document. Use plain text for regular paragraphs and include special commands for mathematical equations, figures, tables, and other elements.

5. End the document environment: Finally, end the document environment using the "" command.

Compiling XeLaTeX documents

Once you have created your XeLaTeX document, you need to compile it to generate the final output. Follow these steps to compile your document:

1. Build your document: Use your chosen IDE to build the document. The IDE will call the necessary XeLaTeX commands to compile your document. You may also need to specify the desired output format (e.g., PDF).

2. Resolve errors and warnings: If there are any errors or warnings during the compilation process, review the corresponding messages and fix the issues in your

document. Common errors include missing packages, undefined commands, or improperly formatted equations.

3. Repeat the compilation: After resolving any errors, compile the document again. This iterative process ensures that your document is correctly formatted and error-free.

4. Review the output: Once the compilation is successful, review the output document to ensure that it matches your expectations. Check for proper formatting, correct page layout, and accurate rendering of equations and figures.

It is important to note that XeLaTeX performs a variety of tasks during the compilation process, such as typesetting text, resolving cross-references, generating the table of contents, and more. Therefore, it may be necessary to compile the document multiple times to ensure all elements are correctly processed.

Troubleshooting common issues in XeLaTeX

While working with XeLaTeX, you may encounter some common issues. Here are a few troubleshooting tips to help you resolve them:

1. Missing packages: If you receive an error indicating a missing package, make sure you have it installed. You can use the "" command to include required packages in the preamble of your document.

2. Undefined commands: If you encounter an error related to an undefined command, ensure that you have spelled it correctly and that the corresponding package is correctly loaded.

3. Improperly formatted equations: XeLaTeX requires proper syntax for mathematical equations. Double-check the formatting of your equations and ensure that all opening and closing delimiters are balanced.

4. File not found: If XeLaTeX cannot locate a file (e.g., an image or a bibliography file), verify that the file is in the specified location and that the path is correctly specified.

5. Rendering issues: If your document does not render as expected, check for any conflicting commands, incompatible packages, or formatting issues.

Remember, troubleshooting is an integral part of the learning process, and don't hesitate to consult official documentation, online forums, or LaTeX communities for help and guidance.

Conclusion

In this section, we have covered the essential steps to get started with XeLaTeX. We explored setting up the XeLaTeX environment, creating a basic document structure, compiling XeLaTeX documents, and troubleshooting common issues. With this foundation, you are ready to delve into more advanced topics and unleash the full potential of XeLaTeX for your document creation needs.

Throughout this book, we will dive deeper into XeLaTeX and explore various techniques and applications to help you become a proficient user. So, let's embark on this exciting journey together!

Basic Document Structure in XeLaTeX

In this section, we will explore the basic document structure in XeLaTeX. Understanding the organization and components of a XeLaTeX document is crucial for creating professional-looking documents. We will cover the preamble, document class, and the main body of the document.

The Preamble

The preamble is the section of the document that comes before the \begin{document} command. It is where you define the document settings and load any necessary packages. Let's take a look at an example of a XeLaTeX preamble:

```
\documentclass[12pt,a4paper]{article}

\setmainfont{Times New Roman}


\title{My XeLaTeX Document}
\author{John Doe}
\date{\today}
```

In this example, we are using the `article` document class with a font size of 12pt and an A4 paper size. We have also loaded the `fontspec`, `graphicx`, and `hyperref` packages. The `fontspec` package allows us to select and use fonts, while the `graphicx` package enables us to include graphics in our document. The `hyperref` package provides hypertext links within the document.

We have also set the main font to be Times New Roman using the `\setmainfont` command. Additionally, we have specified the title, author, and date of the document using the respective commands. Note that the `\date{}` command with the argument `\today` automatically inserts the current date.

While this example covers some commonly used commands in the preamble, there are many more options available depending on your specific needs and preferences.

The Document Class

The document class determines the overall layout and formatting of the document. XeLaTeX provides several built-in document classes such as `article`, `report`, and `book`, each with its own set of predefined styles.

For example, if we use the `article` class, we can set the font size, paper size, and other formatting options in the preamble. The `article` class is suitable for shorter documents such as research papers, reports, or articles.

Here is an example of using the `article` document class:

```
\documentclass[12pt,a4paper]{article}

\setmainfont{Times New Roman}


\title{My XeLaTeX Document}
\author{John Doe}
\date{\today}


\maketitle

% Content goes here
```

In this example, we create a simple document with a title, author, and date using the \maketitle command. The main body of the document falls within the document environment.

The Main Body

The main body of the document contains the actual content such as text, images, equations, and tables. It is placed between the \begin{document} and \end{document} commands.

Here is an example of a basic XeLaTeX document structure with some sample content:

```
\documentclass[12pt,a4paper]{article}

\setmainfont{Times New Roman}


\title{My XeLaTeX Document}
\author{John Doe}
\date{\today}



\maketitle

\section{Introduction}
This is the introduction\index{introduction} of the document\index

\section{Methods}
In this section\index{section}, we describe the methods used\index

\subsection{Experimental Setup}
We explain the experimental setup\index{setup} used\index{used} fo

\section{Results}
The results of our experiments are presented in\index{in} this sec

\section{Conclusion}
We conclude our document\index{document} by summarizing the key\in
```

In this example, we have added some sections and subsections to organize our document. Each section starts with the \section command, followed by the section title. Subsections are created using the \subsection command. You can add as many sections and subsections as needed to structure your document.

Remember to compile the document using XeLaTeX to generate the final output. You can use any text editor or integrated development environment (IDE) with XeLaTeX support to edit and compile your document.

Summary

In this section, we discussed the basic document structure in XeLaTeX. We explored the preamble, which is where you define the document settings, load packages, and specify the title, author, and date. We also covered the document class, which determines the overall layout and formatting, and the main body of the document, where you add content such as text, images, equations, and tables.

Understanding the basic structure of a XeLaTeX document is essential for creating professional-looking documents and organizing your content effectively. In the next sections, we will delve into more advanced techniques and features of XeLaTeX to enhance your document creation process.

Compiling XeLaTeX documents

Compiling XeLaTeX documents is a crucial step in the process of creating high-quality typesetting output. In this section, we will explore the different aspects of compiling XeLaTeX documents, including the necessary commands, options, and troubleshooting techniques.

The XeLaTeX Compiler

XeLaTeX is a command-line program used to compile documents written in the XeLaTeX typesetting language. It is an extension of the LaTeX typesetting system, allowing for enhanced font support and better handling of non-ASCII characters.

To compile a XeLaTeX document, open a terminal or command prompt and navigate to the directory where your document is located. Then, run the following command:

```
xelatex <filename.tex>
```

Replace `<filename.tex>` with the name of your actual file. XeLaTeX will process your document, executing all necessary steps to generate the final output.

Compiling Options

XeLaTeX provides several options that allow you to customize the compilation process. These options can be specified in the command line, either before or after the filename.

- **-interaction=mode:** This option determines the level of interaction between the compiler and the user. Common modes include `batchmode`, `nonstopmode`, and `scrollmode`.

- **-output-directory=dir:** Specifies the directory where the output files will be generated. This is useful for keeping your working directory clean and organized.

- **-jobname=name:** Changes the name of the output file. By default, XeLaTeX uses the same name as the input file.

- **-halt-on-error:** Stops the compilation process if an error is encountered. This can be useful for debugging purposes.

For example, to compile a document named `example.tex` in batch mode and specify an output directory, you can use the following command:

```
xelatex -interaction=batchmode -output-directory=output example.te
```

Troubleshooting Compilation Issues

Sometimes, the compilation process may encounter errors or warnings that need to be addressed. Here are some common issues and their solutions:

- **Missing Packages:** If XeLaTeX complains about missing packages, make sure they are installed on your system. You can use the package manager of your distribution to install them.

- **Undefined Control Sequences:** This error occurs when XeLaTeX encounters a command it does not recognize. Double-check the spelling and syntax of the command, and ensure that any necessary packages are included.

- **Bad Box Warnings:** These warnings indicate that the typesetting result may not be optimal. They can be caused by issues such as overly long lines or inconsistent spacing. Review the warnings and adjust your document accordingly.

- **Font Issues:** If XeLaTeX complains about missing fonts or font-related errors, ensure that the required fonts are installed on your system. You may need to specify the font file or font name using the appropriate commands in your document.

- **Persistent Compilation Errors:** If you encounter persistent errors that you cannot resolve, it can be helpful to comment out parts of your document to identify the source of the problem. This process of trial and error can help isolate and fix the issue.

If you are still having trouble resolving compilation issues, there are several online resources and forums where you can seek assistance from the XeLaTeX community.

Best Practices

To ensure a smooth and efficient compilation process, here are some best practices to follow:

- Keep your document well-organized with separate files for sections, chapters, and other components. This makes it easier to debug and manage the compilation process.

- Update your distribution and packages regularly to benefit from bug fixes and enhancements. Many issues can be resolved by simply installing the latest updates.

- Use version control software to track changes to your document. This allows you to revert to previous versions if problems arise during the compilation process.

- Keep a backup of your document files to avoid potential data loss. This is especially important when working on large and complex projects.

- Take advantage of the extensive documentation available for XeLaTeX. Online resources, books, and forums can provide valuable insights and solutions to common and unique challenges.

- Experiment with different compilation options and packages to optimize the performance and quality of your typesetting output.

+ Test your document on different platforms and configurations to ensure cross-compatibility. This is particularly important when collaborating with others or sharing your work with a wider audience.

+ Seek feedback from others to get different perspectives on the layout, design, and overall presentation of your document. Constructive criticism can help you refine and enhance your work.

By following these best practices and staying proactive in troubleshooting any encountered issues, you can enjoy a smooth and successful compilation process with XeLaTeX.

Conclusion

Compiling XeLaTeX documents involves running the XeLaTeX compiler with appropriate options to process your document and generate the final output. By understanding the compilation process, troubleshooting common issues, and following best practices, you can achieve professional and visually appealing typesetting results. Now that you have a solid foundation in XeLaTeX compilation, let's explore the basics of document structure and formatting in the next chapter.

Troubleshooting common issues in XeLaTeX

In this section, we will cover some common issues that users may encounter when working with XeLaTeX and provide troubleshooting tips to help resolve them. XeLaTeX is a powerful typesetting system, but like any software, it can have its quirks and challenges. Understanding and addressing these issues can save a lot of time and frustration when working on your documents.

Font-related issues

One common issue users may face with XeLaTeX is related to fonts. XeLaTeX has excellent support for system and OpenType fonts, but incorrect font installation or missing font files can cause problems.

Problem 1: Font not found If XeLaTeX cannot find a specified font, it will generate an error message. To troubleshoot this issue, you can follow these steps:

1. Check if the font is installed on your system. Use your operating system's font management tools to verify the installation.

2. Verify the font name and make sure it matches the actual font file name. Typos and case sensitivity can lead to font not found errors.

3. If the font is not installed, you can install it manually. Download the font file from a trusted source and install it using your operating system's font management tools.

Problem 2: Font not rendering properly   Sometimes, the font may not render as expected, causing issues with characters, spacing, or line breaks. Here are a few troubleshooting steps to consider:

1. Check if the font supports the characters you are using. Not all fonts have complete character sets, especially for less common scripts or symbols.

2. Verify that you have the latest version of the font installed. Some font files may have bugs or rendering issues that are fixed in updated versions.

3. Experiment with different font features and settings. XeLaTeX provides various options for font customization, including ligatures, kerning, and spacing adjustments.

Package conflicts and compatibility issues

XeLaTeX offers a wide range of packages and libraries to extend its functionality. However, conflicts between different packages or compatibility issues with specific versions of packages can cause errors or unexpected behavior.

Problem 1: Conflicting packages   If you encounter an error related to conflicting packages, you can try the following troubleshooting steps:

1. Disable or remove any unnecessary packages. Sometimes, packages may have overlapping functionality or conflicting options.

2. Check if there are any known compatibility issues between the packages you are using. Refer to the package documentation or online forums for information on known conflicts and possible workarounds.

3. Update your packages to the latest versions. Package updates often include bug fixes and improved compatibility with other packages.

Problem 2: Compatibility issues with document class options   Certain document class options may not be compatible with specific packages or configurations in XeLaTeX. Here are some troubleshooting tips to address compatibility issues:

1. Experiment with different document class options. Some options may conflict with specific packages, so try disabling or modifying them to see if the issue persists.

2. Check the documentation of the document class and the package for any known compatibility issues. The documentation often provides guidance on how to resolve conflicts or recommends alternative approaches.

3. Seek help from the XeLaTeX community. Online forums and discussion groups can be valuable resources for troubleshooting compatibility issues. Other users may have encountered similar problems and can provide insights or solutions.

Compilation errors and warnings

During compilation, XeLaTeX may generate errors or warnings that indicate issues with the document structure or syntax. Understanding these messages and addressing the underlying problems is crucial for successful compilation.

Problem 1: Undefined control sequence   This error typically occurs when using an unrecognized command or macro. To troubleshoot this issue, you can follow these steps:

1. Check for typos in the command or macro name. The error message often includes the specific location where the undefined control sequence is encountered.

2. Verify that the package or document class defining the command is properly loaded. Some commands are specific to certain packages or classes and may require the appropriate inclusion.

3. Make sure you have correctly spelled the command and used the correct syntax. Check the command's documentation for guidance on its usage and parameters.

Problem 2: Overfull or underfull hbox   These warnings indicate that a line of text in your document extends beyond the specified line width (overfull hbox) or does not fill the line completely (underfull hbox). Here are some troubleshooting tips:

1. Review the affected line of text and check for long words or equations that exceed the line width. Consider adjusting the text, breaking long words, or modifying the line formatting.

2. Check if the line spacing or page layout settings are causing the issue. Adjusting the layout settings or increasing the line spacing may help resolve the warning.

3. Experiment with different document class options or packages that provide better line breaking algorithms. For example, the microtype package can improve the overall typesetting and help reduce hbox warnings.

Troubleshooting resources for XeLaTeX

When encountering issues with XeLaTeX, it's essential to have access to relevant resources for troubleshooting and finding solutions. Here are a few recommended resources:

+ XeLaTeX documentation: The official documentation provides comprehensive information on using XeLaTeX, including troubleshooting tips and common issues.

+ LaTeX forums and communities: Online forums such as *TeX Stack Exchange* and *LaTeX Community* are excellent places to seek help and advice from experienced users and experts.

+ Package documentation: When using specific packages, always refer to the package documentation for guidance on troubleshooting and known issues.

+ Books and tutorials: Various books and online tutorials cover different aspects of XeLaTeX, providing in-depth explanations and troubleshooting tips.

By following these troubleshooting tips and utilizing the available resources, you can effectively resolve common issues with XeLaTeX and ensure a smooth and productive typesetting experience. Remember to always keep a backup of your documents and experiment with small changes to avoid any unexpected complications.

Exercises

1. Identify a font-related issue you have encountered while working with XeLaTeX. Describe the problem and explain how you resolved it.

2. Find a conflicting package combination that generates errors in XeLaTeX. Try different solutions to resolve the conflict and document the steps you took to fix it.

3. Create a sample document that intentionally includes an undefined control sequence error. Explain the cause of the error and provide a solution to resolve it.

4. Experiment with different line breaking algorithms or settings to reduce the occurrence of hbox warnings in your document. Compare the results and summarize your findings.

Further Reading

1. Oetiker, T., Partl, H., Hyna, I., & Schlegl, E. (2020). *The Not So Short Introduction to LaTeX.* Retrieved from https://tobi.oetiker.ch/lshort/lshort.pdf

2. Kottwitz, S. (2011). *LaTeX Beginner's Guide.* Birmingham, UK: Packt Publishing.

3. Griffiths, D., & Higham, N. (2016). *Learning LaTeX.* Philadelphia, PA: Society for Industrial and Applied Mathematics.

Conclusion

Troubleshooting issues in XeLaTeX can be challenging, but with the right knowledge and resources, you can overcome common problems and achieve the desired results. By understanding font-related issues, package conflicts, compilation errors, and warnings, you will be better equipped to identify and resolve issues efficiently. Don't hesitate to seek help from the XeLaTeX community and experiment with different solutions to find the best approach for your specific situation.

XeLaTeX Basics

Packages and libraries in XeLaTeX

In XeLaTeX, packages and libraries play a crucial role in expanding the functionality of the standard LaTeX system. They offer additional features and tools that allow users to customize their documents and create professional-looking outputs. In this section, we will explore some important packages and libraries commonly used in XeLaTeX.

fontspec

The `fontspec` package is a fundamental package for XeLaTeX that provides support for advanced font selection and manipulation. With `fontspec`, you can easily choose and use any system-installed font on your computer. It allows you to specify the font family, style, size, and other attributes directly in your XeLaTeX document.

Here's an example of how to use the `fontspec` package to select a specific font for your document:

```
\setmainfont{Times New Roman}

This is a\index{a} sample\index{sample} XeLaTeX document\index{doc
```

In this example, the `fontspec` package is included using the `usepackage` command, and the `setmainfont` command is used to set the main font of the document to Times New Roman. You can replace "Times New Roman" with any other font installed on your system.

polyglossia

The `polyglossia` package is designed for multilingual typesetting in XeLaTeX. It provides support for various languages and their specific typographic rules, hyphenation patterns, and fonts. With `polyglossia`, you can easily switch between different languages within your XeLaTeX document.

Here's an example of how to use the `polyglossia` package to typeset a document in multiple languages:

```
\setmainfont{Times New Roman}
\setmainlanguage{english}
\setotherlanguage{french}

This is a\index{a} sample\index{sample} XeLaTeX document\index{do
\begin{french}
Ceci est un exemple de document\index{Ceci est un exemple de docu
\end{french}
```

In this example, the `polyglossia` package is included using the `usepackage` command. The `setmainlanguage` command is used to set the main language of the document to English, while the `setotherlanguage` command is used to specify French as the other language. The `french` environment is then used to switch to French language mode within the document.

graphicx

The `graphicx` package is a widely used package for including and manipulating graphics in XeLaTeX documents. It provides commands for inserting images, scaling and rotating them, and applying various transformations. With `graphicx`, you can easily incorporate figures, diagrams, and other visual elements into your XeLaTeX documents.

Here's an example of how to use the `graphicx` package to insert an image into your document:

```
This is a\index{a} sample\index{sample} XeLaTeX document\index{doc
% \begin{figure}[h]
%   \centering
%   \includegraphics[width=0.5\textwidth]{example-image}
%   \caption{An example image}
%   \label{fig:example}
% \end{figure}
```

In this example, the `graphicx` package is included using the `usepackage` command. The `includegraphics` command is used to insert an image named `example-image` with a width of 0.5 times the width of the text. The `figure` environment is used to wrap the image and provide a caption and label for referencing.

These are just a few examples of the many packages and libraries available for use in XeLaTeX. As you explore more, you will discover a wide range of packages and libraries that cater to specific needs, such as typesetting mathematics (`amsmath`), creating tables (`booktabs`), and adding color (`xcolor`). It's important to consult the documentation and resources available for each package to fully understand their capabilities and how to use them effectively in your XeLaTeX documents.

Resources and Further Reading

To dive deeper into the world of packages and libraries in XeLaTeX, here are some recommended resources:

- The Comprehensive TeX Archive Network (CTAN) (`https://ctan.org/`) is the central repository for TeX related packages, and it provides a vast collection of packages and documentation.

- The XeLaTeX Wikibook (`https://en.wikibooks.org/wiki/LaTeX/XeTeX`) offers a comprehensive guide with examples and explanations specifically for XeLaTeX users.

- The Technical Support User Group (`https://tug.org/`) is a community-driven organization that provides support, resources, and documentation for TeX and related systems.

In addition to these resources, it's always beneficial to explore online forums, mailing lists, and social media groups dedicated to TeX and XeLaTeX. These communities are filled with helpful individuals who are often willing to share their knowledge and experiences.

Document class options in XeLaTeX

When working with XeLaTeX, document class options provide a way to customize the overall appearance and layout of your document. These options allow you to control various settings such as font size, paper size, margins, and more. In this section, we will explore some commonly used document class options in XeLaTeX and how to utilize them effectively.

Font Size

One of the fundamental aspects of document formatting is selecting an appropriate font size. XeLaTeX provides the following options for font size:

- 10pt: Sets the default font size to 10 points.
- 11pt: Sets the default font size to 11 points.
- 12pt: Sets the default font size to 12 points.

For example, to set the document font size to 12 points, you would add the following command to the preamble of your document:

```
\documentclass[12pt]{article}
```

Paper Size

Another important aspect of document formatting is choosing the appropriate paper size. XeLaTeX provides several options for paper size, such as:

- a4paper: Sets the paper size to A4, which is the default.
- letterpaper: Sets the paper size to Letter.
- legalpaper: Sets the paper size to Legal.

To set the document paper size to Letter, you would use the following document class option:

```
\documentclass[letterpaper]{article}
```

Margins

Controlling the document margins is crucial for achieving the desired layout. XeLaTeX allows you to adjust the margins using the geometry package. This package provides flexible options for modifying the page layout. Here is an example of how to set the margins to 1 inch on all sides:

```
\usepackage[margin=1in]{geometry}
```

Two-sided Printing

If you want your document to be printed on both sides of the page, you can specify the `twoside` option. This option ensures that the margins and headers are adjusted accordingly for even and odd pages. Here's an example of how to enable the two-sided printing option:

```
\documentclass[twoside]{article}
```

Draft Mode

While working on a large document, it can be useful to enable the draft mode. This mode is helpful for identifying overfull boxes, such as lines of text that extend beyond the margins. To enable draft mode, you can use the `draft` option in the document class declaration:

```
\documentclass[draft]{article}
```

Title Page

If you want to create a separate title page for your document, you can use the `titlepage` option. This option suppresses the automatic page number on the first page and provides additional space at the top of the page for the title and author information. Here's an example of how to enable the title page option:

```
\documentclass[titlepage]{article}
```

Other Options

Aside from the options mentioned above, there are other document class options available in XeLaTeX that can be used to control various aspects of your document. Some of these options include `landscape` for landscape page orientation, `onecolumn` to set the document in a single column layout, and `twocolumn` for a two-column layout.

It is important to note that not all document classes support all options. Therefore, it is essential to refer to the documentation of your chosen document class to ensure compatibility.

In conclusion, document class options in XeLaTeX offer great flexibility for customizing the appearance and layout of your document. Whether it's adjusting font size, paper size, margins, or enabling specific features like two-sided printing or draft mode, understanding and utilizing these options can greatly enhance your document formatting capabilities. Be sure to experiment with different options to find the settings that best suit your needs. Happy typesetting!

Fonts and Typography in XeLaTeX

In this section, we will explore the various aspects of fonts and typography in XeLaTeX. Fonts play a crucial role in document layout and design, and XeLaTeX offers a wide range of options for customizing and enhancing the typographic quality of your documents. We will discuss how to choose and install fonts, how to customize their appearance, and how to handle different font features. We will also explore typographic principles such as kerning, tracking, and ligatures.

Choosing and Installing Fonts

One of the main advantages of using XeLaTeX over traditional LaTeX is its support for system fonts. XeLaTeX allows you to use any font installed on your system, including TrueType, OpenType, and PostScript fonts. This gives you the flexibility to choose from a vast collection of fonts.

When choosing fonts for your document, it is important to consider their readability and appropriateness for the content. Fonts should complement the overall design and enhance the reading experience. There are different categories of fonts, such as serif, sans-serif, and monospaced, each with its own characteristics and use cases.

To use a particular font in XeLaTeX, you need to have it installed on your system. Most operating systems come with a default set of fonts, but you can also download and install additional fonts from various sources, such as Google Fonts or Adobe Fonts. Once the font is installed, you can specify it in your XeLaTeX document using the \setmainfont, \setsansfont, or \setmonofont commands, depending on the font category.

Customizing Font Appearance

XeLaTeX provides several options for customizing the appearance of fonts in your document. You can control the font size, weight, style, and color to achieve the desired typographic effect. The following commands can be used to modify the font properties:

- \fontsize{size}{baselineskip} - Sets the font size and the baselineskip, which determines the spacing between lines of text.

- \textbf{text} - Sets the text in bold.

- \textit{text} - Sets the text in italics.

- \textcolor{color}{text} - Sets the text color.

For example, to set the main font size to 12pt, you can use \fontsize{12pt}{14pt}. You can also combine different font properties, such as \textbf{\textit{bold and italic text}}.

Handling Different Font Features

Fonts often come with various features that can enhance the typography of your document. These features include ligatures, alternative character shapes, and advanced typographic substitutions. XeLaTeX provides the \setmainfont and \newfontfamily commands to specify font features.

To enable ligatures, which are special combinations of characters that are displayed as a single glyph, you can use the following command:

```
\setmainfont[Ligatures=TeX]{fontname}
```

Here, fontname should be replaced with the name of the font you want to use. The Ligatures=TeX option enables standard TeX ligatures, such as fi, fl, and ff.

You can also enable other font features, such as swashes, small caps, and stylistic alternates, using the RawFeature= option. For example, to enable swashes, you can use:

```
\setmainfont[RawFeature={+swsh}]{fontname}
```

This will activate the swash alternate glyphs when available in the chosen font.

Typographic Principles

In addition to font selection and customization, it is important to understand and apply typographic principles to achieve optimal typography in your documents. Let's explore some key principles:

- **Kerning** is the adjustment of the spacing between specific pairs of characters to improve their visual appearance. XeLaTeX automatically applies kerning based on the font metrics, but you can fine-tune it using the \kern command.

- **Tracking** refers to the overall spacing between characters in a block of text. Negative tracking tightens the spacing, while positive tracking loosens it. You can adjust the tracking using the \textls command from the soul package.

- **Ligatures** are special combinations of characters that are substituted with a single glyph. They improve the appearance of certain character combinations, such as "fi" and "fl". XeLaTeX automatically applies ligatures unless it is explicitly disabled.

- **Hyphenation** is the process of breaking words at the end of a line to improve spacing and prevent excessive gaps. XeLaTeX automatically hyphenates words, but you can control this behavior using the \hyphenation command.

These typographic principles, when applied appropriately, enhance the readability and overall aesthetic of your document.

Summary

Fonts and typography are crucial elements of document design, and XeLaTeX provides a powerful platform for customizing and enhancing the typographic quality of your documents. In this section, we explored how to choose and install fonts, customize font appearance, handle font features, and apply typographic principles. By understanding and leveraging these capabilities, you can create visually appealing and professional-looking documents.

Customizing page layout in XeLaTeX

In XeLaTeX, you have the flexibility to customize the layout of your document pages according to your specific requirements. Whether you are aiming for a professional look for your business reports or creating an eye-catching design for your creative projects, XeLaTeX provides powerful tools to help you achieve your desired page layout.

The geometry package

One popular package for customizing page layout in XeLaTeX is the geometry package. This package allows you to set various parameters such as margins, paper size, and page orientation.

To use the geometry package, you need to include the following line in the preamble of your document:

Once you have included the package, you can start customizing your page layout. Here are some common options you can modify:

- **Margins:** You can set the margins of your document using the `margin` option. For example, to set equal margins on all sides, you can use:

  ```
  \geometry{margin=1in}
  ```

- **Paper size:** You can specify the paper size using the `paper` option. For example, to set the paper size to A4, you can use:

  ```
  \geometry{a4paper}
  ```

- **Page orientation:** You can set the page orientation to either portrait or landscape using the `landscape` option. For example, to set the page orientation to landscape, you can use:

  ```
  \geometry{landscape}
  ```

These are just a few examples of the options available in the `geometry` package. You can refer to the package documentation for more details on how to customize your page layout further.

The fancyhdr package

If you want to add headers and footers to your document pages, you can use the `fancyhdr` package. This package provides extensive customization options for headers and footers, allowing you to add page numbers, section names, and other information.

To use the `fancyhdr` package, you need to include the following line in the preamble of your document:

Once you have included the package, you can define your headers and footers using the `fancyhdr` commands. Here's an example:

```
\pagestyle{fancy}
\fancyhf{}
\fancyhead[L]{\leftmark}
\fancyhead[R]{\thepage}
```

In this example, we set the page style to `fancy` and clear the default header and footer using `fancyhf{}`. We then set the left header to display the current section name using `\leftmark`, and the right header to display the page number using `\thepage`.

You can further customize the headers and footers by adjusting the position, font, and style of the text. The `fancyhdr` package provides a wide range of commands and options for this purpose.

Sample Problem: Customizing page layout for a resume

Suppose you are creating a resume using XeLaTeX and you want to customize the page layout to make it visually appealing and professional. You would like to have a narrow margin, a single column layout, and a header with your name and contact information.

To achieve this, you can use the following code:

```
\usepackage[a4paper,margin=0.5in]{geometry}
```

```
\pagestyle{fancy}
\fancyhf{}
\fancyhead[C]{Your Name}
\fancyhead[R]{contact@example.com}
```

```
% Your resume content goes here
```

In this example, we set the paper size to A4 and the margin to 0.5 inches using the `geometry` package. We then define the page style as `fancy` and set the header to display the name and contact information.

You can further customize the layout by adjusting the font style, size, and colors in the header or by adding additional sections as per your resume design.

Summary

Customizing page layout in XeLaTeX allows you to design your document according to your specific requirements. By using packages like `geometry` and `fancyhdr`, you can easily modify margins, paper size, page orientation, headers, and footers. Experiment with different options and styles to create professional and visually appealing documents.

Inserting figures and graphics in XeLaTeX

One of the key features that sets XeLaTeX apart from traditional LaTeX is its enhanced support for handling figures and graphics. In this section, you will learn how to insert images into your XeLaTeX documents, manipulate their size and placement, and add captions and labels for easy referencing.

Including images in XeLaTeX documents

To include an image in your XeLaTeX document, you first need to load the `graphicx` package, which provides the necessary commands for manipulating graphics. This package is part of the standard LaTeX distribution and is automatically installed with XeLaTeX.

To begin, let's assume you have an image file named `myimage.png`. You can use the `includegraphics` command to insert the image into your document. Here's an example:

```
% \begin{figure}
%   \centering
%   \includegraphics[width=0.5\textwidth]{myimage.png}
%   \caption{A beautiful sunset.}
%   \label{fig:sunset}
% \end{figure}
```

In this example, we specify the path and filename of the image in the curly brackets after `includegraphics`. The optional argument `width=0.5\textwidth` sets the width of the image to half of the text width, allowing the image to fit nicely within the document. You can experiment with different values to achieve the desired size.

Manipulating and scaling images in XeLaTeX

Sometimes, you may need to resize or scale an image to fit a specific area of your document. The `includegraphics` command provides several optional arguments to help you achieve this.

- `width=value`: Sets the width of the image to the specified value. For example, `width=3cm` sets the width to 3 centimeters.

- `height=value`: Sets the height of the image to the specified value. For example, `height=4in` sets the height to 4 inches.

- `scale=value`: Scales the image by the specified factor. For example, `scale=0.5` reduces the size of the image to half its original size.

Let's modify our previous example to illustrate these options:

```
% \begin{figure}
%   \centering
%     \includegraphics[width=0.75\textwidth, height=5cm]{my
%     \caption{A beautiful sunset.}
%     \label{fig:sunset}
% \end{figure}
```

In this modified example, we set the width of the image to 75% of the text width and the height to 5 centimeters. You can adjust these values to suit your needs.

Customizing image placement and alignment in XeLaTeX

By default, XeLaTeX places figures at the top or bottom of a page. However, you may want finer control over the placement and alignment of your images. The `figure` environment provides options to achieve this.

- h: Places the figure in approximately the same position as in the source text.

- t: Places the figure at the top of a page.

- b: Places the figure at the bottom of a page.

◆ p: Places the figure on a separate page containing only floats.

◆ !: Overrides internal parameters to allow more flexibility for figure placement.

To specify the placement options, you can add them inside square brackets after `figure`. For example:

```
% \begin{figure}[htbp]
%     \centering
%     \includegraphics[width=0.5\textwidth]{myimage.png}
%     \caption{A beautiful sunset.}
%     \label{fig:sunset}
% \end{figure}
```

In this example, we use the `htbp` options to allow placement of the figure either here (if there is enough space on the current page), at the top, at the bottom, or on a separate page dedicated to floats.

Adding captions and labels to figures in XeLaTeX

To provide a clear description of your figures and enable easy referencing, you can add captions and labels to them. The `caption` command is used to add a caption, and the `label` command assigns a unique label to the figure for referencing.

Here's an example:

```
% \begin{figure}
%     \centering
%     \includegraphics[width=0.5\textwidth]{myimage.png}
%     \caption{A beautiful sunset.}
%     \label{fig:sunset}
% \end{figure}
```

As we can see in Figure `\ref{fig:sunset}`, the sunset is tr

In this example, we use the `caption` command to add the caption "A beautiful sunset." We then assign the label `fig:sunset` to the figure using the `label` command. In the body text, we can reference the figure by using the `ref` command with the label as an argument.

Best practices for using figures in XeLaTeX

When working with figures in XeLaTeX, it is important to adhere to some best practices to ensure the best results:

- Use vector-based graphics whenever possible, such as PDF or SVG formats, to maintain the quality of the images.

- Keep the resolution of raster graphics (e.g., PNG or JPEG) high enough to avoid pixelation when scaling them.

- Use descriptive captions and labels to provide context and aid in referencing.

- Place figures close to their first reference in the text to improve readability.

- Regularly check for and correct any errors or warnings related to missing or incorrectly referenced figures.

By following these best practices, you can effectively integrate figures and graphics into your XeLaTeX documents, enhancing their visual appeal and overall presentation.

Creating tables in XeLaTeX

In scientific, technical, and academic writing, tables play a crucial role in presenting data and information in a structured and organized manner. XeLaTeX provides powerful tools for creating elegant and customizable tables that meet the highest typographic standards. In this section, we will explore various techniques and packages available in XeLaTeX to create and format tables.

Basic table structure

A table in XeLaTeX consists of rows and columns. Each cell within the table contains content such as text, numbers, or even other tables. The basic structure of a table is defined within the `tabular` environment.

To create a simple table with three columns, we can use the following code:

```
\begin{tabular}{|c|c|c|}
  \hline
  Column 1 & Column 2 & Column 3 \\
  \hline
  Cell 1 & Cell 2 & Cell 3 \\
```

```
\hline
Cell 4 & Cell 5 & Cell 6 \\
\hline
\end{tabular}
```

In this example, the tabular environment is enclosed by \begin{tabular} and \end{tabular} tags. The argument |c|c|c| specifies that the table has three columns, each of which is centered (c) and separated by vertical lines (|). The command \hline creates horizontal lines to separate the header row from the content rows.

The ampersand (&) character is used to separate the content in each cell, and the double backslash (\\) represents the end of a row. The header row is typically formatted differently than the content rows, providing visual cues to the reader.

Formatting table contents

XeLaTeX provides various packages to format table contents, such as booktabs, multirow, and multicolumn. These packages enhance the appearance and readability of tables.

The booktabs package offers improved table design with guidelines on the use of horizontal lines. It encourages the use of three horizontal lines: one at the top, one between the header row and the content rows, and one at the bottom. Suppressed vertical lines are recommended, giving the table a cleaner and more professional look.

Here's an example of a table formatted using the booktabs package:

```
\begin{tabular}{ccc}
  \toprule
  Column 1 & Column 2 & Column 3 \\
  \midrule
  Cell 1 & Cell 2 & Cell 3 \\
  Cell 4 & Cell 5 & Cell 6 \\
  \bottomrule
\end{tabular}
```

In this example, the toprule, midrule, and bottomrule commands from the booktabs package are used to create horizontal lines, replacing the standard \hline command.

The multirow package allows for spanning multiple rows within a table. This can be useful when a cell needs to cover multiple rows. The syntax for using multirow is as follows:

```
\begin{tabular}{|c|c|c|}
  \hline
  \multirow{2}{*}{Header 1} & Header 2 & Header 3 \\
  & Subheader & Subheader \\
  \hline
  Content 1 & Cell 2 & Cell 3 \\
  \hline
  Content 4 & Cell 5 & Cell 6 \\
  \hline
\end{tabular}
```

In this example, the multirow command is used to span two rows in the first column of the table. The first argument specifies the number of rows to span, and the second argument defines the content of the cell. The asterisk (*) tells XeLaTeX to automatically determine the height of the row.

The multicolumn package is used to merge cells horizontally within a table. This can be useful when a cell needs to span multiple columns. The syntax for using multicolumn is as follows:

```
\begin{tabular}{|c|c|c|}
  \hline
  Header 1 & Header 2 & Header 3 \\
  \hline
  \multicolumn{2}{|c|}{Merged Cell} & Cell 3 \\
  \hline
  Cell 4 & Cell 5 & Cell 6 \\
  \hline
\end{tabular}
```

In this example, the multicolumn command is used to merge two columns in the table. The first argument specifies the number of columns to merge, and the second argument defines the content of the merged cell.

Enhancing table layout

XeLaTeX provides additional tools and packages to enhance the layout and aesthetics of tables. Two popular packages for this purpose are `tabularx` and `colortbl`.

The `tabularx` package provides an extended version of the `tabular` environment with adjustable column widths. This allows tables to automatically adjust their width to fit the available space. The syntax for using `tabularx` is as follows:

```
\begin{tabularx}{\textwidth}{|X|X|}
  \hline
  Column 1 & Column 2 \\
  \hline
  Cell 1 & Cell 2 \\
  \hline
  Cell 3 & Cell 4 \\
  \hline
\end{tabularx}
```

In this example, the `tabularx` environment is used instead of the standard `tabular` environment. The argument `\textwidth` specifies that the table should occupy the full width of the text area. The X column specifier expands to fill the available space and allows the table to automatically adjust its width.

The `colortbl` package provides support for coloring rows, columns, or individual cells in a table. This can be useful for highlighting specific information or adding visual interest. The syntax for using `colortbl` is as follows:

```
\begin{tabular}{|c|c|}
  \hline
  \rowcolor{gray!20} Column 1 & Column 2 \\
  \hline
  Cell 1 & \cellcolor{blue!20}Cell 2 \\
  \hline
\end{tabular}
```

In this example, the \rowcolor command is used to color the entire row, and the \cellcolor command is used to color individual cells. The color names, such as gray!20 and blue!20, can be adjusted to achieve the desired color.

Conclusion

Tables are a fundamental part of scientific and technical writing, allowing for the clear and organized presentation of data and information. XeLaTeX provides powerful tools and packages for creating and formatting tables, giving you complete control over their structure and appearance. By utilizing packages like booktabs, multirow, multicolumn, tabularx, and colortbl, you can create professional and visually appealing tables that enhance the overall quality of your documents.

While tables may seem simple at first glance, they require careful attention to detail to ensure clarity and readability. Remember to keep your tables neat and well-organized, using appropriate spacing, alignment, and formatting techniques. Always consider the needs of your audience and the purpose of the table, and choose the most suitable format and layout accordingly.

Exercises

1. Create a table to compare the features of different programming languages, including syntax, paradigms, and popularity.

2. Format the following table using the booktabs package:

Student ID	Name	Score
12345	John Smith	85
23456	Jane Doe	92
34567	Alex Johnson	78

Table 0.1: Student Scores

3. Create a table with merged cells to display the average monthly temperatures for different cities.

4. Experiment with different color combinations using the colortbl package to create visually appealing tables.

5. Explore additional packages and techniques for advanced table customization in XeLaTeX and share your findings with others.

Remember to document your code and provide clear explanations for each exercise.

Resources

- The booktabs package documentation: *https://ctan.org/pkg/booktabs*
  - The multirow package documentation: *https://ctan.org/pkg/multirow*
  - The tabularx package documentation: *https://ctan.org/pkg/tabularx*
  - The colortbl package documentation: *https://ctan.org/pkg/colortbl*
  - The LaTeX Wikibook on tables: *https://en.wikibooks.org/wiki/LaTeX/Tables*

Footnotes and endnotes in XeLaTeX

In academic and technical writing, it is common to include additional information or references as footnotes or endnotes. XeLaTeX provides several options for managing and customizing footnotes and endnotes in your documents. In this section, we will explore the different methods and techniques for adding footnotes and endnotes in XeLaTeX.

Basic Footnotes

To add a footnote in XeLaTeX, you can use the \footnote{} command. Simply place the command within the sentence or paragraph where you want the footnote marker to appear, and provide the corresponding footnote text as the argument. XeLaTeX will automatically insert the footnote marker in the text and place the footnote at the bottom of the page.

For example, let's consider the following sentence:

```
The history of XeLaTeX dates back to the early 2000s.\footnote{XeL
```

When compiled, the output will be:

The history of XeLaTeX dates back to the early 2000s.[1]

Note that XeLaTeX automatically assigns a unique marker to each footnote and generates the corresponding footnote text at the bottom of the page. If you have multiple footnotes within a single page, XeLaTeX will handle the numbering and formatting automatically.

Customizing Footnotes

XeLaTeX allows you to customize the appearance and formatting of footnotes according to your requirements. You can change the style, size, and position of the footnote markers as well as the presentation of the footnote text.

---

[1] XeLaTeX was first released in 2004.

To customize the style of the footnote markers, you can use packages like `footmisc` or `fnpct`. These packages provide additional functionalities and options for formatting footnotes. For example, you can change the symbols used for footnote markers or use superscript numbers instead.

To change the positioning of the footnotes, you can use the `\footnote` command with optional arguments. For instance, you can use the `\footnote[num]` command to change the marker to a specific number. Similarly, you can use `\footnotemark[num]` to only print the marker without the corresponding footnote text. Later in the document, you can use `\footnotetext[num]{...}` to specify the footnote text at a desired location.

You can also customize the appearance of the footnote text itself. You can change the font size, style, or even the numbering format using packages like `footmisc` or `manyfoot`.

Endnotes

In addition to footnotes, XeLaTeX also supports the use of endnotes. Endnotes are similar to footnotes, but they are placed at the end of a chapter or the entire document, rather than at the bottom of the page.

To use endnotes in XeLaTeX, you need to load the `endnotes` package in the preamble of your document. Then, you can use the `\endnote{}` command to insert an endnote within the text. The endnotes will be automatically collected and placed in a separate section at the end of the chapter or document.

For example:

```
The main advantage of using XeLaTeX is its support for Unicode.\e
that allows representation of almost all writing systems and symbo
This makes it easier to typeset\index{typeset} multilingual docume
```

When compiled, the endnote will be collected and displayed at the end of the chapter or document. The numbering of the endnotes will be handled automatically.

The `endnotes` package provides several customization options for endnotes, such as changing the title of the endnotes section or changing the format of the endnote markers.

Conclusion

In this section, we explored the methods for adding footnotes and endnotes in XeLaTeX. We learned how to use the `\footnote` command to add footnotes and how to customize their appearance using packages. We also saw how to use the \endnote command to add endnotes and customize their formatting.

Footnotes and endnotes are essential for providing additional information, references, or explanations in academic and technical writing. As an author, it is important to use footnotes and endnotes correctly and consistently to enhance the readability and credibility of your document.

It is recommended to refer to the documentation of the packages mentioned in this section for more detailed information on customization options and best practices for working with footnotes and endnotes in XeLaTeX.

Further Reading:

- The documentation of the footmisc package.

- The documentation of the fnpct package.

- The documentation of the manyfoot package.

Exercise:

1. Add footnotes to a sample document explaining key concepts related to your field of study.

2. Add endnotes to a research article with supplementary information and references.

3. Experiment with different customization options for footnotes and endnotes, such as changing the marker symbols or formatting the text.

Cross-referencing in XeLaTeX

In XeLaTeX, cross-referencing is a powerful tool that allows you to refer to other parts of your document, such as sections, figures, tables, equations, and even citations. Cross-referencing is essential in academic and technical writing as it helps readers navigate through complex documents and locate specific information easily.

To use cross-referencing in XeLaTeX, you need to follow a few steps:

1. Labeling: Begin by labeling the element you want to refer to using the \label{...} command. This label acts as a marker that can be referenced later in the document. For example, if you want to refer to a section titled "Introduction," you can place a label within the section like this:

```
\section{Introduction}
\label{sec:introduction}
...
```

2. Referencing: Once you have labeled an element, you can refer to it by using the `\ref{...}` command. This command retrieves the number or identifier associated with the labeled element and inserts it into the text. For example, if you want to refer to the labeled section "Introduction," you can use the `\ref` command like this:

```
In the \ref{sec:introduction} section, we will discuss...
```

When the document is compiled, the `\ref` command will be replaced with the appropriate number or identifier of the referenced element.

3. Compilation: It's important to compile your XeLaTeX document multiple times to make sure all cross-references are resolved correctly. The initial compilation may not include all the necessary information for cross-referencing, so running XeLaTeX again will update the references.

It's worth noting that XeLaTeX automatically handles the numbering and formatting of cross-references. If you add or remove elements that affect the numbering (such as adding a new section or figure), XeLaTeX will update the cross-references accordingly.

Let's look at a practical example. Suppose we have a document with several sections, figures, and equations, and we want to cross-reference them:

```
\section{Introduction}
\label{sec:introduction}

In this section\index{section}, we will discuss the basic\index{b

\section{Methodology}
\label{sec:methodology}

The methodology\index{methodology} for our study\index{study} is

\subsection{Experimental Setup}
\label{subsec:experimental-setup}

The experimental setup\index{setup} plays a\index{a} crucial role
```

Figure \ref{fig:data} shows the collected data from our experiment

```
\section{Results}
\label{sec:results}
```

The results obtained are presented in\index{in} this section\index

Table \ref{tab:results} summarizes the findings.

The equation \ref{eq:important-equation} represents a vital relati

```
% \begin{figure}[ht]
% \centering
% \includegraphics[width=0.8\textwidth]{data.png}
% \caption{Collected Data}
% \label{fig:data}
% \end{figure}
```

```
\begin{table}[ht]
\centering
\begin{tabular}{|c|c|}
\hline
Parameter & Value \\
\hline
A & 10 \\
B & 20 \\
\hline
\end{tabular}
\caption{Experimental Results}
\label{tab:results}
\end{table}
```

```
\begin{equation}
E = mc^2
\label{eq:important-equation}
\end{equation}
```

In this example, we have labeled the sections, subsection, figure, table, and equation using the `\label` command. Then, we have referred to them using the `\ref` command. When the document is compiled, the cross-references will be updated automatically with the corresponding numbers and labels.

It's essential to keep in mind that when you modify the structure of your document, such as adding or removing sections, figures, or equations, you need to recompile the document to ensure the cross-references are up to date.

Additionally, XeLaTeX provides several packages, such as `hyperref`, that enhance cross-referencing capabilities by adding hyperlinks to the references, making it easier for readers to navigate within the document. The `hyperref` package is highly recommended if your document contains many cross-references.

Cross-referencing is a valuable feature in XeLaTeX that helps readers navigate complex documents and enhances the overall reading experience. By utilizing the `\label` and `\ref` commands, you can create informative and interactive documents.

In summary, cross-referencing in XeLaTeX involves labeling elements within your document using `\label` and then referring to those labels using `\ref`. Regularly recompiling the document ensures that the cross-references are accurate and up to date. Adding the `hyperref` package can enhance the navigation experience by enabling hyperlinks in the cross-references.

Creating bibliographies in XeLaTeX

Bibliographies are an essential part of academic writing, allowing authors to provide references for the sources they have consulted. In this section, we will explore how to create bibliographies in XeLaTeX using the popular BibLaTeX package. We will cover the basics of setting up a bibliography database, citing sources, and generating a bibliography in various citation styles.

Setting up a bibliography database

Before we can start citing sources and generating a bibliography, we need to set up a bibliography database. XeLaTeX uses BibLaTeX, which provides a flexible and powerful way to manage bibliographic data.

To create a bibliography database, we need to create a .bib file that contains the bibliographic entries. Each entry corresponds to a specific source and includes key-value pairs for different fields such as author, title, year, etc. Here is an example of a bibliographic entry for a book:

```
@book{smith2010,
```

```
    author = {John Smith},
    title = {The Art of Writing},
    year = {2010},
    publisher = {Publisher Name}
}
```

In this example, the key "smith2010" is used to uniquely identify the book. We can use this key later to cite the source in our document.

Citing sources

Once we have our bibliography database set up, we can start citing sources in our document. BibLaTeX provides the \cite command for this purpose. This command takes the key of the entry we want to cite as its argument.

For example, to cite the book we defined earlier, we can use the following command:

```
\cite{smith2010}
```

When we compile our document, XeLaTeX will replace the \cite command with the appropriate citation. By default, BibLaTeX uses numeric citations, so the citation in the generated document will be represented as a number enclosed in square brackets, like [1].

Generating a bibliography

To generate a bibliography, we need to include the \printbibliography command in our document. This command tells BibLaTeX to generate the bibliography based on the citations we have used.

By default, the generated bibliography will include all the entries in our bibliography database. However, we can also filter the bibliography to include only the sources we have cited. To do this, we can use the \nocite command to specify which entries should be included in the bibliography, even if they are not explicitly cited in the document.

Here is an example of how to generate a bibliography in XeLaTeX:

```
\printbibliography
```

By default, BibLaTeX uses the "author-year" citation style. However, we can easily change the citation style by providing an optional argument to the

\printbibliography command. BibLaTeX provides various built-in citation styles, such as "numeric", "alphabetic", and "ieee". We can also customize the citation style by modifying the bibliography style.

Customizing the bibliography style

BibLaTeX provides a powerful way to customize the bibliography style. We can modify the appearance of the bibliography by creating a custom bibliography style file (.bbx) and modifying the relevant formatting commands.

For instance, if we want to change the bibliography style to use footnotes instead of in-text citations, we can create a custom .bbx file and define a new bibliography driver for footnotes. We can then load this custom style file in our document using the \bibliographystyle command.

Conclusion

In this section, we have explored how to create bibliographies in XeLaTeX using the BibLaTeX package. We have learned how to set up a bibliography database, cite sources, generate a bibliography, and customize the bibliography style. With this knowledge, you will be able to create professional-looking bibliographies for your academic documents.

Remember to consult the BibLaTeX documentation for more advanced customization options and additional citation styles. Happy typesetting!

Adding Annotations and Comments in XeLaTeX

In this section, we will explore how to add annotations and comments in XeLaTeX documents. Annotations and comments are useful for indicating areas that need revision, giving feedback on specific parts of a document, or providing additional explanations or instructions. XeLaTeX provides several ways to add annotations and comments, including inline comments, margin notes, and text boxes.

Inline Comments

Inline comments are a convenient way to add short annotations directly within the text of a document. These comments are usually not visible in the final output, but they provide valuable information for the author or collaborators. To add an inline comment in XeLaTeX, you can use the % symbol followed by your comment.

For example, consider the following sentence:

```
XeLaTeX is a\index{a} powerful document\index{document} markup\ind
```

You can add an inline comment to highlight a potential issue, like this:

```
XeLaTeX is a powerful document markup language used % Consider add
for typesetting\index{typesetting}.
```

The comment does not affect the compiled document, but it provides a reminder for the author to revisit that particular section.

Margin Notes

Margin notes allow you to add longer annotations or comments in the margins of your document. These can be used for providing additional explanations, references, or suggestions related to specific parts of the content. XeLaTeX provides the \marginpar command to add margin notes.

To add a margin note, use the following syntax:

```
\marginpar{This is a margin note.}
```

Here's an example:

```
XeLaTeX offers powerful features for typesetting documents.\margin
```

When compiled, the margin note will appear in the margin of the respective page. You can customize the appearance and placement of margin notes using package options or by modifying the page layout settings.

Text Boxes

Text boxes are useful for adding longer annotations or comments that require a separate area on the page. XeLaTeX provides various packages, such as tcolorbox or mdframed, that allow you to create customizable text boxes. These packages provide a wide range of options for styling, including borders, background colors, and shadows.

To create a text box using the tcolorbox package, use the following syntax:

```
\begin{tcolorbox}[options]
    This is a\index{a} text\index{text} box\index{box}.
\end{tcolorbox}
```

Here's an example:

```
\begin{tcolorbox}[colback=yellow!10!white,colframe=red!75!black,t
    This is an important note\index{note} regarding the topic\ind
\end{tcolorbox}
```

When compiled, the text box will appear on the page with the specified formatting and title.

It's important to note that text boxes may require additional packages and may affect the overall layout of the document. Ensure that the use of text boxes is consistent with the design and structure of your document.

Best Practices for Annotations and Comments

When adding annotations and comments in XeLaTeX, keep these best practices in mind:

- Be clear and concise: Annotations should provide relevant information without being overly verbose.

- Use a consistent style: Maintain a consistent style for your annotations and comments throughout the document.

- Provide context: If an annotation refers to a specific part of the document or requires additional explanation, make sure to provide enough context for the readers to understand the comment.

- Revise and remove annotations: Regularly review annotations and comments to ensure that they are still relevant. Remove annotations that are no longer necessary.

By following these best practices, you can effectively use annotations and comments to enhance collaboration and improve the quality of your documents.

Summary

In this section, we explored various methods for adding annotations and comments in XeLaTeX documents. We discussed inline comments, margin notes, and text boxes as different options for annotating and commenting on specific parts of a document. We also highlighted the importance of following best practices to ensure clear and effective communication through annotations and comments.

Adding annotations and comments in XeLaTeX can improve collaboration and facilitate the revision process of a document. By utilizing these techniques, you can enhance the readability and clarity of your documents, making them more engaging and impactful for your audience.

Advanced Techniques in XeLaTeX

Customizing document styles in XeLaTeX

In XeLaTeX, document styles play a crucial role in defining the overall appearance and layout of a document. They allow users to customize various elements such as fonts, spacing, headers, footers, and more. Customizing document styles in XeLaTeX involves understanding the structure of a document class, modifying its default settings, and utilizing various packages and commands to achieve the desired style. In this section, we will explore different techniques and best practices for customizing document styles in XeLaTeX.

Understanding document class options

The first step in customizing document styles is to select an appropriate document class. Each document class provides a set of default styles and options that can be modified according to the user's requirements. Some popular document classes in XeLaTeX are `article`, `report`, and `book`.

When choosing a document class, it is essential to consider the type of document you are writing. For example, the `article` class is suitable for shorter documents like research papers, while the `book` class is more suitable for longer documents such as books or theses. The `report` class is a balance between the two.

Document class options allow users to modify global settings such as paper size, font size, and the number of columns. For instance, to set the document font size to 12pt, you can use the following command:

```
\documentclass[12pt]{article}
```

It is also possible to combine multiple options by separating them with commas. For example, to set the paper size to A4 and the font size to 12pt, you can use:

```
\documentclass[a4paper, 12pt]{article}
```

Different document classes have their specific options, so it's important to consult the documentation for each document class to explore the available customization possibilities.

Modifying fonts and typography

One of the most significant advantages of using XeLaTeX is its excellent support for font customization. By default, XeLaTeX can use any font installed on your system. This feature allows users to choose from a wide range of fonts for their documents, including system fonts, OpenType fonts, TrueType fonts, and more.

To set the main font of a document, use the `fontspec` package. This package provides commands like `\setmainfont` and `\setsansfont` to modify the main and sans-serif fonts, respectively. For example, to set the main font to Times New Roman and the sans-serif font to Arial, you can use the following code:

```
\setmainfont{Times New Roman}
\setsansfont{Arial}
```

XeLaTeX also offers additional font features such as ligatures, letterspacing, and more. These features can be enabled using the `fontspec` package. For example, to enable ligatures for the main font, use the command `\setmainfont[Ligatures=TeX]{Times New Roman}`.

In addition to modifying fonts, XeLaTeX provides commands to control typography aspects such as line spacing, paragraph formatting, and justification. The `setspace` package allows users to set custom line spacing using commands like `\singlespacing`, `\onehalfspacing`, and `\doublespacing`. To adjust paragraph indentation, the `parskip` package can be used. For example, to set no indentation and to insert a vertical space between paragraphs, use `\usepackage[parfill]{parskip}`.

Customizing page layout

Customizing the page layout in XeLaTeX involves adjusting parameters such as margin sizes, header and footer styles, page numbering, and more. The `geometry` package is a powerful tool for customizing page dimensions and margins. For example, to set all margins to 1 inch, use the command `\usepackage[margin=1in]{geometry}`.

Header and footer styles can be customized using the `fancyhdr` package. This package provides commands to set the content of the header and footer, as well as the placement of page numbers. For example, to set the page number on the top right corner of each page, use the following code:

```
\pagestyle{fancy}
\rhead{\thepage}
```

XeLaTeX also offers customization options for title pages, including the ability to display a custom title, author, and date. The `titling` package provides commands like `\title{}`, `\author{}`, and `\date{}` to set the corresponding elements. To display the title information on the document, use the command `\maketitle`.

Adding additional packages and styles

To further customize document styles, XeLaTeX allows users to include additional packages and styles. These packages provide various features and functionalities, such as typesetting algorithms, including graphics, creating tables, and more.

For example, the `algorithm2e` package provides commands to create and format algorithms in a document. The `graphicx` package allows users to insert images into the document, and the `tabularx` package provides a flexible environment for creating tables with adjustable columns.

It is important to note that when adding additional packages, users should ensure that there are no conflicts between the packages' functionalities. Some packages may have conflicting settings or require specific loading orders. In such cases, it is recommended to consult the package documentation or seek assistance from the XeLaTeX community.

Best practices for customizing document styles

When customizing document styles in XeLaTeX, it is crucial to follow some best practices to ensure clean and maintainable code. Here are a few tips:

+ Start with a minimal setup: Begin with a simple document class and minimal set of packages relevant to your document. Avoid adding unnecessary packages that may introduce conflicts or affect performance.

+ Separate formatting and content: Keep the formatting and content separate by defining the document structure in the preamble and putting the actual content in the document body.

+ Use stylesheets: Define custom stylesheets, such as CSS-like files, to centralize style definitions and make it easier to apply consistent styles across multiple documents.

+ Comment your code: Commenting your code helps document the intent of specific customizations and aids in future modifications or debugging.

+ Test on different devices: Check the appearance and layout of your document on various devices, including different screen sizes and printers, to ensure the desired output is achieved.

+ Stay up to date: Keep track of updates to packages and document class versions to take advantage of new features, bug fixes, and security improvements.

By following these best practices, you can ensure that your customizations are easy to manage, efficient, and produce the desired visual outcome.

Summary

In this section, we explored the process of customizing document styles in XeLaTeX. We learned about the importance of selecting an appropriate document class, modifying fonts and typography, customizing page layout, and adding additional packages and styles. We also discussed some best practices for ensuring clean and maintainable code.

By mastering document style customization in XeLaTeX, you gain full control over the visual appearance and layout of your documents, allowing you to create professional and aesthetically pleasing publications. Experiment with different styles, be creative, and enjoy the vast possibilities that XeLaTeX offers for customizing your documents.

Creating Complex Mathematical Equations in XeLaTeX

In scientific and technical writing, the ability to typeset complex mathematical equations accurately and elegantly is of utmost importance. XeLaTeX provides a powerful and flexible platform for creating and formatting mathematical expressions with precision. In this section, we will explore various techniques and strategies for creating complex mathematical equations in XeLaTeX.

Math Modes in XeLaTeX

Before we dive into creating complex equations, let's briefly discuss the two math modes available in XeLaTeX: inline math mode and display math mode.

Inline Math Mode   In inline math mode, mathematical expressions are inserted directly within the text. To enter inline math mode, enclose the math expression within a pair of dollar signs (\$). For example, to typeset the equation $E = mc^2$, we can write it as $E = mc^2$ within a paragraph.

Display Math Mode   Display math mode is used for equations that are displayed separately from the surrounding text. To enter display math mode, use the double dollar signs (\$\$) or the \[and \] delimiters. For example:

$$E = mc^2$$

or

$$E = mc^2 \tag{1}$$

Display math mode is especially useful for complex equations or when equation numbers are desired.

Formatting Equations

XeLaTeX provides a wide range of symbols, operators, and commands to format and structure mathematical expressions. Let's explore some of the most commonly used ones:

Superscripts and Subscripts   To include superscripts and subscripts, use the caret ("^") and underscore ("_"), respectively. For example, to write X^2 and X_1, use \^2 and _1.

Fractions   Fractions   can   be   created   using   the \frac{numerator}{denominator} command. For instance, to write $\frac{1}{2}$, use \frac{1}{2}.

Roots and Exponents   To represent square roots or any other Nth root, use the \sqrt{} command. For example, to display $\sqrt{9}$, use \sqrt{9}. Similarly, to represent exponentiation, use the caret symbol ("^"). To write X^3, use X^3.

Greek Letters   XeLaTeX supports the use of Greek letters in mathematical expressions. To write Greek letters, use the backslash ("\") followed by the name of the letter. For example, to write alpha (α), use \alpha.

Matrices and Arrays   To create matrices or arrays in XeLaTeX, we can use the `matrix` or `array` environments. For example:

$$\begin{matrix} 1 & 2 \\ 3 & 4 \end{matrix}$$

or

$$\begin{matrix} 1 & 2 & 3 \\ 4 & 5 & 6 \\ 7 & 8 & 9 \end{matrix}$$

Advanced Equations

Now that we have covered the basics of formatting equations, let's explore some more advanced techniques for creating complex mathematical expressions in XeLaTeX.

Equation Numbering   By default, XeLaTeX numbers equations automatically in display math mode. However, if you want to manually label and reference equations, you can use the \label and \ref commands. For example:

$$E = mc^2 \tag{2}$$

The equation above can be referenced using Equation \ref{eq:einstein}. XeLaTeX will automatically update the equation number if other equations are added or removed.

Aligning Equations   To align multiple equations or lines of an equation, you can use the \align or \align* environment. For instance:

$$x + y = 5 \tag{3}$$
$$2x - y = 1 \tag{4}$$

The ampersand (&) symbol is used to align the equations at a specific point.

Mathematical Symbols and Notations   XeLaTeX provides a vast array of symbols and notations for various mathematical disciplines. For example, the package `amssymb` offers additional mathematical symbols like ∞, $\mathbb{R}$, and $\therefore$. You can include this package by adding \usepackage{amssymb} to the preamble of your document.

Real-World Examples

To solidify our understanding of creating complex mathematical equations in XeLaTeX, let's consider a real-world example in physics.

Example: The Schrödinger Equation The Schrödinger equation is a fundamental equation in quantum mechanics that describes the behavior of quantum systems. It is given by:

$$i\hbar\frac{\partial}{\partial t}\Psi(\mathbf{r}, t) = \hat{H}\Psi(\mathbf{r}, t)$$

where i is the imaginary unit, $\hbar$ is the reduced Planck constant, $\frac{\partial}{\partial t}$ represents the partial derivative with respect to time, Ψ is the wave function, $\mathbf{r}$ represents the position vector, t is time, and $\hat{H}$ is the Hamiltonian operator.

Exercise: Maxwell's Equations Consider Maxwell's equations, a set of four fundamental equations in electromagnetism. Write down each equation and label them using appropriate numbering and referencing.

Additional Resources

To further enhance your skills in creating complex mathematical equations in XeLaTeX, the following resources may be helpful:

+ The Comprehensive LaTeX Symbol List provides an extensive catalog of mathematical symbols and their corresponding LaTeX commands.

+ The LaTeX Stack Exchange (tex.stackexchange.com) is a valuable online community for getting help and guidance on specific issues or questions related to LaTeX and XeLaTeX.

+ Online tutorials and guides, such as the one provided by Overleaf (www.overleaf.com/learn), offer step-by-step instructions and examples for different aspects of XeLaTeX, including mathematical equations.

Summary

In this section, we explored the techniques and strategies for creating complex mathematical equations in XeLaTeX. We discussed the two math modes available in XeLaTeX—inline math mode and display math mode—and learned how to format equations using various mathematical symbols and commands. We also delved into advanced equations, such as equation numbering and alignment. Finally, we examined a real-world example and provided additional resources for further learning. Armed with this knowledge, you are now ready to tackle the challenges of typesetting complex mathematical equations in XeLaTeX.

Typesetting multiple languages in XeLaTeX

In today's globalized world, it is common to encounter documents that contain multiple languages. Whether it is a research paper with citations in different languages, a document with multilingual labels and captions, or a book that requires typesetting in multiple scripts, XeLaTeX provides powerful tools to handle such scenarios seamlessly.

1. **Support for Unicode:** One of the main advantages of using XeLaTeX is its extensive support for Unicode. Unicode is an international standard that assigns a unique code to every character used in human writing systems, including characters from different scripts and languages. With XeLaTeX, you can directly input and display characters from various languages without any extra setup or package installations.

2. **Setting the font:** XeLaTeX allows you to choose fonts from different language families for typesetting your document. This means that you can use a single font for Latin-based languages like English, and switch to a different font for non-Latin scripts like Chinese, Arabic, or Devanagari. To select a font, you can use the fontspec package and specify the font name or system font names.

3. **Switching between languages:** XeLaTeX provides convenient commands to switch between different languages within a document. The polyglossia package is widely used for multilingual typesetting. It allows you to define the main language of the document and then switch to other languages whenever needed. For example, you can use the command \setdefaultlanguage{english} to set English as the main language and \setotherlanguage{french} to switch to French.

4. **Language-specific features:** Different languages have their own typographic rules and conventions. XeLaTeX provides support for language-specific features like hyphenation, quotation marks, date formats, and more. For example, the babel package, along with language-specific modules, offers predefined settings and patterns for various languages. By including the desired language-specific module, you can ensure correct typesetting of the language-specific elements.

5. **Bidirectional typesetting:** XeLaTeX also supports bidirectional typesetting, which is essential for languages that are written from right to left, like Arabic and

Hebrew. The `bidi` package provides commands to switch the text direction and handle bidirectional elements like numbers and punctuation marks.

6. **Combined languages:** XeLaTeX allows you to seamlessly combine multiple languages within the same document. You can mix different languages in paragraphs, titles, captions, and even in mathematical equations without any conflicts. Simply switch the language context using the provided commands, and XeLaTeX will handle the rest.

It is important to note that when typesetting multiple languages, it is crucial to choose appropriate fonts that support the necessary scripts. You should also ensure that your document encoding is set to UTF-8, which supports all Unicode characters, to avoid any encoding issues.

Overall, XeLaTeX provides comprehensive support for typesetting multiple languages, allowing you to create professional and visually appealing documents that are inclusive and accessible to a global audience.

Example:

Let's consider an example of a research paper that includes citations in English and French. We want to ensure that both languages are typeset correctly within the document.

```
\documentclass{article}
\usepackage{fontspec}
\usepackage{polyglossia}
\setdefaultlanguage{english}
\setotherlanguage{french}
\begin{document}
Lorem ipsum dolor sit amet, consectetur adipiscing elit.
\cite{source1} states that the problem can be solved in
polynomial time.
\begin{french}
Ceci est un exemple de citation en français
\cite{source2}.
\end{french}
\end{document}
```

In this example, we start with English as the default language. We then switch to French within the `french` environment to typeset the French citation. XeLaTeX takes care of the language-specific formatting and hyphenation automatically.

This approach allows you to maintain consistency throughout your document, regardless of the number of languages involved.

Resources:

- *The LaTeX Font Catalogue* - Comprehensive information about fonts available for use with XeLaTeX: `https://www.tug.org/FontCatalogue`

- *Polyglossia package documentation* - Detailed documentation on using the `polyglossia` package for multilingual typesetting: `https://ctan.org/pkg/polyglossia`

- *The bidi package* - Documentation for the `bidi` package, which handles bidirectional typesetting: `https://ctan.org/pkg/bidi`

- *UTF-8 encoding* - Information about the UTF-8 character encoding and its importance for multilingual typesetting: `https://en.wikipedia.org/wiki/UTF-8`

- *LaTeX Wikibook* - Provides extensive information and examples on various LaTeX topics, including multilingual typesetting: `https://en.wikibooks.org/wiki/LaTeX`

Incorporating graphics and multimedia in XeLaTeX

In this section, we will explore how to incorporate graphics and multimedia elements into XeLaTeX documents. Visuals and multimedia can greatly enhance the readability and engagement of documents, making them more informative and visually appealing. XeLaTeX provides various packages and tools to seamlessly integrate images, videos, audio, and other multimedia elements into your documents.

Including Images in XeLaTeX Documents

Images are one of the most common forms of visual media used in documents. XeLaTeX supports various image formats, including JPEG, PNG, EPS, PDF, and SVG. To include an image in your document, you need to use the `graphicx` package, which provides the `includegraphics` command.

Syntax:

```
\includegraphics[options]{image_file}
```

The `options` parameter allows you to specify various properties of the inserted image, such as width, height, scale, rotation, and alignment. The `image_file` argument represents the path to your image file.

Example:

. . .

. . .
```
\includegraphics[width=0.5\textwidth]{image.jpg}
```
. . .

In the example above, the `includegraphics` command is used to insert an image called `image.jpg` into the document. The `width` option is set to 0.5 times the width of the text area, which scales the image to half of the text width.

Manipulating and Scaling Images in XeLaTeX

XeLaTeX provides various options to manipulate and scale images to suit your document needs. You can adjust the size, resolution, rotation, and position of the inserted image.

Scaling Images: To scale an image, you can set the `width` or `height` option of the `includegraphics` command. The value can be an absolute length (e.g., 2cm, 50pt) or a relative length (e.g., `0.5\textwidth`, `0.3\textheight`). XeLaTeX automatically resizes the image while maintaining the aspect ratio.

Rotating Images: You can rotate an image by specifying the desired angle in degrees using the `angle` option of the `includegraphics` command.

Positioning Images: By default, images are inserted at the current insertion point in the document. However, you can control the position of the image using the `figure` environment. The `figure` environment allows you to add captions, labels, and references to your images.

Example:
```
% \begin{figure}[htbp]
% \centering
% \includegraphics[width=0.7\textwidth, angle=45]{image.jpg}
% \caption{An example image rotated by 45 degrees}
% \label{fig:image}
```

```
% \end{figure}
```

In the example above, the image is rotated by 45 degrees and centered using the `centering` command. The `figure` environment is used to add a caption and label to the image. The label allows you to reference the image later in the document using the `ref` command.

Customizing Image Placement and Alignment in XeLaTeX

XeLaTeX provides options to control the placement and alignment of images within your document. By default, images are placed at the current insertion point and aligned to the left margin.

Placement Options: The placement options specify where the image can be positioned within the document. The common placement options include:

- **h:** Place the image at the current position
- **t:** Place the image at the top of the page
- **b:** Place the image at the bottom of the page
- **p:** Place the image on a separate page

You can combine these options (e.g., `htbp`) to indicate your preferred placement. However, keep in mind that XeLaTeX will try its best to honor the placement options, but it may not always be possible depending on the content and available space in the document.

Aligning Images: By default, images are aligned to the left margin of the page. However, you can change the alignment using the `floatrow` package. The `floatrow` package allows you to align the image to the left, right, or center of the page.

Example:

```
% \begin{figure}[htbp]
% \centering
% \includegraphics[width=0.7\textwidth]{image.jpg}
% \caption{An example image}
% \label{fig:image}
% \end{figure}
```

The example above demonstrates a typical usage of the `figure` environment. The image is centered using the `centering` command.

Incorporating multimedia in XeLaTeX

In addition to static images, XeLaTeX also supports the inclusion of multimedia elements such as videos, audios, and animations. This can be achieved using the `animate` package and the `media9` package.

Including Videos: To include a video in your XeLaTeX document, you can use the `media9` package. This package provides the `includemedia` command, which allows you to embed a video file in your document.

Syntax:

`\includemedia[options]{video_file}`

The `options` parameter allows you to specify various properties of the embedded video, such as width, height, start time, and playback controls. The `video_file` argument represents the path to your video file.

Example:

```
...

...
\includemedia[
  width=0.6\linewidth,
  height=0.45\linewidth,
  activate=pageopen,
  addresource=video.mp4,
  flashvars={
    source=video.mp4
    &autoPlay=true
  }
]{% \includegraphics{video_poster.jpg}}{VPlayer.swf}
...
```

In the example above, a video file called `video.mp4` is embedded into the document using the `includemedia` command. The video is displayed as a poster image (`video_poster.jpg`) with dimensions specified by `width` and `height`. The `VPlayer.swf` file is used as the video player. The `flashvars` parameter sets the video source and enables auto playback.

Including Audio: To include audio in your XeLaTeX document, you can use the `media9` package. This package provides the `includemedia` command, similar to including videos.

Syntax:

`\includemedia[options]{audio_file}`

The `options` parameter allows you to specify various properties of the embedded audio, such as width, height, autoPlay, and controls. The `audio_file` argument represents the path to your audio file.

Example:

```
...


...
\includemedia[
  width=0.6\linewidth,
  height=1em,
  activate=pageopen,
  addresource=audio.mp3,
  flashvars={
    source=audio.mp3
    &autoPlay=true
  }
]{\fbox{Play Audio}}{APlayer.swf}
...
```

In the example above, an audio file called `audio.mp3` is embedded into the document using the `includemedia` command. The audio is represented by the text "Play Audio" enclosed in a box. The dimensions of the audio player are specified by `width` and `height`. The auto playback is enabled using the `autoplay` parameter.

Best Practices for Using Graphics and Multimedia in XeLaTeX

Here are some best practices for incorporating graphics and multimedia elements in XeLaTeX documents:

- Use vector graphics whenever possible, as they can be scaled without loss of quality.

- Optimize images for size and resolution to balance quality and document size.

- Test the compatibility of multimedia elements across different document viewers and platforms.

- Provide alternative content or descriptions for images and multimedia elements to ensure accessibility.

- Ensure proper attribution and licensing for any external images or multimedia elements used in your document.

- Regularly check for updates and new features in XeLaTeX and related packages used for graphics and multimedia.

By following these best practices, you can effectively incorporate graphics and multimedia elements into your XeLaTeX documents, enhancing their visual appeal and engagement.

Creating professional presentations with XeLaTeX

Creating professional presentations is an essential skill in today's digital age. Whether you are presenting your research findings, pitching a business idea, or delivering a keynote speech, a well-designed and visually appealing presentation can greatly enhance your message and captivate your audience. In this section, we will explore how XeLaTeX can be utilized to create stunning, professional presentations.

Principles of effective presentation design

Before delving into the technical aspects of creating presentations with XeLaTeX, it's important to understand the principles of effective presentation design. Here are some key principles to consider:

- **Simplicity:** Keep your slides clean and uncluttered. Use concise bullet points and limit the amount of text on each slide. Remember, your audience should be focused on your words, not struggling to read a dense slide.

- **Visual appeal:** Use visually engaging elements such as high-quality images, charts, and diagrams. Incorporate a consistent color scheme and typography to create a cohesive visual experience throughout your presentation.

- **Hierarchy and structure:** Organize your content using a logical hierarchy. Utilize headings, subheadings, and slide transitions to guide your audience through your presentation smoothly.

- **Consistency:** Maintain a consistent design style throughout your presentation. Use the same font, color scheme, and layout for all slides to reinforce your brand or message.

- **Engagement:** Incorporate interactive elements, such as hyperlinks, embedded videos, or animations, to make your presentation more engaging and dynamic.

Now that we have established the principles of effective presentation design, let's explore how XeLaTeX can help us bring these principles to life.

Preparing a XeLaTeX document for presentation

To create a presentation with XeLaTeX, we can utilize the Beamer class, which provides a powerful framework specifically designed for creating professional presentations. To get started, we need to set up our document with the Beamer class and define our presentation style.

```
\usetheme{theme_name}

\setmainfont{font_name}
\title{My Presentation}
\author{Your Name}
```

```
\date{\today}
```

```
\begin{frame}
\titlepage
\end{frame}
```

```
\section{Introduction}
\subsection{Overview}
\begin{frame}{Slide Title}
Content of the slide\index{slide}...
\end{frame}
```

```
% More slides...
```

In the above example, we have set the document class as beamer and chosen a presentation theme using the command \usetheme{theme_name}. We have also specified the font for our presentation using the fontspec package and the command \setmainfont{font_name}. The \title, \author, and \date commands are used to customize the title page with your desired information.

To define the structure of our presentation, we use the \section and \subsection commands to create sections and subsections within our presentation. Each \frame environment represents a new slide in the presentation, and we can provide a title and content for each slide.

Adding visual elements to your presentation

Now, let's explore how we can enhance our presentation by adding visual elements such as images, graphs, and animations. XeLaTeX provides various packages that can be utilized for this purpose.

- **Images:** To include images in our presentation, we can use the graphicx package. We can use the \includegraphics command to insert an image file into our slide. For example, to insert an image named image.png, we can use the following command:

```
\includegraphics[width=0.5\textwidth]{image.png}
```

- **Graphs and diagrams:** For creating graphs and diagrams, the TikZ package can be immensely helpful. TikZ is a versatile and powerful tool that allows us to create high-quality graphics directly in our XeLaTeX document. We can draw various types of graphs, flowcharts, and other visual elements using TikZ commands within a `tikzpicture` environment.

- **Animations:** XeLaTeX also supports the inclusion of animations in presentations. We can use the `animate` package to embed animations in our slides. This package allows us to include animated GIFs, SWF (Flash) files, and JavaScript-based animations. To include an animation, we can use the `\animategraphics` command.

Presentation tips and best practices

To deliver an engaging and impactful presentation, here are some additional tips and best practices:

- Practice your presentation to ensure smooth delivery and timing. Familiarize yourself with the content and rehearse your speaking points.

- Use a remote presenter or presenter view to navigate through your slides easily. This will allow you to maintain eye contact with your audience while controlling the presentation.

- Consider using slide transitions and animations sparingly and strategically. Overusing effects can distract and detract from the content of your presentation.

- Keep your audience engaged by involving them through interactive elements, such as polls, quizzes, or questions.

- Use a legible font size and choose high-contrast colors to ensure maximum readability, particularly for larger audiences or projection screens.

- Practice good presentation skills, such as maintaining a confident posture, speaking clearly and audibly, and effectively using visual aids.

Remember, a successful presentation is not solely dependent on the technology or design but also on your delivery and ability to connect with your audience. Utilizing XeLaTeX can help you create visually appealing and professional presentations, but ultimately, your content and presentation skills will determine the overall success.

Exercise: Create a XeLaTeX presentation with at least five slides on a topic of your choice. Incorporate visual elements such as images, graphs, or animations to enhance your presentation. Practice delivering your presentation and gather feedback from your peers or colleagues.

Additional resources

Here are some additional resources to further explore the world of XeLaTeX presentations:

- **Beamer User Guide:** The official Beamer user guide is a comprehensive resource for understanding the capabilities and usage of the Beamer class. It provides detailed documentation and examples.

- **TikZ and PGF Manual:** The TikZ and PGF manual is an extensive guide on using the TikZ package for creating graphics and diagrams. It covers the various commands and options available for drawing complex visual elements.

- **Beamer Theme Gallery:** The Beamer Theme Gallery is a collection of different presentation themes available for Beamer. It showcases various styles and designs to choose from.

- **Presentation Tips and Techniques:** Explore books, articles, and online resources on effective presentation techniques, public speaking, and designing engaging slide decks.

Summary

In this section, we have explored the principles of effective presentation design and how XeLaTeX can be utilized to create professional presentations. We learned how to set up a XeLaTeX document for presentations using the Beamer class and customized our presentation style. We also discussed adding visual elements such as images, graphs, and animations to enhance our presentations. Finally, we provided presentation tips and best practices to ensure a successful delivery. With the knowledge gained from this section, you can now confidently create visually stunning and engaging presentations using XeLaTeX.

Collaborative editing using XeLaTeX with version control

Collaborative editing and version control are essential tools for any project involving multiple authors or contributors. With XeLaTeX, you can take advantage of these tools to streamline the collaborative writing process and ensure the integrity and consistency of your documents. In this section, we will explore the benefits of collaborative editing and how to effectively use version control systems with XeLaTeX.

Benefits of Collaborative Editing

Collaborative editing allows multiple authors to work together on a document simultaneously, eliminating the need for cumbersome file sharing and manual merging of changes. With XeLaTeX, you can leverage the power of version control systems to enable efficient and coordinated collaboration. Some benefits of collaborative editing include:

- **Real-time collaboration:** Collaborators can work on the same document simultaneously, making it easier to coordinate and integrate contributions.

- **Version history:** Version control systems automatically keep track of changes made to the document, allowing you to reference previous versions and undo changes if necessary.

- **Conflict resolution:** Version control systems provide mechanisms to resolve conflicts that may arise when multiple authors modify the same section of a document.

- **Traceability:** Collaborators can leave comments, suggestions, and annotations to facilitate communication and provide feedback on specific parts of the document.

Using Version Control Systems with XeLaTeX

Version control systems such as Git and Mercurial can seamlessly integrate with XeLaTeX to manage document revisions and facilitate collaboration. Here, we will focus on Git as an example version control system.

Step 1: Setting Up a Git Repository

To start using version control with XeLaTeX, you first need to set up a Git repository. This is where the document and its revisions will be stored. You can create a new repository on a local machine or use an online Git hosting service like GitHub or GitLab.

Step 2: Initializing the Repository

After creating the repository, navigate to the root directory of your XeLaTeX project in the command line and run the following command to initialize the repository:

```
\$ git init
```

This command initializes the repository and creates a hidden `.git` folder that stores Git's internal files and configuration.

Step 3: Tracking the Document

Next, you need to tell Git which files to track for changes. In your XeLaTeX project directory, run the following command:

```
\$ git add main.tex
```

This command adds the `main.tex` file to the staging area, indicating that it will be included in the next commit.

Step 4: Committing Changes

To create a new revision of the document, you need to commit your changes. Run the following command:

```
\$ git commit -m ``Initial commit"
```

This command commits the changes made to the `main.tex` file and adds a descriptive message (e.g., "Initial commit") to help identify the purpose of the revision.

Step 5: Collaborating with Others

With the Git repository set up, you can now share it with your collaborators. They can clone the repository to their local machines using the following command:

```
\$ git clone <repository_url>
```

Collaborators can make changes to the document, commit them, and synchronize their revisions with the central repository.

Best Practices for Collaborative Editing with XeLaTeX and Version Control

To ensure smooth collaboration and minimize conflicts, consider the following best practices:

- **Communication:** Maintain constant communication with your collaborators to avoid duplication of work and resolve conflicts in a timely manner. Tools like chat applications or project management platforms can facilitate collaboration.

+ **Branching:** Create separate branches in the Git repository for different features, sections, or authors. This way, each collaborator can work on their respective branch without interfering with others' work. Merging branches can be done later to integrate changes.

+ **Code Review:** As collaborators make changes, it is crucial to review the code and provide feedback. Code review helps maintain the quality and consistency of the document. Tools like GitHub's pull requests can facilitate the code review process.

+ **Regular Committing:** Encourage collaborators to commit changes frequently. Smaller, more focused commits are easier to manage and resolve conflicts than large, monolithic ones.

+ **Conflict Resolution:** When conflicts arise, carefully analyze the changes made by different collaborators and resolve conflicts by merging or making necessary adjustments. Tools like Git's merge or rebase functionalities can help with conflict resolution.

Conclusion

Collaborative editing using XeLaTeX and version control systems provides an efficient and organized approach to document collaboration. By leveraging the power of Git or other version control systems, multiple authors can seamlessly collaborate on a document while maintaining a clear history of changes. Adhering to best practices for collaboration and version control ensures smooth coordination and minimizes conflicts. With these techniques, you can harness the power of collaborative editing and produce high-quality documents with XeLaTeX.

Font Selection and Manipulation in XeLaTeX

In this section, we will explore the various aspects of font selection and manipulation in XeLaTeX. Fonts play a crucial role in the overall look and feel of a document, and with XeLaTeX, we have the flexibility to use a wide range of fonts, including system fonts, OpenType fonts, and TrueType fonts.

Introduction to Fonts in XeLaTeX

Fonts are a fundamental element of typography, and they contribute to the clarity and visual appeal of a document. In XeLaTeX, we can leverage the full power of

TrueType and OpenType fonts, which are widely used and provide extensive typographic capabilities.

Font Selection

Choosing the right font for a document requires careful consideration of factors such as readability, style, and context. XeLaTeX provides several ways to select fonts, including system fonts, installed fonts, and external fonts.

System Fonts XeLaTeX allows us to directly use system fonts installed on our computer. This is particularly useful when we want to match the look and feel of the document to the operating system or to other applications. To use a system font, we can specify its name in the document preamble using the `fontspec` package.

```
\setmainfont{Arial}
```

In this example, we set the main font of the document to Arial. We can use similar commands to set specific fonts for headings, captions, or other elements.

Installed Fonts Besides system fonts, XeLaTeX also allows us to use fonts that we have installed on our system. These fonts can be located in the `texmf` directory or in the local directory of the document. To use an installed font, we can use the `fontspec` package and specify the font file's path and name.

```
\newfontfamily\myfont{MyFont}[Path=./fonts/]{MyFont.ttf}
```

In this example, we define a new font family called `myfont` and specify the path and file name of the font. We can then use `\myfont` to select this font within the document.

External Fonts In addition to system and installed fonts, XeLaTeX also allows us to use external fonts. These fonts can be downloaded from various sources and provide a vast array of design options. To use an external font, we need to first ensure that the font file is accessible to XeLaTeX. We can then use the `fontspec` package to load the font and specify its name in the document.

```
\newfontfamily\awesomefont{FontAwesome}
```

In this example, we load the FontAwesome font and assign it the name `awesomefont`. We can now use `\awesomefont` to select this font and utilize its unique icons and symbols.

Font Manipulation

Once we have selected a font, XeLaTeX provides various techniques to manipulate and modify its appearance. We can adjust font size, style, weight, and even combine multiple fonts for different purposes.

Font Size   In XeLaTeX, we can easily change the size of the selected font using the standard `\fontsize` command. This command takes two arguments: the desired size and the baseline skip. For example, to set the font size to 12pt with a baseline skip of 14pt, we can use:

```
\fontsize{12pt}{14pt}\selectfont
```

This command will change the font size from the point at which it is issued until the end of the current group.

Font Style   XeLaTeX allows us to modify the style of the selected font using various commands. We can switch to italic, bold, or small caps styles easily. For example, to set the font to italic, we can use the `\textit` command:

```
\textit{This is italicized text.}
```

Similarly, we can use `\textbf` for bold and `\textsc` for small caps.

Font Weight   XeLaTeX also provides options to control the weight or thickness of the selected font. We can use `\textmd` for normal weight and `\textbf` for bold weight. For example:

```
\textmd{This is normal weight text.}
\textbf{This is bold weight text.}
```

These commands can be used in combination with style commands to achieve the desired font appearance.

Font Family Switching XeLaTeX allows us to switch between different font families within a document. This can be useful when we want to use different fonts for headings, captions, or specific sections. To switch to a different font family, we can define a new font using \newfontfamily and then use it within the document using its assigned name.

```
\newfontfamily\headingfont{Montserrat}[Path=./fonts/]{Montserrat-B

\section{\headingfont{This is a Heading}}
```

In this example, we define a new font family called headingfont and assign it the Montserrat-Bold font. We then use this font to format a section heading. This allows for greater flexibility and control over the typographic hierarchy of the document.

Conclusion

Font selection and manipulation play a significant role in the visual presentation of a document. With XeLaTeX, we have the power to choose from a wide range of fonts and easily adjust their size, style, weight, and family. By understanding the principles and techniques discussed in this section, you will be able to create visually appealing and professional-looking documents using XeLaTeX.

Exercises

1. Experiment with different font families and styles in your document. Change the font for headings, captions, and body text to create a visually balanced and aesthetically pleasing document.

2. Combine different fonts to create a typographic hierarchy in your document. Use a sans-serif font for headings, a serif font for body text, and a monospaced font for code snippets.

3. Explore the fontspec package documentation to discover more advanced font manipulation techniques, such as fine-tuning of font features and character variants.

Additional Resources

- The LaTeX Font Catalogue: `https://tug.org/FontCatalogue/`

- XeTeX Reference Guide: `https://ctan.org/pkg/xetexref`

- The LaTeX Fontspec Package Documentation: `https://ctan.org/pkg/fontspec`

In this section, we have covered the basics of font selection and manipulation in XeLaTeX. Fonts are a powerful tool in document design, and with XeLaTeX, we have the ability to create visually stunning and professional documents.

Fine-tuning line spacing and paragraph formatting in XeLaTeX

In XeLaTeX, fine-tuning line spacing and paragraph formatting is essential for achieving professional-looking documents. In this section, we will explore various techniques to adjust line spacing, indentations, and alignment to enhance the readability and aesthetics of our documents.

Line spacing

Line spacing refers to the vertical distance between lines of text in a paragraph. By default, XeLaTeX uses a line spacing of 1.2 times the font size. However, in some cases, you may want to increase or decrease the line spacing to improve readability or adhere to specific formatting requirements.

To change the line spacing, we can use the `setspace` package. This package provides the command `\setstretch{}`, which allows us to set the line spacing factor. For example, to set the line spacing to double-spaced, we can use:

```
...

\setstretch{2}
```

If you want to adjust the line spacing to a specific value, you can provide the desired factor as an argument to `\setstretch{}`. For example, `\setstretch{1.5}` will set the line spacing to 1.5 times the font size.

It's important to note that changing the line spacing can affect the overall appearance of the document. Therefore, it's advisable to consult any style guidelines or formatting requirements that you need to follow.

Paragraph indentation

Paragraph indentation is the horizontal space added at the beginning of a paragraph to separate it from the preceding text. By default, XeLaTeX indents the first line of each paragraph, except for the first paragraph after a section heading.

If you want to manipulate paragraph indentation, you can use the `indentfirst` package. This package enables indenting the first paragraph after a heading. To use the `indentfirst` package, simply add `\usepackage{indentfirst}` in the preamble of your document.

To modify the indentation of subsequent paragraphs, you can use the `parskip` package. This package provides the command `\setlength{\parindent}{...}` to set the indentation length. For example, to remove indentation from all paragraphs, you can use:

```
...
\setlength{\parindent}{0pt}
```

On the other hand, if you want to increase the indentation, you can specify a positive length value in the argument, such as `\setlength{\parindent}{1cm}`.

Text alignment

Text alignment refers to the horizontal positioning of the text within a paragraph. XeLaTeX provides four types of alignment: left-aligned, right-aligned, centered, and justified.

By default, XeLaTeX left-aligns the text. To change the alignment, you can use the following commands:

- **Right alignment:** `\raggedleft`

- **Center alignment:** `\centered`

- **Justified alignment:** `\raggedright`

For example, if you want to center-align a paragraph, you can enclose it within the `\centered` environment like this:

```
\begin{centered}
This paragraph\index{paragraph} will be\index{be} centered.
\end{centered}
```

It's worth noting that justified alignment is the default behavior in XeLaTeX. However, if you want to explicitly justify a paragraph, you can use the \raggedright command.

Spacing before and after paragraphs

In addition to adjusting line spacing and indentation, you may also want to control the spacing before and after paragraphs to improve the visual hierarchy and readability of your document.

To add space before a paragraph, you can use the \vspace command with a specified length. For example, \vspace{1cm} adds 1 centimeter of space before the paragraph.

To add space after a paragraph, you can use the \par command followed by the \vspace command. For example:

```
This is a\index{a} paragraph\index{paragraph}.
\par
\vspace{1cm}
This is another paragraph\index{paragraph}.
```

By adjusting the spacing before and after paragraphs, you can enhance the visual structure of your document and guide the reader's eye.

Best practices for line spacing and paragraph formatting

When fine-tuning line spacing and paragraph formatting in XeLaTeX, it's crucial to maintain consistency and adhere to any style guidelines or formatting requirements. Here are some best practices to keep in mind:

- Use line spacing that enhances readability without sacrificing the overall aesthetics of the document.

- Adjust paragraph indentation based on the desired formatting style or guidelines.

- Choose text alignment that aligns with the overall design and purpose of the document.

- Control spacing before and after paragraphs to create a visually appealing layout.

- Regularly review and proofread your document to ensure consistent formatting.

- Test your document on various devices and printing mediums to ensure optimal readability and formatting.

By following these best practices, you can effectively fine-tune line spacing and paragraph formatting to create professional-looking documents in XeLaTeX.

Summary

In this section, we explored techniques for fine-tuning line spacing and paragraph formatting in XeLaTeX. We learned how to adjust line spacing with the setspace package, manipulate paragraph indentation using the indentfirst and parskip packages, change text alignment, and control spacing before and after paragraphs. Additionally, we discussed best practices to ensure consistent and visually appealing formatting. With these tools and guidelines, you can now create well-formatted and aesthetically pleasing documents in XeLaTeX.

Exercises

1. Adjust the line spacing of an existing document to 1.5 times the font size.

2. Create a document with justified alignment and an indentation of 1 inch.

3. Experiment with different paragraph spacing techniques to create a visually appealing layout.

4. Modify the line spacing and alignment of a specific section within a document.

Resources

1. Online documentation for the setspace package: `https://www.ctan.org/pkg/setspace`

2. Online documentation for the indentfirst package: `https://www.ctan.org/pkg/indentfirst`

3. Online documentation for the parskip package: `https://www.ctan.org/pkg/parskip`

Conclusion

In this section, we explored the importance of fine-tuning line spacing and paragraph formatting in XeLaTeX documents. We discussed techniques for adjusting line spacing, paragraph indentation, text alignment, and spacing before and after paragraphs. We also provided best practices and exercises to help you practice and apply these techniques effectively. With a good understanding of these concepts, you can now enhance the readability and aesthetics of your XeLaTeX documents. Happy typesetting!

Creating Custom Templates and Stylesheets in XeLaTeX

In XeLaTeX, one of the powerful features is the ability to create custom templates and stylesheets. Templates provide a predefined structure for your document, while stylesheets allow you to customize the formatting and layout. In this section, we will explore how to create and use these custom templates and stylesheets to streamline your document creation process.

Introduction to Templates in XeLaTeX

Templates in XeLaTeX provide a way to define a set of default formatting options for your document. They are especially useful when you need to maintain a consistent style across multiple documents or when you want to simplify the process of creating new documents with predefined layouts.

Creating a template involves setting up the basic document structure, defining the header and footer, specifying the font styles, and configuring the page layout. Let's explore each aspect in detail.

Setting up the Document Structure

To create a template, start by setting up the basic document structure. This includes specifying the document class, font size, paper size, and margins. For example, you can use the following code snippet as a starting point:

```
\documentclass[12pt]{article}
\usepackage[a4paper, margin=2cm]{geometry}

% Your content here
```

In this example, we have specified the document class as "article" with a font size of 12pt. The "geometry" package is used to set the paper size to A4 and the margin to 2cm on all sides. You can customize these settings according to your requirements.

Defining the Header and Footer

The header and footer of your document contain important information such as the document title, author name, page numbers, and date. To define the header and footer in your template, you can use packages like "fancyhdr" or "titleps". Here's an example using the "fancyhdr" package:

```
\pagestyle{fancy}
\fancyhf{}
\lhead{My Document}
\rhead{\thepage}
\lfoot{Author Name}
\rfoot{\today}
\renewcommand{\headrulewidth}{0.4pt}
\renewcommand{\footrulewidth}{0.4pt}
```

In this code snippet, we are using the "fancyhdr" package to define the page style as "fancy". We then clear the header and footer using the command \fancyhf{}. Next, we set the left header (\lhead) to display the document title, the right header (\rhead) to display the page number using \thepage, the left footer (\lfoot) to display the author name, and the right footer (\rfoot) to display the current date using \today. Finally, we set the header and footer line widths using \renewcommand.

Specifying Font Styles

Customizing the font styles in your document template can help create a unique visual identity for your documents. By default, XeLaTeX supports fonts from your operating system, but you can also use custom font packages or load font files directly.

To load a custom font package, you can use the \usepackage command. For example, to use the "Arial" font, you can use the package \usepackage{fontspec} and set the font family using \setmainfont{Arial}.

If you have font files (.otf or .ttf), you can load them directly using the \newfontfamily command. For example:

```
\newfontfamily\myfont{MyCustomFont.otf}
```

Once you have loaded the font, you can use it in your document by changing the font family. For example, to use the custom font in the entire document, you can use `\usepackage{fontspec}` and `\setmainfont{\myfont}`.

Configuring Page Layout

Configuring the page layout is an essential part of creating a custom template. You can adjust the margins, set the page orientation, and define the column layout using various packages.

To customize the margins, you can use the "geometry" package as mentioned earlier. Additionally, the "changepage" package provides more advanced options like changing the margins on specific pages or sections.

To set the page orientation, you can use the "pdflscape" package to create landscape pages within your document. Simply include the package and use the environment `\begin{landscape}` and `\end{landscape}` to enclose the content you want to display in landscape mode.

For multi-column layouts, you can use the "multicol" package. Simply load the package using `\usepackage{multicol}` and use the environment `\begin{multicols}{2}` and `\end{multicols}` to divide the content into two columns.

Using the Custom Template

Once you have created your custom template, you can use it as a basis for creating new documents. To do this, simply copy the template file and modify it according to your needs. You can change the document title, author name, content, and any other elements required for your specific document.

By using custom templates, you can save time and effort in formatting and setting up the document structure. It ensures consistency across multiple documents and provides a professional look and feel to your work.

Best Practices

Here are a few best practices to keep in mind when creating custom templates and stylesheets in XeLaTeX:

- Keep the template simple and easy to modify.

- Comment your template code to provide explanations and instructions to others.

- Test the template with different types of content to ensure it handles various scenarios.

- Use version control to track changes and manage different versions of your template.

- Share your template with others in the XeLaTeX community to promote collaboration and idea exchange.

Creating custom templates and stylesheets in XeLaTeX can significantly enhance your document creation process. It allows you to establish a consistent style, saves time in formatting, and ensures a professional look for your documents. Experiment with different designs, fonts, and layouts to find the perfect template that fits your needs.

Exercises

1. Create a custom template for a research paper with the following specifications: - Font: Times New Roman, 12pt. - Paper size: A4 with 2cm margins. - Header: Display the paper title on the left side and the page number on the right side. - Footer: Display the author name on the left side and the current date on the right side. - Use the template to create a sample research paper.

2. Design a template for a newsletter using a two-column layout. Customize the font and color scheme to match the branding of your organization. Populate the template with sample content.

3. Modify the template from exercise 1 to include a cover page with the title, author name, and date. Add a table of contents with links to the corresponding sections. Use the template to create a sample document with multiple sections.

Resources

- The LaTeX Wikibook: https://en.wikibooks.org/wiki/LaTeX - The XeLaTeX   Documentation: http://mirrors.ctan.org/info/xetexref/xetex-reference.pdf - Overleaf Templates Gallery: https://www.overleaf.com/gallery

Summary

In this section, we learned how to create custom templates and stylesheets in XeLaTeX. Templates provide a predefined structure for your documents, while stylesheets allow you to customize the formatting and layout. We explored setting up the document structure, defining the header and footer, specifying font styles, configuring page layout, and using the custom templates. We also discussed best practices and provided exercises for practice. With custom templates and stylesheets, you can streamline your document creation process and ensure consistency in your work.

Troubleshooting Advanced Issues in XeLaTeX

In the process of working with XeLaTeX, it is common to encounter various issues and errors that can hinder the successful compilation and generation of your documents. In this section, we will explore some of the common advanced issues that may arise and provide troubleshooting techniques to help you overcome them.

1. Font-related Issues: One of the key advantages of XeLaTeX is its support for a wide range of fonts, including system fonts and non-English fonts. However, working with fonts can sometimes lead to problems. Here are some common font-related issues and their solutions:

1.1 Font Not Found Error: Sometimes, when using a specific font, you may encounter a "Font not found" error during compilation. This error usually occurs when the font you are trying to use is not installed on your system or not accessible to XeLaTeX. To resolve this issue, make sure the necessary font files are installed and accessible. You can check if the font is installed on your system using the font management tools available for your operating system.

1.2 Font Rendering Issues: Occasionally, you may notice that your fonts do not render correctly in the output PDF. This can happen due to a variety of reasons, such as incompatible font formats or missing font features. To troubleshoot this issue, you can try the following steps:

- Verify that the font you are using is a valid OpenType (OTF) or TrueType (TTF) font. XeLaTeX requires these font formats for proper rendering. - Ensure that your font files are not corrupted. Sometimes, downloading fonts from unreliable sources can result in file corruption. Try re-downloading the font files from a trusted source. - Use the fontspec package to specify font options explicitly. This can help in resolving any conflicts or inconsistencies in font rendering.

2. Package Conflicts and Incompatibilities: XeLaTeX relies on various packages and libraries to enhance its functionality. However, using multiple packages together

can sometimes lead to conflicts or incompatibilities. Here are some common issues related to package conflicts:

2.1 Package Loading Order: In some cases, the order in which packages are loaded can affect their functionality or cause conflicts. When faced with a package conflict, try changing the order in which you load the packages. Experimenting with different loading orders can often resolve conflicts and ensure smooth compilation.

2.2 Package Compatibility: Packages are developed independently, and sometimes newer versions of a package may introduce changes that break compatibility with other packages you are using. If you encounter package compatibility issues, consider using older versions of packages or finding alternative packages that provide similar functionality.

2.3 Package Options Conflict: Many packages come with various options that can be customized to suit specific needs. However, conflicting options between different packages can cause compilation errors. To troubleshoot such issues, carefully review the documentation of the packages you are using and ensure that the options you specify are compatible with each other.

3. Debugging and Error Messages: When an error occurs during the compilation process, XeLaTeX provides error messages that can help identify the underlying issue. Understanding these error messages and knowing how to debug them is essential for troubleshooting advanced issues.

3.1 Analyzing Error Logs: XeLaTeX generates error logs that provide detailed information about compilation errors. By analyzing these logs, you can gain insight into the cause of the error and take appropriate steps to resolve it. Look for error messages, warnings, and line numbers mentioned in the log.

3.2 Debugging Tools: XeLaTeX provides various tools that can aid in debugging and troubleshooting issues. One such tool is the `showexpl` package, which allows you to display the content of macros and environments during compilation. This can be helpful in identifying errors related to macro usage. Another tool is the `syntonly` package, which allows you to check the syntax of your document without actually compiling it. This can be useful for catching any syntactical errors early on.

3.3 Commenting and Isolating Code: If you encounter an error, it can be helpful to comment out specific sections of your code to identify the source of the problem. By isolating the problematic code, you can focus on debugging that specific section and potentially resolve the issue more efficiently.

4. Performance Optimization: As your XeLaTeX projects grow in complexity, you may encounter performance issues that impact compilation time or even cause system resource limitations. Here are some techniques to optimize the performance of your XeLaTeX documents:

4.1 Minimize Packages and Libraries: Loading excessive packages and libraries can increase compilation time and resource usage. Review the packages and libraries you are using and ensure that you only include what is essential for your document. Removing redundant or unused packages can significantly improve performance.

4.2 Cache Fonts: XeLaTeX has a font caching mechanism that can enhance the performance by reducing the overhead of font loading. Enable font caching by setting the appropriate option in your XeLaTeX configuration. With font caching enabled, XeLaTeX will only load fonts once, improving compilation speed.

4.3 Optimize Code Structure: By optimizing the structure and organization of your code, you can improve compilation time. Break your document into logical sections and use separate files for different parts, such as figures or tables. This can enable partial compilation and reduce the need to recompile the entire document every time.

4.4 Utilize Compilation Options: XeLaTeX provides various compilation options that allow you to fine-tune the process and optimize performance. Experiment with options like `-draftmode` or `-interaction=batchmode` to suppress unnecessary output and reduce compilation time.

In conclusion, troubleshooting advanced issues in XeLaTeX requires a combination of understanding the underlying principles, analyzing error messages, and using appropriate debugging techniques. By familiarizing yourself with common issues and their solutions, you'll be better equipped to handle any challenges that arise during your XeLaTeX journey.

Remember that troubleshooting often involves trial and error, so don't be discouraged if you don't find an immediate solution. Patience, persistence, and leveraging the extensive resources available in the XeLaTeX community will go a long way in resolving advanced issues. Happy troubleshooting!

XeLaTeX Graphics and Visualization

Introduction to Graphics in XeLaTeX

Overview of graphics formats in XeLaTeX

In XeLaTeX, there are several graphics formats that can be used to include images in documents. Each format has its own characteristics and best use cases. This section provides an overview of the most commonly used graphics formats in XeLaTeX and discusses their advantages and disadvantages.

Raster graphics formats

Raster graphics formats are suitable for representing continuous-tone images, such as photographs or complex illustrations. In XeLaTeX, the most commonly used raster graphics formats are:

+ JPEG (Joint Photographic Experts Group): JPEG is a widely used format for storing compressed photographic images. It provides a good balance between image quality and file size, making it suitable for web publishing or inclusion in electronic documents. However, it is important to note that JPEG is a lossy compression format, which means that image quality may degrade when the file is repeatedly edited or saved.

+ PNG (Portable Network Graphics): PNG is a lossless graphics format that supports full-color images with transparent backgrounds. It is a popular choice for graphics that require sharp edges, such as logos or icons. PNG files tend to be larger than JPEG files, but they preserve image quality without degradation.

- GIF (Graphics Interchange Format): GIF is a graphics format commonly used for small animations, icons, and simple graphics. It supports both transparent backgrounds and a limited number of colors (up to 256), making it suitable for images with large areas of uniform color. However, GIF is not well-suited for photographs or complex illustrations due to its limited color palette.

Vector graphics formats

Vector graphics formats are resolution-independent and can be scaled to any size without loss of quality. In XeLaTeX, the most commonly used vector graphics formats are:

- PDF (Portable Document Format): PDF is a versatile format that can contain both raster and vector elements. It is widely supported and can be easily generated from various applications. PDF is an ideal format for high-quality printing and is commonly used for diagrams, schematics, and other graphics that require precise control over lines, shapes, and colors.

- EPS (Encapsulated PostScript): EPS is a vector graphics format that encapsulates PostScript commands. It is commonly used in professional publishing workflows, especially for graphics that need to be included in other documents. EPS files can be scaled without loss of quality, making them suitable for print and other high-resolution output.

- SVG (Scalable Vector Graphics): SVG is an XML-based vector graphics format that is widely supported by modern web browsers. It is commonly used for graphics on the web, as well as for integration with other web technologies such as JavaScript and CSS. SVG files can be manipulated and animated using scripting languages, making them suitable for interactive visualizations.

Choosing the right format

When choosing a graphics format in XeLaTeX, it is important to consider the specific requirements of your document and the characteristics of each format. Here are some general guidelines to help you make an informed decision:

- For photographs or complex illustrations with a large number of colors, JPEG or PNG formats are suitable choices. JPEG offers better compression for photographic images, while PNG provides lossless compression and supports transparency.

+ For graphics with sharp edges, such as logos or icons, PNG or vector formats like PDF or SVG are recommended. PNG allows for transparent backgrounds, while vector formats ensure scalability without loss of quality.

+ When working with external applications or integrating graphics into other documents, PDF or EPS formats are commonly used for their wide compatibility and versatility.

+ If you are targeting web or interactive platforms, SVG is a good choice due to its scalability and support for interactivity.

It is also worth noting that XeLaTeX supports automatic detection of graphics formats, so you generally do not need to specify the format explicitly when including images in your documents. However, it is good practice to specify the file extension to prevent any potential issues.

In the next section, we will explore the process of including images in XeLaTeX documents and discuss techniques for manipulating and scaling images to fit your document's requirements.

Including images in XeLaTeX documents

In XeLaTeX, incorporating images into your documents is a common requirement, whether it's for adding visual elements to enhance the content or for including graphs, charts, or diagrams to support your explanations. In this section, we will explore different methods for including images in XeLaTeX documents.

Graphics Formats in XeLaTeX

Before we dive into the specifics of including images, let's take a moment to understand the different graphics formats that are supported in XeLaTeX.

Three commonly used graphics formats in XeLaTeX are:

1. **PDF**: Portable Document Format (PDF) is the preferred format for including images in XeLaTeX documents. PDF images are vector-based, which means they can be scaled without losing quality. They also support transparency, layers, and interactive elements.

2. **EPS**: Encapsulated PostScript (EPS) is a widely used format in the publishing industry. EPS images are also vector-based and can be scaled without loss of quality. However, they do not support transparency or interactive elements.

3. **PNG/JPEG**: Portable Network Graphics (PNG) and Joint Photographic Experts Group (JPEG) are raster formats commonly used for photographs and graphics with complex color gradients. Raster images are pixel-based, which means they can lose quality when scaled. PNG supports transparency, while JPEG does not.

Now that we understand the different graphics formats, let's explore how to include images in XeLaTeX documents.

The \includegraphics Command

The most common way to include an image in XeLaTeX is by using the \includegraphics command, provided by the graphicx package. This command allows you to insert an image into your document with various customization options.

The basic syntax for the \includegraphics command is as follows:

```
\includegraphics[<options>]{<filename>}
```

Here, ⬚options⬚ are optional parameters to customize the image, and ⬚filename⬚ is the name of the image file.

The ⬚filename⬚ can include the file extension (e.g., image.png), or you can omit the extension if it's a known image format and XeLaTeX can recognize it (e.g., image).

Let's consider an example to illustrate how to use the \includegraphics command:

Suppose we have an image named "example.png" in the same directory as our XeLaTeX document. We can include this image in our document as follows:

```
\includegraphics[width=0.5\textwidth]{example}
```

In this example, we set the width of the image to occupy 50% of the text width by specifying `width=0.5\textwidth` as the option. We provide the filename without the file extension.

The \includegraphics command offers various other options, such as scaling the image, rotating it, cropping it, and adjusting its position. You can explore these options in the documentation of the graphicx package.

Organizing Image Files

When working with multiple images, it is advisable to organize them in a separate directory, such as an "images" folder, to keep your project directory clean and organized.

To include an image in a nested directory, you can specify the relative path to the image file from the main document using forward slashes (/). For example:

```
% \includegraphics{images/example}
```

In this example, the image is located in the "images" folder within the same directory as the main document.

Captioning and Referencing Images

In some cases, you may want to add a caption to your images and refer to them within the text. The caption and subcaption packages provide convenient ways to achieve this.

To add a caption to your image, you can use the \caption command. For example:

```
% \begin{figure}
%   \centering
```

```
%    \includegraphics[width=0.5\textwidth]{example}
%    \caption{A sample image}
%    \label{fig:sample}
% \end{figure}
```

In this example, we wrap the \includegraphics command within a figure environment, which allows us to add a caption using the \caption command. We also provide a label using the \label command, which allows us to refer to the image later in the document.

To refer to the image within the text, we can use the \ref command followed by the label. For example:

"As shown in Figure \ref{fig:sample}, the image demonstrates..."

Make sure to compile the document multiple times to ensure that the caption and reference numbers are updated correctly.

Best Practices for Including Images

Here are some best practices to consider when including images in your XeLaTeX documents:

1. Use vector-based formats like PDF or EPS whenever possible, as they provide better scalability and quality.

2. Keep the resolution of raster images (PNG/JPEG) high enough for print or screen display.

3. Specify the width or height of the image using relative units, such as \textwidth or \linewidth, for better flexibility across different devices and document layouts.

4. Always include a caption and label for your images to provide context and enable easy referencing.

5. Avoid excessive image sizes that may impact document loading time or page layout.

By following these best practices, you can ensure that your images are seamlessly integrated into your XeLaTeX documents, enhancing the visual appeal and clarity of your content.

Conclusion

Including images in XeLaTeX documents is a fundamental technique to enhance the visual presentation and support the content with graphical elements. In this section, we explored different methods for including images, such as the \includegraphics command, and discussed best practices for organizing, captioning, and referencing images. By following these techniques, you can effectively incorporate visual content into your XeLaTeX documents and create professional-looking outputs.

Manipulating and Scaling Images in XeLaTeX

In XeLaTeX, you can easily manipulate and scale images to suit your document's needs. This section will cover various techniques and commands to perform these tasks effectively.

Including Images in XeLaTeX Documents

Before we delve into manipulating and scaling images, let's first understand how to include images in a XeLaTeX document. To incorporate an image, you need to use the graphicx package, which provides the necessary commands.

To include an image, use the \includegraphics command followed by the image file name and its path. For example, to include an image named example.jpg located in the images folder, use the following command:

```
% \includegraphics{images/example.jpg}
```

By default, XeLaTeX looks for images in the same folder as the main .tex file. If your image files are located in a different folder, specify the path relative to the main document or provide an absolute path.

Scaling Images

While including images, you often need to adjust their size to fit your document layout. XeLaTeX allows you to scale images both proportionally and non-proportionally.

To proportionally scale an image, use the width or height options with the desired dimension specified. For example, to scale an image to a width of 0.5\textwidth, use the following command:

```
\includegraphics[width=0.5\textwidth]{example.jpg}
```

Similarly, you can scale an image to a specific height using the height option. For example, to scale an image to a height of 5cm, use the following command:

```
\includegraphics[height=5cm]{example.jpg}
```

If you want to non-proportionally scale an image, you can use the scale option. The scale value indicates the factor by which the image will be scaled. For example, to scale an image to twice its original size, use the following command:

```
\includegraphics[scale=2]{example.jpg}
```

Manipulating Images

In addition to scaling, XeLaTeX provides some other options to manipulate images. Let's explore a few of them:

- **Rotation:** You can rotate an image by specifying the angle in degrees using the `angle` option. For example, to rotate an image by 45 degrees, use the following command:

  `\includegraphics[angle=45]{example.jpg}`

- **Clipping:** If you want to show only a portion of an image, you can use the `trim` and `clip` options. The `trim` option allows you to specify the amount to trim from the left, bottom, right, and top of the image. The `clip` option clips the image to the specified dimensions. For example, to trim 1cm from the left and bottom sides and show only the central part of an image, use the following command:

  `\includegraphics[trim=1cm 1cm 1cm 1cm, clip]{example.jpg}`

- **Flipping:** XeLaTeX also provides options to flip or mirror an image. The `scaleX` and `scaleY` options allow you to flip an image horizontally or vertically, respectively. For example, to horizontally flip an image, use the following command:

  `\includegraphics[scaleX=-1]{example.jpg}`

Resolution and Image Formats

When including images in XeLaTeX, it's important to consider their resolution and format. Higher resolution images generally result in better print quality but may increase the document size. On the other hand, lower resolution images may reduce the document size but compromise the print quality.

XeLaTeX supports various image formats, including JPEG, PNG, PDF, and EPS. When choosing an image format, consider the requirements of your document and the capabilities of the output device.

JPEG is suitable for photographs and complex images with continuous color gradients. PNG is better for images with sharp edges and transparency. For vector-based graphics, such as diagrams or illustrations, PDF and EPS formats are preferable.

Best Practices for Manipulating and Scaling Images

Here are some best practices to keep in mind when manipulating and scaling images in XeLaTeX:

+ Maintain the aspect ratio: Proportional scaling ensures that the image doesn't get distorted. Avoid non-proportional scaling unless it's necessary.

+ Optimize image size and resolution: Use appropriate resolution images for the intended output. Compress images without compromising quality to reduce document size.

+ Keep the document size manageable: Be mindful of the overall size of the document when including multiple images. Large documents with many high-resolution images may take longer to compile and process.

+ Use vector graphics whenever possible: Whenever suitable, use vector graphics (PDF, EPS) instead of raster images (JPEG, PNG) for better scalability and sharpness, especially for diagrams and illustrations.

+ Use external image editing tools when required: Complex image manipulations, such as merging or extensive cropping, are often better handled with external software tools. Export the modified images in the desired format and include them in XeLaTeX.

Now that you're familiar with the techniques to manipulate and scale images in XeLaTeX, you can confidently incorporate visuals into your documents and customize them to suit your needs. Experiment with different options and explore further possibilities to enhance the visual appeal of your XeLaTeX documents.

Customizing image placement and alignment in XeLaTeX

In XeLaTeX, one of the key aspects of creating visually appealing documents is the ability to customize the placement and alignment of images. By carefully controlling the position and alignment of images, you can enhance the overall aesthetic of your document and improve readability. In this section, we will explore various techniques and commands that can be used to customize image placement and alignment in XeLaTeX.

Controlling image placement

When it comes to placing an image in a XeLaTeX document, there are several options available. By default, XeLaTeX will try to find the best location for the image based on the surrounding text and other elements. However, in some cases, you may want to have more control over where the image is positioned.

One way to control the placement of an image is to use the figure environment. The figure environment allows you to add a caption and label to the image, and also provides options for controlling the vertical and horizontal placement.

To use the figure environment, simply enclose your image code within the figure tags. For example:

```
% \begin{figure}[h]
%     \centering
%     \includegraphics[scale=0.5]{image.png}
%     \caption{Example image}
%     \label{fig:example}
% \end{figure}
```

In the above example, the [h] placement option specifies that the image should be placed at the current location in the document. Other placement options include t for top, b for bottom, and p for a dedicated page for floats. Note that these placement options are suggestions rather than guarantees, as XeLaTeX will try to find the best placement based on the document layout.

Controlling image alignment

In addition to controlling the placement of an image, you may also want to adjust its alignment within the document. XeLaTeX provides several commands and options for adjusting the alignment of images.

To align an image horizontally, you can use the \centering command within the figure environment. This command centers the image horizontally within the available space. For example:

```
% \begin{figure}[h]
%      \centering
%      \includegraphics[scale=0.5]{image.png}
%      \caption{Example image}
%      \label{fig:example}
% \end{figure}
```

In the above example, the \centering command is used to center the image horizontally.

To align an image vertically within the available space, you can use the floatrow package. This package provides the \ffigbox command, which allows you to specify both the horizontal and vertical alignment for an image. For example:

```
\ffigbox[\FBwidth]
  {\caption{Example image}\label{fig:example}}
  {\includegraphics[height=3cm]{image.png}}
```

In the above example, the \ffigbox command is used to align the image vertically within the available space. The \FBwidth option specifies that the image should be centered both horizontally and vertically.

Wrapping text around images

Another common requirement in document design is to wrap text around an image. XeLaTeX provides the wrapfig package, which allows you to achieve this effect.

To wrap text around an image, you need to use the wrapfigure environment provided by the wrapfig package. This environment takes two parameters: the placement and size of the image, and the width of the wrapped text.

Here is an example of how to use the wrapfigure environment:

```
\begin{wrapfigure}{r}{0.5\textwidth}
  \centering
  \includegraphics[width=0.4\textwidth]{image.png}
  \caption{Example image}
  \label{fig:example}
\end{wrapfigure}

Lorem\index{Lorem} ipsum dolor sit amet, consectetur\index{consect
```

In the above example, the `wrapfigure` environment is used to wrap the text around the image. The `r` parameter specifies that the image should be aligned to the right of the text, and the `0.5\textwidth` parameter specifies that the image should occupy 50% of the available width.

Best practices for image placement and alignment

When customizing image placement and alignment in XeLaTeX, it is important to follow some best practices to ensure that your document looks professional and visually appealing.

Here are some best practices to consider:

+ Provide meaningful captions and labels for images to enhance their accessibility and make it easier for readers to refer to them.

+ Use consistent placement and alignment throughout your document to maintain a cohesive visual style.

+ Avoid excessive use of floating images, as they can disrupt the flow of the document. Reserve floating images for cases where manual placement is not feasible.

+ Optimize image size and resolution to balance visual quality with file size. This is particularly important for digital publishing where file size can impact loading times.

+ Test your document layout on different devices and screen sizes to ensure that the images are displayed properly across various platforms.

By following these best practices, you can effectively customize image placement and alignment in XeLaTeX and create visually stunning documents.

Summary

In this section, we explored various techniques and commands for customizing image placement and alignment in XeLaTeX. We learned how to control the placement of an image using the `figure` environment, and how to adjust horizontal and vertical alignment using the `\centering` command and the `floatrow` package. We also learned how to wrap text around images using the `wrapfig` package. Finally, we discussed best practices for achieving professional results when customizing image placement and alignment.

With the knowledge gained from this section, you can now confidently customize the placement and alignment of images in your XeLaTeX documents, adding visual appeal and enhancing readability.

Creating Diagrams and Flowcharts in XeLaTeX

Creating diagrams and flowcharts is an essential skill for many professional and technical fields. In XeLaTeX, we can use the powerful TikZ package to create diagrams and flowcharts with ease. TikZ provides a flexible and comprehensive set of tools for drawing high-quality graphic elements directly within LaTeX documents.

Introduction to Diagrams and Flowcharts

Diagrams and flowcharts are visual representations used to represent complex ideas, processes, or systems. They help in understanding relationships, sequences, and connections between different elements. Diagrams can be useful in various fields, such as computer science, engineering, mathematics, and business.

In XeLaTeX, we can use TikZ to create a wide range of diagrams and flowcharts, including:

- Flowcharts: Used to represent the logical flow of a process or system, with different shapes representing different steps or decisions.

- Block diagrams: Used to represent systems or processes as interconnected blocks or nodes, with arrows indicating the flow between them.

- UML diagrams: Used in software engineering to model the structure and behavior of object-oriented systems.

- Circuit diagrams: Used in electrical engineering to represent circuits and their components.

- Network diagrams: Used to represent various types of networks, such as computer networks or social networks.

Getting Started with TikZ

Before we delve into creating diagrams and flowcharts, let's set up our XeLaTeX environment and include the necessary packages.

First, we need to load the TikZ package by adding the following line to the preamble of our document:

Next, we can define the necessary TikZ libraries and settings. For example, to include the library for flowchart and block diagram shapes, we can add the following line:

Now we are ready to start creating our diagrams and flowcharts using TikZ.

Creating Flowcharts

Flowcharts are valuable tools for visualizing the steps and decisions involved in a process. Let's consider an example of a simple flowchart representing a decision-making process.

By default, the `caption` package will automatically number the captions and format them according to the document's class style. However, we can customize the numbering and formatting by using the options provided by the package.

Caption Styling

The `caption` package allows us to customize the styling of captions by providing options in the `captionsetup` command.

For example, to change the font size of the caption to `Large`, we can add the following line to our preamble:

```
\captionsetup[figure]{font=Large}
```

This will make the caption text larger for all figures in our document. Similarly, we can modify other aspects of the caption, such as the font family, color, alignment, and spacing.

Labeling and Referencing

Labels are essential for referencing figures within the text. XeLaTeX automatically assigns a number to each figure caption, and we can use the `label` command to assign a unique label to a figure.

To refer to a labeled figure, we can use the `ref` command followed by the label name. For example, to refer to the sample figure from earlier, we can use:

```
As shown in Figure \ref{fig:sample}, ...
```

This will automatically insert the correct figure number when the document is compiled.

Best Practices

When adding captions and labels to figures in XeLaTeX, it is important to follow some best practices:

- Always provide a concise and descriptive caption that explains the content of the figure.

- Use labels that are meaningful and help in easily identifying and referencing the figures.

- Place the `caption` command before the `label` command within the `figure` environment to ensure proper referencing.

- Customize the styling of captions to match the overall document style and readability.

- Use consistent formatting and numbering for captions throughout the document.

By following these best practices, we can ensure that our figures are well-documented and easily understandable within our XeLaTeX documents.

Summary

In this section, we explored the techniques and best practices for adding captions and labels to figures in XeLaTeX. We learned how to use the `caption` package to customize the styling of captions and how to assign labels to figures for referencing within the text. By following the best practices, we can enhance the readability and clarity of our XeLaTeX documents that contain figures.

Creating Vector Graphics in XeLaTeX

In this section, we will explore the powerful capabilities of XeLaTeX for creating vector graphics. Vector graphics are composed of geometric shapes that are defined by mathematical expressions. They have numerous advantages over raster or bitmap images, such as scalability, resolution independence, and the ability to edit and manipulate individual elements. XeLaTeX provides a range of tools and libraries that allow us to create high-quality and customizable vector graphics directly within our documents.

Introduction to Vector Graphics

Before delving into the details of creating vector graphics in XeLaTeX, let's first understand the basic concepts and principles of vector graphics.

Vector graphics are created using mathematical equations that describe the shape, position, and attributes of the graphic elements. These elements can be simple geometric shapes like lines, curves, and polygons, or more complex objects like illustrations, diagrams, and charts. The main advantage of vector graphics is that they can be scaled to any size without loss of quality, making them ideal for high-resolution printing and display on various devices.

In contrast, raster or bitmap images consist of a grid of pixels, each with a specific color value. When a bitmap image is scaled up or down, the pixels are either duplicated or removed, leading to a loss of image quality. Raster images are best suited for realistic images like photographs or detailed artwork.

The TikZ Package

To create vector graphics in XeLaTeX, we will make use of the TikZ package. TikZ is a versatile and powerful tool that allows us to create and manipulate vector graphics directly within our LaTeX documents. It provides a simple and intuitive syntax for specifying shapes, paths, colors, and other visual properties.

To use the TikZ package, we need to include the following line in the preamble of our document:

Once the package is included, we can start using TikZ commands to create our vector graphics.

Drawing Basic Shapes

Let's start by drawing some basic shapes using TikZ. We can draw shapes like rectangles, circles, lines, and polygons by specifying their coordinates and dimensions.

To draw a rectangle, we use the `draw` command followed by the coordinates of the bottom-left and top-right corners:

```
\begin{tikzpicture}
  \draw (0, 0) rectangle (2, 1);
\end{tikzpicture}
```

This code will draw a rectangle with the bottom-left corner at coordinates $(0, 0)$ and the top-right corner at coordinates $(2, 1)$.

Similarly, we can draw a circle using the `circle` command, specifying the center coordinates and the radius:

```
\begin{tikzpicture}
  \draw (0, 0) circle (1);
\end{tikzpicture}
```

This code will draw a circle with center coordinates $(0, 0)$ and a radius of 1.

To draw a line, we specify the coordinates of the starting and ending points:

```
\begin{tikzpicture}
  \draw (0, 0) -- (1, 1);
\end{tikzpicture}
```

This code will draw a line starting from coordinates $(0, 0)$ and ending at coordinates $(1, 1)$.

We can also draw polygons by specifying the coordinates of the vertices:

```
\begin{tikzpicture}
  \draw (0, 0) -- (0, 1) -- (1, 1) -- cycle;
\end{tikzpicture}
```

This code will draw a triangle with vertices at coordinates (0, 0), (0, 1), and (1, 1).

Applying Styles and Colors

In addition to drawing basic shapes, we can also apply various styles and colors to our vector graphics.

To change the line style, we can use commands like dashed, dotted, and thick:

```
\begin{tikzpicture}
  \draw[thick, dashed] (0, 0) rectangle (2, 1);
\end{tikzpicture}
```

This code will draw a dashed rectangle with a thick border.

We can specify the fill color of a shape using the fill command:

```
\begin{tikzpicture}
  \draw[fill=blue] (0, 0) circle (1);
\end{tikzpicture}
```

This code will draw a filled blue circle.

Additionally, we can customize the stroke color, line width, and opacity using the stroke, line width, and opacity commands:

```
\begin{tikzpicture}
  \draw[stroke=red, line width=2pt, opacity=0.5]
      (0, 0) rectangle (2, 1);
\end{tikzpicture}
```

This code will draw a rectangle with a red stroke, a line width of 2 points, and 50% opacity.

Complex Paths and Transformations

TikZ allows us to create complex paths by combining multiple basic shapes and applying various transformations.

We can create curves using the `.. controls ..` syntax, where we specify control points that define the shape of the curve:

```
\begin{tikzpicture}
  \draw (0, 0) .. controls (1, 1) and (2, 1) .. (3, 0);
\end{tikzpicture}
```

This code will draw a curved line from coordinates $(0, 0)$ to $(3, 0)$, with control points at $(1, 1)$ and $(2, 1)$.

We can also apply transformations like scaling, rotation, and translation to our shapes:

```
\begin{tikzpicture}
  \draw (0, 0) rectangle (2, 1);
  \draw[xscale=2, rotate=30, translate={(3, 1)}] (0, 0) rectangle
\end{tikzpicture}
```

This code will draw two rectangles, one without any transformations and another one with a horizontal scale of 2, a rotation of 30 degrees, and a translation of $(3, 1)$.

Advanced Vector Graphics Techniques

TikZ provides numerous advanced techniques for creating vector graphics in XeLaTeX. Some of these techniques include:

- Clipping and masking: We can define custom paths to limit the visibility of certain parts of our graphics.

- Transparencies and blending: We can control the transparency and blending of different shapes and colors.

- Decorations and patterns: We can apply decorative elements and patterns to our shapes, such as borders, shadows, and hatching.

- Text annotations: We can add text labels and annotations to our vector graphics, including advanced typography and mathematical equations.

These techniques allow us to create visually appealing and complex vector graphics for various purposes, such as scientific illustrations, data visualizations, and technical diagrams.

Conclusion

In this section, we have explored the capabilities of XeLaTeX for creating vector graphics. We have learned the basic concepts of vector graphics and how they differ from raster images. We have also seen how to use the TikZ package to draw basic shapes, apply styles and colors, create complex paths, and perform transformations. Furthermore, we have touched upon some advanced techniques for vector graphics creation. With the knowledge gained from this section, you can now create your own professional and customizable vector graphics directly within your XeLaTeX documents. Experiment with different shapes, styles, and effects to achieve the desired visual impact. The possibilities are limitless when it comes to creating vector graphics in XeLaTeX!

Creating animations and interactive visualizations in XeLaTeX

In this section, we will explore how to create dynamic and interactive visualizations using XeLaTeX. While XeLaTeX is primarily used for typesetting documents, it also provides powerful tools and packages to generate animations and interactive graphics.

Introduction to animations in XeLaTeX

Animations are a great way to present complex ideas, demonstrate processes, or illustrate concepts in an engaging manner. XeLaTeX allows us to create animations by combining static frames at different time intervals. By using the `animate` package, we can easily define the animation parameters and generate the desired output.

Using the `animate` package

The `animate` package provides a simple and intuitive interface for creating animations in XeLaTeX. To use this package, we need to include it in the preamble of our document by adding the following line:

The `animate` package provides several commands and options to control the animation settings, such as the frame rate, playback controls, and looping behavior. Let's explore some of the key functionalities.

Creating simple animations

To create a simple animation, we first need to generate a series of frames that represents the desired motion. Each frame is a separate image or graphic that we want to display at a particular time interval. We can then use the `animateinline` environment to include these frames and specify the animation parameters.

Here's an example of a bouncing ball animation:

```
\begin{animateinline}[controls,autoplay,loop]{24}
    \multiframe{36}{n=0+1}{
        \begin{tikzpicture}
            \draw (0,0) circle (1);
            \fill (0,\n/10) circle (0.1);
        \end{tikzpicture}
    }
\end{animateinline}
```

In this example, we use the `tikzpicture` environment from the TikZ package to draw a ball at different positions (`\n/10`) at each frame. The `multiframe` command is used to specify the total number of frames and the increment value for each frame. The animation parameters (`[controls,autoplay,loop]`) control the playback and looping behavior.

Adding interactivity

XeLaTeX also allows us to add interactivity to our animations, enabling the viewer to interact with the graphics or control the animation playback. This can be achieved using the `media9` package and the multimedia capabilities of PDF viewers.

To use the `media9` package, we need to include it in the preamble of our document:

With `media9`, we can include interactive elements such as buttons, sliders, and checkboxes in our animations. We can also define actions triggered by user interactions, such as switching between scenes or pausing the animation.

Examples and resources

To learn more about creating animations and interactive visualizations in XeLaTeX, here are some useful resources:

- The animate package documentation provides detailed information on the various options and commands: https://ctan.org/pkg/animate

- The TikZ manual offers a comprehensive guide to creating graphics and animations with TikZ: http://www.texample.net/media/pgf/builds/pgfmanualCVS2012-11-04T19-38-51Z.pdf

- The media9 package documentation provides examples and guidance on adding interactivity to PDF documents: https://ctan.org/pkg/media9

Summary

In this section, we explored how to create animations and interactive visualizations in XeLaTeX. We learned about the animate package for generating animations and the media9 package for adding interactivity. With these tools, we can engage our audience and present our ideas in a dynamic and captivating manner. By combining XeLaTeX's typesetting capabilities with animation and interactivity, we can create visually appealing and informative documents. So go ahead, unleash your creativity, and bring your documents to life using XeLaTeX!

Troubleshooting Image-related Issues in XeLaTeX

In this section, we will explore some common image-related issues that may occur when working with XeLaTeX. Images play an essential role in many documents, including figures, diagrams, and graphics, so it's crucial to know how to troubleshoot and resolve any problems that may arise.

Image Format Compatibility

One common issue when working with images in XeLaTeX is compatibility with different image formats. XeLaTeX supports a variety of image formats, including PNG, JPEG, EPS, and PDF. However, certain formats may require additional packages or settings to be used properly.

Problem: XeLaTeX fails to include the desired image in the document, and the compilation process generates an error.

Solution: Here are a few steps you can take to troubleshoot and resolve this issue:

1. Check the image file extension: Ensure that the image file extension matches the format specified in your XeLaTeX code. For example, if you are including a PNG image, make sure the file extension is ".png".

2. Confirm the file path: Verify that the path to the image file is correct. Ensure that the file is located in the specified directory or provide the full path to the image file.

3. Enable necessary packages: Depending on the image format you are using, you may need to include additional packages in the preamble of your document. For example, the graphicx package is commonly used for including images, while the epstopdf package is required for EPS images.

4. Convert incompatible image formats: If you encounter issues with a specific image format, consider converting it to a compatible format. For example, you can use external tools or online converters to convert an image to PNG or JPEG formats, which are widely supported by XeLaTeX.

Image Scaling and Positioning

Another common issue with images in XeLaTeX is scaling and positioning. It is essential to correctly resize and position images within the document to ensure optimal visual presentation.

Problem: The included image appears too large or too small in the document, or it is not positioned as desired.

Solution: Here are some troubleshooting steps to address image scaling and positioning issues:

1. Adjust image size: Specify the desired dimensions for the image using the width and height parameters in the \includegraphics command. Experiment with different values to find the appropriate size for your document.

```
\includegraphics[width=0.5\textwidth]{example.png}
```

2. Maintain aspect ratio: To preserve the image's aspect ratio while resizing, use only one dimension parameter and let XeLaTeX automatically adjust the other dimension proportionally.

```
\includegraphics[width=0.5\textwidth]{example.png}
```

3. Position the image: Utilize the \begin{figure} and \end{figure} environment to control the positioning of the image within the document. You can use options such as h, t, b, and p to specify the desired location (e.g., here, top, bottom, page).

```
% \begin{figure}[h]
%     \centering
%     \includegraphics[width=0.5\textwidth]{example.png}
%     \caption{Sample image}
%     \label{fig:sample}
% \end{figure}
```

4. Avoid absolute measurements: Instead of using fixed dimensions, consider using relative measurements (e.g., percentages of the text width) to make the image more adaptive to different document sizes.

Image Resolution and Quality

Image resolution and quality are essential aspects when including graphics in documents. Low-resolution or distorted images can negatively affect the overall document quality.

Problem: The included image appears pixelated or of poor quality in the document.

Solution: Here are some steps to ensure high image resolution and quality:

1. Use high-resolution images: When possible, use images with higher resolutions to improve their quality. This is particularly important when printing the document.

2. Check image file quality: Verify that the source image files have sufficient quality before including them in the document. If the image quality is poor from the start, no amount of resizing or editing can improve it significantly.

3. Adjust image compression: Some image formats (e.g., JPEG) apply compression, which can reduce the image quality. Adjust the compression level to retain the desired image quality.

```
\includegraphics[width=0.5\textwidth, quality=100]{example.jpg}
```

4. Avoid excessive resizing: Avoid excessive resizing of images, as it can lead to a loss of image quality. Ideally, use images that are close to the desired dimensions to minimize the amount of scaling required.

Image File Missing or Corrupted

There may be instances where an image file is missing from its intended location or has become corrupted. These issues can affect the document's visual presentation.

Problem: The image does not appear in the document, and XeLaTeX generates an error indicating a missing or corrupted image file.

Solution: Here are some steps to address missing or corrupted image files:

1. Verify file existence: Check if the image file exists in the specified location. Confirm the file name and extension match the filename specified in your XeLaTeX code.

2. Restore or replace missing files: If the image file is missing or has been accidentally deleted, restore it from a backup or obtain a new copy from the original source.

3. Repair corrupted files: If the image file is corrupted or damaged, try using file recovery tools or obtain a new, uncorrupted copy.

4. Check file permissions: Ensure that the image file has appropriate permissions that allow XeLaTeX to access it. If necessary, adjust the file permissions to grant the necessary access rights.

Resource Limitations

When working with a large number of images or high-resolution graphics, XeLaTeX may encounter resource limitations related to memory usage or disk space.

Problem: XeLaTeX fails to compile the document or generates errors related to resource limitations when including multiple or large images.

Solution: Here are some steps to address resource limitations when working with images:

1. Optimize image file sizes: Reduce the file size of images using compression tools or image editing software without significantly sacrificing image quality. This can help reduce the overall resource usage.

2. Limit image resolution: If high-resolution images are not necessary for the intended output, consider reducing the resolution before including them in the document. This can help conserve memory and disk space.

3. Increase resource limits: If you continually encounter resource limitations, consider increasing the memory allocation or disk space available to XeLaTeX. Consult the XeLaTeX documentation or your system administrator for guidance on adjusting resource limits.

4. Prioritize image inclusion: If memory constraints are still an issue, prioritize the inclusion of the most critical images and exclude or downsize less important ones.

Conclusion

Understanding and troubleshooting image-related issues in XeLaTeX is essential for creating visually appealing and professional documents. By addressing common problems related to image format compatibility, scaling and positioning, resolution and quality, missing or corrupted files, and resource limitations, you can ensure that your images enhance the overall visual impact of your documents. Remember to experiment, test, and iterate to achieve the desired results. Happy typesetting!

Best practices for using graphics in XeLaTeX

Graphics play a crucial role in enhancing the visual appeal and understanding of documents. In this section, we will discuss the best practices for incorporating and manipulating graphics in XeLaTeX documents. We will cover various aspects, including graphics formats, image manipulation, customization, and troubleshooting.

Choosing the right graphics format

A key consideration when working with graphics in XeLaTeX is choosing the appropriate graphics format. XeLaTeX supports multiple graphics formats, such as PDF, PNG, JPEG, and EPS. Each format has its advantages and usage scenarios.

- PDF (Portable Document Format): PDF is a versatile format that is particularly suitable for vector graphics and complex diagrams. It offers high-quality output and scalability without loss of details. Whenever possible, it is recommended to use PDF for graphics in XeLaTeX.

- PNG (Portable Network Graphics): PNG is a bitmap format that is well-suited for images with transparency and sharp edges. It is ideal for screenshots, icons, and graphics with solid colors. However, PNG images tend to have larger file sizes compared to other formats.

- JPEG (Joint Photographic Experts Group): JPEG is a widely used format for photographs and natural images. It provides efficient compression for continuous-tone images, but it is not suitable for images with sharp edges or text. JPEG images are lossy compressed, which means that some details may be lost during compression.

+ EPS (Encapsulated PostScript): EPS is a vector graphics format widely used in the print industry. It supports high-quality typography and scalable graphics. However, EPS files may not be directly supported by XeLaTeX and may require conversion to PDF or another compatible format.

To include graphics in a XeLaTeX document, use the `graphicx` package and the `includegraphics` command. For example, to include a PDF image named `example.pdf`:

...

```
% \includegraphics{example.pdf}
```

Manipulating and scaling images

XeLaTeX provides several options for manipulating and scaling images to fit the document layout and design. Here are some best practices to consider:

+ Scaling: To scale an image proportionally, use the `width` or `height` options in the `includegraphics` command. For example, `\includegraphics[width=0.5\linewidth]{example.pdf}` scales the image to half the width of the text block.

+ Rotating: To rotate an image, use the `angle` option in the `includegraphics` command. For example, `\includegraphics[angle=45]{example.pdf}` rotates the image by 45 degrees.

+ Cropping: If you need to crop an image, you can use external tools like ImageMagick to create a cropped version of the image and include it in the document. Alternatively, you can use the `trim` and `clip` options in the `includegraphics` command to crop the image directly. For example, `\includegraphics[trim=0 0 100 0, clip]{example.pdf}` trims 100 units from the right side of the image.

+ Captioning: To add a caption and label to an image, you can use the `caption` and `label` commands in combination with the `figure` environment. This helps with cross-referencing and improves the overall structure of your document.

Customizing image placement and alignment

Controlling the placement and alignment of images in XeLaTeX documents is essential for maintaining a consistent and visually appealing layout. Here are some best practices for customizing image placement:

+ Floating images: To allow XeLaTeX to automatically position images, you can enclose them within a `figure` environment. This enables the images to float along with the surrounding text, maintaining the document's overall flow. Use the `[htbp]` placement options to suggest preferred locations for the images (i.e., here, top, bottom, or on a separate page).

+ Alignment: XeLaTeX provides different options for aligning images within the document. The `\centering` command centers the image horizontally, while the `\raggedleft` and `\raggedright` commands align the image to the left or right, respectively. Experiment with these alignment options to achieve the desired visual effect.

+ Wrapping text around images: To wrap text around an image, use the `wrapfig` package. This package provides the `wrapfigure` environment, which allows you to specify the location and alignment of the image and the surrounding text. Wrapping text around images can improve the readability and aesthetics of your document.

Troubleshooting image-related issues

Working with graphics in XeLaTeX can sometimes present challenges. Here are some common issues and their solutions:

+ Image not found: If XeLaTeX is unable to find the image file, ensure that the file is located in the correct directory relative to your main LaTeX document. Double-check the spelling and capitalization of the file name. Additionally, make sure that the file extension matches the actual format of the image.

+ Poor image quality: If an image appears pixelated or low-quality, ensure that you are using a high-resolution version of the image. Avoid resizing images in a way that reduces their quality. If possible, use vector graphics formats like PDF, which can be scaled without loss of quality.

+ Slow compilation: Including large or complex images in a XeLaTeX document can significantly increase compilation time. Consider optimizing your images by reducing their file size or resolution. You can use external tools to compress images without sacrificing too much visual quality.

+ Overlapping images or text: If you experience issues with images overlapping with text or other graphical elements, adjust the placement options or refer to the documentation of the packages you are using. It may be necessary to fine-tune the position or use additional packages to handle complex layouts.

Summary

In this section, we explored best practices for using graphics in XeLaTeX. We discussed choosing the right graphics format, manipulating and scaling images, customizing image placement, and troubleshooting common issues. By following these best practices, you can effectively incorporate graphics into your XeLaTeX documents, enhancing their visual appeal and overall quality. Remember to experiment, iterate, and consult the documentation of the packages you are using to explore further possibilities and refine the visual design of your documents.

Visualization and Data Analysis with XeLaTeX

Introduction to data visualization in XeLaTeX

Data visualization is a vital component of data analysis and presentation. It involves the representation of data in graphical or visual forms to facilitate understanding, interpretation, and communication of complex information. XeLaTeX, a powerful extension of LaTeX, offers various tools and techniques for creating visually appealing and effective data visualizations.

In this section, we will explore the fundamentals of data visualization in XeLaTeX and the different approaches you can take to create informative and compelling visual representations of your data.

Principles of Data Visualization

Before diving into the technical aspects of data visualization in XeLaTeX, it is essential to understand the fundamental principles that guide effective data visualization design. These principles help ensure that your visualizations are clear, accurate, and visually engaging.

1. **Simplicity:** Keep your visualizations simple, avoiding unnecessary clutter and distractions. Focus on conveying the key message and insights effectively.

2. **Clarity:** Strive for clarity in your visualizations by using appropriate labels, titles, and annotations. Make sure that the intended message is easily understandable by the target audience.

3. **Accuracy:** Ensure that your visualizations accurately represent the underlying data. Choose appropriate scales, axes, and units to avoid distorting or misrepresenting the information.

4. **Consistency:** Maintain consistency in visual elements such as colors, fonts, and styles throughout your visualizations. Consistency helps establish a cohesive and coherent visual narrative.

5. **Relevance:** Focus on displaying relevant information and avoid including unnecessary details that may confuse or overwhelm the audience. Show only what is necessary to support your message.

6. **Interactivity:** Consider incorporating interactive elements in your visualizations to allow users to explore and interact with the data. Interactive visualizations can enhance engagement and provide a more immersive experience.

By adhering to these principles, you can create effective data visualizations that communicate information accurately and engage your audience.

Types of Data Visualization

Data visualization in XeLaTeX can take various forms, depending on the type of data and the message you want to convey. Here are some common types of data visualizations:

1. **Bar charts and line graphs:** Bar charts and line graphs are useful for comparing values or trends across different categories or time periods. They are effective in presenting numerical data in a visually appealing and easy-to-understand manner.

2. **Scatter plots and heatmaps:** Scatter plots and heatmaps are ideal for visualizing relationships and distributions in multivariate data. They can reveal patterns and correlations between different variables.

3. **Pie charts and donut charts:** Pie charts and donut charts are useful for depicting proportions or percentages of a whole. They are excellent for highlighting the relative contributions of different categories.

4. **Area charts and stacked bar charts:** Area charts and stacked bar charts are effective in showcasing the cumulative contribution of different categories over time or across various dimensions.

5. **Tree maps and trellis charts:** Tree maps and trellis charts are suitable for visualizing hierarchical or nested data structures. They provide a clear overview of the proportions and relationships within the hierarchy.

6. **Network diagrams and social graphs:** Network diagrams and social graphs are valuable for representing connections and relationships between entities. They are commonly used in social network analysis and network visualization.

7. **Box plots and violin plots:** Box plots and violin plots are effective in visualizing summary statistics and distribution characteristics of a dataset. They provide a concise overview of the central tendency, spread, and skewness of the data.

8. **Choropleth maps and cartograms:** Choropleth maps and cartograms are useful for representing spatial data and geographical distributions. They can effectively depict variations across different regions.

These are just a few examples of the types of data visualizations that can be created using XeLaTeX. Choosing the appropriate visualization type depends on the nature of the data and the insights you want to convey.

Creating Data Visualizations in XeLaTeX

In XeLaTeX, data visualizations can be created using various packages and libraries. One of the most popular packages for data visualization is PGF/TikZ, which provides a powerful and flexible set of tools for drawing high-quality graphics directly in your XeLaTeX documents.

To create a basic bar chart using PGF/TikZ, you can use the `axis` environment from the `pgfplots` package:

```
\begin{tikzpicture}
  \begin{axis}[
    width=0.8\textwidth,
    height=0.4\textheight,
    xlabel={Category},
    ylabel={Value},
    xmin=0,
    ymin=0,
    ymax=100,
    xtick=data,
    ytick={0,20,...,100},
    legend style={at={(0.5,-0.15)},
      anchor=north,legend columns=-1},
    ymajorgrids=true,
    grid style=dashed
  ]
    \addplot[ybar,fill=blue!40] coordinates {
      (Category 1,70)
      (Category 2,30)
      (Category 3,80)
      (Category 4,50)
    };
    \legend{Values}
  \end{axis}
\end{tikzpicture}
```

In this example, we create a bar chart with four categories and their corresponding values. The xmin, ymin, ymax, xtick, and ytick options are used to customize the axis limits and tick marks. The legend command adds a legend to the chart.

By customizing the axis labels, colors, styles, and other options, you can create a wide range of visualizations with PGF/TikZ.

Tips and Best Practices

Here are some tips and best practices to keep in mind when creating data visualizations in XeLaTeX:

+ Use appropriate color schemes and palettes to enhance the readability and aesthetics of your visualizations. Consider using colorblind-friendly palettes to ensure accessibility.

+ Label your axes and provide clear titles and captions to provide context and aid interpretation of your visualizations.

+ Consider the audience and purpose of your visualizations. Tailor your visuals to effectively communicate the intended message to your specific target audience.

+ Experiment with different visualization techniques and styles to find the most suitable representation for your data. Don't be afraid to iterate and refine your visualizations.

+ Use appropriate scaling and transformations to present your data accurately. Consider using logarithmic scales or normalization techniques to address data skewness or outliers.

+ Adhere to Data-Ink Ratio principles pioneered by Edward Tufte to minimize non-essential graphical elements and maximize the data-ink ratio in your visualizations.

+ Test your visualizations on different devices and screen sizes to ensure responsiveness and legibility across various platforms.

By following these tips and best practices, you can create compelling and effective data visualizations in XeLaTeX.

Conclusion

Data visualization is a powerful tool for communicating complex information and insights. With XeLaTeX and packages like PGF/TikZ, you have the flexibility and capabilities to create a wide range of visually appealing visualizations. By understanding the principles of data visualization design, choosing appropriate visualization types, and following best practices, you can effectively convey your data-driven narratives and engage your audience.

Creating Bar Charts and Line Graphs in XeLaTeX

In this section, we will explore how to create bar charts and line graphs in XeLaTeX. These visualizations are widely used in various fields to represent and analyze data. We will start by discussing the principles of bar charts and line graphs and then demonstrate how to create them using the TikZ package.

Principles of Bar Charts

Bar charts are used to compare different categories or groups by representing data using rectangular bars. The length of each bar corresponds to the value of the data it represents. Bar charts are excellent for visualizing categorical data and showing comparisons between different groups.

When creating a bar chart, there are a few key components to consider:

- Category Labels: Each category or group should have a label associated with it. These labels are usually placed on the x-axis of the chart.

- Value Axis: The y-axis represents the values of the data being measured. It is typically scaled according to the range of the data values.

- Bars: Each bar represents a specific category and indicates the value associated with that category. The height or length of the bar corresponds to the value.

- Bar Colors: You can choose different colors for each bar or group to distinguish them visually.

- Legends: If there are multiple groups or datasets, it's helpful to include a legend to explain the colors or patterns used in the chart.

Creating Bar Charts with TikZ

To create bar charts in XeLaTeX, we can use the powerful TikZ package, which allows for precise control over graphical elements. Let's start by loading the necessary packages and defining the data that we want to visualize:

```
% Define data
\pgfplotstableread[row sep=\\,col sep=&]{
    Category & Value \\
```

```
    A & 10 \\
    B & 15 \\
    C & 8 \\
    D & 12 \\
}\datatable
```

In the above code, we load the TikZ and pgfplots packages, which are essential for creating graphics. We also define our data using the `pgfplotstableread` command, where the categories and values are separated by & and each row is terminated by

.

Next, we can create the actual bar chart using the `axis` environment within a `tikzpicture` environment:

```
\begin{tikzpicture}
    \begin{axis}[
        ybar,
        width=\textwidth,
        height=8cm,
        ymin=0,
        ylabel=Values,
        symbolic x coords={A,B,C,D},
        xtick=data,
        nodes near coords,
        nodes near coords align={vertical},
        legend style={at={(0.5,-0.15)},
           anchor=north,legend columns=-1},
        ]
        \addplot table[x=Category,y=Value]{\datatable};
        \legend{Data}
    \end{axis}
\end{tikzpicture}
```

Let's go through some important parameters used in the code:

+ `ybar`: This option specifies that we want to create a vertical bar chart. If you prefer a horizontal bar chart, you can use the `xbar` option instead.

+ `width` and `height`: These options specify the dimensions of the chart.

+ `ymin`: This sets the lower limit of the value axis.

+ `ylabel`: This sets the label for the value axis.

+ `symbolic x coords` and `xtick`: These specify the categories or groups for the x-axis.

+ `nodes near coords`: This enables each bar to display its value near its top.

+ `nodes near coords align`: This aligns the value labels vertically.

+ `legend style`: This positions the legend at the bottom center of the chart.

Finally, we use the `\addplot` command to plot the data from our table, and the `\legend` command to add a legend to the chart.

By compiling the code, we can generate a bar chart that visually represents the data we specified. It should include labeled bars for each category, as well as a legend explaining the colors or patterns used.

Principles of Line Graphs

Line graphs, also known as line charts, are used to represent trends or changes over time. They are particularly effective for visualizing continuous data sets. Line graphs typically consist of points connected by lines, with the x-axis representing time or another continuous variable and the y-axis representing the values of the data.

When creating a line graph, it's important to consider the following:

+ Data Points: Each data point represents a specific value at a given time or point in the dataset.

+ Trend Lines: The lines connecting the data points help visualize the trend or change over time.

+ Axes Labels: The x-axis should display the time or other continuous variable, while the y-axis represents the values being measured.

+ Scaling: The scaling of the axes should be appropriate for the range of the data being plotted.

+ Gridlines: Including gridlines can help readers interpret the values more easily.

+ Legends: If there are multiple lines or datasets, a legend can provide information about the different lines or patterns used.

Creating Line Graphs with TikZ

To create line graphs in XeLaTeX, we can again use the TikZ package. Let's start by defining the data that we want to plot:

```
% Define data
\pgfplotstableread[row sep=\\,col sep=&]{
    Time & Value \\
    1 & 10 \\
    2 & 15 \\
    3 & 8 \\
    4 & 12 \\
}\datatable
```

In the above code, we define the time points and corresponding values in a table similar to what we did for the bar chart example.

Next, we can create the line graph using the `axis` environment within a `tikzpicture` environment:

```
\begin{tikzpicture}
    \begin{axis}[
        width=\textwidth,
        height=8cm,
        xlabel=Time,
        ylabel=Values,
        xtick=data,
        ytick={5,10,...,25},
        grid=major,
        legend style={at={(0.5,-0.15)},
          anchor=north,legend columns=-1},
        ]
        \addplot table[x=Time,y=Value]{\datatable};
        \legend{Data}
    \end{axis}
\end{tikzpicture}
```

The parameters used in this code are similar to those used for the bar chart example, with a few differences:

+ `xlabel`: This sets the label for the x-axis.

- `ytick`: This specifies the values for the y-axis ticks.

- `grid=major`: This adds major gridlines to the chart.

Again, we use the `\addplot` command to plot the data and the `\legend` command to add a legend.

By compiling the code, we can generate a line graph that visually represents the data we provided. It should include labeled data points connected by lines, with axes labeled appropriately and gridlines for ease of interpretation.

It is worth noting that both bar charts and line graphs can be customized extensively using the TikZ package. You can adjust colors, line styles, axis labels, legends, and other elements to suit your specific needs. The TikZ documentation provides a wealth of examples and options for customization.

Conclusion

In this section, we explored how to create bar charts and line graphs in XeLaTeX using the TikZ package. We discussed the principles behind these two types of graphs and provided code examples for generating them. By following the outlined steps and customizing the options, you can create visually appealing and informative bar charts and line graphs for your data. Remember to experiment with different styles and layouts to find the best representation for your specific needs.

Now that you have learned how to create bar charts and line graphs, you can apply this knowledge to visualize your own data and enhance your scientific or technical documents with informative and compelling visuals. Happy typesetting!

Creating Scatter Plots and Heatmaps in XeLaTeX

In scientific and data analysis research, scatter plots and heatmaps are commonly used to visualize and analyze relationships between variables. XeLaTeX provides powerful tools and libraries to create high-quality scatter plots and heatmaps in your documents. In this section, we will explore the principles, techniques, and best practices of creating scatter plots and heatmaps in XeLaTeX.

Introduction to Scatter Plots

A scatter plot is a graphical representation of a collection of points, where each point represents the values of two different variables. The x-axis represents one variable, while the y-axis represents the other variable. Scatter plots are used to identify trends, patterns, and correlations between the variables.

Creating Scatter Plots with TikZ

TikZ is a powerful package in XeLaTeX for creating high-quality graphics. To create a scatter plot using TikZ, we need to define the coordinates of the data points and customize the plot appearance.

Let's consider an example of plotting the relationship between the hours studied and the exam scores of a group of students. We have the following data:

Hours Studied	Exam Score
2	75
4	85
6	92
8	88
10	95

First, we need to load the TikZ package:

Next, we can create the scatter plot by defining the coordinates of the data points:

```
\begin{tikzpicture}
  \begin{axis}[
    axis lines = left,
    xlabel = {Hours Studied},
    ylabel = {Exam Score},
  ]
    \addplot[
      mark=*,
      only marks,
      nodes near coords,
      point meta=explicit symbolic,
    ] table[meta=label] {
      x     y     label
      2     75    A
      4     85    B
      6     92    C
      8     88    D
      10    95    E
```

```
  };
 \end{axis}
\end{tikzpicture}
```

In the above code, we used the `axis` environment from TikZ to set up the coordinate system with labeled x-axis and y-axis. We used the `addplot` command to plot the data points using the `table` method. The `mark` option specifies the shape of the data points (in this case, asterisks), and the `only marks` option removes connecting lines.

We also added the `nodes near coords` option to display the labels of the data points and the `point meta` option to specify the meta information for each point. Finally, we used the `table` environment to define the data points and their labels.

This code will generate a scatter plot of the hours studied versus the exam scores, with data points labeled as A, B, C, D, and E. You can customize the appearance of the plot by modifying the axis labels, data points, colors, and other options according to your requirements.

Introduction to Heatmaps

A heatmap is a graphical representation of data where values are represented as colors in a matrix. Heatmaps are commonly used to visualize the intensity, density, or distribution of a variable across different categories or dimensions. They are particularly useful for visualizing large datasets and identifying patterns or clusters.

Creating Heatmaps with TikZ

TikZ provides several libraries and options to create heatmaps in XeLaTeX. We can use the `pgfplots` package, which is built on top of TikZ, to generate high-quality heatmaps.

Let's consider an example of visualizing the average monthly temperatures for different cities over a year. We have the following data:

City	Jan	Feb	Mar	Apr	May	Jun	Jul	Aug	Sep	Oct	Nov
New York	32	36	46	58	68	76	82	81	73	62	49
London	43	45	49	53	59	64	69	68	63	56	47
Tokyo	46	49	54	61	66	72	77	80	75	67	54

To create a heatmap using TikZ and `pgfplots`, we need to load the necessary packages:

Next, we can create the heatmap by defining the matrix of data:

```
\begin{tikzpicture}
  \begin{axis}[
    title = {Average Monthly Temperatures},
    xticklabels = {Jan,Feb,Mar,Apr,May,Jun,Jul,Aug,Sep,Oct,Nov,De
    yticklabels = {New York,London,Tokyo},
    xlabel = {Month},
    ylabel = {City},
    colorbar,
    colorbar style={
      title=Temperature (\textdegree F),
      ylabel=Temperature,
    },
    point meta min=32,
    point meta max=82,
    colormap={mymap}{color=(blue); color=(yellow)},
  ]
    \addplot[
      matrix plot*,
      mesh/color input=explicit,
      mesh/rows=3,
      mesh/cols=12,
    ] table {
      32 36 46 58 68 76 82 81 73 62 49
      43 45 49 53 59 64 69 68 63 56 47
      46 49 54 61 66 72 77 80 75 67 54
    };
  \end{axis}
\end{tikzpicture}
```

In the above code, we used the axis environment to set up the heatmap. We specified the x-axis and y-axis labels using the xticklabels and yticklabels options, respectively. The colorbar option adds a color legend to the heatmap, and we used the colormap option to define the color scheme.

We used the addplot command with the matrix plot* option to create the heatmap. The table environment is used to define the matrix of data. The point `meta min` and `point meta max` options set the minimum and maximum values for the color mapping.

This code will generate a heatmap of the average monthly temperatures for New York, London, and Tokyo. The color intensity represents the temperature, with blue indicating lower temperatures and yellow indicating higher temperatures. You can customize the appearance of the heatmap by modifying the axis labels, color scheme, legend, and other options according to your requirements.

Best Practices and Tips

When creating scatter plots and heatmaps in XeLaTeX, here are some best practices and tips to keep in mind:

- Choose appropriate variable types and scales for more meaningful visualizations.

- Use clear labels and titles to provide context and enhance understanding.

- Customize the appearance of plots with colors, markers, titles, legends, and other visual elements.

- Test different visualization options to find the most suitable representation of your data.

- Consider the overall design and composition of your document when placing or integrating the plots.

- Use consistent styles and conventions throughout your document for a professional and cohesive look.

It is always a good practice to experiment with different settings, options, and visualization techniques to find the most effective and visually appealing representations of your data. Additionally, keep in mind the principles of effective data visualization, such as avoiding clutter, choosing appropriate scales, and focusing on relevant information.

In the next sections, we will explore more advanced techniques and applications of XeLaTeX in scientific and technical writing. Stay tuned!

Exercises

1. Plot the relationship between the prices of different stocks and their corresponding daily trading volumes.

2. Create a heatmap to visualize the distribution of crime rates across different neighborhoods in a city.

3. Experiment with different color schemes and styles to enhance the visual impact of your scatter plots and heatmaps.

Resources

+ The TikZ and pgfplots documentation: https://www.ctan.org/pkg/pgf

+ The Visual Display of Quantitative Information by Edward R. Tufte

+ Data Visualization: A Practical Introduction by Kieran Healy

+ https://tikz.netlify.com/

Remember to practice and explore different features and techniques to improve your skills in creating scatter plots and heatmaps in XeLaTeX.

Creating Interactive Visualizations with JavaScript in XeLaTeX

In this section, we will explore how to create interactive visualizations using JavaScript within a XeLaTeX document. JavaScript is a powerful programming language that allows us to dynamically manipulate HTML elements and add interactivity to our web-based visualizations. By leveraging the capabilities of JavaScript, we can create engaging and interactive graphics directly within our XeLaTeX documents.

Introduction to Interactive Visualizations

Interactive visualizations are a great way to present data and engage your audience. With JavaScript, we can add a wide range of interactive features to our visualizations, such as tooltips, zooming, panning, and animations. These interactive elements enhance the user experience, allowing them to explore the data in a more immersive and interactive way.

Benefits of Using JavaScript

Integrating JavaScript into your XeLaTeX document for creating interactive visualizations offers several benefits:

- **Enhanced User Experience:** JavaScript allows you to create interactive and dynamic visualizations that can respond to user actions, providing a rich and engaging experience.

- **Real-time Data Updates:** JavaScript enables you to update your visualizations in real-time based on changing data or user input. This is particularly useful for live data feeds or interactive dashboards.

- **Cross-platform Compatibility:** JavaScript is supported by all modern web browsers, making your interactive visualizations accessible to a wide range of devices and platforms.

- **Extensive Visualization Libraries:** There are numerous JavaScript libraries, such as D3.js, Chart.js, and Plotly, that provide a wide range of pre-built visualization components and features, saving you time and effort in developing complex interactive visualizations.

Integrating JavaScript with XeLaTeX

To integrate JavaScript into a XeLaTeX document, we need to use the `embedjs` package. This package allows us to include JavaScript code directly within the XeLaTeX document, enabling us to create interactive visualizations.

First, we need to load the `embedjs` package in the preamble of our document:

Next, we can use the `embedjs` environment to include our JavaScript code:

```
\begin{embedjs}
// JavaScript code goes here
\end{embedjs}
```

Within the `embedjs` environment, we can write our JavaScript code, which will be executed when the document is rendered in a web browser. We can use JavaScript to manipulate the HTML elements generated by XeLaTeX and add interactivity to our visualizations.

Creating Interactive Visualizations

Let's consider an example where we want to create an interactive bar chart using JavaScript within our XeLaTeX document. We will use the D3.js library, which provides powerful tools for creating dynamic and interactive visualizations.

First, we need to include the D3.js library in our document. We can do this by embedding the necessary JavaScript code within the embedjs environment:

```
\begin{embedjs}
// Include D3.js library
<script src="https://d3js.org/d3.v7.js"></script>

// JavaScript code for interactive bar chart goes here
\end{embedjs}
```

Next, we need to define the data for our bar chart. We can use a JSON object to store the data values:

```
\begin{embedjs}
// Define data for the bar chart
var data = [
  { label: 'Apple', value: 10 },
  { label: 'Banana', value: 20 },
  { label: 'Orange', value: 15 },
  { label: 'Grape', value: 30 }
];

// JavaScript code for interactive bar chart goes here
\end{embedjs}
```

Now, we can write the JavaScript code to create the interactive bar chart using D3.js:

```
\begin{embedjs}
// Define data for the bar chart
var data = [
  { label: 'Apple', value: 10 },
  { label: 'Banana', value: 20 },
  { label: 'Orange', value: 15 },
  { label: 'Grape', value: 30 }
```

```
];

// Select the SVG element
var svg = d3.select('svg');

// Set the dimensions of the canvas
var width = 500;
var height = 300;

// Set the scale for the x-axis
var xScale = d3.scaleBand()
  .domain(data.map(function(d) { return d.label; }))
  .range([0, width])
  .padding(0.1);

// Set the scale for the y-axis
var yScale = d3.scaleLinear()
  .domain([0, d3.max(data, function(d) { return d.value; })])
  .range([height, 0]);

// Add the bars to the chart
svg.selectAll('rect')
  .data(data)
  .enter()
  .append('rect')
  .attr('x', function(d) { return xScale(d.label); })
  .attr('y', function(d) { return yScale(d.value); })
  .attr('width', xScale.bandwidth())
  .attr('height', function(d) { return height - yScale(d.value); })
  .attr('fill', 'steelblue');

// Add tooltips to the bars
svg.selectAll('rect')
  .append('title')
  .text(function(d) { return 'Label: ' + d.label + ', Value: ' + d
\end{embedjs}
```

In the above code, we first select the SVG element on which we want to create the bar chart. We then define the scales for the x-axis and y-axis, which map the data values to the visual dimensions of the chart. Finally, we add the bars to the chart based on the data values, and append tooltips to each bar for additional information.

To include the visualization in our XeLaTeX document, we can use the includegraphics command to embed an SVG image generated by the JavaScript code:

```
% \begin{figure}[htbp]
%    \centering
%    \includegraphics[width=0.8\textwidth]{bar_chart.svg}
%    \caption{Interactive bar chart created with JavaScript}
%    \label{fig:bar_chart}
% \end{figure}
```

By following these steps, we can easily create interactive visualizations using JavaScript within our XeLaTeX documents.

Summary

In this section, we learned how to create interactive visualizations with JavaScript in XeLaTeX. We explored the benefits of using JavaScript for creating interactive visualizations, and saw how to integrate JavaScript code into our XeLaTeX document using the embedjs package. We also demonstrated an example of creating an interactive bar chart using the D3.js library. By leveraging JavaScript's capabilities, we can enhance our visualizations and provide a more engaging experience for our readers.

Creating 3D visualizations and animations in XeLaTeX

In this section, we will explore how to create stunning 3D visualizations and animations using XeLaTeX. 3D graphics can greatly enhance the presentation of complex data, making it easier to understand and visualize. We will start by discussing the basic principles of 3D graphics, followed by an introduction to the relevant packages and libraries in XeLaTeX. Then, we will cover techniques for creating basic 3D objects, customizing their appearance, and animating them.

Introduction to 3D Graphics

Before we delve into the technical details of creating 3D visualizations in XeLaTeX, let's take a moment to understand the basic principles behind 3D graphics. 3D graphics involve representing objects and scenes using three-dimensional coordinates, which allow for a more realistic depiction of space. In a 3D coordinate system, points are defined by their x, y, and z coordinates, representing their position along the three axes.

In XeLaTeX, 3D graphics are typically created using the `tikz-3dplot` package, which provides a set of commands and utilities for working with 3D coordinates and transformations. This package is built on top of the powerful TikZ graphics system, which allows for the creation of high-quality graphics directly within the LaTeX document.

Getting Started with 3D Graphics in XeLaTeX

To get started with 3D graphics in XeLaTeX, we need to load the necessary packages and set up a 3D coordinate system. The following code snippet demonstrates how to achieve this:

```
\tdplotsetmaincoords{70}{110} % Set the viewing angles

\begin{tikzpicture}[scale=2]
  \tdplotsetrotatedcoords{0}{0}{45} % Set the rotation angles

  % Draw axes
  \draw[->] (-1,0,0) -- (4,0,0) node[below]{\$x\$};
  \draw[->] (0,-1,0) -- (0,4,0) node[right]{\$y\$};
  \draw[->] (0,0,-1) -- (0,0,4) node[above]{\$z\$};

  % Draw a 3D object
  \draw[fill=blue!50!black] (1,1,1) -- (3,1,1) -- (3,3,1) -- cycle
\end{tikzpicture}
```

In the above code, we first load the `tikz` and `tikz-3dplot` packages, which are essential for creating 3D graphics. We then set the main viewing angles using the `tdplotsetmaincoords` command. Next, we define a new `tikzpicture` environment and set the rotation angles using the `tdplotsetrotatedcoords` command. Inside the `tikzpicture`, we can draw the 3D object using standard TikZ commands. In this example, we draw a triangle and fill it with a blue color.

Customizing 3D Objects and Appearance

In XeLaTeX, we have full control over the customization of 3D objects and their appearance. We can change the shape, color, transparency, and other properties of 3D objects to achieve the desired visual effect. This can be done using various TikZ options and commands.

To customize the shape of a 3D object, we can use the available TikZ commands to draw different geometrical shapes, such as cubes, spheres, cones, and cylinders. For example, to draw a cube, we can use the `\draw` command followed by a series of `--` commands to define the vertices of the cube. We can then use the `fill` option to specify the color of the cube.

```
\begin{tikzpicture}[scale=2]
  \tdplotsetrotatedcoords{0}{0}{45}

  % Draw a cube
  \draw[fill=red!50!black] (0,0,0) -- (1,0,0) -- (1,1,0) -- (0,1,
  \draw[fill=green!50!black] (0,0,0) -- (0,1,0) -- (0,1,1) -- (0,
  \draw[fill=blue!50!black] (0,0,0) -- (0,0,1) -- (1,0,1) -- (1,0
  \draw[fill=yellow!50!black] (1,1,1) -- (0,1,1) -- (0,1,0) -- (1
  \draw[fill=cyan!50!black] (1,1,1) -- (1,0,1) -- (1,0,0) -- (1,1
  \draw[fill=magenta!50!black] (1,1,1) -- (1,0,1) -- (0,0,1) -- (
\end{tikzpicture}
```

In the above code, we create a cube by drawing six rectangles that form its six faces. We use different colors to distinguish the faces of the cube.

We can also apply transformations to the 3D objects to change their position, rotation, and scale. The `scale`, `shift`, and `rotate` options can be used to achieve these transformations. For example, to scale an object by a factor of 2 and rotate it by 45 degrees around the z-axis, we can use the following code:

```
\begin{tikzpicture}[scale=2]
  \tdplotsetrotatedcoords{0}{0}{45}

  % Draw a 3D object
  \draw[fill=blue!50!black] (1,1,1) -- (3,1,1) -- (3,3,1) -- cycl
```

```
\end{tikzpicture}
```

Animating 3D Objects in XeLaTeX

One of the unique features of XeLaTeX is the ability to create animated 3D graphics directly within the LaTeX document. This can be accomplished using the `animate` package, which allows for the creation of frame-based animations.

To create an animation, we need to define a series of frames that represent different states of the animation. Each frame can contain different 3D objects or different positions of the same objects. The `animateinline` environment can be used to encapsulate the frames and define the animation settings.

Here's an example that demonstrates how to create a rotating cube animation using XeLaTeX:

```
\begin{animateinline}[controls]{10} % Set the frame rate and enabl
  \multiframe{36}{i=0+10}{ % Create 36 frames, incrementing the an
    \tdplotsetmaincoords{70+\i}{110+\i} % Update the viewing angle
    \begin{tikzpicture}[scale=2]
      \tdplotsetrotatedcoords{0}{0}{45} % Set the rotation angles

      % Draw a rotating cube
      \tdplotdrawpolytopearc[fill=red!50!black,draw=black,dashed]{
      \tdplotdrawpolytope[fill=green!50!black]{1,1,0}{2,1,0}{2,2,0
      \tdplotdrawpolytopearc[fill=blue!50!black,draw=black,dashed]
      \tdplotdrawpolytopearc[fill=yellow!50!black,draw=black,dashe
      \tdplotdrawpolytopearc[fill=cyan!50!black,draw=black,dashed]
      \tdplotdrawpolytope[fill=magenta!50!black]{0,1,1}{1,1,1}{1,0
    \end{tikzpicture}
  }
\end{animateinline}
```

In the above code, we define an animation with a frame rate of 10 frames per second using the `animateinline` environment. We then create 36 frames, each incrementing the viewing angles by 10 degrees. Inside each frame, we draw a rotating cube using the `tdplotdrawpolytope` and `tdplotdrawpolytopearc` commands. The `multiframe` command is used to specify the number of frames and the increment of the angle.

Conclusion

In this section, we have explored how to create stunning 3D visualizations and animations using XeLaTeX. We started by understanding the basic principles of 3D graphics and then learned how to use the `tikz-3dplot` package to create a 3D coordinate system and draw 3D objects. We customized the appearance of the objects by changing their shape, color, and transparency. Finally, we discovered how to create frame-based animations using the `animate` package. With the knowledge gained in this section, you can now create impressive 3D visualizations and animations directly within your XeLaTeX documents. Enjoy the freedom and creativity that XeLaTeX offers in the world of 3D graphics!

Incorporating statistical analysis and regression models in XeLaTeX

Introduction to statistical analysis

Statistical analysis plays a crucial role in various fields such as economics, social sciences, biology, and many others. It helps to understand data, extract meaningful insights, and make informed decisions. In this section, we will explore how XeLaTeX can be used to incorporate statistical analysis and regression models into documents.

Overview of regression models

Regression analysis is a statistical technique used to model the relationship between a dependent variable and one or more independent variables. It helps us understand how changes in the independent variables affect the dependent variable. XeLaTeX provides various packages and libraries that allow us to perform regression analysis and visualize the results.

Linear regression

Linear regression is a widely used regression model that assumes a linear relationship between the dependent variable and the independent variables. In XeLaTeX, we can use the lm function from the stats package to fit a linear regression model to our data. We can then use the summary function to display the summary statistics of the model, including the coefficients, standard errors, t-values, and p-values.

Example: Predicting house prices

Let's consider an example of predicting house prices based on their size and location. We have a dataset with information about the size of houses in square feet and their corresponding prices in dollars. We can use XeLaTeX to perform a linear regression analysis on this dataset.

First, we load the necessary packages and import the dataset:

```
\pgfplotstableread[
    col sep=comma,
    columns={Size,Price},
    ]{house_data.csv}\mydata
```

Next, we fit a linear regression model to the data:

```
\begin{table}[h]
\centering
\pgfplotstabletypeset[
    columns={Size,Price},
    create on use/Slope/.style={
        create col/linear regression={y=Price}
    },
    ]{\mydata}
\caption{Linear regression results for predicting house prices}
\label{tab:linear_regression}
\end{table}
```

The table in Figure ?? shows the results of the linear regression analysis. We can see that the estimated slope coefficient for the Size variable is 103.33, indicating that, on average, each additional square foot increases the house price by $103.33.

Non-linear regression

Sometimes, the relationship between the dependent and independent variables is non-linear. In such cases, we can use non-linear regression models to capture the relationship. XeLaTeX provides various statistical packages that offer methods for fitting non-linear regression models.

Example: Fitting a polynomial regression model

Consider a dataset that represents the growth of a plant over time. We hypothesize that the growth can be modeled by a polynomial function. To fit a polynomial regression model in XeLaTeX, we can use the nls function from the stats package.

Here is an example of how to fit a quadratic regression model to the plant growth data:

```
% \begin{figure}[h]
% \centering
% \begin{tikzpicture}
% \begin{axis}[
%     xlabel={Time},
%     ylabel={Growth},
%     ]
% \addplot+[only marks] table [x=Time, y=Growth] {\mydata};
% \addplot+[no markers] table [x=Time,
%     y={create col/linear regression={y=Growth}}] {\mydata};
% \addplot [domain=0:10, samples=100] {0.5*x^2 + 2*x + 1};
% \legend{Data, Linear regression, Quadratic regression}
% \end{axis}
% \end{tikzpicture}
% \caption{Quadratic regression model for plant growth}
% \label{fig:quadratic_regression}
% \end{figure}
%
```

By integrating XeLaTeX with R in this way, we can easily update the grade analysis and plot by recompiling the XeLaTeX document whenever new data becomes available. This allows us to generate dynamic and informative reports based on the latest data analysis.

Conclusion

Integrating XeLaTeX with data analysis tools and APIs opens up a world of possibilities for creating data-driven documents. By seamlessly combining the power of XeLaTeX for typesetting with the capabilities of data analysis tools, we can easily generate visually appealing and informative reports, research papers, and presentations that are always up-to-date with the latest data analysis results. Whether it's incorporating dynamic visualizations, statistical analyses, or machine learning outputs, the integration of XeLaTeX with data analysis tools is an essential skill for anyone involved in data-driven document generation.

Further Reading and Resources

To further explore the integration of XeLaTeX with data analysis tools and APIs, consider exploring the following resources:

- *R Markdown: The Definitive Guide* by Yihui Xie, J. J. Allaire, and Garrett Grolemund

- *Python for Data Analysis* by Wes McKinney

- *Learning SQL* by Alan Beaulieu

- *API Design Patterns* by JJ Geewax

- *Practical API Design* by Jaroslav Tulach

By delving into these resources, you can enhance your knowledge and explore advanced techniques for integrating XeLaTeX with various data analysis tools and APIs.

Best practices for data visualization in XeLaTeX

Data visualization is a powerful tool for communicating information effectively. In this section, we will discuss best practices for creating visually appealing and informative data visualizations using XeLaTeX. We will cover various techniques and approaches to enhance the readability and effectiveness of your visualizations.

Choose the Right Chart Type

The first step in creating a successful data visualization is selecting the appropriate chart type. Different chart types are suitable for different types of data and messaging. Here are some common chart types and their recommended use cases:

1. Bar charts: Suitable for comparing categorical data or displaying trends over time.

2. Line charts: Ideal for depicting continuous data and showing trends over time.

3. Scatter plots: Useful for visualizing the relationships between two continuous variables.

4. Pie charts: Effective for displaying proportions or percentages of a whole.

5. Heatmaps: Great for illustrating the density or distribution of data in a matrix format.

When choosing a chart type, consider the message you want to convey and the characteristics of your data. Avoid using complicated or unnecessary chart types that may confuse your audience.

Simplify and Streamline

One of the key principles of data visualization is simplicity. Avoid cluttering your visualizations with unnecessary elements that can distract or confuse your audience. Keep the following tips in mind when simplifying your visualizations:

- Use a limited color palette: Choose a coherent color scheme that enhances readability and maintains consistency throughout your visualizations.

- Remove unnecessary labels and gridlines: Only include labels and gridlines when they are essential for understanding the data.

- Minimize chart junk: Avoid adding embellishments and decorative elements that do not serve a purpose.

- Use white space effectively: Utilize white space to separate elements and improve overall visual clarity.

By simplifying your visualizations, you can highlight the key information and create a more impactful presentation.

Ensure Readability

Readability is crucial in data visualization. Make sure that your visualizations can be easily understood by your audience. Consider the following tips to improve readability:

- Use appropriate font sizes: Ensure that the text in your visualizations, such as axis labels or data labels, is readable without straining the eyes.

- Label your axes clearly: Clearly label your axes with concise and descriptive labels to provide context for your data.

- Provide appropriate units: Include units of measurement for your data to provide clarity and prevent misinterpretation.

Additionally, make sure that your visualizations are accessible to individuals with visual impairments by providing alt text for images and using high contrast colors.

Tell a Compelling Story

Data visualizations are most effective when they tell a compelling story. Consider the narrative you want to convey and structure your visualizations accordingly. Use the following tips to enhance the storytelling aspect of your visualizations:

- Use annotations: Add annotations or call-outs to draw attention to important data points or trends.

- Provide context: Include a title or a brief description that provides context and explains the purpose of your visualization.

- Incorporate storytelling elements: Consider incorporating elements of storytelling, such as a beginning, middle, and end, to engage your audience.

By crafting a compelling narrative, you can engage your audience and ensure that your data visualizations have a lasting impact.

Use Interactive Visualizations

Interactive visualizations can provide a richer and more engaging experience for your audience. Consider using interactive elements in your visualizations to allow users to explore the data in more detail. Some ways to incorporate interactivity in your visualizations include:

✦ Tooltips: Display additional information or context when the user hovers over specific data points.

✦ Filters: Enable users to select specific data subsets or filter the visualization based on different criteria.

✦ Zoom and pan: Allow users to zoom in on specific areas of the visualization or pan across a large dataset.

Interactive visualizations can help users understand the data more effectively and encourage deeper exploration.

Keep it Honest and Accurate

Data integrity is crucial in data visualization. Ensure that your visualizations accurately represent the underlying data and avoid misleading or misrepresenting information. Here are some guidelines to maintain data integrity:

✦ Use appropriate scaling: Ensure that axis scales are chosen carefully to prevent distorting the data and creating misleading impressions.

✦ Provide a clear data source: Always clearly state the source of your data to maintain transparency and credibility.

✦ Avoid distorting visuals: Be cautious of using 3D effects or exaggerated perspectives that can distort the perception of the data.

By presenting data honestly and accurately, you can build trust with your audience and strengthen the impact of your visualizations.

Experiment and Iterate

Lastly, don't be afraid to experiment and iterate with your data visualizations. Try different chart types, color schemes, and layouts to discover what works best for your data and message. Get feedback from others and be willing to make improvements based on constructive criticism.

Remember that data visualization is a continuous learning process, and there is always room for improvement. Embrace the opportunity to refine your skills and create even more compelling and effective visualizations.

Conclusion

In this section, we have explored best practices for creating effective data visualizations in XeLaTeX. By selecting the right chart type, simplifying and streamlining your visualizations, ensuring readability, storytelling, incorporating interactivity, maintaining data integrity, and embracing experimentation, you can create visualizations that are impactful and engaging. Keep these best practices in mind as you embark on your data visualization journey in XeLaTeX. Happy visualizing!

XeLaTeX for Scientific and Technical Writing

Introduction to Scientific and Technical Writing with XeLaTeX

Common challenges in scientific and technical writing

Scientific and technical writing presents a unique set of challenges that both novice and experienced writers often encounter. In this section, we will explore some of the common difficulties faced by writers in these fields and provide strategies to overcome them.

1.1 Writing for a specific audience

One of the most important aspects of scientific and technical writing is tailoring the content to the intended audience. Writers must consider the readers' level of knowledge, background, and expectations. It can be challenging to strike the right balance between providing sufficient detail for experts while ensuring clarity for non-experts.

To address this challenge, writers should thoroughly research their target audience and create a clear profile of their readers. This process will help determine the appropriate level of technicality, terminology, and depth of explanation required. Additionally, including real-world examples and analogies can effectively bridge the gap between technical information and the readers' understanding.

1.2 Organizing complex information

Scientific and technical writing often deals with intricate concepts, data, and experimental results. Effectively organizing and presenting this information in a logical and coherent manner can be a challenge. Poor organization can lead to confusion and make it difficult for readers to follow the writer's arguments.

To tackle this challenge, writers should start by creating a comprehensive outline. This outline should include main headings, subheadings, and key points to guide the writing process. Utilizing bullet points, numbered lists, and paragraph breaks can help break down complex information into manageable chunks.

Another helpful strategy is to use clear and concise section headings that accurately reflect the content. This allows readers to navigate the document easily and locate specific information. Additionally, writers should consider using visual aids such as tables, graphs, and illustrations to enhance the understanding of complex concepts.

1.3 Balancing technical accuracy and readability

Scientific and technical writing requires a high level of technical accuracy. However, striking a balance between technical rigor and readability can be a challenge. While it is important to present accurate information, using overly complex language and jargon can hinder comprehension and alienate readers.

To address this challenge, writers should use plain language and avoid unnecessary technical terms where possible. Technical terms that are essential to the understanding of the topic should be defined in a clear and concise manner. Additionally, writers should make extensive use of examples, analogies, and visuals to simplify complex ideas.

1.4 Ensuring logical flow and coherence

Maintaining a logical flow and coherence throughout a scientific or technical document is essential to facilitate readers' comprehension. Writers often struggle with transitions between ideas and ensuring that each section builds upon the previous one in a coherent manner.

To overcome this challenge, writers should pay attention to the overall organization of the document as mentioned earlier. Additionally, the use of transition words and phrases, such as "however," "therefore," and "in contrast," can help smoothly connect different ideas and concepts.

Furthermore, writers should consistently refer back to earlier sections or concepts when introducing new information. This technique reinforces connections and promotes a better understanding of the overall structure of the document.

1.5 Citing and referencing sources accurately

Scientific and technical writing heavily relies on citing and referencing sources to support claims and provide evidence. However, ensuring accurate and consistent citation can be a time-consuming and error-prone process.

To overcome this challenge, writers should familiarize themselves with the citation style required by their field or institution (e.g., APA, MLA, IEEE). Using reference management software such as EndNote or Zotero can streamline the citation process and ensure consistent formatting.

Additionally, writers should double-check all references for accuracy and completeness. Missing or incorrect citations can undermine the credibility of the document. It is also essential to properly attribute ideas, data, and figures to their respective sources to avoid plagiarism.

In conclusion, scientific and technical writing poses several challenges, including writing for a specific audience, organizing complex information, balancing technical accuracy and readability, ensuring logical flow and coherence, and citing and referencing sources accurately. By understanding and addressing these challenges, writers can produce clear, concise, and effective scientific and technical documents.

Writing mathematical equations and expressions in XeLaTeX

As XeLaTeX is a powerful tool for typesetting scientific and technical documents, it provides extensive support for writing mathematical equations and expressions. In this section, we will explore the various features and techniques available in XeLaTeX for expressing mathematical concepts effectively.

Introduction to mathematical typesetting in XeLaTeX

Mathematical typesetting requires a separate environment in XeLaTeX known as the math mode. This mode allows you to write mathematical expressions and equations using a specific syntax and provides various commands and symbols for representing mathematical concepts.

To enter the math mode, you can either use the dollar signs ($) for inline equations or the double dollar signs ($$) for displayed equations. For example:

```
In inline text: \$E = mc^2\$
In displayed equation: \$\$E = mc^2\$\$
```

It is recommended to use the 'amsmath' package, which provides additional functionality and improved equation formatting. To use this package, simply add the following line to the preamble of your document:

Equation formatting and alignment

In XeLaTeX, the 'amsmath' package provides several environments for typesetting equations and aligning them properly.

The 'equation' environment is used for single-line equations. For example:

```
\begin{equation}\label{eq:mass-energy}
    E = mc^2
\end{equation}
```

This equation will be automatically numbered and can be referenced using the '\ref' command.

The 'align' environment is used for aligning multiple equations in columns. For example:

```
\begin{align}
    a &= b + c \\
    d &= e + f
\end{align}
```

This will align the equations at the equal sign. If you want to align the equations at a different symbol, you can use the `alignat` environment.

Symbols and operators

XeLaTeX supports a wide range of mathematical symbols and operators that can be used to represent various mathematical concepts. Below are some examples of frequently used symbols and operators:

- Greek letters: α, β, γ, etc.

- Trigonometric functions: $\sin$, $\cos$, $\tan$, etc.

- Exponents and logarithms: x^2, $\log(x)$, etc.

- Summation and integration: $\sum_{i=1}^{n}$, $\int_a^b$, etc.

- Fractions and binomial coefficients: $\frac{1}{2}$, $\binom{n}{k}$, etc.

To use these symbols and operators in your equations, simply enter the corresponding command or expression in math mode.

Matrices and vectors

XeLaTeX provides special environments for typesetting matrices and vectors. The `matrix` environment can be used to create matrices with custom brackets or parentheses. For example:

$$\begin{matrix} 1 & 2 \\ 3 & 4 \end{matrix}$$

This will create a 2x2 matrix.

The `pmatrix`, `bmatrix`, and `vmatrix` environments can be used to typeset matrices with different types of brackets or parentheses.

To represent vectors, you can use the `\vec` command. For example:

$$\vec{v} = \begin{pmatrix} x \\ y \\ z \end{pmatrix}$$

This will create a vector with components x, y, and z.

Numbering and referencing equations

XeLaTeX automatically numbers equations by default. However, you can suppress the numbering by using the `equation*` environment instead of the `equation` environment.

To reference an equation within your document, you can use the `\label` and `\ref` commands. For example:

$$E = mc^2 \tag{5}$$

According to equation `\ref{eq:mass-energy}`, the energy of an object is equal to its mass times the speed of light squared.

The `\label` command assigns a unique identifier to the equation, and the `\ref` command is used to refer to that equation elsewhere in the document.

Mathematical fonts

XeLaTeX allows you to use a wide variety of mathematical fonts to typeset your equations. By default, it uses the Computer Modern font. However, you can change the font by using the appropriate package and font commands in the preamble of your document.

For example, to use the Euler math font, you can add the following lines to your preamble:

. . .

This will change the font used for mathematical equations throughout your document.

Advanced mathematical typesetting

XeLaTeX provides advanced functionality for typesetting complex mathematical expressions and equations. For example, the 'amsmath' package provides commands for writing multiline equations, displayed fractions, and more.

Moreover, various packages like 'amssymb', 'amsfonts', and 'mathtools' enhance XeLaTeX's mathematical typesetting capabilities by providing additional symbols, fonts, and tools.

To learn more about these advanced features and techniques, refer to the documentation of the 'amsmath' package and other relevant packages.

Conclusion

In this section, we explored the basics of writing mathematical equations and expressions in XeLaTeX. We discussed how to enter the math mode, format and align equations, use symbols and operators, create matrices and vectors, number and reference equations, choose mathematical fonts, and utilize advanced mathematical typesetting features.

XeLaTeX provides a rich set of tools and functionalities that make it an excellent choice for typesetting mathematical content in scientific and technical documents. With a good understanding of these techniques, you can effectively communicate complex mathematical concepts in your XeLaTeX documents.

Remember to practice and experiment with different mathematical expressions to develop a better understanding of XeLaTeX's capabilities.

Formatting and Typesetting Scientific Papers in XeLaTeX

Scientific papers require precise formatting and typesetting to effectively communicate research findings and facilitate easy comprehension by the readers.

XeLaTeX, with its powerful features and flexible capabilities, is an excellent tool for writing scientific papers. In this section, we will explore the various techniques and best practices for formatting and typesetting scientific papers in XeLaTeX.

Document Structure

Like any other LaTeX document, a scientific paper in XeLaTeX follows a similar structure with a few additional elements specific to scientific writing.

Title and Author Information The title and author information of the paper play a crucial role in capturing the reader's attention. To format the title, you can use the \title command followed by the \author command to specify the author's name. It is also common practice to include the date of publication. For example:

```
\title{The Impact of Climate Change on Biodiversity}
\author{John Doe}
\date{\today}
```

Abstract The abstract provides a concise summary of the paper's main objectives, methodology, and findings. In XeLaTeX, you can create the abstract using the abstract environment. For example:

```
\begin{abstract}
This study\index{study} investigates the effects of climate\index{
data\index{data} collected from various ecological surveys. The re
in\index{in} species richness\index{richness} and population\index
measures.
\end{abstract}
```

Sections and Subsections To organize the content of your scientific paper, you can utilize sections and subsections. Use the \section command to create a new section, and the \subsection command for subsections. For example:

```
\section{Introduction}
Lorem\index{Lorem} ipsum dolor sit amet, consectetur\index{consect
molestie, consequat\index{consequat} nunc\index{nunc} nec, tincidu

\subsection{Background}
Cras ac nulla non\index{non} nulla vestibulum convallis. Donec dic
```

```
sed fringilla\index{sed fringilla} lorem aliquet.
```

. . .

Equations and Mathematical Expressions

Scientific papers typically include mathematical equations to express hypotheses, models, and calculations. XeLaTeX provides robust support for typesetting equations using the popular `amsmath` package. Here are some examples of commonly used mathematical environments and symbols:

Inline Equations   For short mathematical expressions within the text, you can use the $ symbol to delimit the math mode. For example:

```
The equation \$E=mc^2\$ proposed by Einstein revolutionized the
```

Display Equations   For longer equations that require additional space, you can use the `equation` environment. This environment automatically numbers the equations. For example:

$$E = mc^2 \qquad (6)$$

Equation 6 represents the mass-energy equivalence.

Aligning Equations   To align a series of equations, use the `align` environment. This environment allows you to align equations based on operators or specific alignment points using the & symbol. For example:

```
\begin{align}
    f(x) &= x^2 + 2x + 1 \\
    g(x) &= \sqrt{x+1}
\end{align}
```

Tables and Figures

Tables and figures are essential components of scientific papers as they present data and visualizations. XeLaTeX provides several packages, such as `booktabs`, `tabularx`, and `graphicx`, to enable the creation of high-quality tables and figures.

Tables   To create a table in XeLaTeX, you can use the `tabular` environment within a `table` environment. The `tabular` environment allows you to define the number of columns, their alignment, and the table content. Here's an example:

```
\begin{table}[ht]
    \centering
    \caption{Sample Table}
    \begin{tabular}{ccc}
        \toprule
        Column 1 & Column 2 & Column 3 \\
        \midrule
        Data 1   & Data 2   & Data 3   \\
        Data 4   & Data 5   & Data 6   \\
        \bottomrule
    \end{tabular}
    \label{tab:sample}
\end{table}
```

Figures   To include figures in your scientific paper, you can use the `graphicx` package. This package provides the `\includegraphics` command, which allows you to insert images in various formats (e.g., PDF, PNG, JPEG). Here's an example usage:

```
% \begin{figure}[ht]
%     \centering
%     \includegraphics[width=0.5\textwidth]{figure.png}
%     \caption{Sample Figure}
%     \label{fig:sample}
% \end{figure}
```

Citations and References

Scientific papers rely heavily on citations and references to support claims and credit the original authors. In XeLaTeX, you can use the `biblatex` package with a BibTeX file (.bib) to manage your references. Here's an example for citing references:

```
According to \cite{einstein1905}, the theory of relativity shook t
of classical physics\index{physics}.
```

. . .

```
\printbibliography
```

Best Practices

To ensure that scientific papers in XeLaTeX adhere to the highest standards, consider the following best practices:

- Use consistent and visually pleasing typography.

- Follow the appropriate citation style (e.g., APA, MLA, IEEE).

- Proofread and edit your paper for grammar and spelling mistakes.

- Consider collaborating with colleagues and seeking feedback for improvement.

- Use version control systems (e.g., Git) to track changes and collaborate.

Conclusion

Formatting and typesetting scientific papers in XeLaTeX requires attention to detail and a thorough understanding of the tools and techniques available. By following the guidelines outlined in this section, you will be able to create visually appealing and well-structured scientific papers that effectively communicate your research findings. Remember to constantly review and refine your work to ensure its accuracy and readability. Happy scientific writing!

Incorporating data tables, figures, and diagrams in technical documents

In technical documents, data tables, figures, and diagrams play a crucial role in presenting complex information in a concise and visually appealing manner. In this section, we will explore various techniques to incorporate these elements into your XeLaTeX documents effectively.

Data Tables

Data tables are commonly used to present numerical or tabular data in a structured format. XeLaTeX provides several packages and commands for creating and formatting data tables.

One popular package is `tabularx`, which allows you to create tables with flexible column widths. To use this package, you need to include `tabularx` in your document preamble:

To create a basic data table, use the `tabular` environment within a `table` environment. Here's an example:

```
\begin{table}[ht]
\centering
\begin{tabular}{|c|c|c|}
\hline
\textbf{Name} & \textbf{Age} & \textbf{Profession} \\
\hline
John Doe & 30 & Engineer \\
\hline
Jane Smith & 25 & Scientist \\
\hline
\end{tabular}
\caption{Example data table}
\label{tab:example-table}
\end{table}
```

In this example, we have a simple data table with three columns: Name, Age, and Profession. The | characters define vertical lines for the table's borders, and the & symbol separates the entries within each row. The \hline command adds horizontal lines to separate the header row from the data rows.

You can also use the booktabs package for more professional-looking tables. This package provides commands like \toprule, \midrule, and \bottomrule to create top, middle, and bottom lines, respectively.

Figures

Figures, such as images, plots, and charts, are often used to enhance the visual appeal and understandability of technical documents. XeLaTeX supports various packages and commands for including and formatting figures.

To include figures in your document, you need to use the graphicx package:

You can insert a figure using the \includegraphics command within a figure environment:

```
% \begin{figure}[ht]
% \centering
% \includegraphics[width=0.5\textwidth]{example-image}
% \caption{Example figure}
% \label{fig:example-figure}
% \end{figure}
```

In this example, we include an image file named example-image with a width of 0.5 times the width of the text area. You can adjust the width to fit your requirements.

It's important to provide a meaningful caption for your figures using the \caption command. This caption appears below the figure. The \label command allows you to reference the figure within your document.

Diagrams

Diagrams are valuable tools for illustrating processes, structures, or relationships in technical documents. XeLaTeX offers the TikZ package, which provides a versatile and powerful framework for creating high-quality diagrams programmatically.

To use TikZ, include the tikz package:

Here's an example of a simple diagram created using TikZ:

```
% \begin{figure}[ht]
% \centering
% \begin{tikzpicture}
% \draw (0,0) circle (1cm);
% \node at (0,0) {A};
% \draw (2,0) circle (1cm);
% \node at (2,0) {B};
% \draw (0.5,0.5) -- (1.5,0.5);
% \end{tikzpicture}
% \caption{Example diagram}
% \label{fig:example-diagram}
% \end{figure}
%
```

Similarly, to include a table, you can use the `table` environment along with the `tabular` environment. Here's an example:

```
\begin{table}
    \centering
    \begin{tabular}{ccc}
        \hline
        Column 1 & Column 2 & Column 3 \\
        \hline
        Value 1 & Value 2 & Value 3 \\
        Value 4 & Value 5 & Value 6 \\
        \hline
    \end{tabular}
    \caption{Example table}
    \label{tab:example_table}
\end{table}
```

This will insert a table with three columns and two rows and add a caption and label. You can refer to the table using the `\ref` command like this:

```
Table \ref{tab:example_table} shows an example table.
```

This will produce:
Table ?? shows an example table.

Citing and referencing

Citing and referencing sources is a critical part of scientific writing. XeLaTeX supports various citation styles through the `biblatex` package, which allows you to manage your references efficiently.

To include a bibliography in your article, you can use the `\printbibliography` command. Here's an example:

```
\printbibliography
```

This will print the bibliography at the desired location in your document. The references should be stored in a separate `.bib` file, which can be created using software like JabRef or managed with online tools like Zotero.

To cite a reference within the document, you can use the `\cite` command. For example:

```
According to Doe et al. \cite{doe2019}, the results are significa
```

This will produce:
According to Doe et al. [1], the results are significant.

Writing and organizing content

When writing mathematical and scientific articles, it is essential to maintain a clear and organized structure to convey your ideas effectively.

Here are some tips to consider:

- Start with a clear and concise introduction that outlines the research problem and motivation.

- Present your methodology and experimental design in a logical and sequential manner.

- Use sections and subsections to divide your article into coherent parts.

- Clearly label and explain all figures, tables, and equations.

- Use proper notation and provide definitions for any specialized terms or symbols.

- Include references to related work and cite them appropriately.

- Proofread your article carefully for grammar, spelling, and formatting errors.

It is also helpful to seek feedback from colleagues or experts in your field to ensure the clarity and correctness of your content.

Resources and tools

Writing mathematical and scientific articles can require the use of various resources and tools. Here are some handy resources and tools that can enhance your writing experience in XeLaTeX:

- Overleaf: An online collaborative LaTeX editor that provides a rich set of templates and features.

- LaTeX templates: Various websites offer LaTeX templates specifically designed for scientific articles.

- Zotero: A free reference management tool that can help you organize and cite your references efficiently.

- Mathpix: A tool that allows you to take pictures of handwritten or printed equations and converts them into LaTeX code.

Using these resources and tools can streamline your writing workflow and improve the overall quality of your mathematical and scientific articles.

Mastering the art of scientific writing

Scientific writing is a skill that requires practice, patience, and attention to detail. Here are some additional tips to help you master the art of scientific writing:

- Read widely in your field to familiarize yourself with the conventions and writing styles of scientific articles.

- Pay close attention to the structure, organization, and clarity of published papers.

- Strive for concise and precise writing, avoiding unnecessary jargon and wordiness.

- Proofread your work carefully to eliminate errors and ensure accuracy.

- Seek feedback from colleagues or mentors to improve the quality of your writing.

Remember, scientific writing is not just about presenting research findings but also about effectively communicating your ideas to a wider audience.

Example problem

Now let's work on an example problem to practice writing mathematical and scientific articles in XeLaTeX.

Problem: A researcher wants to investigate the growth rate of a certain plant species under different temperature conditions. The plant's height (in centimeters) is recorded at various time points, as shown in Table 0.2.

Time (days)	Height (cm)
0	5
5	8
10	12
15	15
20	17

Table 0.2: Plant growth under different temperature conditions

The researcher wants to determine the growth rate of the plant over the observation period.

Solution: To calculate the growth rate, we can use the formula:

$$\text{Growth rate} = \frac{\text{Change in height}}{\text{Change in time}}$$

Using the data from Table 0.2, we can calculate the growth rate as follows:

$$\text{Growth rate} = \frac{17 - 5}{20 - 0} = \frac{12}{20} = 0.6 \text{ cm/day}$$

Therefore, the growth rate of the plant is 0.6 cm/day.

Conclusion

In this section, we have explored the techniques and best practices for writing mathematical and scientific articles in XeLaTeX. We have discussed typesetting mathematical equations, including figures and tables, citing and referencing, organizing content, and mastering the art of scientific writing. By following these guidelines and using the recommended resources and tools, you can create professional and visually appealing articles in XeLaTeX. With practice and diligence, you can become proficient in writing mathematical and scientific articles that effectively communicate your research findings to the scientific community.

Best practices for collaborative authoring in XeLaTeX

Collaborative authoring in XeLaTeX can greatly enhance productivity and enable efficient teamwork. Here are some best practices to ensure smooth collaboration:

1. Version Control: Utilize a version control system like Git, along with a platform like GitHub, to manage changes, track history, and facilitate collaboration. This allows multiple authors to work on the same document simultaneously without conflicts.

2. Overleaf Collaboration: Overleaf is a popular online platform for collaborative authoring in XeLaTeX. It provides real-time synchronization and enables multiple users to work on the document simultaneously. Use Overleaf's built-in collaboration features for smoother teamwork.

3. Document Structure: Design a clear and organized document structure to make collaboration easier. Divide the document into logical sections and use separate files for each chapter or section. This helps in managing changes, avoiding conflicts, and simplifying the collaboration process.

4. Communication: Establish effective communication channels with your collaborators. Use project management tools like Slack or Microsoft Teams to discuss ideas, assign tasks, and share progress. Regular communication ensures everyone is on the same page and reduces misunderstandings.

5. Writing Style and Formatting: Maintain a consistent writing style and formatting to maintain the document's coherence. Set guidelines for headings, font styles, section numbering, figure placement, and citation style. This streamlines the collaboration process and creates a professional-looking document.

6. Commenting and Reviewing: Encourage collaboration through commenting and reviewing. Use XeLaTeX's built-in commenting features or tools like Adobe Acrobat or Google Docs to provide feedback, suggest edits, and discuss changes. This facilitates a constructive and iterative collaborative process.

7. Handling Bibliographies: When collaborating on a document with references, it is crucial to manage bibliographies efficiently. Consider using a reference management tool like Zotero or Mendeley to organize citations, insert them into the document, and generate bibliographies automatically.

8. Troubleshooting Collaborative Issues: Collaborative authoring may introduce challenges like conflicting edits or incompatible packages. Create a troubleshooting guide specific to collaborative writing in XeLaTeX. This guide

should address common issues, recommend solutions, and provide tips for resolving conflicts.

9. Training and Support: Provide training and support to all collaborators to familiarize them with the collaborative workflow, version control system, and XeLaTeX-specific practices. This ensures that everyone is equipped with the necessary skills to collaborate effectively.

10. Continuous Integration: Consider implementing continuous integration processes for your XeLaTeX project. This ensures that the document builds successfully after each commit, avoiding errors or compatibility issues. Tools like Travis CI or GitLab CI can be used for automated builds and testing.

Remember, collaborative authoring in XeLaTeX requires effective communication, coordination, and adherence to agreed-upon guidelines. By following best practices and leveraging collaborative tools, you can enhance productivity and produce high-quality documents with ease.

XeLaTeX for Web and Mobile Publishing

Introduction to Web and Mobile Publishing with XeLaTeX

Overview of web and mobile publishing technologies

Web and mobile publishing have revolutionized the way content is created, distributed, and consumed. In this section, we will provide an overview of the key technologies and concepts behind web and mobile publishing, including responsive design, interactivity, and optimization for different devices.

Responsive Design

Responsive design is an approach to web and mobile publishing that aims to create websites and applications that adapt to different screen sizes and orientations. With the proliferation of smartphones, tablets, and various other devices, it has become crucial for content to be accessible and readable across a wide range of platforms.

One of the key techniques used in responsive design is the use of fluid grids. Instead of fixed layouts, fluid grids allow content to resize and reposition based on the available screen space. This ensures that users have a consistent and optimal viewing experience regardless of the device they are using.

Another important aspect of responsive design is flexible images. Images are resized proportionally and can change their position based on the screen size. This prevents images from becoming too large or small on different devices, maintaining the overall visual integrity of the webpage.

Media queries are used to apply different styles based on the device's characteristics. By using CSS rules, specific styles can be applied to different screen widths, resolutions, or even device types. This allows content creators to tailor the user experience to different devices and optimize the presentation of their content.

Interactivity

The web and mobile landscape has shifted from static pages to dynamic and interactive experiences. Interactivity engages users, enhances the overall experience, and enables users to interact with content in meaningful ways.

JavaScript is the primary language used for client-side interactivity on the web. It allows for the manipulation of webpage elements, handling user input, and facilitating communication with servers. JavaScript frameworks, such as React or Angular, provide additional abstractions and tools to build complex and interactive web applications.

Mobile applications often rely on native development approaches, where applications are developed specifically for a particular platform, such as iOS or Android. These platforms provide developers with access to native APIs and functionality, enabling highly interactive and performant applications.

Web technologies, such as HTML5 and CSS3, have introduced new features that enable richer interactivity. HTML5 introduced the canvas element, which allows for drawing graphics and animations directly within a webpage. CSS3 added support for advanced animations and transitions, turning static pages into more dynamic and engaging experiences.

Optimization for Different Devices

Publishing content on the web and mobile platforms requires considering the unique characteristics and limitations of each device. To ensure a seamless experience, optimization techniques are employed to address device-specific challenges.

Performance optimization focuses on reducing the load time and improving the overall performance of web and mobile applications. Techniques such as minification, compression, and caching are used to reduce file sizes and minimize the number of network requests. This results in faster loading times and improved user experience.

Mobile devices often have limited processing power, memory, and battery life. Therefore, optimization techniques to reduce CPU and memory usage are necessary to ensure smooth performance on these devices. This includes optimizing JavaScript code, minimizing the use of animations and effects, and reducing unnecessary processing.

Compatibility with different browsers and devices is another critical aspect of web and mobile publishing. Cross-browser testing ensures that the content is displayed correctly and functions as expected across various web browsers. Similarly, device testing helps identify any issues related to different screen sizes, resolutions, and operating systems.

Accessibility is another important consideration in web and mobile publishing. It involves making content accessible to users with disabilities, ensuring that they can perceive, understand, and navigate through the content. This includes providing alternative text for images, using proper semantic markup, and enabling keyboard navigation.

In conclusion, understanding the technologies behind web and mobile publishing is essential for creating engaging, interactive, and accessible content. Responsive design, interactivity, and optimization techniques play a crucial role in delivering a seamless user experience across different devices and platforms.

Creating interactive and multimedia-rich documents in XeLaTeX

In this section, we will explore the powerful features of XeLaTeX that allow us to create interactive and multimedia-rich documents. With XeLaTeX, we can create documents that go beyond static text and images, by incorporating interactive elements such as hyperlinks, buttons, and multimedia content like audio and video. These interactive features enhance the reading experience, making the document more engaging and dynamic.

Interactive Elements

XeLaTeX provides several packages and libraries that enable the inclusion of interactive elements in documents. One commonly used package is 'hyperref', which allows us to add hyperlinks to different parts of the document as well as external URLs. We can use the 'command to create a hyperlink, specifying the URL and the text that will be displayed.

For example, to create a hyperlink to a website, we can use the following code:

```
Welcome to my website! Check it out \href{http://www.example.c
```

Another package that provides interactive elements is 'pdfcomment'. It enables us to add annotations and comments to the document. These annotations can be displayed as pop-ups or tooltips when the reader hovers over a certain area.

```
This is an important concept.\pdfcomment{Remember to review
```

With the 'media9' package, we can embed multimedia content into our documents, such as video and audio files. This package supports a wide range of multimedia formats and provides extensive customization options.

Interactive Presentations

XeLaTeX also allows us to create interactive presentations that include animations, transitions, and automatic content playback. The 'beamer' document class is a popular choice for creating such presentations. It provides a variety of themes, layouts, and formatting options that make it easy to create professional-looking slides.

To create a basic interactive presentation using 'beamer', we start with a document setup:

```
\usetheme{default}

\begin{frame}
    \titlepage
\end{frame}
```

We can then add slides with content:

```
\begin{frame}
    \frametitle{Introduction}
    Welcome to my presentation\index{presentation}!
\end{frame}
```

In addition to static content, we can also add interactive elements to our slides. For example, we can create buttons that navigate to different slides within the presentation using the 'command:

```
\begin{frame}
   \frametitle{Interactive Slide}
   Click \hyperlink{target}{here} to go to a different slide.
\end{frame}

\begin{frame}[label=target]
   \frametitle{Target Slide}
   This is the slide\index{slide} that will be\index{be} displaye
\end{frame}
```

With the combination of interactive elements provided by XeLaTeX and the features of the 'beamer' class, we can create engaging and interactive presentations that captivate the audience.

Best Practices

When creating interactive and multimedia-rich documents, there are some best practices to keep in mind:

+ Use interactive elements sparingly: While interactive elements can enhance the reading experience, it is important not to overwhelm the reader with too many distractions. Be selective and use interactive elements only when they add value to the content.

+ Test cross-platform compatibility: Since XeLaTeX documents can be viewed on different devices and operating systems, it is essential to test the interactive elements on multiple platforms to ensure they function as intended.

+ Consider accessibility: Make sure that interactive elements are accessible to users with disabilities. Provide alternative text for images, include captions and transcripts for multimedia content, and ensure that hyperlinks are descriptive and can be activated using keyboard navigation.

+ Optimize media files: Compress multimedia files to reduce file size and improve loading times. Use appropriate file formats and consider the capabilities of different devices when embedding media content.

In conclusion, XeLaTeX provides extensive capabilities for creating interactive and multimedia-rich documents. By incorporating interactive elements and multimedia content, we can create engaging and dynamic documents that enhance the reader's experience. Following best practices ensures that the interactive elements are used effectively and that the documents are accessible and compatible across different platforms.

Optimizing XeLaTeX for web and mobile performance

In today's digital age, web and mobile publishing have become increasingly important for reaching a wider audience. However, delivering high-quality and responsive documents on these platforms can be a challenge. In this section, we will explore techniques to optimize XeLaTeX for web and mobile performance, ensuring that your documents load quickly and display properly across different devices and screen sizes.

Understanding web and mobile publishing

Before we dive into optimization techniques, let's briefly understand the principles of web and mobile publishing. When it comes to digital content, performance is crucial. Users expect websites and mobile apps to load quickly and be highly responsive. Slow loading times and sluggish performance can result in a poor user experience and discourage visitors from engaging with your content.

When publishing documents on the web or mobile platforms, it's important to consider the following factors:

- **Page weight:** The total size of all the resources (HTML, CSS, JavaScript, images, fonts) that need to be downloaded to render the document.

- **Network latency:** The time it takes for requests to reach the server and for the server to respond. This is affected by factors such as distance, network congestion, and server load.

- **Render time:** The time it takes for the browser or mobile app to process and display the document once it has been downloaded.

- **Device capabilities:** Different devices have varying processing power, memory, and screen sizes. Optimizing for a range of devices ensures a consistent user experience across platforms.

Now that we understand the challenges and considerations of web and mobile publishing, let's explore optimization techniques specific to XeLaTeX.

Minimizing page weight

Reducing the size of your XeLaTeX documents is the first step in optimizing for web and mobile performance. Here are some strategies to minimize page weight:

- **Remove unnecessary packages and libraries:** Evaluate the packages and libraries you are using in your document. Remove any that are not required, as each package adds extra overhead to the document.

- **Compress PDF output:** When compiling your document, consider using compression options to reduce the size of the resulting PDF file. XeLaTeX provides options to optimize PDF output, such as compressing images and fonts.

- **Externalize graphics:** If your document contains a large number of graphics or images, consider externalizing them. This means storing the graphics as separate files and including them in the document using the \includegraphics command. This prevents the graphics from being embedded in the final PDF, reducing the overall file size.

- **Optimize image size and format:** Ensure that the images you include in your document are properly optimized for the web. Use image editing tools to compress and resize images before including them. Additionally, consider using more efficient image formats such as JPEG for photographs and PNG for graphics with transparency.

By minimizing the page weight of your XeLaTeX documents, you can significantly improve the load time and responsiveness on the web and mobile platforms.

Improving render time

In addition to reducing page weight, optimizing the render time of your XeLaTeX documents is essential for a smooth user experience. Here are some techniques to improve render time:

- **Enable font subsetting:** XeLaTeX allows you to include only the necessary glyphs and characters from your fonts, reducing the file size and improving render time. Use the fontspec package to enable font subsetting in your document.

- **Use system fonts:** System fonts are pre-installed on most devices and can be rendered more quickly compared to custom fonts. Consider using system fonts for your document to improve render time, especially for web and mobile platforms.

- **Limit JavaScript usage:** If your document includes JavaScript code, be mindful of its impact on render time. JavaScript can introduce delays in page rendering, especially on mobile devices with limited processing power. Minimize or optimize JavaScript usage wherever possible.

By implementing these techniques, you can ensure that your XeLaTeX documents render quickly and smoothly on web and mobile platforms.

Responsive design and media queries

With the wide range of devices and screen sizes available today, it's important to optimize your XeLaTeX documents for responsiveness. Responsive design ensures that your documents adapt to different screen sizes and orientations, providing an optimal viewing experience for users. Here's how you can achieve responsive design:

- **CSS media queries:** Use CSS media queries to apply different stylesheets or styles to your document based on the characteristics of the device, such as screen width. This allows you to adjust the layout and formatting of your document dynamically.

- **Flexible layouts:** Design your document with flexible layouts using techniques like CSS grids and flexbox. This allows elements to resize and reflow based on the available screen space, accommodating different screen sizes and orientations.

- **Optimize image and media delivery:** Use techniques such as lazy loading and adaptive image loading to ensure that images and media are delivered in the appropriate format and size based on the user's device and network conditions. This helps reduce page weight and improve load times.

By implementing responsive design strategies, you can ensure that your XeLaTeX documents deliver an optimal viewing experience across a wide range of web and mobile devices.

Accessibility considerations

When optimizing XeLaTeX documents for web and mobile, it's important to consider accessibility. Designing documents that are accessible to users with disabilities ensures inclusivity and a better user experience for all. Here are some tips for optimizing accessibility:

+ **Semantic markup:** Use semantic markup to provide structure and meaning to your document. This helps assistive technologies properly interpret and navigate through the content.

+ **Alternative text:** Provide descriptive alternative text for images, charts, and other visual elements. This allows screen readers to convey the information to visually impaired users.

+ **Keyboard navigation:** Ensure that your document can be navigated using a keyboard alone, without relying on mouse or touch interactions. This is particularly important for users with motor disabilities who may have difficulty using a mouse or touchscreen.

+ **Color contrast:** Use sufficient color contrast to ensure that text is readable for users with visual impairments. Consider using tools and guidelines to check the color contrast ratios in your document.

By considering accessibility in your XeLaTeX documents, you can make them more inclusive and usable for a wider audience.

Testing and optimization tools

To ensure the best possible performance for your XeLaTeX documents on the web and mobile, it's important to test and optimize them using appropriate tools. Here are some tools that can help in the process:

+ **PageSpeed Insights:** A web-based tool by Google that analyzes the performance of web pages and provides suggestions for optimization. It can help identify performance bottlenecks and provide actionable insights.

+ **Lighthouse:** Another web-based tool by Google that offers comprehensive performance audits for web pages, including accessibility, search engine optimization, and best practices. Lighthouse generates detailed reports and provides recommendations for improvement.

+ **WebPageTest:** A free and open-source tool that allows you to test the performance of web pages from multiple locations around the world. It provides detailed analysis and offers optimization suggestions.

+ **Browser developer tools:** Modern web browsers come with built-in developer tools that allow you to analyze network activity, inspect page elements, and profile performance. These tools can be valuable in identifying and fixing performance issues.

By utilizing these testing and optimization tools, you can fine-tune the performance of your XeLaTeX documents and ensure a seamless user experience on the web and mobile platforms.

Conclusion

Optimizing XeLaTeX for web and mobile performance involves reducing page weight, improving render time, implementing responsive design, considering accessibility, and utilizing appropriate testing and optimization tools. By following the techniques outlined in this section, you can deliver high-quality and responsive documents that load quickly and display properly across a wide range of devices. So go ahead, optimize your XeLaTeX documents, and make an impact on the web and mobile platforms!

Creating Accessible Documents for Web and Mobile with XeLaTeX

In today's digital age, accessibility is of utmost importance. It is crucial to ensure that all individuals, regardless of their abilities, can access and interact with content on the web and mobile platforms. XeLaTeX provides robust support for creating accessible documents, allowing you to produce content that can be easily consumed by a wide range of users, including those with visual impairments or other disabilities.

Understanding Accessibility

Accessibility refers to the design and development of content and technologies that can be used by individuals with disabilities. In the context of web and mobile publishing, accessibility involves creating documents that can be easily navigated, understood, and interacted with, even by individuals who use assistive technologies such as screen readers or braille displays.

When creating accessible documents, it is important to comply with international accessibility standards and guidelines, such as the Web Content Accessibility Guidelines (WCAG) developed by the World Wide Web Consortium (W3C). These standards provide a set of recommendations for making web content more accessible to people with disabilities.

Key Principles of Accessible Design

To ensure that your XeLaTeX documents are accessible, it is important to adhere to the following key principles of accessible design:

- **Perceivable:** Provide alternative ways for users to perceive content, such as adding captions to images or providing transcripts for audio or video content.

- **Operable:** Ensure that users can navigate and interact with your document using a variety of input methods, including keyboard-only or voice commands.

- **Understandable:** Make your document's structure and content clear and easy to understand, using headings, lists, and other organizing elements.

- **Robust:** Ensure that your document is compatible with a wide range of assistive technologies and can be correctly interpreted by different user agents.

By following these principles, you can create documents that are accessible to a wider audience, including individuals with disabilities.

Key Techniques for Creating Accessible Documents

There are several techniques you can employ in XeLaTeX to ensure the accessibility of your documents. Let's explore some key techniques:

1. **Provide Alternative Text for Images:** When including images in your document, make sure to provide alternative text (alt text) that describes the content of the image. This allows users who cannot see the image to understand its context and meaning.

% \begin{figure}

```
%    \centering
%    \includegraphics[width=0.5\textwidth]{image.png}
%    \caption{A sample image}
%    \label{fig:image}
% \end{figure}
```

2. **Use Semantic Structure:** Structure your document using semantic elements, such as headings, lists, and paragraphs. This helps users navigate through the content more easily and understand its structure.

```
\section{Introduction}
Lorem\index{Lorem} ipsum dolor sit amet, consectetur\ind
\subsection{Benefits of Accessibility}
Vestibulum rutrum elit nec neque mattis, vitae lobortis\
\subsubsection{Accessible Design Principles}
Pellentesque habitant\index{habitant} morbi tristique se
```

3. **Ensure Sufficient Color Contrast:** When using colors to convey information, ensure that there is enough contrast between the foreground and background colors. This ensures that individuals with visual impairments can perceive the content.

```
\definecolor{foreground}{RGB}{0, 0, 0}
\definecolor{background}{RGB}{255, 255, 255}
\pagecolor{background}
\color{foreground}
```

. . .

4. **Include Descriptive Links:** When adding hyperlinks to your document, make sure to use descriptive link texts that convey the purpose or destination of the link. Screen readers can then provide users with more meaningful information about the links.

```
For more information, please visit the \hyperref[https:/
```

Best Practices for Accessible Web and Mobile Publishing

To ensure that your XeLaTeX documents are as accessible as possible, consider the following best practices:

- Use high-quality and resizable fonts to ensure readability for individuals with visual impairments.

- Use logical and meaningful heading hierarchies to structure your content.

- Provide captions for images, videos, and other multimedia content.

- Add alternative text for complex or informative visuals.

- Ensure that forms and interactive elements are accessible using keyboard navigation.

- Incorporate the ability to resize text and images for users with visual impairments.

- Test your documents using assistive technologies to ensure compatibility and usability.

By following these best practices, you can create accessible documents that cater to the needs of a diverse user base.

Conclusion

Creating accessible documents is not only important for complying with accessibility standards but also for ensuring that your content reaches a wider audience. By leveraging the features and capabilities of XeLaTeX, you can create documents that are perceivable, operable, understandable, and robust. By adhering to the principles and techniques of accessible design, you can make your XeLaTeX documents accessible to users with disabilities and provide a more inclusive user experience. Remember to consider the best practices and continually test your documents to ensure ongoing accessibility compliance.

Publishing XeLaTeX documents as web pages and ebooks

In this section, we will explore how to publish XeLaTeX documents as web pages and ebooks. With XeLaTeX, we can create beautiful and professional-looking documents that can be easily shared and distributed online. Whether you want to create a personal website or publish an ebook, XeLaTeX provides the necessary tools and features to make your content shine.

Overview of web and mobile publishing technologies

Before we delve into the specifics of publishing XeLaTeX documents, let's first have a brief overview of web and mobile publishing technologies. In the digital age, it is essential to consider the different platforms and devices on which your content will be accessed.

When it comes to web publishing, there are several technologies and formats to consider. HTML (Hypertext Markup Language) is the standard markup language used for creating web pages. It is versatile and supports various elements and features such as text formatting, images, hyperlinks, and multimedia.

CSS (Cascading Style Sheets) is another crucial technology for web publishing. It allows you to control the presentation and layout of your web pages. With CSS, you can define styles for fonts, colors, spacing, and more.

For mobile publishing, EPUB (Electronic Publication) and MOBI (Mobipocket) are popular formats used for ebooks. EPUB is an open standard format that is widely supported by ebook readers and devices. MOBI, on the other hand, is the format used by Amazon Kindle devices.

Creating responsive designs for web and mobile with XeLaTeX

With the increasing popularity of mobile devices, it is crucial to create web pages and ebooks that are responsive and adapt to different screen sizes. XeLaTeX provides several packages and techniques to achieve responsive designs.

The **geometry** package can be used to specify the page size and margins of your document. By setting appropriate values for these parameters, you can ensure that your content fits well on different devices.

To create responsive designs for web pages, you can use CSS media queries in conjunction with XeLaTeX. Media queries allow you to apply different styles based on the characteristics of the device or screen size. By defining different CSS rules for different screen sizes, you can create a layout that adjusts dynamically.

For ebooks, you can utilize the capabilities of EPUB and MOBI formats to create responsive designs. These formats support CSS styling, allowing you to define responsive styles for different screen sizes directly in your XeLaTeX document. By using media queries and CSS rules specific to EPUB and MOBI, you can ensure that your ebook looks great on a variety of devices.

Creating interactive and multimedia-rich documents in XeLaTeX

In addition to responsive designs, you may also want to incorporate interactive and multimedia elements into your web pages and ebooks. XeLaTeX, with its support for different graphics formats and integration with other technologies, allows you to create engaging and interactive content.

To include images and multimedia elements in your web pages, you can use the **graphicx** package and HTML tags. With the graphicx package, you can easily include images in various formats such as JPEG, PNG, and PDF. HTML tags such as <img> and <video> can be used to embed images, videos, and audio files directly in your XeLaTeX-generated HTML pages.

For ebooks, EPUB and MOBI formats support multimedia elements as well. By using XeLaTeX, you can include images, videos, and audio files in your document and specify their placement and formatting. This allows you to create rich and interactive reading experiences for your readers.

Optimizing XeLaTeX for web and mobile performance

When publishing XeLaTeX documents as web pages and ebooks, it is essential to optimize your content for performance. Slow-loading web pages and bulky ebooks can lead to a poor user experience. Here are some tips for optimizing XeLaTeX documents for web and mobile:

- Use efficient graphics formats: Choose image formats that strike a balance between quality and file size. JPEG is suitable for photographs, while PNG is better for graphics and illustrations with fewer colors.

- Compress images: Before including images in your XeLaTeX document, consider compressing them to reduce file size. This can be done using various image optimization tools.

- Minimize CSS and JavaScript: Keep your CSS and JavaScript code as concise as possible. Avoid unnecessary styles and scripts that can slow down page rendering.

- Consider using a content delivery network (CDN): CDNs can help deliver your web pages and ebooks faster by distributing content across multiple servers located geographically closer to your readers.

- Test on different devices and platforms: Ensure that your web pages and ebooks appear correctly on various devices and browsers. Test for compatibility and responsiveness.

By following these optimization techniques, you can ensure that your XeLaTeX documents load quickly and provide a smooth experience for your readers.

Creating accessible documents for web and mobile with XeLaTeX

Accessibility is an important aspect of publishing content on the web and mobile devices. It ensures that your documents can be accessed and understood by users with disabilities. XeLaTeX provides support for creating accessible documents through various techniques and standards.

For web pages, you can leverage HTML standards to enhance accessibility. HTML provides semantic elements such as <header>, <nav>, <main>, <footer>, and more, which help in structuring your content and making it accessible to screen readers. Properly labeling form elements and providing alternative text for images also contribute to accessibility.

When it comes to ebooks, EPUB format supports accessibility features. By using XeLaTeX to generate EPUB files, you can take advantage of these features. EPUB supports semantic markup, text-to-speech functionality, and assistive technologies. By properly structuring and labeling your content, you can make your ebooks accessible to a wider audience.

It is important to follow accessibility guidelines, such as the Web Content Accessibility Guidelines (WCAG), when publishing documents. These guidelines provide best practices and recommendations for making your content accessible. By adhering to these guidelines, you can ensure that your XeLaTeX documents are inclusive and usable by all.

Publishing XeLaTeX documents as web pages

Publishing XeLaTeX documents as web pages involves converting your XeLaTeX-generated output to HTML format. There are several tools and methods to accomplish this.

One way is to use the **tex4ht** package, which can convert XeLaTeX documents to HTML. Tex4ht provides a customizable conversion process, allowing you to control the output HTML structure and formatting. It supports various command-line options to fine-tune the conversion process according to your requirements.

Another option is to use online services, such as Overleaf, which provide built-in support for exporting XeLaTeX documents to HTML. With Overleaf, you can seamlessly convert your XeLaTeX documents to web pages without the need for additional tools or installations.

Once you have converted your XeLaTeX document to HTML, you can further refine and customize the output by applying CSS styles and JavaScript interactivity. This allows you to create visually appealing and functional web pages from your XeLaTeX content.

Publishing XeLaTeX documents as ebooks

To publish XeLaTeX documents as ebooks, you need to convert your XeLaTeX-generated output to EPUB or MOBI format. Just like converting to HTML, there are different tools and methods available for this purpose.

One common tool is **Pandoc**, which is a versatile document converter. Pandoc supports XeLaTeX as an input format and can generate EPUB and MOBI files. By using Pandoc, you can convert your XeLaTeX documents to ebooks with ease.

Another option is to use dedicated EPUB creation tools such as **Calibre** or **Sigil**. These tools provide a user-friendly interface for creating and editing EPUB files. You can import your XeLaTeX-generated output into these tools and customize the layout, formatting, and metadata of your ebook.

Once your XeLaTeX document is converted to EPUB or MOBI format, you can distribute it through various platforms such as Amazon Kindle Direct Publishing (KDP), Apple Books, or your own website. These platforms allow readers to purchase and download your ebook onto their devices.

Designing and formatting digital magazines and newsletters with XeLaTeX

In addition to web pages and ebooks, XeLaTeX can be used to create digital magazines and newsletters. With its powerful typesetting and design capabilities, XeLaTeX offers a flexible and professional solution for producing visually appealing publications.

To design digital magazines and newsletters, you can utilize XeLaTeX document classes and templates specifically tailored for these purposes. There are several packages available, such as **memoir**, **tufte-latex**, and **classicthesis**, that provide customizable layouts and styles for magazine-style publications.

XeLaTeX allows you to easily include images, graphics, and custom layouts to create visually stunning pages. By leveraging the power of TikZ and other packages, you can design complex and artistic visual elements for your digital magazines and newsletters.

Furthermore, XeLaTeX provides support for creating interactive features in digital publications. You can include hyperlinks, interactive buttons, and multimedia elements to enhance the reading experience of your audience.

By combining XeLaTeX's typesetting capabilities with its support for interactive and multimedia elements, you can create engaging and visually impressive digital magazines and newsletters that captivate your readers.

Creating mobile apps and e-learning materials with XeLaTeX

Beyond web pages and ebooks, XeLaTeX can also be used to create mobile apps and e-learning materials. With the rise of mobile devices and the increasing demand for educational content, XeLaTeX provides a powerful platform for developing mobile applications and e-learning resources.

XeLaTeX allows you to leverage its robust typesetting capabilities to create educational materials such as textbooks, lecture notes, and quizzes. By integrating interactive features, such as quizzes and exercises, you can make the learning experience more engaging and interactive for students.

To create mobile apps, you can utilize frameworks such as React Native or Flutter, which allow you to build cross-platform mobile applications using JavaScript or Dart, respectively. These frameworks enable you to incorporate XeLaTeX-generated content seamlessly into your mobile app, providing a rich and cohesive user experience.

By combining XeLaTeX-generated educational materials with a mobile app framework, you can create interactive and personalized learning experiences for students. The app can include features such as search, bookmarks, and note-taking, enhancing the usability and practicality of the educational content.

Integrating XeLaTeX with content management systems and web frameworks

Integrating XeLaTeX with content management systems (CMS) and web frameworks can streamline the publishing process and provide a dynamic and scalable platform for managing and delivering XeLaTeX documents.

For web publishing, CMSs such as WordPress, Drupal, and Joomla offer plugins and extensions that facilitate the integration of XeLaTeX-generated content. These plugins convert your XeLaTeX documents to HTML and provide tools for managing and displaying the content on your website. They allow you to create dynamic web pages and enable features such as search, user comments, and user management.

Web frameworks, such as Ruby on Rails, Django, or Laravel, provide a more flexible and customizable option for integrating XeLaTeX documents into web applications. By leveraging the capabilities of these frameworks, you can develop custom solutions that meet your specific requirements for rendering and displaying XeLaTeX-generated content.

These integrations enable you to manage, organize, and publish your XeLaTeX documents efficiently. They provide a seamless workflow for creating, editing, and updating your content, allowing you to focus on the substance of your documents rather than the technical aspects of publishing.

Best practices for web and mobile publishing in XeLaTeX

When publishing XeLaTeX documents as web pages and ebooks, it is essential to follow best practices to ensure the quality and usability of your content. Here are some tips to consider:

- Design with mobile in mind: Mobile devices are becoming the primary platform for accessing web content and ebooks. Therefore, it is important to prioritize mobile-friendly designs and responsive layouts to deliver an optimal reading experience.

- Optimize images and multimedia: Compress images to reduce file size and optimize load times. Choose appropriate formats for different types of content. Ensure that multimedia elements are properly encoded and compatible with target devices.

- Test on multiple devices and browsers: Verify that your web pages and ebooks render correctly across different devices, operating systems, and browsers. Test for responsiveness, compatibility, and accessibility.

- Follow accessibility guidelines: Adhere to WCAG and other accessibility guidelines to make your content accessible to a wide range of users, including those with disabilities.

- Validate your output: Use validation tools to ensure that your HTML and EPUB files adhere to the relevant standards. This helps to identify and fix issues early in the publishing process.

By following these best practices, you can create web pages and ebooks that are visually appealing, accessible, and optimized for both web and mobile platforms.

Designing and Formatting Digital Magazines and Newsletters with XeLaTeX

In today's digital age, the publishing industry has seen a significant shift towards online platforms. Digital magazines and newsletters have become popular choices for delivering content to a wide audience in an interactive and engaging way. XeLaTeX, with its powerful typesetting capabilities and support for multi-language and complex scripts, can be an excellent tool for designing and formatting digital publications. In this section, we will explore various techniques and best practices for creating stunning digital magazines and newsletters using XeLaTeX.

Understanding the Digital Publication Landscape

Before we dive into the details of designing and formatting digital magazines and newsletters, it is essential to understand the unique characteristics and requirements of the digital publication landscape. Here are a few key points to consider:

+ **Responsive Design:** Digital publications need to adapt to different screen sizes, from desktop computers to tablets and smartphones. Designing with responsiveness in mind ensures that your content looks and functions well across devices.

+ **Interactive Features:** Unlike their print counterparts, digital magazines and newsletters can take advantage of interactive elements such as hyperlinks, multimedia content (videos, audio), image galleries, and animations. Incorporating these features can enhance the reader's experience.

+ **Accessibility:** Making your digital publications accessible to all users, including those with disabilities, is crucial. Consider using alt text for images, providing transcripts for media files, and ensuring proper reading order for screen reader users.

+ **Optimized Performance:** Users expect fast-loading and smooth-scrolling digital publications. Optimizing the performance of your document, such as reducing the file size of images and controlling the complexity of interactive elements, can improve the overall user experience.

+ **Cross-platform Compatibility:** Digital publications should be compatible with various operating systems and web browsers. Test your document on different platforms to ensure consistent rendering and functionality.

Keeping these considerations in mind, let's explore the steps to design and format digital magazines and newsletters using XeLaTeX.

Choosing a Document Class

To start, we need to choose a suitable document class that provides the necessary features and layout options for a digital publication. The `article` class is commonly used for newsletters, while the `scrartcl` class from the KOMA-Script bundle offers more advanced options for magazine layouts.

For example, to use the `scrartcl` class:

```
\documentclass[a4paper]{scrartcl}
```

This sets the document class to `scrartcl` with the paper size set to A4. You can customize additional options as per your requirements, such as setting the font size, margins, and columns.

Layout and Design

When designing the layout of your digital magazine or newsletter, it is essential to consider the visual hierarchy of content, readability, and aesthetics. Here are some tips to achieve an appealing layout:

- **Grid-based Design:** Use a grid to guide the placement of elements and ensure consistency throughout the publication. The `grid` package in XeLaTeX can assist in creating a grid system.

- **Typography:** Choose appropriate fonts and font sizes for headings, subheadings, body text, and captions. XeLaTeX provides extensive font support, enabling you to use a wide range of open-source and commercial fonts. Ensure that the fonts you choose are web-safe and viewable across various devices.

- **Color Scheme:** Select a color scheme that complements your content and aligns with your brand identity. Use colors strategically to draw attention to important elements and create visual hierarchy.

- **Images and Graphics:** Incorporate high-quality images, illustrations, and graphics to enhance your digital publication's visual appeal. Use the `graphicx` package in XeLaTeX to include images in various formats (e.g., JPEG, PNG, PDF) and manipulate their placement and size.

+ **Interactive Elements:** Take advantage of XeLaTeX's capabilities to include interactive elements such as hyperlinks and multimedia content. The `hyperref` package allows you to create hyperlinks within your document, while the `media9` package supports embedding multimedia files.

Handling Multiple Layouts and Device Adaptation

Digital publications often require different layouts for different devices (e.g., one layout for desktop and another for mobile). This adaptation can be achieved using responsive design techniques. Here's how:

+ **Media Queries:** Use CSS media queries within your XeLaTeX document to specify different styles based on the device's screen size. The `cssmedia` package in XeLaTeX provides support for media queries.

+ **Flexibility in Content:** Consider the flexibility of content placement and adaptability when designing your document. You can make use of XeLaTeX's capabilities to automatically adjust layout and styling based on screen size.

+ **Testing and Optimization:** Test your document on different devices and screen sizes to ensure a seamless user experience. Optimize the performance by optimizing images, minimizing dependencies, and reducing unnecessary JavaScript.

Exporting as Web Pages and Ebooks

Once you have designed and formatted your digital magazine or newsletter in XeLaTeX, the next step is to export it as web pages or ebooks. Here are a few options to consider:

+ **HTML and CSS:** XeLaTeX can export your document as HTML and CSS, allowing you to host it on a web server. Use the `tex4ht` package to convert your XeLaTeX document into HTML.

+ **EPUB and MOBI Formats:** XeLaTeX can also export your document as EPUB and MOBI formats, compatible with ebook readers and platforms. The `tex4ebook` package can convert your XeLaTeX document into EPUB and MOBI formats.

- **Online Publishing Platforms:** Consider utilizing online publishing platforms such as Issuu, Joomag, or Calaméo to publish and distribute your digital magazines or newsletters. These platforms offer easy-to-use interfaces for uploading and sharing your publications.

Best Practices for Digital Publishing with XeLaTeX

Here are some additional best practices to keep in mind when designing and formatting digital magazines and newsletters with XeLaTeX:

- **File Size Optimization:** Optimize the file size of your digital publication by compressing images, minimizing external dependencies, and removing unnecessary code. This ensures faster loading times and a smoother user experience.

- **Testing and Cross-platform Compatibility:** Test your digital publication on different devices, operating systems, and web browsers to ensure consistently rendered content and functionality.

- **Accessibility:** Follow accessibility guidelines to make your digital publications accessible to all users. Use alternative text for images, provide closed captions for multimedia content, and ensure proper heading structure and navigation.

- **User Analytics and Feedback:** Incorporate user analytics and feedback mechanisms to gather insights on user engagement and preferences. This feedback can help you refine your design and content strategy.

- **Regular Updates and Maintenance:** Stay up-to-date with new technologies, best practices, and security considerations. Regularly update and maintain your digital publications to provide an optimal experience for your audience.

Conclusion

Designing and formatting digital magazines and newsletters with XeLaTeX opens up a world of possibilities for creating visually stunning and interactive publications. By understanding the unique requirements of the digital publication landscape and leveraging the power of XeLaTeX, you can design and publish engaging content that captivates your audience across various devices and platforms. Whether you are a professional publisher or an individual enthusiast, XeLaTeX provides the tools and flexibility to bring your digital publications to life.

Creating mobile apps and e-learning materials with XeLaTeX

In today's digital age, mobile apps and e-learning materials have become increasingly popular for education and training purposes. XeLaTeX, with its powerful typesetting capabilities and support for multiple languages, is a great tool for creating visually appealing and interactive content for mobile apps and e-learning platforms. In this section, we will explore various techniques and best practices for designing and developing mobile apps and e-learning materials with XeLaTeX.

Designing mobile app interfaces

When designing mobile app interfaces, it is important to consider the unique constraints and requirements of mobile devices. XeLaTeX provides a flexible and customizable framework for creating responsive designs that adapt to different screen sizes. Here are some key considerations when designing mobile app interfaces with XeLaTeX:

- **Layout:** Use the `geometry` package to define the layout of the app interface. Consider the screen size, aspect ratio, and orientation of the device to create a user-friendly and visually appealing layout. The `multicol` package can be used to create multi-column layouts for displaying content.

- **Typography:** Choose appropriate fonts and font sizes that are legible on small screens. XeLaTeX allows you to easily customize the typography of your app using different font families, font weights, and font styles.

- **Color scheme:** Select a color scheme that is visually appealing and accessible. Use the `xcolor` package to define and apply colors consistently throughout your app.

- **Navigation:** Design intuitive navigation elements, such as menus, tabs, and buttons, to ensure easy interaction and smooth user experience. The `hyperref` package can be used to add hyperlinks and interactive elements to your app.

- **Graphics and media:** Incorporate relevant images, icons, and multimedia content to enhance the visual appeal and engagement of your app. Use the `graphicx` package to include image files and the `media9` package for embedding audio and video files.

+ **User feedback:** Provide visual cues and feedback to guide users and inform them of their actions. XeLaTeX offers various packages, such as `tcolorbox` and `animate`, for creating tooltips, pop-ups, and other interactive elements.

By leveraging these design principles and the extensive customization options in XeLaTeX, you can create visually stunning and user-friendly interfaces for your mobile apps.

Developing e-learning materials

XeLaTeX is also a powerful tool for developing e-learning materials, such as interactive textbooks, online courses, and educational websites. With its support for mathematical equations, scientific notation, and multi-language typesetting, XeLaTeX is well-suited for creating content across various fields of study. Here are some key techniques for developing e-learning materials with XeLaTeX:

+ **Structuring content:** Use the `titlesec` package to define clear and consistent sectioning styles for your e-learning materials. This helps in organizing the content and providing a logical flow.

+ **Mathematical equations:** XeLaTeX's built-in support for mathematical equations, through packages like `amsmath` and `mathtools`, allows you to typeset complex mathematical expressions and formulas. Be sure to label and reference equations for easy navigation and comprehension.

+ **Interactive elements:** Enhance the learning experience by incorporating interactive elements, such as quizzes, exercises, and simulations. The `exam` package can be used to create interactive assessments, while the `animate` package enables the inclusion of interactive animations and visualizations.

+ **Multilingual support:** XeLaTeX's ability to handle multiple languages and scripts makes it ideal for creating e-learning materials that cater to a global audience. Consider using language-specific fonts and settings to ensure accurate rendering of different scripts.

+ **Accessibility:** Follow accessibility guidelines and standards, such as the Web Content Accessibility Guidelines (WCAG), to ensure that your e-learning materials are accessible to users with disabilities. Use appropriate markup and alternative text for images, and provide captions for multimedia content.

- **Collaboration and version control:** Take advantage of collaboration tools, such as Overleaf and Git, to facilitate teamwork and version control when developing e-learning materials. These tools enable multiple contributors to work on the same project simultaneously and track changes effectively.

By leveraging these techniques, you can create engaging and interactive e-learning materials that effectively convey educational content to learners.

Example: Developing a Physics Interactive App

To illustrate the techniques discussed, let's consider an example of developing an interactive physics app using XeLaTeX. The app aims to assist students in understanding the concepts of projectile motion.

The app interface can consist of different sections, such as theory, simulations, and practice problems. The theory section provides a concise explanation of projectile motion, accompanied by equations and diagrams rendered using XeLaTeX's mathematical typesetting capabilities. The simulations section incorporates interactive animations that visualize projectile motion under various conditions, allowing students to experiment and observe the effects of different parameters.

To enhance the learning experience, the app can include practice problems with immediate feedback. Students can input their answers, and the app can automatically check the solutions and provide explanations for incorrect responses. This can be implemented using XeLaTeX's programming capabilities and packages like exam or exercise.

Incorporating real-world examples and context-specific problems into the app can make the learning experience more engaging and practical. For instance, the app can present scenarios where projectile motion is applicable, such as calculating the trajectory of a basketball shot or a ball thrown from a moving vehicle.

By combining the principles of mobile app design, e-learning content development, and the customization options in XeLaTeX, you can create an interactive and educational app that effectively teaches the principles of projectile motion.

Additional Resources

Here are some additional resources that can help you further explore the development of mobile apps and e-learning materials with XeLaTeX:

- Overleaf's documentation on mobile app development: `https://www.overleaf.com/learn/mobile-apps`

- The XeLaTeX GitHub repository: `https://github.com/latex3/xetex`

- The animate package documentation: `https://ctan.org/pkg/animate`

- The exam package documentation: `https://ctan.org/pkg/exam`

These resources provide examples, tutorials, and documentation to help you delve deeper into creating mobile apps and e-learning materials using XeLaTeX.

In conclusion, XeLaTeX offers a versatile and powerful platform for designing and developing mobile apps and e-learning materials. By leveraging its typesetting capabilities, customization options, and support for multiple languages, you can create visually appealing, interactive, and educational content for a wide range of devices and platforms. So, get started with XeLaTeX and unlock the potential of mobile learning and e-education!

Integrating XeLaTeX with Content Management Systems and Web Frameworks

In this section, we will explore how to integrate XeLaTeX with content management systems (CMS) and web frameworks to streamline the process of publishing and managing documents on the web. We will discuss the benefits of using XeLaTeX in conjunction with popular CMS platforms such as WordPress and Drupal, as well as web frameworks like Django and Ruby on Rails. We will also explore the different approaches to integrating XeLaTeX with these systems and frameworks, including pre-rendering, on-the-fly rendering, and dynamic rendering.

Benefits of Integrating XeLaTeX with CMS and Web Frameworks

Integrating XeLaTeX with CMS and web frameworks offers several benefits for content creators and publishers.

1. Consistent Formatting: XeLaTeX's powerful typesetting capabilities ensure that documents maintain consistent formatting across different platforms and devices, providing a professional and polished appearance.

2. Automatic Compilation: By integrating XeLaTeX with CMS and web frameworks, documents can be automatically compiled and rendered upon request, saving time and effort for content creators.

3. Seamless Collaboration: CMS and web frameworks provide an environment for multiple users to collaborate on document creation and management. Integrating XeLaTeX ensures that documents are rendered consistently for all users, regardless of their platform or device.

4. Versatility: XeLaTeX's support for different fonts, languages, and typographic features allows for the creation of visually appealing and engaging content that caters to a global audience.

Integrating XeLaTeX with Content Management Systems

Content management systems (CMS) provide a centralized platform for creating, editing, and publishing content on the web. Integrating XeLaTeX with popular CMS platforms such as WordPress and Drupal allows for seamless integration of XeLaTeX-rendered documents into the CMS workflow.

To integrate XeLaTeX with a CMS, follow these steps:

1. Install XeLaTeX: Ensure that XeLaTeX is installed on your server or local machine, depending on where your CMS is hosted.

2. Configure CMS: Configure the CMS to recognize XeLaTeX-rendered documents by defining the file extension, MIME type, and rendering options for XeLaTeX files.

3. Pre-rendering Approach: With the pre-rendering approach, XeLaTeX documents are compiled and rendered offline, and the resulting PDF files are uploaded to the CMS. This approach ensures fast rendering times on the web since the documents are already in a format that is optimized for display.

4. On-the-fly Rendering Approach: With the on-the-fly rendering approach, XeLaTeX documents are compiled and rendered dynamically upon user request. This approach allows for real-time updates and avoids the need to pre-render documents. However, it requires server-side resources and may result in slightly slower rendering times.

5. Dynamic Rendering Approach: The dynamic rendering approach combines pre-rendering and on-the-fly rendering. XeLaTeX documents are compiled and rendered offline, and the resulting PDF files are cached. When a user requests a document, the cached PDF file is served, ensuring fast rendering times. If the document has been updated, the cache is invalidated and the document is re-rendered.

Integrating XeLaTeX with Web Frameworks

Web frameworks provide a foundation for building dynamic web applications. Integrating XeLaTeX with web frameworks such as Django and Ruby on Rails allows for the seamless generation and rendering of XeLaTeX documents within the web application.

To integrate XeLaTeX with a web framework, follow these steps:

1. Set up XeLaTeX Environment: Ensure that XeLaTeX is properly installed and configured on your server or local development environment.

2. Configure Routes and URLs: Define routes and URLs within the web framework to handle requests for XeLaTeX-rendered documents. These routes will trigger the compilation and rendering process.

3. Generate LaTeX Templates: Create LaTeX templates within your web framework that define the structure and layout of the XeLaTeX documents. These templates can be customized to include dynamic content from your application's database or user input.

4. Bind Data and Render Documents: Bind the necessary data from your application's database or user input to the LaTeX templates and execute the XeLaTeX compilation process. Save the resulting PDF file or provide it as a download for the user.

5. Handle Error Handling: Implement error handling in case the XeLaTeX compilation process fails. Proper error messages should be displayed to users, and steps should be taken to log and diagnose any issues.

Examples and Resources

Here are a few examples and resources to help you get started with integrating XeLaTeX with CMS and web frameworks:

1. WordPress Plugin: "XeLaTeX Publisher" is a popular WordPress plugin that enables the integration of XeLaTeX with WordPress. It provides features for pre-rendering, on-the-fly rendering, and caching of XeLaTeX documents.

2. Drupal Module: "XeLaTeX Module" is a Drupal module that allows for the integration of XeLaTeX with Drupal. It provides integration with the WYSIWYG editor, batch rendering, and options for caching rendered documents.

3. Django Application: "DjangoXeLaTeX" is a Django application that enables the generation and rendering of XeLaTeX documents within a Django web application. It provides a set of template tags and filters for seamless integration.

4. Ruby on Rails Gem: "XeLaTeX-Rails" is a Ruby on Rails gem that provides seamless integration of XeLaTeX within a Ruby on Rails application. It includes

generators for creating LaTeX templates and provides options for on-the-fly rendering and caching.

5. Overleaf: Overleaf is an online LaTeX editor with collaboration features that can be integrated with popular CMS systems or web frameworks. It allows for real-time collaborative editing, version control, and seamless integration with online publishing platforms.

6. LaTeX for WordPress: The "LaTeX for WordPress" plugin allows for the integration of XeLaTeX-rendered equations and expressions within WordPress posts and pages. It provides a simple and user-friendly interface for inserting mathematical content.

These examples and resources provide a starting point for integrating XeLaTeX with content management systems and web frameworks, but there are many more options and tools available depending on your specific requirements and preferences.

Best Practices

When integrating XeLaTeX with content management systems and web frameworks, consider the following best practices:

1. Performance Optimization: Optimize the XeLaTeX compilation process for performance by using caching, pre-rendering, and incremental rendering techniques. This will ensure fast loading times for XeLaTeX-rendered documents on the web.

2. Security Considerations: When allowing user-generated content to be rendered by XeLaTeX, ensure that proper security measures are in place to prevent malicious code execution. Validate and sanitize user inputs and implement sandboxing techniques to limit the actions that can be performed by the XeLaTeX rendering engine.

3. Version Control: Use version control systems such as Git to manage changes to XeLaTeX documents and track revisions. This ensures that a history of changes is maintained and allows for easy collaboration and rollback to previous versions if needed.

4. Documentation and Training: Provide documentation and training materials to content creators and developers on how to use XeLaTeX within the CMS or web framework. This will help foster adoption and ensure that best practices are followed.

5. Community Support: Utilize online forums, mailing lists, and communities to seek help and advice from experienced XeLaTeX users. The XeLaTeX community is vibrant and can provide valuable insights and solutions to common integration challenges.

By following these best practices, you will be able to seamlessly integrate XeLaTeX with content management systems and web frameworks, providing a powerful platform for publishing and managing documents on the web.

Summary

Integrating XeLaTeX with content management systems and web frameworks allows for the seamless generation and rendering of professional-quality documents on the web. By following the steps outlined in this section and considering the best practices, you can harness the power of XeLaTeX in conjunction with popular CMS platforms and web frameworks. This integration provides consistent formatting, automatic compilation, seamless collaboration, and versatility in content creation. With the examples and resources provided, you have a starting point for integrating XeLaTeX with your preferred CMS or web framework. Keep exploring and experimenting to find the best approach for your specific needs and requirements.

Best practices for web and mobile publishing in XeLaTeX

Web and mobile publishing have become increasingly important in today's digital world. With XeLaTeX, you can create documents that are optimized for web and mobile platforms, ensuring a seamless reading experience for your audience. In this section, we will discuss the best practices for web and mobile publishing in XeLaTeX, including responsive design, interactivity, performance optimization, accessibility, and distribution.

Responsive designs for web and mobile

One of the key considerations in web and mobile publishing is creating responsive designs that adapt to different screen sizes and orientations. With XeLaTeX, you can use packages like `geometry` and `hyperref` to define the layout and incorporate hyperlinks, respectively.

To ensure a responsive design, it is crucial to use relative units for defining page dimensions, such as percentages or em units, instead of fixed values. This allows the content to adjust dynamically based on the available screen space. Additionally, leveraging CSS media queries through the `media9` package enables you to customize the document layout for specific devices or resolutions.

Creating interactive and multimedia-rich documents

XeLaTeX provides powerful tools for creating interactive and multimedia-rich documents for web and mobile platforms. The media9 package allows you to embed audio, video, and 3D content directly into your document, making it more engaging for the readers.

To ensure a seamless experience across different devices and browsers, it is recommended to use widely supported file formats, such as MP4 for video and MP3 for audio. You can also customize the player controls and appearance using the options provided by the media9 package.

Optimizing XeLaTeX for web and mobile performance

Web and mobile platforms demand efficient performance and fast loading times. To optimize the performance of XeLaTeX documents for web and mobile publishing, you can follow these best practices:

+ Minimize the use of large images or use image compression techniques like JPEG for photographs and PNG for graphics.

+ Utilize lazy loading techniques to defer the loading of non-essential content, especially for mobile devices with limited bandwidth.

+ Group related resources, such as CSS and JavaScript files, and load them asynchronously to reduce the number of server requests and improve loading speed.

+ Take advantage of XeLaTeX's caching mechanism to store precompiled versions of your document, reducing compilation time when generating subsequent versions.

+ Optimize the document structure, reducing unnecessary nested elements and using semantic markup for better search engine optimization (SEO) and screen reader compatibility.

Creating accessible documents for web and mobile

Accessibility is another important aspect of web and mobile publishing. XeLaTeX provides features to enhance the accessibility of your documents, ensuring they can be accessed and understood by a wider audience, including people with disabilities.

To create accessible documents, consider the following practices:

* Provide alternative text descriptions for images using the `alt` attribute. This allows screen readers to describe the image to visually impaired users.

* Ensure proper document structure with headings (`h1` to `h6`) and semantic markup (`article`, `main`, `nav`, etc.) to aid in screen reader navigation.

* Use high contrast color schemes and avoid relying solely on color to convey important information.

* Test your document with assistive technologies, such as screen readers and screen magnifiers, to ensure compatibility and usability for users with disabilities.

Publishing XeLaTeX documents as web pages and ebooks

XeLaTeX provides various options for publishing documents as web pages or ebooks. You can convert your XeLaTeX document to HTML using tools like `tex4ht` or directly export to EPUB format.

When publishing as web pages, it is important to maintain the document's structure and styling. Use CSS frameworks like Bootstrap to ensure consistency and responsiveness across devices. Moreover, consider using content delivery networks (CDNs) to serve static resources, ensuring better loading speed.

For ebooks, ensure that the document's layout and formatting adapt well to different e-reader devices. Test your ebook on popular platforms like Amazon Kindle or Apple iBooks to verify compatibility and correct any formatting issues.

Designing and formatting digital magazines and newsletters

XeLaTeX can be a powerful tool for designing and formatting digital magazines and newsletters, which often require rich multimedia content and complex layouts.

To create visually appealing and interactive digital publications, consider these best practices:

* Use the `tcolorbox` package to create attractive boxes, sidebars, and callouts.

* Incorporate CSS styles and animations to enhance the visual appeal of your digital magazine or newsletter.

* Ensure that the document's layout and typography adapt well to different screen sizes, using responsive design techniques.

- Include hyperlinks and navigation aids to improve the user experience and facilitate easy navigation between different sections or articles.

- Test the digital magazine or newsletter on various devices and platforms to ensure a consistent and enjoyable reading experience.

Creating mobile apps and e-learning materials

XeLaTeX can also be utilized for creating mobile apps and e-learning materials, providing a versatile and customizable platform for educational content.

Consider the following best practices when designing mobile apps and e-learning materials:

- Use the `animate` package to create interactive and engaging educational animations.

- Utilize interactivity frameworks like JavaScript and HTML5 to enhance the learning experience with quizzes, interactive exercises, or simulations.

- Optimize the app or e-learning materials for performance by minimizing file sizes and utilizing caching techniques.

- Incorporate feedback mechanisms, such as user surveys or quizzes, to gather feedback and assess learning outcomes.

- Test the mobile app or e-learning materials on different platforms, such as iOS and Android, to ensure compatibility and usability.

Integrating XeLaTeX with content management systems and web frameworks

To streamline your web and mobile publishing workflow, consider integrating XeLaTeX with content management systems (CMS) and web frameworks.

Popular CMS platforms like WordPress or Drupal offer plugins or modules that facilitate the conversion of XeLaTeX documents to web pages or ebooks. These integrations provide a seamless workflow, allowing you to focus on the content creation aspect.

Similarly, web frameworks like React or Angular can be used to build web applications that render XeLaTeX documents dynamically. By leveraging the power of JavaScript frameworks, you can create interactive web experiences that seamlessly incorporate XeLaTeX-generated content.

Best practices for web and mobile publishing

To sum up, here are some key best practices for web and mobile publishing in XeLaTeX:

- Use responsive design techniques to create documents that adapt to different screen sizes and orientations.

- Incorporate interactivity and multimedia elements to enhance the user experience.

- Optimize the performance of your XeLaTeX documents for web and mobile platforms.

- Ensure accessibility by incorporating features that make your documents usable for people with disabilities.

- Choose the appropriate format (web page or ebook) for publishing your XeLaTeX document and consider the specific requirements of each format.

- Design and format digital magazines and newsletters with visually appealing layouts.

- Create mobile apps and e-learning materials that provide interactive and engaging educational content.

- Integrate XeLaTeX with content management systems and web frameworks to streamline your publishing workflow.

By following these best practices, you can leverage the power of XeLaTeX to create professional and optimized documents for web and mobile publishing.

XeLaTeX for Ebooks and Digital Publishing

Introduction to digital publishing with XeLaTeX

In today's digital age, traditional methods of publishing have evolved to meet the demands of a rapidly changing world. With the advent of digital publishing, content creators now have the ability to distribute their work across multiple platforms, such as the web and mobile devices. XeLaTeX, a powerful typesetting system built on top of LaTeX, offers a versatile and efficient solution for digital publishing.

Digital publishing refers to the creation, distribution, and consumption of content in electronic formats, such as web pages, ebooks, and digital documents. It encompasses a wide range of media, including text, images, videos, and interactive elements. XeLaTeX, with its support for Unicode and modern font technologies, allows authors to create attractive and beautifully typeset documents tailor-made for digital platforms.

In this section, we will explore the various aspects of digital publishing with XeLaTeX. We will discuss the benefits and challenges of publishing in digital formats, as well as the techniques and best practices to create visually appealing and interactive documents. We will also delve into the process of optimizing XeLaTeX documents for performance and compatibility with different devices and platforms.

Before we dive into the specifics of digital publishing with XeLaTeX, let us first understand the advantages it offers over traditional publishing methods.

Benefits of digital publishing with XeLaTeX

1. **Flexibility and adaptability:** XeLaTeX provides the ability to create documents that seamlessly adapt to different screen sizes and resolutions. This allows content creators to cater to a wide range of devices, from smartphones and tablets to desktop computers and e-readers.

2. **Interactive and multimedia-rich content:** XeLaTeX enables the integration of interactive elements, multimedia files, and dynamic visualizations into digital documents. This opens up new possibilities for creating engaging and immersive reading experiences.

3. **Hyperlinking and cross-referencing:** XeLaTeX supports hyperlinks and cross-referencing, making it easy to navigate within the document and reference external resources. This enhances the user experience and enables effortless access to additional information.

4. **Accessibility and inclusivity:** XeLaTeX provides robust support for accessibility features, such as alternative text for images and proper semantic markup. This ensures that content is accessible to individuals with disabilities and complies with accessibility standards.

5. **Ease of distribution:** Digital documents created with XeLaTeX can be easily distributed and shared across various platforms, such as websites, online repositories, and ebook stores. This eliminates the need for physical printing and shipping, reducing costs and environmental impact.

Now that we have explored the advantages of digital publishing with XeLaTeX, let us delve into the techniques and best practices for creating effective and visually appealing digital documents.

Design considerations for digital publishing

When creating digital documents with XeLaTeX, it is important to keep in mind the specific requirements of digital platforms. Here are some design considerations to ensure optimal readability and user experience:

1. **Responsive design and layout:** Design your document to adapt to different screen sizes and orientations. Use responsive techniques to ensure that the content is displayed optimally on various devices.

2. **Font selection and readability:** Choose fonts that are legible on screens of different sizes and resolutions. Pay attention to text size, line spacing, and contrast to ensure readability.

3. **Optimizing image and media files:** Compress images and videos to reduce file sizes without compromising quality. Use appropriate file formats and resolutions to balance visual appeal and performance.

4. **Navigation and user interface:** Create clear navigation elements and interactive features to facilitate easy navigation and enhance the user experience. Use hyperlinks, bookmarks, and table of contents to provide seamless navigation within the document.

5. **Accessibility and inclusivity:** Ensure that your document meets accessibility standards by providing alternative text for images, proper headings, and appropriate semantic markup. Consider colorblindness and other visual impairments when designing visual elements.

6. **Interactive and multimedia elements:** Leverage the capabilities of digital platforms by incorporating interactive elements, such as quizzes, animations, and audio/video content, to make your document engaging and interactive.

By considering these design principles, you can create digital documents with XeLaTeX that are visually appealing, user-friendly, and accessible to a wide audience.

Resources for digital publishing with XeLaTeX

To further enhance your understanding of digital publishing with XeLaTeX, here are some recommended resources:

1. *The LaTeX Companion* by Frank Mittelbach et al. provides comprehensive coverage of LaTeX, including XeLaTeX and digital publishing techniques.

2. *Digital Publishing with XeLaTeX* by Jonathan Kew explores the intricacies of digital publishing using XeLaTeX, with a focus on typography and design for digital platforms.

3. The *XeTeX mailing list* and the *TeX Stack Exchange* are excellent online communities where you can seek advice, ask questions, and learn from experienced users.

4. Official documentation and user guides for XeLaTeX and related packages provide detailed information on specific features and functionalities.

Remember, digital publishing with XeLaTeX is a constantly evolving field, and it is essential to stay updated with the latest trends and techniques. Experiment, explore, and harness the power of XeLaTeX to create visually stunning and interactive digital documents.

Creating and formatting ebooks in EPUB and MOBI formats with XeLaTeX

In this section, we will explore how XeLaTeX can be used to create and format ebooks in EPUB and MOBI formats. Ebooks have gained immense popularity in recent years, as they provide a convenient and portable way to access digital content on various devices such as e-readers, tablets, and smartphones. XeLaTeX, with its powerful typesetting capabilities and support for Unicode, is well suited for creating high-quality ebooks that are visually appealing and easy to read.

Overview of EPUB and MOBI Formats

Before we delve into the details of ebook creation with XeLaTeX, let's first understand the two most commonly used ebook formats: EPUB and MOBI.

EPUB (Electronic Publication) is an open standard format for ebooks developed by the International Digital Publishing Forum (IDPF). EPUB files are based on HTML and CSS, making them reflowable and adaptable to different screen sizes and orientations. EPUB supports a wide range of metadata, interactive features, and multimedia content, making it suitable for various types of ebooks.

MOBI (Mobipocket) is an ebook format developed by Mobipocket SA. It is primarily used for Amazon Kindle devices and applications. MOBI files are similar to EPUB files in terms of reflowability and support for interactive features. However, MOBI uses a proprietary format and has some limitations compared to EPUB.

Now that we have a basic understanding of EPUB and MOBI formats, let's see how we can leverage the power of XeLaTeX to create and format ebooks in these formats.

Setting Up XeLaTeX for Ebook Creation

To begin creating ebooks with XeLaTeX, we need to set up our XeLaTeX environment accordingly. We assume that you have already installed a distribution of LaTeX that includes XeLaTeX.

First, we need to create a new XeLaTeX document. Create a new .tex file and add the following code at the beginning:

```
\setmainfont{Times New Roman}
```

In this example, we are using the article document class, which is suitable for most ebook projects. We are also loading the fontspec package to enable font customization, the graphicx package for image inclusion, and the hyperref package for hyperlinking within the document. The \setmainfont command specifies the main font to be used in the ebook (in this case, Times New Roman).

Structuring the Ebook Document

Next, let's structure our ebook document by adding sections, chapters, and subsections. XeLaTeX provides commands for creating these structural elements, which will be converted into navigational elements in the final ebook.

Add the following code after the document class declaration:

```
\title{My Ebook}
\author{John Doe}
\date{\today}


\maketitle

\section{Introduction}
This is the introduction\index{introduction} section\index{section

\subsection{Overview}
This subsection\index{subsection} provides an overview\index{overv
```

```
\section{Chapter 1}
This is the content\index{content} of chapter\index{chapter} 1.

\subsection{Section 1}
This is section\index{section} 1 of chapter\index{chapter} 1.

\section{Chapter 2}
This is the content\index{content} of chapter\index{chapter} 2.

% Add more chapters and sections as needed
```

In this example, we set the title, author, and date of the ebook using the \title, \author, and \date commands, respectively. The \maketitle command is used to generate the title page with the provided information.

The document is then wrapped within the \begin{document} and \end{document} tags. Within this environment, we create sections using the \section command and subsections using the \subsection command.

Feel free to add more chapters, sections, and subsections as required for your ebook.

Including Text Content

Once we have structured our ebook document, we can start adding text content. Simply type your content within the appropriate sections and subsections.

For example, within the Introduction section, we can add the following:

```
\section{Introduction}
This is the introduction\index{introduction} section\index{secti
```

Similarly, you can add content to other sections and subsections.

Including Images

To include images in your ebook, you can use the \includegraphics command provided by the graphicx package. This command allows you to insert images in various formats such as PNG, JPEG, and PDF.

For example, suppose you have an image named "example.png" that you want to include in your ebook. You can use the following code to insert the image:

```
% \begin{figure}[ht]
%     \centering
%     \includegraphics[width=0.5\textwidth]{example.png}
%     \caption{Example image}
%     \label{fig:example}
% \end{figure}
```

In this code, we wrap the \includegraphics command within a figure environment to ensure proper placement of the image. We use the \centering command to horizontally center the image. The \caption command is used to provide a caption for the image, and the \label command is used to give the image a label that can be referenced later.

Creating Hyperlinks

Hyperlinks are an essential feature of ebooks, as they enable users to navigate within the document and access external resources. XeLaTeX provides the \href command from the hyperref package to create hyperlinks.

To create a hyperlink, use the following syntax:

```
\href{URL}{link text}
```

For example, suppose you want to create a hyperlink to a website called "example.com" with the text "Click here to visit example.com." You can use the following code:

```
\href{http://example.com}{Click here to visit example.com}
```

Adding Metadata to the Ebook

EPUB and MOBI formats support metadata such as title, author, description, and cover image. To add metadata to your ebook, you can use the \title, \author, and \date commands at the beginning of your XeLaTeX document. Additionally, you can customize the cover image by including an image file using the \coverimage command from the hyperref package.

For example, let's add metadata and a cover image to our ebook:

```
\title{My Ebook}
\author{John Doe}
\date{\today}
```

```
\coverimage{cover.jpg}
```

```
\maketitle
```

```
% Rest of the ebook document
```

In this example, we set the title, author, and date as before. We also include a cover image named "cover.jpg" using the \coverimage command.

Compiling the Ebook

To compile the XeLaTeX document into EPUB and MOBI formats, we need to use additional tools such as Pandoc or Calibre.

Pandoc is a versatile document converter that supports various input and output formats, including EPUB and MOBI. Calibre, on the other hand, is a powerful ebook management tool that includes conversion capabilities.

Once you have either Pandoc or Calibre installed, you can use them to convert your XeLaTeX document into EPUB and MOBI formats.

For example, using Pandoc, you can use the following command to convert your XeLaTeX document into EPUB:

```
pandoc -s my_ebook.tex -o my_ebook.epub
```

Similarly, you can use the following command to convert your XeLaTeX document into MOBI:

```
pandoc -s my_ebook.tex -o my_ebook.mobi
```

Note that you may need to install additional LaTeX packages and fonts to ensure compatibility with Pandoc or Calibre.

Best Practices for Ebook Creation

When creating ebooks with XeLaTeX, consider the following best practices:

- Use a clean and minimalist design to enhance readability and user experience.

- Optimize images for different screen sizes and resolutions to reduce file size and improve rendering performance.

- Test your ebook on multiple devices and e-reader applications to ensure proper display and functionality.

- Include a table of contents and navigation links to make it easy for readers to navigate through your ebook.

- Validate your EPUB and MOBI files using online validators to ensure compliance with the respective standards.

By following these best practices, you can create ebooks that provide an enjoyable reading experience across different devices and platforms.

Conclusion

In this section, we explored how XeLaTeX can be used to create and format ebooks in EPUB and MOBI formats. We discussed the basics of EPUB and MOBI formats, set up our XeLaTeX environment for ebook creation, structured our ebook document, included text content, images, and hyperlinks, added metadata, and compiled the ebook into EPUB and MOBI formats.

Creating ebooks with XeLaTeX gives you full control over the typesetting and design, allowing you to create visually appealing and high-quality digital publications. With the versatility of XeLaTeX and the popularity of ebooks, you can leverage these skills to share your knowledge, stories, and ideas with a wide audience. So, go ahead and start creating your own ebooks with XeLaTeX!

Adding interactivity and multimedia to ebooks with XeLaTeX

In today's digital age, ebooks have become increasingly popular as a medium for publishing and sharing content. With XeLaTeX, you can not only create beautifully formatted ebooks but also add interactivity and multimedia elements to enhance the reading experience. In this section, we will explore various techniques and tools that allow you to incorporate interactive features and multimedia content into your XeLaTeX ebooks.

The Importance of Interactivity and Multimedia in Ebooks

Ebooks offer a unique advantage over traditional print books by allowing readers to engage with the content in interactive ways. Interactivity can enhance comprehension, engagement, and the overall reading experience. Multimedia elements, such as audio, video, and interactive graphics, provide additional context and can help convey information more effectively.

For example, in a language learning ebook, interactive quizzes and exercises can test the reader's understanding and provide instant feedback. In a textbook, videos can demonstrate complex concepts or experiments that are challenging to explain with text alone. By adding interactivity and multimedia to ebooks, you can create a more engaging and immersive learning experience.

Techniques for Adding Interactivity

XeLaTeX provides several techniques for adding interactivity to ebooks. Let's explore some of the most commonly used techniques:

Hyperlinks   Hyperlinks are the simplest form of interactivity in ebooks. They allow readers to navigate between sections, chapters, or external resources. XeLaTeX provides the `hyperref` package, which enables the inclusion of hyperlinks in your ebook. For example, you can create a link to a glossary term or a reference to another section within the document.

To add a hyperlink, use the `\href{URL}{text}` command. For instance, `\href{https://www.example.com}{Visit our website}` will create a hyperlink with the text "Visit our website" that points to `https://www.example.com`.

Interactive Forms   Interactive forms allow readers to input data or make selections within the ebook. This feature is useful for creating surveys, questionnaires, or interactive exercises. The `hyperref` package also provides commands for creating interactive forms. You can use form elements such as text fields, checkboxes, radio buttons, and combo boxes.

To create a text field, use the `\TextField{label}` command. For example, `\TextField{Enter your name:}` will create a text field with the label "Enter your name:". The user can then input their name directly in the ebook.

Animations and Interactive Graphics   Animations and interactive graphics can bring your ebook to life. One way to include animations and interactive graphics is by using the `animate` package. This package allows you to incorporate animated GIFs into your ebook.

To include an animated GIF, use the `\animategraphics` command, specifying the file name, width, and height. For example, `\animategraphics[width=0.5\textwidth]{300px}{animation.gif}` will insert an animated GIF called `animation.gif` with a width of 50% of the text width.

You can also create interactive graphics using the `tikz` package. With TikZ, you can design interactive diagrams, charts, and visualizations. By adding interactivity to these elements, readers can explore the data or interact with the graphical elements.

Best Practices for Adding Interactivity and Multimedia

While incorporating interactivity and multimedia can greatly enhance the ebook experience, it is important to consider a few best practices:

+ Use interactivity and multimedia sparingly. Too many interactive elements can be overwhelming and distract from the main content.

+ Ensure that interactivity is intuitive and enhances the learning experience. Make sure that interactive elements serve a purpose and are easy to use.

+ Test your ebook across different devices and platforms to ensure that interactive elements are compatible and work as intended.

+ Consider accessibility when incorporating multimedia. Provide alternative text for images and captions for videos to make your ebook accessible to all readers.

Resources for Adding Interactivity and Multimedia

Here are some resources that can help you learn more about adding interactivity and multimedia to your XeLaTeX ebooks:

+ The `hyperref` package documentation provides a comprehensive guide to using hyperlinks and interactive forms in XeLaTeX.

+ The `animate` package documentation offers detailed instructions on including animated GIFs in your ebooks.

+ The TikZ documentation provides examples and tutorials for creating interactive graphics with TikZ.

+ The XeLaTeX Stack Exchange community is a valuable resource for asking questions and getting assistance with specific issues related to adding interactivity and multimedia in XeLaTeX.

Conclusion

Adding interactivity and multimedia to your XeLaTeX ebooks can significantly enhance the reader's engagement and learning experience. By incorporating hyperlinks, interactive forms, animations, and interactive graphics, you can create dynamic and immersive digital publications. Remember to use interactivity and multimedia judiciously, keeping the purpose and accessibility of the ebook in mind.

Designing and formatting interactive textbooks and educational materials

In today's digital age, traditional textbooks are not the only way to deliver educational content. With the advancement of technology, interactive textbooks and educational materials are gaining popularity due to their dynamic and immersive learning experiences. In this section, we will explore the principles and techniques of designing and formatting interactive textbooks using XeLaTeX.

Introduction to Interactive Textbooks

Interactive textbooks go beyond the static nature of traditional printed textbooks by incorporating multimedia elements, such as videos, audio clips, animations, and interactive exercises. They provide a more engaging and interactive learning experience for students, enhancing their understanding and retention of the subject matter.

Interactive textbooks can be developed for various subjects and educational levels, including K-12 education, university courses, professional training, and self-learning materials. With XeLaTeX, we have the flexibility to create interactive content that merges text, images, interactive elements, and multimedia seamlessly.

Designing Interactive Elements

When designing interactive textbooks, it is essential to consider the overall instructional design principles. Here are some key elements to consider:

- **Clear learning objectives:** Define clear learning objectives for each section or module to guide the development of interactive elements.

- **Engaging multimedia content:** Incorporate relevant multimedia elements, such as images, videos, and audio, to reinforce concepts and engage learners.

- **Interactive exercises:** Include interactive exercises, such as quizzes, drag-and-drop activities, and simulations, to promote active learning and knowledge application.

- **Adaptability:** Design the interactive elements to be adaptable to different devices, screen sizes, and accessibility needs.

- **Intuitive navigation:** Ensure that the interactive textbook has a user-friendly navigation system to help learners easily move between sections and interactive elements.

Formatting Interactive Textbooks

Formatting interactive textbooks in XeLaTeX involves combining traditional typesetting principles with interactive elements. Here are some guidelines for formatting interactive textbooks:

- **Document class selection:** Choose a suitable document class for your interactive textbook project. The document class should support multimedia embedding and interactivity options.

- **Page layout and design:** Develop an aesthetically pleasing layout that balances text, images, and interactive elements. Use XeLaTeX's extensive typographic capabilities to enhance the readability of the text.

- **Embedding multimedia:** Utilize XeLaTeX packages, such as `media9`, `animate`, or `movie15`, to embed multimedia content, such as videos, audio clips, and animations, into your interactive textbook.

- **Hyperlinks and cross-references:** Include hyperlinks and cross-references within the interactive textbook to allow users to navigate between different sections, interactive exercises, and external resources.

- **Interactive exercises:** Develop interactive exercises using XeLaTeX packages like `exsheets` or `exam` to create quizzes, fill-in-the-blanks, and other interactive learning activities.

- **Accessibility considerations:** Ensure that the interactive textbook is accessible to all learners, including those with disabilities. Follow accessibility guidelines such as WCAG (Web Content Accessibility Guidelines).

Example: Interactive Mathematics Textbook

To illustrate the concepts discussed above, let's take an example of an interactive mathematics textbook created using XeLaTeX. In this textbook, we want to explain the concept of quadratic equations and provide interactive exercises for students.

We start by designing the layout of the textbook with clear headings, subheadings, and paragraphs. Within the content, we can embed interactive elements such as sliders for changing the coefficients of quadratic equations and buttons to solve them. We can also include interactive graphs that dynamically change as students modify the equations.

Furthermore, we can add interactive exercises where students can input the solutions to quadratic equations and receive immediate feedback on their answers. These exercises can be designed using XeLaTeX packages like `exsheets` to provide customizable and interactive question and answer environments.

By incorporating multimedia elements like instructional videos and audio explanations, we provide additional resources to support learners' understanding of quadratic equations.

This interactive mathematics textbook not only enhances the learning experience for students but also allows educators to assess their progress through the interactive exercises.

Conclusion

Designing and formatting interactive textbooks using XeLaTeX opens up new possibilities in education. By incorporating multimedia elements, interactive exercises, and adaptable content, interactive textbooks offer a modern and engaging way of learning.

With XeLaTeX's flexibility and powerful typesetting capabilities, educators and content creators can design interactive materials that foster active learning and promote better comprehension and retention of the subject matter.

In the next section, we will explore the process of publishing XeLaTeX documents as web pages and ebooks, further expanding the possibilities for sharing and distributing interactive educational content.

Creating and Formatting Comic Books and Graphic Novels in XeLaTeX

Comic books and graphic novels are popular forms of visual storytelling that have gained widespread recognition in modern literature and entertainment. With their unique blend of words and images, they offer a visually captivating and immersive reading experience. In this section, we will explore how XeLaTeX can be used to create and format comic books and graphic novels, combining the power of typesetting with the art of storytelling.

Introduction to Comic Book and Graphic Novel Production

Comic book and graphic novel production involves creating sequential visual narratives using a combination of illustrations, dialogues, and captions. The process typically involves several stages, including scriptwriting, sketching, inking, coloring, and lettering. XeLaTeX can streamline this workflow by providing a comprehensive set of tools for precise typesetting, flexible layout design, and seamless integration of visual elements.

Structuring the Comic Book Layout

A well-designed layout is crucial for a comic book or graphic novel, as it guides the reader's eye and enhances the storytelling experience. XeLaTeX offers various packages and customization options to define the panel layout, manage multi-page compositions, and ensure consistent spacing between panels and pages.

To create a comic book layout, we can use the `tikzpicture` environment from the TikZ package. We start by defining the dimensions of our page and panel sizes. Then, we can use TikZ nodes and shapes to create panels, speech bubbles, and captions.

For example, let's consider a simple layout with a grid-based panel structure. Each page consists of a certain number of panels arranged in rows and columns. We can use lines and rectangles to delineate the panels and add text nodes for dialogue and captions.

```
\begin{tikzpicture}[scale=1]
  % Setting dimensions
  \def\panelwidth{5cm}
  \def\panelheight{5cm}
  \def\panelsep{0.5cm}

  % Drawing panels
  \foreach \x in {0,...,2} {
```

```
\foreach \y in {0,...,3} {
  \draw[thick] (\x*\panelwidth+\x*\panelsep,\y*\pane
}
}
```

```
% Adding text nodes
\node[align=center] at (1.75*\panelwidth+\panelsep,1.2
\node at (2.25*\panelwidth+\panelsep,0.8*\panelheight)
\end{tikzpicture}
```

This code snippet generates a simple comic book page layout with 3 rows and 4 columns of equally sized panels. You can customize the dimensions and add more panels to suit your specific needs. Experiment with different layouts and arrangements to create visually appealing compositions.

Importing Artwork and Images

Comic books and graphic novels often consist of a combination of hand-drawn illustrations and digitally created artwork. XeLaTeX provides various methods to import and incorporate these visual elements into your document.

To include hand-drawn illustrations, you can scan or photograph the drawings and save them in widely supported image formats such as PNG, JPEG, or SVG. Once you have digital versions of the artwork, you can use the `graphicx` package to include them in your document.

...

```
\includegraphics[width=\textwidth]{artwork.png}
```

For digitally created artwork, you can export the images from design software such as Adobe Photoshop or Illustrator into compatible formats. Again, use the `graphicx` package to include them in your document.

Typography and Lettering

Typography plays a crucial role in comic books and graphic novels, as it helps convey the tone, emotion, and personality of the characters. XeLaTeX offers extensive support for typography, allowing you to choose from a wide range of fonts and customize their appearance.

To ensure consistent and visually appealing lettering, it is recommended to use fonts specifically designed for comic book lettering, such as Comic Sans MS or Blambot fonts. These fonts are optimized for readability and mimic the handwritten style commonly used in comics.

. . .

```
\setmainfont{Comic Sans MS}
```

In addition to the main font used for dialogues and captions, you can use different fonts for onomatopoeias, emphasis, or special effects. Experiment with font styles and sizes to create visually engaging lettering that complements the overall artwork.

Adding Speech Bubbles and Captions

Speech bubbles and captions are essential elements in comic books and graphic novels, as they convey the dialogue and narration. XeLaTeX provides several techniques to create speech bubbles and captions with customizable styles and positioning.

To create speech bubbles, you can use the TikZ package and its shapes library. The cloud shape in TikZ resembles a typical speech bubble shape. Combine it with text nodes to insert the dialogue or narration.

```
\draw[thick] (2*\panelwidth+\panelsep,1.5*\panelheight+\pa
```

This code snippet creates a speech bubble in the middle panel of the layout. Adjust the coordinates and properties to position the speech bubble in different panels and modify its appearance.

For captions, you can simply add text nodes within the panels or next to the artwork using the TikZ node command. Customize the font, size, and alignment to match the intended style.

Coloring and Shading

Coloring and shading play a significant role in enhancing the visual impact of comic books and graphic novels. XeLaTeX allows you to incorporate colors into your artwork, panels, and text, adding depth and richness to the overall composition.

To add colors to your document, you can use the `xcolor` package. It provides a wide range of predefined color names and allows you to define your own custom colors.

. . .

```
\definecolor{myred}{RGB}{255,0,0}
```

With defined colors, you can use them in various elements of your comic book, such as filling shapes, outlining panels, or coloring text. Experiment with different color combinations to create a visually pleasing and cohesive color scheme.

For shading and adding visual effects, TikZ offers a multitude of options. You can apply gradients, shadows, and transparency to elements within your artwork or panels. These effects can be achieved through a combination of TikZ styles, such as `shading`, `drop shadow`, and `opacity`.

Exporting to PDF and Digital Formats

Once you have created and formatted your comic book or graphic novel in XeLaTeX, you can export it to a PDF file for digital distribution or printing. XeLaTeX ensures high-quality output, precise rendering of fonts and graphics, and compatibility with various devices and platforms.

To export your document to a PDF, simply compile your XeLaTeX source code using any TeX distribution. The resulting PDF file can be easily shared online, read on digital devices, or printed for physical distribution.

Additionally, XeLaTeX provides options to export your document directly to popular ebook formats, such as EPUB or MOBI, using external conversion tools. This enables you to distribute your comic book or graphic novel through ebook platforms and reach a broader audience.

Best Practices for Comic Book and Graphic Novel Production in XeLaTeX

To ensure a smooth and efficient comic book production workflow in XeLaTeX, consider the following best practices:

- Organize your project by dividing it into separate files for each component, such as the script, artwork, and lettering.

- Utilize version control systems like Git to track changes, collaborate with others, and maintain a history of revisions.

- Optimize the use of packages and external resources to minimize compilation time and ensure stability.

- Regularly test your document on different devices and platforms to ensure compatibility and visual consistency.

- Seek inspiration from existing comic books and graphic novels, analyze their layout and design choices, and incorporate them into your own work.

By following these best practices, you can harness the full potential of XeLaTeX for creating visually stunning and professional-grade comic books and graphic novels.

Conclusion

XeLaTeX provides a powerful platform for creating and formatting comic books and graphic novels with precise typesetting, versatile layout design, and seamless integration of visuals. By leveraging its extensive features and customization options, you can bring your visual stories to life, captivate readers, and explore the endless possibilities of this medium. So, grab your pen, unleash your creativity, and let XeLaTeX be your companion on the journey of storytelling through comics and graphic novels.

Publishing and distributing XeLaTeX ebooks on major platforms

Publishing and distributing ebooks has become increasingly popular in recent years, offering authors and publishers a flexible and cost-effective way to reach a wide audience. In this section, we will explore how to publish and distribute ebooks created using XeLaTeX on major platforms such as Amazon Kindle, Apple iBooks, and Google Play Books. We will discuss the specific requirements and guidelines for each platform and provide step-by-step instructions on how to prepare your XeLaTeX documents for publication.

Understanding ebook formats for major platforms

Before we dive into the process of publishing and distributing XeLaTeX ebooks, it is important to understand the different ebook formats supported by major platforms. Each platform has its own preferred format, and it is essential to convert your XeLaTeX document into the appropriate format before submission.

1. **Amazon Kindle:** The Amazon Kindle platform primarily uses the MOBI format for ebooks. MOBI files are based on the Open eBook format and are optimized for Kindle devices and Kindle apps. To publish your XeLaTeX ebook on Kindle, you will need to convert it to the MOBI format using tools like Calibre or KindleGen.

2. **Apple iBooks:** Apple iBooks supports the EPUB format, which is an open standard for ebooks. EPUB files can be read on various devices, including iPhones, iPads, and Macs. To publish your XeLaTeX ebook on iBooks, you will need to convert it to EPUB format using tools like Pandoc or Sigil.

3. **Google Play Books:** Google Play Books accepts both EPUB and PDF formats for ebooks. EPUB files offer a more interactive reading experience, while PDF files preserve the original layout and formatting. To publish your XeLaTeX ebook on Google Play Books, you can either convert it to EPUB format or upload it directly as a PDF file.

Preparing your XeLaTeX document for conversion

Now that you understand the ebook formats for major platforms, let's discuss how to prepare your XeLaTeX document for conversion.

1. **Clean up your document:** Before converting your XeLaTeX document, it is important to clean up the code and ensure that there are no errors or warnings.

Remove any unnecessary packages, commands, or customizations that are not supported in the ebook format. Test your document by compiling it to PDF and make sure that it looks and functions as intended.

2. **Convert to HTML or EPUB**: To convert your XeLaTeX document to the required formats, you can start by converting it to HTML using tools like Pandoc. HTML provides a flexible and accessible format that can be easily converted to EPUB or MOBI. Alternatively, you can directly convert your XeLaTeX document to EPUB format using tools like Pandoc or Sigil.

3. **Check the formatting**: After the conversion, make sure to check the formatting of your ebook. Pay attention to the layout, fonts, images, tables, and equations to ensure they are properly rendered. Adjust any formatting issues and make sure the content is readable on different devices and screen sizes.

Publishing on Amazon Kindle

To publish your XeLaTeX ebook on Amazon Kindle, follow these steps:

1. **Create an Amazon Kindle Direct Publishing (KDP) account**: Start by creating a KDP account on the Amazon Kindle Direct Publishing website. Provide the necessary details and set up your account.

2. **Create a new ebook**: In your KDP account, click on "Create a new Kindle eBook" and enter the required information, such as the title, author name, and book description. You can also upload a cover image for your ebook.

3. **Upload your converted MOBI file**: Once you have filled in the necessary details, upload your converted MOBI file. KDP will automatically convert it to the Kindle format and provide a preview for you to review.

4. **Set the pricing and distribution**: Choose the pricing and distribution options for your ebook. Set the list price, select the royalty options, and choose the territories where you want your ebook to be available.

5. **Submit for publication**: Review all the details and click on "Publish Your Kindle eBook" to submit it for publication. Your ebook will go through a review process, and once approved, it will be available for purchase on the Kindle Store.

Publishing on Apple iBooks

To publish your XeLaTeX ebook on Apple iBooks, follow these steps:

1. **Join the Apple Developer Program:** Before publishing on iBooks, you need to join the Apple Developer Program. This program allows you to distribute your ebooks on iBooks and other Apple platforms. Sign up for the program and complete the necessary enrollment steps.

2. **Prepare your EPUB file:** Make sure your XeLaTeX document is converted to the EPUB format. Use tools like Pandoc or Sigil to convert it if needed. Ensure that all the formatting, images, and interactive elements are properly converted.

3. **Sign in to iTunes Connect:** Sign in to iTunes Connect using your Apple ID. This is the platform to manage your iBooks content.

4. **Create a new book:** In iTunes Connect, navigate to "My Books" and click on the "+" button to create a new book. Enter the required details such as the title, author name, and book description.

5. **Upload your EPUB file:** Upload your converted EPUB file and fill in the metadata such as the cover image, pricing, and categorization. iTunes Connect will perform a validation check to ensure the file meets the required standards.

6. **Submit for review:** Review all the details and click on "Submit for Review" to submit your ebook for Apple's review process. This process ensures that your book meets Apple's content and quality guidelines.

7. **Wait for approval:** Once your ebook passes the review process, it will be available on the iBooks Store for users to purchase and download.

Publishing on Google Play Books

To publish your XeLaTeX ebook on Google Play Books, follow these steps:

1. **Create a Google Play Books Partner account:** Start by creating a Google Play Books Partner account. Provide the necessary details and set up your account.

2. **Prepare your EPUB or PDF file**: Convert your XeLaTeX document to either the EPUB or PDF format. EPUB files offer a more interactive reading experience, while PDF files preserve the original layout and formatting.

3. **Sign in to the Google Play Books Partner Center**: Sign in to the Google Play Books Partner Center using your Google account. This is the platform to manage your ebooks on Google Play Books.

4. **Add a new book**: In the Partner Center, click on "Add book" and enter the required information, including the title, author name, and book description.

5. **Upload your EPUB or PDF file**: Upload your converted EPUB or PDF file and fill in the metadata such as the cover image, pricing, and categorization. Google Play Books will perform a validation check to ensure the file meets the required standards.

6. **Set the pricing and distribution**: Choose the pricing and distribution options for your ebook. Set the list price, select the revenue share options, and choose the territories where you want your ebook to be available.

7. **Submit for publication**: Review all the details and click on "Submit for publication" to submit your ebook. Google Play Books will review your submission, and once approved, it will be available for purchase on the Google Play Store.

Best practices for publishing and distributing XeLaTeX ebooks

Here are some best practices to consider when publishing and distributing XeLaTeX ebooks:

+ **Test and preview your ebook**: Before submitting your ebook for publication, make sure to thoroughly test and preview it on different devices and platforms. Check for any formatting issues, broken links, or missing elements.

+ **Invest in professional editing and proofreading**: To ensure the highest quality for your ebook, consider investing in professional editing and proofreading services. This will help eliminate any grammar or spelling errors and improve the overall readability.

+ **Optimize your ebook for different devices**: Keep in mind that readers will be using various devices with different screen sizes and resolutions. Make sure your ebook is optimized for different devices by testing it on multiple platforms and adjusting the formatting if necessary.

+ **Promote and market your ebook:** Once your ebook is published, make sure to promote and market it to reach your target audience. Utilize social media, email marketing, and other promotional channels to generate visibility and increase sales.

+ **Stay up to date with platform guidelines:** Major ebook platforms may update their guidelines and requirements periodically. Stay informed about any changes and ensure that your ebooks comply with the latest guidelines to avoid any issues with publication or distribution.

Conclusion

Publishing and distributing XeLaTeX ebooks on major platforms like Amazon Kindle, Apple iBooks, and Google Play Books opens up new avenues for authors and publishers to reach a global audience. By understanding the specific requirements and guidelines for each platform, converting your XeLaTeX document into the appropriate format, and following the submission process, you can successfully publish and distribute your ebooks on these platforms. Remember to test, optimize, and promote your ebooks to maximize their impact and reach. Happy publishing!

Building custom ebook readers and applications with XeLaTeX

Creating custom ebook readers and applications with XeLaTeX offers a unique opportunity to design and tailor digital reading experiences to suit specific needs and preferences. In this section, we will explore the principles and techniques involved in building custom ebook readers and applications using XeLaTeX.

Overview of ebook readers and applications

Ebook readers and applications provide a platform for digital reading, allowing users to access and interact with ebooks in various formats. These applications offer features such as bookmarking, highlighting, searching, and annotation, enhancing the reading experience for users.

Building a custom ebook reader using XeLaTeX involves leveraging its powerful typesetting capabilities to create visually appealing and interactive interfaces. By integrating XeLaTeX with other technologies, such as JavaScript and CSS, we can design and develop rich, user-friendly ebook readers tailored to specific requirements.

Design considerations for custom ebook readers

When designing a custom ebook reader, it is essential to consider the following factors:

+ **Layout and navigation:** Choose a layout that presents the content in a readable and intuitive manner. Design navigation controls, such as table of contents, page scrolling, and bookmarking, to facilitate easy access to different sections of the ebook.

+ **Customizability:** Provide options for users to personalize the reading experience by customizing font sizes, background colors, and other display settings. Implement features like night mode and screen brightness adjustment for enhanced readability in different lighting conditions.

+ **Accessibility:** Ensure that the ebook reader adheres to accessibility standards, making it usable for users with disabilities. Implement features like text-to-speech, screen reader compatibility, and support for alternative navigation methods.

+ **Interactivity:** Incorporate interactive features like clickable hyperlinks, inline multimedia content, and interactive quizzes to engage readers and provide a more immersive experience.

+ **Cross-platform compatibility:** Build the custom ebook reader to be compatible with multiple platforms and devices, including desktops, tablets, and smartphones, to reach a wider audience. Utilize responsive design techniques to ensure optimal display on different screen sizes and resolutions.

Developing a custom ebook reader with XeLaTeX

To develop a custom ebook reader using XeLaTeX, we can follow these steps:

1. **Define the document structure:** Create a document with a suitable document class, such as `book` or `article`, and set up the necessary document parameters, including page size, margins, and headers/footers.

2. **Import the ebook content:** Import the ebook content into the XeLaTeX document using the \input or \include command. Ensure that the imported content is properly formatted and organized for easy readability.

3. **Design the interface:** Design the interface elements, such as navigation bars, buttons, and menus, using XeLaTeX's layout and typesetting capabilities. Utilize packages like tikz to create custom graphics and icons that enhance the visual appeal of the ebook reader.

4. **Implement interactivity:** Use JavaScript to add interactivity to the ebook reader. For example, you can implement clickable hyperlinks, interactive quizzes, and dynamic content loading to enhance the reading experience.

5. **Customize the reading experience:** Allow users to customize the reading experience by providing options to adjust font sizes, change background colors, and switch between different reading modes (e.g., day mode and night mode). Use CSS to style the ebook reader interface elements dynamically based on user preferences.

6. **Deploy the ebook reader:** Package the custom ebook reader as a standalone application or a web-based reader. For standalone applications, consider using technologies like Electron to package the XeLaTeX document along with the necessary dependencies. For web-based readers, make sure to host the application on a reliable and secure server.

Examples and resources

To further explore the development of custom ebook readers and applications with XeLaTeX, you can refer to the following resources:

+ **Ebook-Reader template:** Utilize existing XeLaTeX templates specifically designed for building ebook readers, such as the Ebook-Reader template available on GitHub. This template provides a starting point with pre-designed interface elements and interactivity features.

+ **XeLaTeX and JavaScript integration:** Learn how to integrate XeLaTeX with JavaScript using packages like pdfpages and media9 to embed interactive content, such as audio and video, directly into the ebook reader.

+ **CSS customization:** Explore CSS customization techniques to style the ebook reader's interface elements. Online resources like W3Schools and

Mozilla Developer Network (MDN) provide comprehensive guides on CSS properties and selectors.

Best practices and considerations

When building custom ebook readers and applications with XeLaTeX, keep the following best practices and considerations in mind:

- **Performance optimization:** Optimize the performance of the ebook reader by minimizing resource usage and optimizing code. Use techniques like lazy loading to improve loading times for large ebooks with many pages or interactive elements.

- **Testing and debugging:** Thoroughly test the ebook reader for compatibility across different platforms, devices, and screen sizes. Utilize debugging tools and techniques to identify and fix any issues before deployment.

- **Security:** Take appropriate measures to ensure the security of the ebook reader. Protect user data, validate user inputs, and implement secure communication channels if the reader requires interaction with external services.

- **User feedback and updates:** Encourage users to provide feedback on the ebook reader's functionality and usability. Regularly update the reader with bug fixes, feature enhancements, and security patches based on user feedback and emerging requirements.

Building custom ebook readers and applications with XeLaTeX opens up endless possibilities for creating unique and immersive reading experiences. Whether it's for personal use, educational purposes, or commercial distribution, the combination of XeLaTeX's powerful typesetting capabilities and other web technologies allows for the creation of highly customizable and engaging digital reading platforms.

Monetizing XeLaTeX ebooks and digital publications

In this section, we will explore various strategies and techniques for monetizing XeLaTeX ebooks and digital publications. With the increasing popularity of digital content, it has become essential for authors and publishers to find ways to generate revenue from their creations. We will examine different monetization models and discuss best practices for maximizing profitability while delivering high-quality content to readers.

Understanding the Market

Before diving into monetization strategies, it is crucial to have a deep understanding of the market. Conduct thorough market research to identify the target audience, their preferences, and their willingness to pay for digital content. Analyze the demand for the specific niche or topic covered in your XeLaTeX ebook or publication.

Consider the following factors when assessing the market:

+ Existing competition: Study the competing products in your niche and identify areas where you can offer unique value to readers.

+ Pricing trends: Look at the pricing models for similar ebooks and publications. Determine whether readers are more inclined to purchase individual ebooks or subscribe to a membership or subscription service.

+ Target audience demographics: Identify the characteristics of your target audience, such as age, occupation, interests, and level of expertise. This information will help you tailor your monetization strategy to their specific needs and preferences.

By gaining a comprehensive understanding of the market, you will be better equipped to develop effective monetization strategies.

Choosing the Right Monetization Model

There are several monetization models available for XeLaTeX ebooks and digital publications. Let's explore some popular options:

1. **Pay-per-download (PPD):** In this model, readers pay a one-time fee to download the ebook or publication. This is a common approach for selling individual ebooks. Consider pricing your ebook based on factors like content length, niche, and perceived value.

2. **Subscription-based:** This model involves offering readers access to a library of ebooks or publications for a recurring fee. Subscriptions can be monthly, quarterly, or annual, depending on your target audience and content frequency. This model encourages customer loyalty and provides a stable revenue stream.

3. **Freemium:** With the freemium model, you offer a basic version of your ebook or publication for free and provide additional premium content for a fee. This allows readers to get a taste of your work before deciding to invest in the premium features. Consider providing exclusive chapters, bonus materials, or advanced content to incentivize readers to upgrade to the premium version.

4. **Crowdfunding:** Crowdfunding platforms allow you to raise funds to support the creation of your ebook or publication. You can offer different tiers of rewards to backers, such as early access to the ebook, personalized content, or limited edition versions. Crowdfunding not only provides financial support but also helps build a community around your work.

It is essential to choose a monetization model that aligns with your target audience's preferences and expectations. Consider experimenting with different models and gathering feedback to refine your strategy.

Marketing and Promotion

To maximize the monetization potential of your XeLaTeX ebooks and digital publications, it is crucial to develop a robust marketing and promotion strategy. Here are some effective techniques to consider:

+ **Create a compelling cover and description:** Invest in professional cover design and write a captivating description that highlights the unique value your ebook or publication offers. A visually appealing cover combined with persuasive copy can significantly impact your sales.

+ **Leverage social media and content marketing:** Build a strong online presence by utilizing social media platforms and creating engaging content related to your ebook's topic. Share sneak peeks, behind-the-scenes content, and expert tips to generate interest and attract potential readers.

+ **Collaborate with influencers and experts:** Partner with influencers or experts in your niche to promote your ebook or publication. Their endorsement can significantly impact your visibility and credibility among their followers.

+ **Run targeted advertising campaigns:** Utilize online advertising platforms to reach your target audience effectively. Platforms like Google Ads and social media advertising allow you to target specific demographics, interests, and locations.

+ **Offer limited-time discounts and promotions:** Create a sense of urgency by offering time-limited discounts or promotions. This can encourage potential readers to make a purchase decision sooner rather than later.

+ **Collect and leverage customer reviews:** Encourage readers to leave reviews and ratings for your ebook or publication. Positive reviews act as social proof and can significantly influence potential readers' purchasing decisions.

Remember that marketing and promotion are ongoing processes. Continuously evaluate the effectiveness of your strategies and make adjustments based on reader feedback and market trends.

Protecting Intellectual Property

When monetizing XeLaTeX ebooks and digital publications, it is crucial to safeguard your intellectual property rights. Consider the following steps to protect your work:

+ **Copyright registration:** Register your ebook or publication with the relevant copyright authorities to establish your ownership and protect against unauthorized use.

+ **Digital rights management (DRM):** Implement DRM technologies to prevent unauthorized copying, printing, or sharing of your content. DRM tools encrypt the ebook or publication, making it accessible only to legitimate buyers.

+ **Watermarking:** Apply digital watermarks to your XeLaTeX documents to deter unauthorized dissemination. Watermarks help identify the original owner and discourage piracy.

+ **License agreements:** Clearly define the terms and conditions of use through license agreements. Specify how readers are allowed to use the content and any restrictions on sharing or reproducing it.

By taking proactive measures, you can reduce the risk of piracy and protect your intellectual property rights.

Analyzing and Optimizing Performance

To ensure the success of your monetization efforts, it is essential to regularly analyze and optimize your ebook's performance. Consider the following metrics and strategies:

- **Sales and revenue tracking:** Monitor the performance of your ebook or publication by tracking sales and revenue metrics. Identify patterns and trends to understand which monetization strategies are most effective.

- **Reader feedback and reviews:** Pay close attention to reader feedback and reviews. Identify areas for improvement and make necessary revisions to enhance the overall quality of your content.

- **Conversion rate optimization (CRO):** Continuously optimize your ebook's landing page or sales funnel to improve conversion rates. Experiment with different layouts, copywriting techniques, and calls-to-action to identify what resonates best with your target audience.

- **A/B testing:** Conduct A/B tests to compare different elements of your ebook or publication, such as cover design, pricing, or promotional strategies. Collect data to identify the approach that yields the highest conversions.

- **Engage with your audience:** Interact with your readers, gather feedback, and address any concerns or issues promptly. Building a strong relationship with your audience fosters trust and loyalty, leading to repeat purchases and positive word-of-mouth.

Regularly analyze your ebook's performance, experiment with optimization strategies, and adapt your approach based on reader insights to maximize monetization potential.

Case Study: Successful XeLaTeX Ebook Monetization

To illustrate the concepts discussed in this section, let's take a look at a case study of a successful XeLaTeX ebook monetization:

Title: "Mastering Scientific Writing with XeLaTeX"

Monetization Model: Pay-per-download

Marketing Strategy: The author collaborated with renowned scientific bloggers and researchers to promote the ebook and gain endorsements.   They created informative blog posts, guest articles, and social media content to generate interest and direct potential readers to a dedicated landing page.

Pricing Strategy: The author conducted extensive market research and priced the ebook competitively based on the length, quality, and niche expertise. They offered a discounted price during the initial launch period to incentivize early adoption.

Performance Optimization: The author continuously tracked sales metrics, solicited reader feedback, and implemented iterative improvements.   They conducted A/B tests for the cover design and landing page layout, resulting in a significant increase in conversion rates.

Upselling Strategy: To further monetize the content, the author developed an online course based on the ebook's concepts.   Readers who purchased the ebook were offered a special discount for enrolling in the course, creating an additional revenue stream.

Protection of Intellectual Property: The author employed DRM technologies to protect against unauthorized distribution and implemented a comprehensive license agreement that specified permitted usage and prohibited sharing.

Continuous Engagement: The author actively engaged with readers through a dedicated email newsletter and social media channels.   They responded to reader queries promptly, addressed concerns, and provided additional bonus materials and resources to build a loyal community.

This case study highlights the importance of implementing a well-rounded monetization strategy, continuous performance optimization, and engaging directly with the target audience.

Conclusion

Monetizing XeLaTeX ebooks and digital publications requires a deep understanding of the market, a well-defined monetization model, effective marketing strategies, and ongoing performance optimization. By leveraging the right strategies and analyzing reader feedback, authors and publishers can generate revenue while providing valuable content to readers. With careful planning and diligent execution, your XeLaTeX ebook or publication can become a profitable venture. Remember to continuously adapt to market trends and maintain a strong connection with your readers to maximize long-term success.

Integrating XeLaTeX with ebook authoring tools and publishing platforms

In this section, we will explore how to integrate XeLaTeX with ebook authoring tools and publishing platforms. With the increasing popularity of ebooks, it is important for authors to have a seamless workflow that allows them to create and publish their content efficiently. XeLaTeX, with its powerful typesetting capabilities and flexible features, can be a great tool for generating high-quality ebooks. We will discuss the different ebook formats, tools for creating and formatting ebooks, and how to optimize XeLaTeX for ebook publishing.

Overview of ebook formats

Before we dive into the integration of XeLaTeX with ebook authoring tools, let's briefly discuss the different ebook formats you might encounter in the publishing industry. The two most common formats are EPUB and MOBI.

EPUB (Electronic Publication) is a free and open ebook standard that is widely supported across different platforms and devices. It is based on HTML and CSS, making it suitable for text-heavy content with basic formatting requirements. EPUB supports reflowable text, which means that the content can adapt to different screen sizes and orientations.

MOBI is a proprietary ebook format developed by Amazon for their Kindle devices. It is based on the older Mobipocket format, which in turn is based on HTML and CSS. MOBI files are typically used for Kindle ebooks and offer similar features to EPUB, including reflowable text and basic formatting options.

Tools for creating and formatting ebooks

To integrate XeLaTeX with ebook authoring tools, we need to consider the different software and frameworks available for creating and formatting ebooks. Here are some popular options:

1. Calibre: Calibre is a free and open-source ebook management tool that allows you to convert, edit, and organize your ebooks. It supports a wide range of formats, including EPUB and MOBI, making it a versatile tool for ebook production.

2. Sigil: Sigil is a free and open-source WYSIWYG ebook editor that allows you to create and edit EPUB ebooks. It provides a user-friendly interface for

designing and formatting your ebook's layout, making it a great tool for authors who prefer a visual approach.

3. Pandoc: Pandoc is a command-line tool that allows you to convert files from one format to another. It supports a wide range of input and output formats, including EPUB and MOBI. You can use Pandoc to convert your XeLaTeX documents to EPUB or MOBI format, allowing for easy integration with ebook authoring workflows.

4. LaTeX packages: There are several LaTeX packages available specifically for ebook production. For example, the reledmac package allows you to typeset critical editions with parallel texts, while the pandoc-citeproc package helps with bibliography management. These packages can enhance your workflow when creating ebooks with XeLaTeX.

Optimizing XeLaTeX for ebook publishing

When integrating XeLaTeX with ebook authoring tools and publishing platforms, it is important to optimize your XeLaTeX code for ebook production. Here are some tips to consider:

1. Use a lightweight document class: Choose a lightweight document class, such as `memoir` or `scrbook`, to minimize the overhead in your ebook. These document classes provide flexible layout options while keeping the file size manageable.

2. Limit the use of packages: Minimize the number of packages you use in your XeLaTeX document, as each package can add extra overhead to the final ebook. Only include packages that are essential for your content.

3. Optimize images: If your ebook includes images, make sure to optimize them for ebook publishing. Use image formats such as JPEG or PNG, and reduce the image resolution to an appropriate level for screen display.

4. Use scalable fonts: Choose scalable fonts that can be easily resized without losing quality. This ensures that your text remains legible on different devices and screen sizes.

5. Test on different ebook readers: Before publishing your ebook, test it on different ebook readers to ensure that the formatting and layout are consistent across devices. This will help you identify any issues that may arise due to variations in rendering capabilities.

Example: Converting a XeLaTeX document to EPUB format

To illustrate the integration of XeLaTeX with ebook authoring tools, let's walk through an example of converting a XeLaTeX document to EPUB format using

Pandoc.

First, ensure that you have Pandoc installed on your system. You can download it from the official website (https://pandoc.org/) and follow the installation instructions.

Next, create a XeLaTeX document using your preferred editor. Include the necessary packages and document class for your content. For this example, we will use the `memoir` document class and the `graphicx` package for including images.

Once your XeLaTeX document is ready, save it as a .tex file (e.g., `mybook.tex`). Open a terminal or command prompt, navigate to the directory where your .tex file is located, and run the following command:

```
pandoc -s mybook.tex\index{tex} -o\index{o} mybook.epub\index{epub
```

This command tells Pandoc to convert the XeLaTeX document (`mybook.tex`) to EPUB format (`mybook.epub`). Pandoc will handle the conversion process and generate the EPUB file for you.

You can then open the EPUB file in an ebook reader or use an ebook authoring tool like Calibre to make further adjustments to the formatting and metadata.

Conclusion

Integrating XeLaTeX with ebook authoring tools and publishing platforms can greatly streamline the process of creating and publishing ebooks. By understanding the different ebook formats, utilizing the right tools, and optimizing your XeLaTeX code, you can produce high-quality ebooks with ease. Whether you are an author or a publisher, incorporating XeLaTeX into your ebook workflow will allow you to leverage its powerful typesetting capabilities and produce visually appealing and professionally formatted ebooks.

Best practices for ebook and digital publishing in XeLaTeX

In this section, we will explore the best practices for creating high-quality ebooks and digital publications using XeLaTeX. With the increasing popularity of digital reading devices and online publishing platforms, it is essential to understand the techniques and strategies for designing and formatting content that translates well into the digital realm. We will cover various aspects of digital publishing, including file formats, interactivity, accessibility, and optimization for different platforms.

Choosing the Right File Format

When it comes to ebook publishing, choosing the right file format is crucial for compatibility and readability across different devices and platforms. XeLaTeX provides support for generating ebooks in EPUB and MOBI formats, which are widely used by most digital reading devices.

EPUB (Electronic Publication) is an open standard format that allows dynamic content, including multimedia elements, to be embedded within the document. This format is widely supported by e-readers and modern web browsers. On the other hand, MOBI (Mobipocket) is a format developed by Amazon specifically for Kindle devices. While EPUB is generally more versatile, MOBI offers better compatibility with Kindle devices.

Before finalizing the file format, it is essential to consider the publishing platform and target audience. If you are planning to distribute the ebook through multiple platforms, EPUB is usually the recommended format. However, if you are primarily targeting Kindle users, generating the ebook in MOBI format will ensure better compatibility and optimization for the platform.

Designing Interactive and Multimedia-rich Documents

One of the advantages of digital publishing is the ability to enhance the reading experience with interactive and multimedia elements. XeLaTeX provides support for embedding various types of interactive content, such as audio, video, hyperlinks, and interactive quizzes.

To include audio and video files in your ebook, you can use the `media9` package in XeLaTeX. This package allows you to embed audio and video files in popular formats, such as MP3 and MP4, directly into your document. You can also customize the playback controls and set different options, such as autoplay and looping.

Hyperlinks are fundamental for navigation within an ebook. XeLaTeX provides the `hyperref` package, which allows you to create hyperlinks for cross-references, URLs, footnotes, and table of contents entries. It is essential to ensure that all hyperlinks are properly formatted and linked to the correct destinations within the ebook.

Adding interactive quizzes or exercises can enhance the engagement of readers. XeLaTeX provides several packages, such as `exercise` and `exam`, for creating different types of exercises, such as multiple-choice questions, fill-in-the-blanks, and matching exercises. These packages enable you to generate interactive questionnaires and evaluate the reader's progress.

Optimizing Performance for Web and Mobile

In the digital publishing world, optimizing performance is crucial to ensure fast loading times and smooth reading experiences on various devices. XeLaTeX offers several optimization techniques to enhance the performance of ebooks and digital publications.

One of the key aspects of optimization is image compression. Large image sizes can significantly slow down the loading time of an ebook. XeLaTeX provides the graphicx package, which allows you to control the resolution and compression of embedded images. It is recommended to compress images without compromising their visual quality to reduce file size.

Another effective technique is asynchronous loading of resources. XeLaTeX allows you to load resources, such as images, scripts, and stylesheets, asynchronously. This means that these resources will be loaded in the background while the ebook is being displayed, improving the overall performance.

Furthermore, it is vital to ensure that the ebook is responsive and adaptively displays content on different devices. XeLaTeX provides support for responsive design using CSS media queries. By using media queries, you can define different stylesheets for different screen sizes, ensuring that the ebook looks and functions well on various devices, including smartphones, tablets, and desktop computers.

Creating Accessible Documents

Accessibility is a critical consideration when publishing ebooks and digital content. It ensures that all readers, regardless of their abilities or assistive technologies, can access and navigate the content effectively. XeLaTeX provides support for creating accessible documents through proper markup and metadata.

To make an ebook accessible, it is important to provide alternative text descriptions for images and other visual elements. XeLaTeX allows you to include alt text for images using the graphicx package. This alt text is read aloud by screen readers, enabling visually impaired readers to understand the content.

Additionally, providing proper structure and headings within the ebook is crucial for accessibility. XeLaTeX supports semantic markup using packages like titlesec and enumerate. By using appropriate headings and hierarchical structures, readers can navigate the ebook more efficiently.

Publishing and Distribution

Once your ebook is ready, it is important to consider the publishing and distribution process. XeLaTeX provides various options for publishing and distributing ebooks to different platforms and marketplaces.

EPUB and MOBI files generated with XeLaTeX can be directly uploaded to popular digital marketplaces like Amazon Kindle Direct Publishing (KDP) and Apple Books. These platforms allow you to reach a wide audience and distribute your ebook to readers around the world.

If you prefer self-publishing, you can host the ebook on your own website or create a dedicated landing page for it. XeLaTeX-generated PDF files can also be distributed digitally and downloaded by readers.

Additionally, it is essential to keep track of sales, reviews, and user feedback. This information can help you understand your readership, make improvements to future editions, and promote your ebook effectively.

Resources and Further Reading

To delve deeper into the world of ebook and digital publishing, here are some recommended resources:

- *EPUB Straight to the Point* by Elizabeth Castro

- *Kindle Publishing Guidelines* by Amazon

- *Accessible EPUB 3* by Laura Brady

- *The Book Designer* - online resource for ebook design and formatting

- *Digital Publishing 101* - comprehensive guide to digital publishing

These resources cover various aspects of ebook creation, digital publishing standards, and best practices for designing and distributing digital content.

Tricks and Caveats

When publishing ebooks with XeLaTeX, there are a few tricks and caveats to keep in mind:

- Test your ebook on multiple devices and e-readers to ensure compatibility and consistent rendering.

- Check for any copyright restrictions or licensing requirements when including multimedia content in your ebook.

- Consider offering different formats (EPUB, MOBI, PDF) to cater to readers with different devices and preferences.

- Regularly update and optimize your ebook to fix any issues and accommodate evolving reading devices and platforms.

- Keep an eye on the latest trends and advancements in ebook publishing to stay ahead of the competition and provide the best reading experience for your audience.

By following these best practices and considering the specific needs and preferences of your target audience, you can create professional, visually appealing, and engaging ebooks and digital publications using XeLaTeX.

XeLaTeX Extensions and Customization

Introduction to XeLaTeX Extensions and Customization

Overview of XeLaTeX Extensions and Packages

In this section, we will explore the various extensions and packages available in XeLaTeX that enhance its functionality and offer additional features for document creation and customization. These extensions and packages allow users to extend the capabilities of XeLaTeX and tailor it to their specific needs. We will cover some popular and useful options that can be used to customize document styles, manage macros, handle fonts, create bibliographies, and more.

Customizing Document Styles with XeLaTeX Extensions

XeLaTeX offers several extensions that enable users to customize document styles and layouts. One widely used extension is `titlesec`, which allows for the easy customization of sectioning titles such as chapter, section, and subsection headings. With `titlesec`, users can modify font styles, spacing, alignment, and other formatting options to create visually appealing document styles.

Another popular extension is `fancyhdr`, which provides tools for customizing headers and footers in documents. Users can set headers and footers to display page numbers, chapter or section titles, and other information. Additionally, `fancyhdr` allows for customization of header and footer styles, such as font selection, alignment, and positioning.

For those who want to create professional-looking tables, the `booktabs` package is a great tool. It provides additional table formatting options, such as the ability to create horizontal lines with different thicknesses, improved spacing, and guidelines for creating visually appealing table layouts.

Creating and Managing Macros and Custom Commands in XeLaTeX

XeLaTeX allows users to define their own macros and custom commands to streamline document creation and simplify repetitive tasks. The newcommand and renewcommand commands are used to define new macros or overwrite existing ones. Macros can be used to define custom shorthand for frequently used text, formatting commands, or complex operations.

Moreover, the xparse package provides more advanced macro creation and management capabilities. It allows users to define macros with optional arguments, default values, and even complex argument structures. The xparse package is especially useful when creating macros that require flexible inputs, such as commands for generating customized tables or mathematical equations.

Extending XeLaTeX with New Fonts and Font Families

One of the most significant advantages of using XeLaTeX is its extensive support for a wide range of fonts and font families. XeLaTeX natively supports TrueType, OpenType, and PostScript fonts, which allows users to utilize a vast collection of high-quality fonts.

To extend the font options even further, the fontspec package can be used. The fontspec package provides commands for specifying fonts, changing font styles, sizes, and applying advanced font features such as ligatures and kerning. It also allows users to define font families and assign specific fonts to different document elements.

Creating and Managing Bibliographic Databases in XeLaTeX

XeLaTeX offers excellent support for bibliography management using the BibTeX system. The biblatex package provides a flexible and robust framework for creating and managing bibliographic databases in XeLaTeX documents. It supports multiple citation styles, automatic generation of reference lists, and customizable bibliography formatting options.

With biblatex, users can easily handle complex referencing requirements, such as citing specific pages, including multiple bibliographies, and managing citations for different languages. Additionally, biblatex integrates well with popular reference management tools, making it easier to import and maintain bibliographic data.

Writing and Using Custom Document Classes in XeLaTeX

XeLaTeX allows users to define their own document classes, which serve as templates for creating custom document layouts and styles. Custom document classes are particularly useful for academic institutions or organizations that require a specific document format for reports, theses, or papers.

The doc package provides essential tools for creating and documenting custom document classes. It offers commands for specifying class options, defining default settings, and documenting the class usage. With the doc package, users can create well-documented, reusable document classes that streamline document creation and ensure consistent formatting.

Creating and Using Custom Packages in XeLaTeX

Apart from defining custom document classes, users can also create custom packages to encapsulate sets of commands and functions that can be easily reused across multiple documents. Custom packages are particularly useful for handling document-specific macros or for sharing common macros and settings across a team or organization.

To create custom packages, users need to define a package file that contains the necessary commands and configurations. The package file should be properly documented using the doc package or other documentation tools. Once created, custom packages can be easily loaded into XeLaTeX documents using the usepackage command.

Best Practices for XeLaTeX Extensions and Customization

While XeLaTeX offers great flexibility for extending its capabilities, it is essential to follow some best practices to ensure smooth document processing and compatibility. Here are some key tips to keep in mind:

- Carefully choose and evaluate the extensions and packages you include in your document. Unused packages can increase compilation time and potentially introduce conflicts between packages.

- Always consult the documentation and user guides for extensions and packages to understand their usage, limitations, and potential conflicts with other packages.

- Test your document at different stages of customization to identify and resolve any issues or errors. Regular testing is crucial to ensure that modifications made using extensions and packages do not introduce unexpected behavior.

+ Keep your customizations modular and well-documented. This makes it easier to reuse or modify them in the future and simplifies collaboration with other users or projects.

+ Update your packages and extensions regularly to benefit from bug fixes, performance improvements, and new features. Keeping your packages up to date also helps ensure compatibility with the latest versions of XeLaTeX.

By following these best practices, you can make the most of XeLaTeX's extension and customization capabilities while maintaining a stable and efficient document processing workflow.

Conclusion

XeLaTeX offers a wide range of extensions and packages that enhance its functionality and allow for extensive customization. These extensions and packages enable users to create professional-looking documents, manage bibliographic data, handle fonts, and streamline document creation through macros and custom commands. By following best practices and staying updated with the latest developments in XeLaTeX, users can leverage these extensions and packages to create high-quality documents tailored to their specific needs.

Customizing document styles with XeLaTeX extensions

In XeLaTeX, document styles play a crucial role in defining the overall appearance and layout of your document. While XeLaTeX provides several built-in document classes and style options, you may sometimes need to customize the document styles to better suit your specific requirements. This is where XeLaTeX extensions come into play.

XeLaTeX extensions are additional packages and libraries that provide enhanced functionality and customization options beyond what is available in the standard XeLaTeX distribution. These extensions allow you to modify various aspects of the document style, such as fonts, headers and footers, margins, section headings, and more.

In this section, we will explore some popular XeLaTeX extensions for customizing document styles and learn how to use them effectively.

Customizing Fonts

One of the key aspects of document style customization is font selection. XeLaTeX offers great flexibility and support for using custom fonts in your documents. With the fontspec package, you can easily specify custom fonts for different elements of your document, such as the main text, headings, captions, and so on.

To use a custom font in your document, you first need to install it on your system or download it from a trusted source. Once you have the font files, you can load them into your document using the fontspec package and its setmainfont command. For example, to use the "Arial" font as the main text font, you can add the following code to your preamble:

```
\setmainfont{Arial}
```

You can also specify additional font features, such as bold, italic, small caps, and different font sizes, using the fontspec package. For example, to use the "Arial" font in bold and italic styles, you can modify the code as follows:

```
\setmainfont[
    BoldFont = Arial Bold,
    ItalicFont = Arial Italic
]{Arial}
```

Furthermore, XeLaTeX supports various font formats, including TrueType (.ttf), OpenType (.otf), and PostScript Type 1 (.pfb). This means you have a wide range of fonts to choose from when customizing your document style.

Adjusting Page Layout

Another important aspect of document style customization is adjusting the page layout. With the geometry package, you can easily modify the page margins, paper size, and other layout parameters to achieve the desired look for your document.

To change the page margins, you can use the geometry package and its margin command. For example, to set the left and right margins to 1 inch, and the top and bottom margins to 0.75 inches, you can add the following code to your preamble:

```
\geometry{
```

```
    left=1in,
    right=1in,
    top=0.75in,
    bottom=0.75in,
}
```

You can also adjust the paper size using the geometry package. For example, to set the paper size to A4, you can modify the code as follows:

```
\geometry{
    a4paper,
    left=1in,
    right=1in,
    top=0.75in,
    bottom=0.75in,
}
```

The geometry package provides many other options for fine-tuning the page layout, including adjusting the header and footer heights, specifying the binding offset for double-sided printing, and setting the page style for different sections of your document.

Customizing Section Headings

Section headings play a crucial role in organizing the content of your document. By default, XeLaTeX provides a set of predefined sectioning commands, such as
chapter,
section,
subsection, etc., which you can use to structure your document.

However, if you want to customize the appearance of section headings, you can use the titlesec package. This package provides a flexible and easy-to-use interface for customizing sectioning commands.

To modify the appearance of section headings, you first need to load the titlesec package in your preamble:

Once the package is loaded, you can use the various commands provided by the package to customize the section headings. For example, to change the font size of the section headings to 14pt and make them bold, you can add the following code to your preamble:

```
\titleformat{\section}
{\normalfont\fontsize{14}{16}\bfseries}{\thesection}{1em}{}
```

Similarly, you can customize the appearance of other sectioning commands, such as
`subsection`,
`subsubsection`, etc., by using the appropriate
`titleformat` command.

In addition to modifying the font size and style, the `titlesec` package also allows you to adjust the spacing before and after the section headings, add decorative lines or boxes, change the numbering style, and much more.

Overall, XeLaTeX extensions provide a rich set of tools for customizing document styles. By leveraging these extensions effectively, you can create professional-looking documents that are tailored to your specific needs.

Resources and Further Reading

To learn more about customizing document styles with XeLaTeX extensions, the following resources are highly recommended:

+ The `fontspec` package documentation: This comprehensive guide provides detailed information on using custom fonts in XeLaTeX documents. It covers various font-related features and options supported by the package.

+ The `geometry` package documentation: This documentation provides comprehensive information about adjusting the page layout in XeLaTeX using the `geometry` package. It explains the various parameters and options available for fine-tuning the page dimensions and margins.

+ The `titlesec` package documentation: This documentation offers a detailed overview of customizing section headings in XeLaTeX using the `titlesec` package. It provides examples and explanations of the various `titleformat` commands and options available for customizing the appearance of sectioning commands.

By referring to these resources and experimenting with the different options provided by XeLaTeX extensions, you can explore the endless possibilities of customizing document styles and create visually stunning documents tailored to your specific needs.

Exercises

1. Customize the font size and style of subsection headings to be italicized and underlined.

2. Adjust the page margins of your document to have equal left and right margins, and larger top and bottom margins.

3. Create a custom sectioning command called "Introduction" that uses a larger font size and a different font family.

4. Experiment with different fonts and typography features to create a unique document style that matches your personal preference.

5. Explore other XeLaTeX extensions, such as `fancyhdr` for customizing headers and footers, and `tocloft` for customizing the table of contents.

Note: Make sure to refer to the documentation and resources mentioned above for further guidance.

Summary

In this section, we have explored how to customize document styles in XeLaTeX using extensions. We discussed how to customize fonts, adjust page layout, and modify section headings. By using XeLaTeX extensions effectively, you can create visually appealing and personalized documents that meet your specific requirements. Remember to refer to the documentation and resources provided for further information and guidance.

Creating and managing macros and custom commands in XeLaTeX

In XeLaTeX, macros and custom commands are powerful tools that allow you to define your own commands and automate repetitive tasks. Macros are defined using the \newcommand or \renewcommand commands, and they can take arguments and perform specific actions based on those arguments. In this section, we will explore how to create and manage macros and custom commands in XeLaTeX.

Introduction to macros and custom commands

Macros in XeLaTeX allow you to define your own commands to simplify and automate common tasks. They are especially useful when you find yourself repeating a particular sequence of commands or when you want to create a shortcut for a complex set of instructions. Custom commands, on the other hand, are macros that you define with specific functionality in mind.

Macros and custom commands have the following benefits:

- They improve code readability and maintainability by abstracting complex or repetitive code into a single command.

- They allow for consistency and standardization in document formatting.

- They make it easier to modify the document structure or style by making changes to a single command definition.

- They enable the creation of new commands specific to your needs, enhancing the functionality of XeLaTeX.

Defining macros in XeLaTeX

To define a new macro in XeLaTeX, you can use the \newcommand or \renewcommand command. The basic syntax for defining a macro is as follows:

```
\newcommand{\commandname}[numargs]{definition}
```

Here, \commandname is the name of your command, numargs is the number of arguments your command takes, and definition is the code that gets executed when the macro is called.

Let's say you frequently use the phrase "Lorem ipsum dolor sit amet" in your document. Instead of typing it out every time, you can define a macro to save time and effort. Here's an example:

```
\newcommand{\lipsum}{Lorem ipsum dolor sit amet}
```

Now, whenever you want to use the phrase "Lorem ipsum dolor sit amet", you can simply type \lipsum.

Passing arguments to macros

Macros can also take arguments, allowing for greater flexibility. You can specify the number of arguments your macro takes by adding an optional argument to the \newcommand or \renewcommand command.

For example, let's say you want to create a macro for formatting vectors. You can define a macro called \vec that takes one argument representing the vector. Here's how you can define it:

```
\newcommand{\vec}[1]{\mathbf{\#1}}
```

Now, whenever you want to typeset a vector, you can simply use the `\vec` command with the vector as the argument. For example, `\vec{v}` will produce v.

You can define macros with multiple arguments as well. For instance, if you want to create a macro for typesetting derivatives, you can define a macro called `\der` that takes two arguments: the function and the variable. Here's an example:

```
\newcommand{\der}[2]{\frac{d\#1}{d\#2}}
```

Now, you can use the `\der` command to typeset derivatives. For example, `\der{f}{x}` will produce $\frac{df}{dx}$.

Managing macros and custom commands

If you want to modify an existing macro, you can use the `\renewcommand` command. This is useful when you want to change the behavior of a predefined macro or override an existing command. The syntax is similar to `\newcommand`.

To redefine the `\lipsum` macro we defined earlier, you can use the following command:

```
\renewcommand{\lipsum}{Lorem ipsum dolor sit amet, consectetur a
```

If you define a lot of macros or have a complex document with many custom commands, it's good practice to organize them in a separate file and include it using the `\input` command.

Best practices for creating macros and custom commands

When creating macros and custom commands in XeLaTeX, it's important to follow best practices to ensure code readability and maintainability. Here are some tips to keep in mind:

- Choose meaningful names for your macros and custom commands to make their purpose clear.

- Document your macros and custom commands, explaining what they do and how they should be used.

- Use comments within your code to explain complex or non-intuitive parts.

- Test your macros and custom commands to ensure they work as expected.

- Avoid redefining existing macros unless necessary, and use `\renewcommand` sparingly.

- Consider using packages like `etoolbox` or `xparse` for more advanced macro and command management.

By creating and managing macros and custom commands effectively, you can significantly enhance your productivity and make your XeLaTeX documents more readable and maintainable.

Summary

In this section, we explored the creation and management of macros and custom commands in XeLaTeX. We learned that macros and custom commands are powerful tools that allow us to define our own commands and automate repetitive tasks. We discussed the syntax for defining macros, passing arguments to macros, and managing macros and custom commands. Additionally, we provided some best practices for creating macros and custom commands. By applying these techniques, you can improve the efficiency and maintainability of your XeLaTeX documents.

Extending XeLaTeX with new fonts and font families

In this section, we will explore how to extend XeLaTeX's font capabilities by incorporating new fonts and font families into your documents. Fonts play a crucial role in the overall look and feel of your document, and XeLaTeX offers great flexibility in terms of font selection and customization.

Introduction to Fonts in XeLaTeX

Fonts are a fundamental aspect of typesetting, allowing you to express your content in different styles and visual representations. XeLaTeX, unlike its predecessor LaTeX, has native support for TrueType (TTF) and OpenType (OTF) fonts, making it easier to use a wide range of fonts in your documents.

With XeLaTeX, you can utilize system fonts installed on your computer or include custom font files directly in your document. This flexibility opens up a world of possibilities for experimenting with different font styles and creating unique typographic designs.

Installing Fonts in XeLaTeX

Before you can use a particular font in XeLaTeX, you need to make sure it is installed on your system. System fonts are typically stored in specific directories, such as `/usr/share/fonts`, `/Library/Fonts`, or `C:\Windows\Fonts`.

To check if a font is installed, you can use the `fc-list` command on Linux and macOS or the Fonts Control Panel on Windows. This will provide you with a list of all available fonts on your system.

If you have a custom font file that is not already installed, you can add it to your XeLaTeX project directory. XeLaTeX provides the `fontspec` package, which allows you to specify custom font files using their file path.

For example, to include a font file named `MyFont.otf`, you can use the following command:

```
\setmainfont{MyFont.otf}
```

This command sets the main font of your document to `MyFont.otf`. You can also specify different font styles, such as `Bold`, `Italic`, or `BoldItalic`, by appending them to the font name:

```
\setmainfont{MyFont-Bold.otf}[BoldFont=MyFont-Bold.otf]
\setromanfont{MyFont-Italic.otf}[ItalicFont=MyFont-Italic.otf]
```

This way, you can use different font variations within your document.

Loading Font Families in XeLaTeX

In addition to individual fonts, XeLaTeX allows you to load font families into your document. A font family typically consists of related fonts with different weights, styles, and variants. For instance, a font family may include Regular, Bold, Italic, and Bold Italic variations.

To load a font family in XeLaTeX, you can use the command `newfontfamily` provided by the `fontspec` package. For example, let's say you have a font family named `MyFont` with the following font files:

- `MyFont-Regular.otf`

- `MyFont-Bold.otf`

- `MyFont-Italic.otf`

- `MyFont-BoldItalic.otf`

You can load this font family in your document using the following commands:

```
\newfontfamily{\myfontregular}{MyFont-Regular.otf}
\newfontfamily{\myfontbold}{MyFont-Bold.otf}
\newfontfamily{\myfontitalic}{MyFont-Italic.otf}
\newfontfamily{\myfontbolditalic}{MyFont-BoldItalic.otf}
```

Now, you can use the font family commands to switch between different font styles within your document. For example:

```
{\myfontregular This is regular text.}
{\myfontbold This is bold text.}
{\myfontitalic This is italic text.}
{\myfontbolditalic This is bold italic text.}
```

By defining font families like this, you can easily apply consistent styles throughout your document.

Customizing Fonts in XeLaTeX

XeLaTeX provides various options for customizing fonts to suit your specific needs. Some common customization techniques include:

- Adjusting font size: You can change the font size using commands like `\Large` or `\Huge`. Alternatively, you can use `\fontsize{size}{baseline_skip}` to set a specific font size.

- Changing font color: The `xcolor` package allows you to change the color of the text using commands like `\textcolor{color}{text}`.

- Setting font features: XeLaTeX offers the `fontspec` package, which allows you to specify various font features such as letter-spacing, ligatures, or small caps. For example, you can enable ligatures using the command `\defaultfontfeatures{Ligatures=Common}`.

- Combining fonts: XeLaTeX makes it easy to combine multiple fonts within a document. You can define different font families and switch between them at different points in your document to create a visually appealing layout.

Experimenting with these customization options will help you achieve the desired typographic effects and enhance the visual impact of your document.

Resources for Fonts in XeLaTeX

Finding the right font for your document can be overwhelming due to the vast number of choices available. Here are some resources to help you discover and use high-quality fonts in XeLaTeX:

- Google Fonts (`https://fonts.google.com`): Offers a wide range of high-quality, open-source fonts that can be easily integrated into your XeLaTeX documents.

- Adobe Fonts (`https://fonts.adobe.com`): Provides a vast collection of professional fonts, including both free and paid options. Adobe Fonts offers seamless integration with XeLaTeX.

- Font Squirrel (`https://www.fontsquirrel.com`): A platform that curates a diverse selection of free fonts for commercial use. You can find a variety of styles and categories, making it easier to find the perfect font for your project.

- The LaTeX Font Catalogue (`https://tug.org/FontCatalogue`): An extensive catalog of fonts specifically designed for LaTeX and XeLaTeX. This resource provides detailed information about each font, including usage and installation instructions.

Remember to always respect font licensing terms when using custom fonts in your documents.

Conclusion

In this section, we explored how to extend XeLaTeX's font capabilities by incorporating new fonts and font families into your documents. We discussed the importance of fonts in typesetting and the flexibility that XeLaTeX offers in terms of font selection and customization.

We learned how to install fonts on your system and how to include custom font files in your XeLaTeX document. We also explored loading font families and customizing fonts using various options provided by XeLaTeX packages.

Additionally, we provided some resources to help you discover and utilize high-quality fonts in your XeLaTeX projects. By leveraging these font capabilities, you can create visually stunning and personalized documents with XeLaTeX.

Creating and managing bibliographic databases in XeLaTeX

Creating and managing bibliographic databases is an essential task for researchers, academics, and anyone involved in scholarly writing. XeLaTeX provides powerful tools and packages for handling bibliographic information, making it a popular choice for producing professional-looking documents with accurate and well-organized citations and references.

In this section, we will explore the principles and techniques of creating and managing bibliographic databases in XeLaTeX. We will cover the basics of bibliographic data organization, integration with citation management software, generating citations and references in XeLaTeX documents, and troubleshooting common issues. Let's dive in!

Basics of bibliographic data organization

Before we delve into the technical aspects of managing bibliographic databases in XeLaTeX, let's first understand the core principles of bibliographic data organization.

A bibliographic database is a collection of bibliographic records that contain all the necessary information about a publication, such as the author(s), title, journal or book title, publication year, and other relevant metadata. Typically, bibliographic data is stored in a structured format, such as the BibTeX or BibLaTeX format, which allows for easy manipulation and integration with XeLaTeX documents.

When creating a bibliographic database, it's important to ensure consistency and accuracy in the data. This includes verifying the correctness of author names, capitalization, and punctuation. It's also a good practice to include unique identifiers for each record, such as DOIs (Digital Object Identifiers) or ISBNs (International Standard Book Numbers), to facilitate easy referencing and citation retrieval.

Additionally, organizing bibliographic data into categories or tags can greatly simplify searching and filtering within the database. Categories can be based on the subject area, publication type, or any other relevant criteria. Using a consistent and logical naming convention for these categories will allow for efficient retrieval of specific references when needed.

Now that we have a basic understanding of bibliographic data organization, let's explore how to integrate and manage bibliographic databases in XeLaTeX.

Integration with citation management software

One of the advantages of using XeLaTeX for creating scholarly documents is the seamless integration with citation management software. Popular reference managers such as Zotero, Mendeley, and EndNote allow users to create and organize bibliographic databases and export them in various formats, including BibTeX and BibLaTeX.

To integrate a bibliographic database from a reference manager into XeLaTeX, you can export the database as a .bib file and include it in your XeLaTeX project. The .bib file contains all the necessary information to generate citations and references in your document.

To include the .bib file in your XeLaTeX document, you can use the \bibliographystyle command to specify the desired citation style and the \bibliogrphy command to define the location of the .bib file. For example:

```
\bibliographystyle{apa}
\bibliography{references.bib}
```

In this example, `apa` is the chosen bibliographic style, and `references.bib` is the name of the .bib file containing the bibliographic data.

Generating citations and references

Once the bibliographic database is integrated into your XeLaTeX document, you can easily generate citations and references using the \cite and \citep commands.

The \cite command is used for in-text citations, while the \citep command is used for parenthetical citations. You can specify one or multiple citation keys within the commands to generate the corresponding citations. For example:

```
According to \cite{smith2021}, ...
Several studies have shown similar results \citep{johnson2019, d
```

In the above example, the citation keys `smith2021`, `johnson2019`, and `doe2020` correspond to specific entries in the bibliographic database.

To generate a list of references at the end of your document, you can use the \printbibliography command. This command will automatically format the references based on the chosen bibliographic style. For example:

```
\printbibliography
```

With just a few commands, you can easily generate properly formatted citations and references in your XeLaTeX document, saving you precious time and effort.

Troubleshooting common issues

While managing bibliographic databases in XeLaTeX is generally straightforward, you may encounter some common issues along the way. Let's explore a few troubleshooting tips to help you resolve these issues.

Missing or incorrect citations: If you notice that citations are missing or incorrect in your document, the first step is to ensure that the citation keys used in the `\cite` or `\citep` commands match the keys in your bibliographic database. Additionally, double-check the formatting of the citation commands to ensure they are correct.

Missing or incorrect references: If references are missing or displayed incorrectly in the generated bibliography, make sure that the entries in your .bib file are properly formatted. Check for any missing or incorrect fields, such as missing author names or publication titles. Also, verify that the chosen bibliographic style is compatible with the fields in your database.

Inconsistent capitalization or formatting: In some cases, the capitalization or formatting of titles or author names in the generated bibliography may be inconsistent or incorrect. This can usually be resolved by ensuring that the fields in your .bib file are consistently formatted. Use curly braces () to preserve capitalization or special formatting when necessary.

Missing or incorrect bibliographic style: If the references are not formatted as expected or if you want to change the bibliographic style, make sure that the chosen style is available and correctly specified in the `\bibliographystyle` command.

Citation style customization: If you need to customize the citation style further, such as adding additional information or modifying the citation format, you can refer to the documentation of the chosen bibliographic style or explore additional XeLaTeX packages, such as `natbib` or `biblatex`, which offer more advanced customization options.

Best practices for managing bibliographic databases in XeLaTeX

To ensure smooth and efficient management of bibliographic databases in XeLaTeX, here are some best practices to keep in mind:

+ Regularly backup your bibliographic database to avoid any data loss.

+ Use a consistent naming convention for citation keys to facilitate easy referencing.

+ Verify the accuracy and completeness of bibliographic data before including it in your .bib file.

+ Regularly update your bibliographic database to include new publications and remove outdated references.

+ Utilize dedicated reference management software to streamline the process of organizing and exporting bibliographic data.

+ Periodically review and clean up your .bib file to remove duplicate entries or incorrect information.

+ Keep a record of any modifications or customizations made to the bibliographic style for future reference.

+ Familiarize yourself with the various options and capabilities of XeLaTeX packages, such as `natbib` or `biblatex`, to customize the citation style and formatting.

By following these best practices, you will be able to efficiently create and manage bibliographic databases in XeLaTeX, ensuring accurate and well-formatted citations and references in your scholarly documents.

Conclusion

In this section, we explored the principles and techniques of creating and managing bibliographic databases in XeLaTeX. We discussed the basics of bibliographic data organization, integration with citation management software, generating citations and references, troubleshooting common issues, and best practices for efficient database management.

With XeLaTeX and its seamless integration with bibliographic data, you can effortlessly generate professional-looking citations and references in your scholarly documents. Proper management of bibliographic databases will not only save you time and effort but also ensure accuracy and consistency in your research work. So go ahead and embrace XeLaTeX's powerful tools for managing bibliographic databases to enhance your scholarly writing experience.

Writing and using custom document classes in XeLaTeX

In XeLaTeX, document classes are used to define the overall structure and formatting of a document. While there are several built-in document classes available, such as article, report, and book, it is often necessary to create custom document classes to meet specific requirements. Custom document classes allow users to define their own document layouts, styles, and functionalities.

Creating a custom document class

To create a custom document class in XeLaTeX, we need to follow a few steps.

First, we need to create a new file with a `.cls` extension, for example, `myclass.cls`. This file will contain the definition of our custom document class.

Next, we need to start the file with the `\NeedsTeXFormat{LaTeX2e}` command, which specifies the minimum version of LaTeX required for the class.

We also need to declare our class using the `\ProvidesClass` command. The syntax for this command is `\ProvidesClass{<classname>}[<date> <version> <description>]`. For example, we can declare our custom class as follows:

```
\ProvidesClass{myclass}[2022/01/01 v1.0 Custom document class]
```

After declaring the class, we can proceed to define its structure and options.

Defining class options

Class options allow users to customize the behavior of the document class. We can define options using the `\DeclareOption` command. The syntax for this command is `\DeclareOption{<option>}{<code>}`.

For example, let's define a class option called `twoside` which sets the document to have two-sided printing:

```
\DeclareOption{twoside}{\@twosidetrue}
```

We can also set default values for options using the `\ExecuteOptions` command. For example, let's set the default value of the `twoside` option to false:

```
\ExecuteOptions{oneside}
```

Setting up the class environment

Next, we need to set up the class environment by defining the `\LoadClass` command. The `\LoadClass` command loads a basic document class, such as `article`, `report`, or `book`, and inherits its default settings.

For example, if we want our custom class to be based on the 'article' class, we can use the following command:

```
\LoadClass[a4paper,12pt]{article}
```

Customizing the class layout and styles

We can customize various aspects of the class layout and styles by redefining existing commands or defining new ones.

For example, we can set the page margins using the 'geometry' package:

```
\RequirePackage[a4paper, margin=1in]{geometry}
```

We can also define new environments or modify existing ones to add custom functionality. For example, let's define a new environment called 'mybox':

```
\newenvironment{mybox}{\begin{mdframed}[backgroundcolor=gray!20]
```

Using the custom document class

Once the custom document class is defined, we can use it in our LaTeX documents by adding the `\documentclass` command at the beginning of the document:

```
\documentclass{myclass}
```

We can also pass options to the custom class using the `\documentclass` command. For example, to enable two-sided printing, we can use:

```
\documentclass[twoside]{myclass}
```

Example Usage

Let's consider an example where we want to create a custom document class for conference papers. We want the papers to be formatted in a two-column layout, with specific fonts, headers, and footers.

We can start by creating a new file called `conference.cls` and defining our custom class as follows:

```
\NeedsTeXFormat{LaTeX2e}
\ProvidesClass{conference}[2022/01/01 v1.0 Custom conference class
\DeclareOption{twocolumn}{\@twocolumntrue}
\DeclareOption{oneside}{\@twocolumnfalse}
\ExecuteOptions{oneside}
\LoadClass[a4paper, 12pt]{article}

% Custom layout and styles code here
...
```

In this example, we have defined a class option `twocolumn` for enabling the two-column layout. By default, the class uses the `oneside` option, which sets the document to single-column layout.

We can further customize the class by adding additional code for setting specific fonts, headers, footers, and other formatting requirements.

To use our custom class, we can create a new LaTeX document and add the following line at the beginning:

```
\documentclass[twocolumn]{conference}
```

This will load our custom document class and format the document according to its specifications.

Resources

Learning XeLaTeX and creating custom document classes can be challenging, but there are many resources available to help you get started. Here are some recommended resources:

- **XeLaTeX:** A comprehensive guide on XeLaTeX can be found in the book "XeLaTeX for Beginners" by ShareLaTeX.

- **LaTeX Wikibook:** The LaTeX Wikibook provides extensive documentation on LaTeX, including information on custom document classes.

- **TeX Stack Exchange:** The TeX Stack Exchange is a community-driven Q&A site where you can ask questions about LaTeX and get answers from experienced LaTeX users.

These resources, along with practice and experimentation, will help you master the art of creating custom document classes in XeLaTeX.

Exercises

1. Create a custom document class for a scientific journal article with the following features:

   - Two-column layout

   - Customized fonts and spacing

   - Numbered sections and subsections

   - Author affiliations and contact information

   - References section with proper formatting

2. Modify the custom document class from the previous exercise to support multiple languages. Add support for displaying article titles, section headings, and figure captions in different languages based on user preferences.

Conclusion

Custom document classes in XeLaTeX provide flexibility and customization options for creating documents with unique layouts, styles, and functionalities. By defining our own document classes, we can tailor the LaTeX environment to suit specific requirements. With practice and experimentation, we can create professional and aesthetically pleasing documents using XeLaTeX's powerful features.

In the next section, we will explore advanced techniques for extending XeLaTeX's capabilities through custom packages and extensions.

Creating and using custom packages in XeLaTeX

Custom packages in XeLaTeX allow users to extend the functionality of the standard LaTeX packages or create entirely new ones to suit their specific needs. In this section, we will explore the process of creating and using custom packages in XeLaTeX, providing step-by-step instructions and examples.

Creating a custom package

To create a custom package in XeLaTeX, follow these steps:

1. Create a separate .sty file for your package. This file should have a unique name that reflects the purpose of the package (e.g., mypackage.sty).

2. Open the .sty file in a text editor and start by adding the necessary package documentation. This documentation should include a brief description of the package, its version number, and the author's name and contact information.

3. Next, define any new commands, environments, or options that your package will provide. For example, if your package is intended to simplify the inclusion of code snippets in a document, you might define a new environment called "codebox" and a command called "inlinecode."

Here's an example of how you can define a new command in your custom package:

```
\newcommand{\hello}[1]{Hello, \#1!}
```

4. After defining the commands and environments, you can include any necessary external packages or libraries that your package depends on. This is done using the \RequirePackage command.

5. Finally, save the .sty file and place it in a location where LaTeX can find it. One common location is the same directory as your main LaTeX document. Alternatively, you can place it in the local texmf tree or in a separate folder dedicated to custom packages.

Using a custom package

Once you have created a custom package, you can use it in your LaTeX document by following these steps:

1. Start by loading the package using the \usepackage command. For example, if your custom package is called "mypackage," you can load it using:

2. After loading the package, you can now use any commands, environments, or options provided by the package in your LaTeX document. For example, if your custom package defined a command called "hello," you can use it like this:

```
\hello{XeLaTeX Secrets}
```

3. Remember to compile your LaTeX document with XeLaTeX to ensure that the custom package is properly loaded and applied.

Best practices for creating and using custom packages

Here are some best practices to keep in mind when creating and using custom packages in XeLaTeX:

1. Name your custom package file with a .sty extension to indicate that it is a LaTeX package.

2. Use descriptive and unique names for your package to avoid conflicts with existing packages.

3. Include comprehensive documentation within your package file, explaining its purpose, usage, and any additional dependencies.

4. Test your package thoroughly before using it in production documents to ensure its compatibility and reliability.

5. Consider sharing your custom packages with the LaTeX community by uploading them to CTAN (Comprehensive TeX Archive Network) or other package repositories.

6. When using custom packages created by others, ensure that you have the latest version and that it is compatible with your current LaTeX distribution.

Example: Creating a custom package for code listings

Let's say we want to create a custom package for including code listings in our LaTeX documents. We'll call our package "codelistings."

1. Create a file called "codelistings.sty" and open it in a text editor.

2. Add the package documentation:

```
% codelistings.sty
% A package for including code listings in LaTeX documents
% Version: 1.0
% Author: John Doe (johndoe@example.com)
```

3. Define the necessary commands and environments:

```
\RequirePackage{listings}

\newenvironment{codelisting}
{
    \lstset{basicstyle=\ttfamily}
    \begin{lstlisting}
}
{
    \end{lstlisting}
}

\newcommand{\inlinecode}[1]{\lstinline{\#1}}
```

4. Save the file and place it in the same directory as your main LaTeX document.
5. In your main LaTeX document, load the package:

6. Now you can use the "codelisting" environment to include code listings:

```
\begin{codelisting}
\#include <stdio.h>

int main() {
    printf("Hello, World!");
    return 0;
}
\end{codelisting}
```

By creating and using custom packages in XeLaTeX, you can greatly enhance the functionality and flexibility of your documents. Whether it's simplifying complex tasks or adding new features, custom packages are a powerful tool for XeLaTeX users.

Additional Resources

- The LaTeX Wikibook: https://en.wikibooks.org/wiki/LaTeX
    - The Comprehensive TeX Archive Network (CTAN): https://ctan.org
    - "TeX Stack Exchange" Q&A community: https://tex.stackexchange.com

Customizing the XeLaTeX Compiler and Build Process

In this section, we will explore how to customize the XeLaTeX compiler and build process to suit your specific needs and preferences. We will cover various aspects such as compiler options, build tools, and automation techniques. By the end of this section, you will have a better understanding of how to optimize your XeLaTeX workflow and achieve efficient and streamlined document compilation.

Compiler Options

The XeLaTeX compiler provides a variety of options that allow you to customize the compilation process. These options can be specified either through command-line arguments or within the document itself. Let's take a look at some commonly used compiler options:

+ **-interaction:** This option controls the interaction mode of the compiler. The possible values are *batchmode, nonstopmode, scrollmode,* and *errorstopmode.* By default, XeLaTeX runs in *errorstopmode,* which halts compilation on the first error. You can use other modes for automated or batch processing when you don't need user interaction.

+ **-output-directory:** This option allows you to specify the output directory for generated files. By default, XeLaTeX creates output files in the same directory as the source file. You can use this option to organize your project files and keep the source directory clean.

+ **-aux-directory:** This option sets the directory for auxiliary files generated during compilation. Auxiliary files include .aux, .log, and .toc files, among others. You can use this option to separate auxiliary files from the main document files.

+ **-jobname:** This option lets you specify a custom name for the output file. By default, XeLaTeX generates an output file with the same base name as the source file. This option is useful when you want to generate output files with specific names.

+ **-draftmode:** This option tells XeLaTeX to compile the document in draft mode. In this mode, images and other expensive operations are skipped, resulting in faster compilation. This is helpful when you are working on a large document and want to save compilation time during the development phase.

+ **-halt-on-error:** This option causes XeLaTeX to stop immediately if an error occurs during compilation. By default, XeLaTeX continues compilation despite errors and generates a document with error messages. Using this option ensures that the compilation stops at the first error, which can be useful for debugging purposes.

These are just a few examples of the options available for customizing the XeLaTeX compiler. You can explore the complete list of options in the XeLaTeX documentation.

Build Tools

While XeLaTeX provides a command-line interface for compilation, you can streamline and automate the build process using various build tools. These tools simplify the compilation workflow and allow you to define custom build configurations. Let's discuss some popular build tools and their features:

+ **latexmk:** latexmk is a powerful build tool that automates the compilation process. It automatically detects changes in source files and triggers recompilation only when necessary. It also takes care of multiple passes required by LaTeX to resolve cross-references, bibliographies, and tables of contents. latexmk supports XeLaTeX and provides a wide range of configuration options.

+ **arara:** arara is another build automation tool specifically designed for LaTeX. It uses YAML-based configuration files to define build rules. You can specify the desired compiler, output directories, and other options in the configuration file. arara automatically determines the correct sequence of compilation commands based on the dependencies and orders the tasks accordingly.

+ **Make:** Make is a general-purpose build tool that can be used with any programming language, including XeLaTeX. It allows you to define build rules and dependencies in a Makefile. Make automatically rebuilds the target files when their dependencies change. You can use Make to control the entire compilation process, including invoking XeLaTeX with the desired options.

+ **CMake:** CMake is a cross-platform build system generator that simplifies the building and compiling of projects. Although primarily used for C/C++

projects, it can be adapted to handle XeLaTeX projects as well. CMake allows you to define build configurations and generate platform-specific build scripts. This can be particularly useful when working on multi-platform projects that involve different build environments.

These build tools provide flexibility and automation to the XeLaTeX compilation process. Choosing the right tool depends on your specific requirements and preferences.

Automation Techniques

To further enhance your workflow and eliminate manual intervention, you can employ automation techniques for XeLaTeX document compilation. These techniques help save time and maintain consistency throughout the build process. Let's explore some commonly used automation techniques:

+ **Scripts:** You can write custom scripts to automate the compilation process. Scripts can be written in languages like Python, Bash, PowerShell, or any other scripting language of your choice. Scripts allow you to define custom compilation steps, handle dependencies, and perform additional tasks such as cleaning up temporary files or creating backups.

+ **Continuous Integration/Continuous Deployment (CI/CD):** CI/CD systems like Jenkins, Travis CI, or GitHub Actions can be used to automate the compilation and deployment of XeLaTeX documents. These systems continuously monitor your project repository, triggering compilation whenever changes are pushed. They help maintain a consistent build environment and can integrate with version control systems to keep track of changes and manage revision history.

+ **Makefile Integration:** If you are already using Make as a build tool, you can Integrate XeLaTeX compilation into the Makefile. Create build rules that invoke XeLaTeX with the desired options, specify dependencies, and handle common tasks like cleaning intermediate files or generating output formats like PDF, HTML, or ePub.

+ **Version Control Hooks:** If you are using version control systems like Git, you can utilize pre-commit and pre-push hooks to automatically trigger compilation when changes are committed or pushed. This ensures that your XeLaTeX documents are always up to date and in a buildable state.

These automation techniques are crucial for maintaining an efficient and productive workflow. They help reduce human error, speed up compilation times, and ensure that your documents are always in sync with the latest changes.

Best Practices

When customizing the XeLaTeX compiler and build process, it is essential to follow some best practices to ensure smooth and efficient document compilation. Here are some best practices to consider:

* **Use Version Control:** Keep your XeLaTeX project under version control to track changes, maintain a history, and collaborate with others. Version control systems like Git provide powerful features for branching, merging, and resolving conflicts.

* **Modularize Your Project:** Break your document into modular components, such as chapters or sections, and organize them in separate files. This makes it easier to manage and update specific parts of the document without affecting the entire project.

* **Document Dependencies:** Make sure to identify dependencies in your project, such as referenced files, images, or external packages. Provide clear instructions for installing and managing these dependencies to ensure reproducibility.

* **Perform Regular Testing:** Test your document regularly, especially after making significant changes or introducing new components. Automated tests, such as checking for compilation errors or verifying document structure and layout, can catch issues early.

* **Keep Backup Copies:** Create backup copies of your project files at different stages to ensure that you can revert to previous versions if necessary. This is especially important before making extensive changes or trying out experimental features.

* **Optimize Compilation Time:** As your project grows, compilation time may increase significantly. To optimize compilation time, consider employing techniques such as precompiling or using incremental builds to avoid recompiling unchanged parts of the document.

Following these best practices will help you maintain a well-organized and efficient XeLaTeX workflow, allowing you to focus on content creation rather than mundane compilation tasks.

Summary

In this section, we explored the various ways to customize the XeLaTeX compiler and build process. We discussed compiler options, build tools, automation techniques, and best practices. By leveraging these customization options, you can enhance your XeLaTeX workflow, improve efficiency, and achieve faster and more accurate document compilation.

Exercises

To test your understanding of customizing the XeLaTeX compiler and build process, try the following exercises:

1. Experiment with different compiler options such as changing the output directory, enabling draft mode, or specifying a custom job name. Observe the effects of these options on the compilation process and output files.

2. Choose one of the build tools mentioned in this section (latexmk, arara, Make, or CMake) and set up a simple build configuration for your XeLaTeX project. Use the tool to automate the compilation process and observe the benefits of automated builds.

3. Write a Bash or Python script that automates specific tasks related to your XeLaTeX project. For example, you can write a script that compiles the document and generates a PDF, HTML, and ePub version simultaneously.

4. Explore the integration of XeLaTeX compilation with a CI/CD system such as Jenkins or Travis CI. Set up a basic pipeline that triggers compilation upon every push to the repository and generates a report on successful builds.

These exercises will help you practice and reinforce the concepts covered in this section, enabling you to become proficient in customizing the XeLaTeX compiler and build process.

Additional Resources

To further expand your knowledge on customizing the XeLaTeX compiler and build process, you can refer to the following resources:

- *The LaTeX Companion* by Frank Mittelbach, Michel Goossens, Johannes Braams, David Carlisle, Chris Rowley. This comprehensive guide covers all aspects of LaTeX, including customization and automation techniques.

- XeLaTeX documentation: The official XeLaTeX documentation provides detailed information on compiler options, command-line arguments, and other customization features.

- Online forums and communities: Joining LaTeX forums or communities such as TeX.StackExchange or LaTeX.org can provide a wealth of knowledge and practical tips from experienced users.

- Official documentation of build tools: Refer to the official documentation of build tools like latexmk, arara, Make, or CMake for detailed information on their usage and configuration options.

With these resources, you can further explore and fine-tune your XeLaTeX workflow according to your specific requirements. Happy customizing and building!

Troubleshooting and debugging XeLaTeX extensions and customization

In this section, we will explore common issues that users may encounter when working with XeLaTeX extensions and customization. We will discuss various debugging techniques and offer troubleshooting tips to help resolve these issues. Debugging and troubleshooting are important skills for XeLaTeX users to master, as they will inevitably encounter challenges when working with complex documents and customizations.

Identifying Errors

One of the first steps in troubleshooting XeLaTeX extensions and customization is identifying the source of errors. XeLaTeX provides error messages that can help in pinpointing the issue. When encountering an error, it is important to carefully read the error message and understand its meaning.

Errors can occur for various reasons, such as syntax errors, missing packages, incorrect formatting, or conflicts between packages. It is crucial to pay attention to line numbers mentioned in the error messages, as they often indicate where the error originates. Once the error is identified, it becomes easier to address and resolve the issue.

Testing with Minimal Examples

When facing an issue with XeLaTeX extensions or customization, it can be helpful to create a minimal example that reproduces the problem. A minimal example should include the minimum amount of code necessary to recreate the issue. By isolating the problem in a minimal example, it becomes easier to identify the cause and find a solution.

Creating a minimal example involves removing any unnecessary code and packages from your document until the issue persists. This process helps in narrowing down the possible causes of the problem. It is important to create minimal examples that are self-contained and can be easily shared with others who may assist in troubleshooting.

Verifying Package Compatibility

XeLaTeX offers a wide range of packages and customization options. However, not all packages are compatible with each other, and conflicts can arise when multiple packages are used simultaneously. When encountering issues with XeLaTeX extensions, it is important to verify the compatibility of the packages being used.

One way to do this is to comment out packages one at a time and recompile the document to see if the issue persists. By selectively activating and deactivating packages, you can identify which one is causing the conflict. Once the conflicting package is identified, you can explore alternative packages or seek assistance from package maintainers or online forums.

Checking Document Structure

Another common source of issues when working with XeLaTeX extensions and customization is a malformed document structure. XeLaTeX relies on a specific document structure to properly process and display the document. If the document structure is incorrect or inconsistent, it can lead to errors and unexpected behavior.

When troubleshooting, it is important to check the structure of your document, paying attention to opening and closing tags, and appropriate nesting of elements. For example, if you are working with custom macros or environments, ensure that they are properly defined and used in the document. Verifying the document structure can often help in identifying and resolving issues related to XeLaTeX extensions.

Consulting Documentation and Online Resources

Troubleshooting and debugging XeLaTeX extensions and customization can be challenging, especially for complex issues. In such cases, it is helpful to consult the documentation of the packages or extensions being used. Documentation often provides troubleshooting guides, tips, and examples that can assist in resolving common issues.

Additionally, online resources such as forums, mailing lists, and Stack Exchange websites dedicated to LaTeX and XeLaTeX can be valuable sources of information and assistance. Many experienced users and developers actively participate in these platforms and are willing to help troubleshoot and resolve issues. When seeking assistance from online resources, be sure to provide a clear and thorough explanation of the problem and include any relevant code or error messages.

Debugging Tools

XeLaTeX provides several debugging tools that can assist in troubleshooting and identifying issues. The \typeout{} command can be used to print diagnostic messages to the log file during compilation. This command allows you to output information about the state of variables, package loading, or specific parts of your code.

Another useful tool is the ltxdoc and ltxdebug packages, which provide additional commands for debugging and tracing your code. These packages enable you to set breakpoints, step through code, and inspect variables during compilation.

Testing Cross-platform Compatibility

XeLaTeX allows for the creation of documents that can be compiled on different operating systems and platforms. However, issues related to cross-platform compatibility can occasionally arise. When troubleshooting, it is important to test your document on multiple platforms to ensure consistent behavior.

If issues are encountered on a specific platform, it may be necessary to investigate platform-specific differences in file handling, package versions, or font availability.

For example, font-related issues can often be resolved by ensuring that the required fonts are installed and accessible on all platforms.

Summary

In this section, we have explored various techniques for troubleshooting and debugging XeLaTeX extensions and customization. By carefully identifying errors, creating minimal examples, verifying package compatibility, checking the document structure, consulting documentation, utilizing debugging tools, and testing cross-platform compatibility, you can effectively resolve issues and improve the stability of your XeLaTeX projects.

Remember that troubleshooting and debugging are iterative processes that require patience and a systematic approach. It is important to document encountered issues and their solutions to build knowledge and reference material for future troubleshooting. With practice and experience, you will become more proficient in identifying and resolving issues, allowing you to fully leverage the power of XeLaTeX for your projects.

Best practices for XeLaTeX extensions and customization

In this section, we will explore some best practices for extending and customizing XeLaTeX to enhance its functionality and meet specific document requirements. XeLaTeX provides several powerful tools and packages that allow users to create unique and customized document styles, manage complex bibliographic databases, and more. By following these best practices, users can optimize their workflow, ensure compatibility with different systems, and avoid common pitfalls.

Overview of XeLaTeX extensions and packages

XeLaTeX offers a wide range of extensions and packages that extend its functionality and customize the document layout. These extensions and packages are built on top of the LaTeX core and provide additional features and tools for specific purposes. Some of the commonly used extensions and packages include:

- **fontspec:** This package allows users to select and customize fonts in their XeLaTeX documents. It provides various commands and options to manage font families, font sizes, font styles, and more.

- **biblatex:** This package is a modern replacement for traditional BibTeX. It provides enhanced functionality for managing bibliographic databases, generating citations, and creating bibliographies. With biblatex, users can customize citation styles, handle multiple bibliographies, and use different citation schemes.

* **graphicx:** This package enables users to include and manipulate graphics in their XeLaTeX documents. It supports various graphic formats, such as PNG, JPEG, and PDF, and provides commands to scale, rotate, and crop images.

* **geometry:** This package allows users to customize the page layout of their XeLaTeX documents. It provides options to set margins, paper size, headers, footers, and other parameters related to document geometry.

* **hyperref:** This package facilitates the creation of hyperlinks within the XeLaTeX documents. It enables users to include clickable links, bookmarks, and metadata in the final PDF output.

These are just a few examples of the extensions and packages available for XeLaTeX. It is important to explore and understand the functionality provided by each extension or package before incorporating them into your document.

Customizing document styles with XeLaTeX extensions

One of the significant advantages of using XeLaTeX is the ability to create and customize document styles to meet specific requirements. XeLaTeX extensions provide various options and commands to modify the layout, font, spacing, and other aspects of the document. Here are some best practices for customizing document styles with XeLaTeX extensions:

* **Understand the document class options:** When customizing the document style, it is essential to understand the available options provided by the document class. These options control the overall layout and formatting of the document. For example, the `article` document class provides options to set the font size, paper size, and column layout. Similarly, the `book` document class offers options for chapters, sections, and page numbering. Familiarize yourself with these options to tailor the document style according to your needs.

* **Choose and customize fonts:** XeLaTeX allows users to select fonts from their system fonts and use them in their documents. The `fontspec` package provides commands and options to set the main font, serif font,

sans-serif font, and monospace font. Additionally, it allows for customizing font features like ligatures, kerning, and letter spacing. Choose fonts that complement your document's content and purpose and customize them to achieve the desired typographic effect.

+ **Define and modify custom commands:** XeLaTeX enables users to define custom commands and macros to streamline document production and make it easier to reuse content. These commands can encapsulate frequently used phrases, complex equations, or formatting styles. By defining custom commands, users can maintain consistency across the document and save time and effort in the long run. Avoid using generic names for custom commands to prevent conflicts with existing commands or packages.

+ **Explore specialized packages:** XeLaTeX offers numerous specialized packages that cater to specific document requirements. For example, the `amsmath` package provides commands for typesetting mathematical equations, while the `listings` package facilitates the inclusion of source code listings. Research and explore these specialized packages to enhance the functionality and appearance of your document.

+ **Maintain flexibility and modularity:** When customizing document styles, it is crucial to keep the design flexible and modular. This allows for easy modifications and future updates. Avoid hardcoding specific values or styles directly in the document code. Instead, define variables or settings that can be easily altered or extended. By maintaining flexibility, you can quickly adjust the document style to adapt to changing requirements or different publishing platforms.

These best practices will help you create custom document styles effectively while ensuring the maintainability and flexibility of your XeLaTeX code.

Creating and managing macros and custom commands in XeLaTeX

Macros and custom commands are essential tools for extending the functionality of XeLaTeX and automating repetitive tasks. By defining custom commands, users can simplify complex formatting, reuse content, and improve the overall document structure. Here are some best practices for creating and managing macros and custom commands in XeLaTeX:

+ **Choose meaningful and descriptive names:** When creating macros and custom commands, it is essential to choose names that accurately reflect their purpose and functionality. Use descriptive names that are easy to understand and remember. This practice enhances code readability and ensures that others collaborating on the document can comprehend and use your custom commands effectively.

- **Plan and organize command syntax:** Before defining custom commands, plan and consider the desired syntax and parameters. Ensure that the command syntax is intuitive and follows a consistent pattern. Think about the expected input and output of the command and design the syntax accordingly. By planning and organizing the command syntax, you can avoid confusion and improve the usability of your custom commands.

- **Check for command conflicts:** Before defining a custom command, check if the command name is already in use by another package or document class. Command conflicts can lead to unexpected behavior or errors in your document. To avoid conflicts, choose unique and less generic names, or use prefixes to differentiate your custom commands from the existing ones. Additionally, make use of package-specific or document-specific namespaces, if available, to further minimize conflicts.

- **Document and comment your custom commands:** Documenting your custom commands is essential for maintaining the code and aiding collaborators or future users of your document. Add comments to explain the purpose, usage, and parameters of each custom command. Include examples and provide clear instructions on how to use the command effectively. Proper documentation ensures that your custom commands can be easily understood and utilized by others.

- **Revisit and refactor custom commands:** As your document evolves, revisit your custom commands to ensure they still serve their intended purpose and remain compatible with any new packages or extensions you might introduce. Refactor or update your custom commands as needed to improve clarity, address conflicts, or handle new requirements. Regularly reviewing and updating your custom commands will ensure that they continue to enhance your XeLaTeX workflow effectively.

By following these best practices, you can create and manage macros and custom commands efficiently in XeLaTeX, simplifying complex formatting and automating recurring tasks.

Extending XeLaTeX with new fonts and font families

One of the strengths of XeLaTeX is its ability to utilize a wide range of fonts beyond the traditional TeX fonts. XeTeX's native support for Unicode and OpenType fonts allows users to incorporate custom font families into their documents. Here are best practices for extending XeLaTeX with new fonts and font families:

- **Choose fonts that enhance readability and aesthetics:** When selecting custom fonts, prioritize readability and aesthetics. Consider the purpose and target audience of your document when choosing fonts. Select fonts that convey the intended tone and style while maintaining readability. Avoid using too many fonts within a single document and ensure that the selected fonts complement each other.

- **Install and load fonts properly:** To use new fonts in XeLaTeX, they must be installed and properly loaded into your system. Installing fonts on different operating systems can vary, so consult the documentation provided by the font's distributor for specific installation instructions. Once the fonts are installed, load them using the `fontspec` package. The `fontspec` package provides commands to select and configure fonts based on their file name or font family name.

- **Explore font features and options:** OpenType fonts come with various features and options that can be utilized in XeLaTeX. These features include ligatures, stylistic alternates, small caps, and more. The `fontspec` package provides commands to activate and control these font features. Experiment with different features and options to enhance the typographic qualities of your document.

- **Consider font licensing restrictions:** When using custom fonts, be mindful of any licensing restrictions associated with the font. Ensure that you have the necessary permissions to use the font in the intended context, such as personal use, commercial use, or redistribution. Familiarize yourself with the font's license terms and comply with any applicable requirements.

- **Test font compatibility across platforms:** Different operating systems and versions may render fonts differently. It is crucial to test your document's font compatibility across different platforms to ensure consistent appearance. Share your document with others and verify that the fonts are correctly displayed on their systems. If necessary, explore alternative font options or provide fallback fonts to maintain consistency in case a specific font is not available.

By following these practices, users can extend XeLaTeX with new fonts and font families, allowing for greater flexibility and creativity in document design.

Creating and managing bibliographic databases in XeLaTeX

XeLaTeX, combined with the `biblatex` package, offers powerful tools to manage bibliographic databases and generate citations and bibliographies. Here are some best practices for creating and managing bibliographic databases in XeLaTeX:

- **Use a reference management software:** Reference management software, such as Zotero, Mendeley, or JabRef, provides an efficient way to manage and organize bibliographic data. These tools help collect, import, and export references in various formats compatible with XeLaTeX. Utilize the features provided by reference management software to maintain a clean and organized bibliographic database.

- **Choose a citation style that meets your needs:** XeLaTeX, with `biblatex`, supports a wide range of citation styles out of the box. Choose a citation style that aligns with the citation requirements of your field or publication. Customize the citation style further if necessary by modifying `biblatex` options or using additional packages.

- **Regularly update and maintain your bibliographic database:** Keep your bibliographic database up-to-date by regularly reviewing and updating the references. Check for any missing information, incorrect formatting, or outdated entries. Remove duplicates or consolidate entries for the same source.

- **Organize your bibliographic database logically:** Organize your bibliographic database in a logical and consistent manner to make it easy to find and manage references. Consider using appropriate tags, keywords, or categories to classify references based on topics, authors, or publication types. Utilize the search and filtering capabilities provided by reference management software to quickly retrieve relevant references as needed.

- **Check and verify citations and bibliographies:** Before finalizing your document, thoroughly check the generated citations and bibliographies for accuracy and consistency. Ensure that each citation corresponds to the correct entry in the bibliographic database. Verify the formatting of citations and bibliographies according to the chosen citation style.

+ **Handle unique citation requirements:** Some fields or publications may have unique citation requirements not covered by standard citation styles. In such cases, consider customizing the citation style using `biblatex` options or creating a new citation style altogether. Consult the `biblatex` documentation or seek guidance from the community for implementing custom citation styles.

By following these best practices, users can effectively create and manage bibliographic databases in XeLaTeX, ensuring accurate and consistent citations and bibliographies.

Troubleshooting and debugging XeLaTeX extensions and customization

While implementing extensions and customizations in XeLaTeX, it is common to encounter issues or errors that require troubleshooting and debugging. Here are some best practices for efficiently resolving issues related to XeLaTeX extensions and customization:

+ **Check for package conflicts:** Package conflicts are a common source of XeLaTeX issues. If you encounter unexpected behavior or errors, check if any of the loaded packages are conflicting. Disable or load packages one by one to identify the conflicting package. Consult the documentation or online resources for guidance on resolving package conflicts.

+ **Review and verify code syntax:** Syntax errors can disrupt the compilation process and cause issues in XeLaTeX. Carefully review and verify your code syntax, paying attention to proper formatting and structure. Use proper indentation, closing parentheses, and brackets. Consider using an integrated development environment (IDE) that provides syntax highlighting and error checking to identify any syntax errors early on.

+ **Use verbose error messages:** By default, XeLaTeX provides concise error messages that may not provide enough information to debug complex issues. To obtain more detailed error messages, pass the `--interaction=errorstopmode` flag when compiling your document. This helps identify the precise location and cause of the error, making it easier to debug and resolve the issue.

+ **Simplify code for isolated debugging:** When troubleshooting complex issues, it can be helpful to simplify your code and isolate the problem. Remove unnecessary packages, custom commands, or formatting until you reach a minimal working example (MWE) that reproduces the issue. This process helps identify the specific code or component causing the problem, making it easier to debug and find a solution.

+ **Consult community resources:** The XeLaTeX community is a valuable resource for troubleshooting and debugging issues. Visit online forums, such as TeX.SX or the XeLaTeX Stack Exchange, to seek assistance from experienced users and developers. When seeking help, provide a minimal working example (MWE) that reproduces the issue and explain the problem in detail. The community can provide insights, solutions, or pointers to relevant documentation or resources.

+ **Update and maintain packages:** Outdated or incompatible packages can lead to issues in XeLaTeX. Regularly update your XeLaTeX installation and packages to the latest versions to benefit from bug fixes and compatibility updates. If you encounter issues with a specific package, check if an updated version or alternative package is available. Additionally, keep track of breaking changes or deprecated features, as they may require modifications to your custom code or extensions.

By following these best practices, users can effectively troubleshoot and debug issues related to XeLaTeX extensions and customization, ensuring smooth and error-free document production.

Conclusion

In this section, we have explored best practices for extending and customizing XeLaTeX to enhance its functionality and meet specific document requirements. We discussed the importance of understanding XeLaTeX extensions and packages, customizing document styles, creating and managing macros and custom commands, extending XeLaTeX with new fonts and font families, managing bibliographic databases, and troubleshooting and debugging extensions and customization. By applying these best practices, users can optimize their workflow, achieve desired document styles and layouts, and resolve issues effectively. Experiment with these practices, explore further resources, and stay engaged with the XeLaTeX community to continue expanding your knowledge and expertise in XeLaTeX extensions and customization.

XeLaTeX for Automation and Workflow Optimization

Introduction to Automation and Workflow Optimization in XeLaTeX

In the modern world, where time is of the essence, efficient workflow management and automation play a crucial role in increasing productivity and optimizing processes. XeLaTeX, with its powerful features and flexible capabilities, offers several options for automating tasks and streamlining document generation. In this section, we will explore the fundamentals of automation and workflow optimization in XeLaTeX, and learn how to leverage these tools to enhance our document creation process.

Importance of Automation and Workflow Optimization

Automation and workflow optimization are essential in any field of work, as they help reduce manual effort, minimize errors, and enhance efficiency. In the context of XeLaTeX, automation refers to the process of automating repetitive tasks, such as compilation, document generation, and formatting. Workflow optimization, on the other hand, involves organizing and structuring tasks in the most efficient way possible, ensuring smooth coordination and seamless integration of various components.

By automating and optimizing XeLaTeX workflows, we can achieve the following benefits:

+ Increase productivity: Automation eliminates the need for manual intervention, allowing us to focus on more important tasks and complete them faster.

+ Improve accuracy: Manual tasks are prone to human errors, while automation ensures consistency and reduces the chances of mistakes.

+ Enhance collaboration: Automating workflows enables smoother collaboration among team members, ensuring that everyone is on the same page.

+ Reduce turnaround time: With faster compilation and document generation, we can quickly iterate and produce high-quality output.

+ Maintain consistency: Automation ensures that documents are formatted consistently, adhering to predefined templates and styles.

In the next few sections, we will explore various techniques and tools for automating and optimizing XeLaTeX workflows.

Writing and Using XeLaTeX Scripts and Automation Tools

XeLaTeX provides a powerful scripting interface that allows us to automate various aspects of the document generation process. Scripts are written in a programming language, such as Python or Bash, and can be used to execute a series of XeLaTeX commands or perform custom actions. These scripts can be utilized to automate repetitive tasks, such as batch compilation of multiple files or generation of reports based on data inputs.

To write and use XeLaTeX scripts, we need to follow these steps:

1. Choose a scripting language: Select a programming language that best suits your requirements and familiarity. Common choices include Python, Bash, Perl, or Ruby.

2. Install necessary tools: Install the required dependencies and packages for executing the scripts in your chosen programming language. For example, if you are using Python, you may need to install the *subprocess* or *os* module.

3. Write the script: Define the sequence of actions or commands you want the script to perform. This can include invoking XeLaTeX with specific arguments, manipulating files or directories, or executing additional post-processing tasks.

4. Run the script: Execute the script in your chosen programming environment. This can be done through the command line or an integrated development environment (IDE).

Let's consider an example to illustrate the usage of a XeLaTeX script. Suppose we have a directory containing multiple XeLaTeX files, and we want to compile all of them into PDF documents. We can write a Python script to automate this task:

```
import os
import\index{import} subprocess\index{subprocess}

input_directory = ''/path/to/latex/files"
output_directory = ''/path/to/output/pdf"

\# Get all .tex files in the input directory
```

```
tex_files = [
    file for file in os.listdir(input_directory) if file
]

\# Iterate over the tex files and compile into PDF
for tex_file in tex_files:
    \# Generate the command for XeLaTeX compilation
    latex_command = ["xelatex", "-output-directory", ou

     \#␣Execute␣the␣command␣using␣subprocess␣module
     subprocess.run(latex_command)

print("Compilation complete!")
```

In this script, we first specify the input and output directories. We then retrieve all .tex files from the input directory using the `os.listdir()` function. Finally, we iterate over the list of tex files, construct the XeLaTeX compilation command, and execute it using the `subprocess.run()` function. Once the compilation is complete, we print a message indicating the successful execution of the script.

This is just a basic example to demonstrate the usage of a XeLaTeX script. In practice, you can extend and customize the functionality of your scripts as per your requirements. XeLaTeX scripting provides endless possibilities for automating tasks and optimizing workflows.

Automating Document Generation and Compilation with XeLaTeX

Document generation and compilation often involve several steps, such as preprocessing data, generating figures, and compiling the final document. To automate these tasks, we can use build systems and make tools that facilitate the seamless integration of various stages in the document generation process.

One such popular tool is GNU Make, which allows us to define rules and dependencies between files. By specifying the relationships between different components of the document, we can automatically trigger specific actions whenever a file is modified or updated. This enables incremental compilation, avoiding redundant re-compilation of files.

To utilize GNU Make for automating document generation with XeLaTeX, we need to follow these steps:

1. Create a Makefile: A Makefile is a configuration file that defines the rules and dependencies for building the document. It contains a set of instructions used

by the make tool to execute the necessary commands.

2. Specify dependencies: Define the relationships between the source files, intermediate files, and the final document. This ensures that changes in any file trigger the appropriate actions required for generating the updated output.

3. Define the rules: Specify the commands to be executed at each stage of the document generation process. This can include running XeLaTeX, generating auxiliary files, compiling bibliographies, or any custom post-processing steps.

4. Run make: Execute the make command in the terminal, which reads the Makefile, analyzes the dependencies, and performs the required actions to build the document.

Let's consider an example Makefile to automate the compilation of a XeLaTeX document:

```
TEX_FILES := main.tex
OUTPUT_DIR := build

.PHONY: all clean

all: \$(OUTPUT_DIR)/main.pdf

\$(OUTPUT_DIR)/main.pdf: \$(TEX_FILES)
        @mkdir -p \$(OUTPUT_DIR)
        xelatex -output-directory=\$(OUTPUT_DIR) main.tex
        bibtex \$(OUTPUT_DIR)/main
        xelatex -output-directory=\$(OUTPUT_DIR) main.tex
        xelatex -output-directory=\$(OUTPUT_DIR) main.tex

clean:
        rm -rf \$(OUTPUT_DIR)
```

In this example, we specify the input tex files and the output directory. We define the target `all`, which depends on the target `$(OUTPUT_DIR)/main.pdf`. This target is responsible for generating the final PDF document.

We then define the commands to be executed for building the document. In this case, we first create the output directory, followed by three XeLaTeX compile cycles and a bibtex command. Finally, we define the `clean` target to remove the generated output directory.

By running the command `make` in the terminal, GNU Make reads the Makefile, analyzes the dependencies, and executes the commands necessary to build the document. Subsequent runs of `make` only recompile the necessary components based on the modified files, resulting in faster build times.

Building and Managing XeLaTeX Projects with Build Tools and Makefiles

For larger XeLaTeX projects with multiple files and complex compilation requirements, build tools and Makefiles provide a robust solution for managing and automating document generation.

Build tools, such as *latexmk* and *arara*, simplify the build process by automatically determining the required number of compile cycles and invoking the necessary commands. These tools intelligently handle dependencies, auxiliary files, bibliographies, and index generation, resulting in a hassle-free compilation experience.

To utilize *latexmk* in your XeLaTeX project, follow these steps:

1. Install *latexmk*: Depending on your operating system, you can install *latexmk* using package managers like *apt*, *yum*, *brew*, or by downloading the binary from the *latexmk* website.

2. Create a *latexmk* configuration file: The configuration file (`latexmkrc`) contains the settings and rules for *latexmk*. It allows you to customize the compilation process and handle specific requirements of your project.

3. Run *latexmk*: Execute the *latexmk* command in your project directory. *latexmk* automatically detects the necessary input files and compiles the document accordingly.

Here's an example `latexmkrc` file for a XeLaTeX project:

```
\# Use XeLaTeX compiler
\$pdflatex = 'xelatex';

\# Enable continuous preview mode
\$pdf_previewer = 'open -a /Applications/Preview.app';

\# Clean up auxiliary files
\$clean_ext = '-b %R.run.xml %R-blx.bib %R-blx.bbl %R.b
```

In this example, we set the compiler to `xelatex` and enable continuous preview mode using the Preview application. We also define the list of auxiliary files to be removed during the cleanup process.

By running the *latexmk* command in the project directory, *latexmk* automatically detects the necessary input files, performs the compilation, and handles all dependencies and post-processing tasks.

Makefiles and build tools like *latexmk* provide a convenient and efficient way to manage and automate the build process of XeLaTeX projects. They handle complex compilation requirements, dependencies, and auxiliary file management, freeing us from the burden of manual intervention.

Integrating XeLaTeX with Continuous Integration and Deployment Pipelines

In a collaborative or production environment, it is often necessary to automate the build and deployment processes through Continuous Integration and Deployment (CI/CD) pipelines. CI/CD pipelines enable automatic building, testing, and deployment of code, ensuring faster and more reliable release cycles.

To integrate XeLaTeX with CI/CD pipelines, we need to follow these steps:

1. Choose a CI/CD platform: Select a CI/CD platform that suits your requirements and integrates well with your version control system. Popular choices include Jenkins, Travis CI, GitLab CI/CD, and GitHub Actions.

2. Define the build steps: Create a configuration file (e.g., `.yml` for GitHub Actions) detailing the necessary build steps and dependencies. This can include installing XeLaTeX, fetching the project code, setting up the environment, and executing the compilation commands.

3. Configure the CI/CD pipeline: Connect your CI/CD platform to your version control system and configure the pipeline triggers based on your requirements (e.g., on every push, pull requests, or specific branch updates).

4. Execute the pipeline: As per the defined triggers, the CI/CD platform automatically executes the pipeline, fetching the latest code, and executing the specified build steps. The output, such as the generated PDF documents, can be stored as artifacts or deployed to designated locations.

Here's an example `.yml` file for integrating XeLaTeX with GitHub Actions:

```
name\index{name}:  Build  LaTeX  Document

on:
  push:
    branches:
      - main
  pull_request:

jobs:
  build:
    runs-on:  ubuntu-latest

    steps:
    - name\index{name}:  Check  out\index{out}  code\index{
      uses:  actions/checkout@v2

    - name\index{name}:  Setup  TeXLive
      uses:  xu-cheng/texlive-action@v2
      with:
        scheme\index{scheme}:  basic\index{basic}
        packages:  xelatex\index{xelatex}

    - name\index{name}:  Build  PDF
      run\index{run}:  xelatex\index{xelatex}\index{xelat
```

In this example, we define a workflow to trigger on every push to the main branch and for all pull requests. The workflow consists of three steps:

1. **Check out code:** Fetches the repository code.

2. **Setup TeXLive:** Sets up the TeXLive LaTeX distribution with the required packages. In this case, we specify xelatex as the package.

3. **Build PDF:** Executes the xelatex command to compile the main.tex file into a PDF document.

By configuring this workflow in GitHub Actions, the platform automatically triggers the build process whenever a change is made to the main branch or a pull request is opened. This ensures that the XeLaTeX document is built and verified automatically, providing quick feedback and reducing the risk of errors.

Integrating XeLaTeX with CI/CD pipelines allows for seamless and reliable document generation and deployment. It ensures that the latest changes are quickly reflected in the output and reduces the chances of manual errors during the build process.

Automated Testing and Continuous Integration for XeLaTeX Projects

Automated testing and continuous integration (CI) are vital components of any software development process. Testing ensures that the code functions as expected, catches potential issues, and helps maintain a high standard of quality. By incorporating automated testing and CI into XeLaTeX projects, we can validate the correctness and consistency of the generated documents.

To implement automated testing and CI for XeLaTeX projects, follow these steps:

1. Identify testing requirements: Determine the types of tests you want to perform on your XeLaTeX documents. This can include validation of the document structure, checking for missing references, verifying cross-references, or analyzing the generated output.

2. Choose a testing framework: Select a suitable testing framework that caters to your requirements. Some popular options are *latexunit* and *arara*.

3. Define the tests: Create test cases that cover different aspects of your documents. For example, you can test for the presence of specific sections, verify the formatting of equations, or ensure the accuracy of bibliographic references.

4. Integrate with the CI process: Modify your CI pipeline configuration to include the tests. This ensures that the tests are automatically executed as part of the build process, providing feedback on the correctness of the generated documents.

Let's consider an example of using the *latexunit* package to perform automated testing on XeLaTeX documents.

First, install the *latexunit* package using your package manager or `tlmgr`:

```
\$ tlmgr install latexunit
```

Next, write test cases in a separate file, e.g., `tests.tex`, using the provided macros from *latexunit*:

```
\test{Verifying section heading}{

  \section{Introduction}
}{
  \AssertSection{Introduction}
}

\test{Validating equations}{


  An equation: \$x^2 + y^2 = z^2\$.

}{
  \AssertMath{An equation: \$x^2 + y^2 = z^2\$.}
}

% Additional test cases...
```

In this example, we define two test cases: one to verify the section heading and another to validate the equation. For each test case, we include the expected output using \AssertSection and \AssertMath macros provided by *latexunit*.

Finally, execute the *latexunit* command to run the tests:

```
\$ latexunit tests.tex
```

The output will indicate the results of the tests, including any failures or errors. This allows you to identify and resolve issues in your XeLaTeX documents with confidence.

By integrating automated testing with your CI process, you can ensure the consistency and correctness of your XeLaTeX documents. It helps catch errors early, maintains a high level of quality, and provides assurance that the documents adhere to the desired specifications.

Best Practices for Automation and Workflow Optimization in XeLaTeX

To make the most of automation and workflow optimization in XeLaTeX, it is essential to follow some best practices:

- **Plan and automate repetitive tasks:** Identify the tasks that can be automated and plan for their implementation. Automating repetitive tasks saves time and improves consistency.

- **Modularize your workflow:** Break down complex processes into smaller, manageable units. This allows for easier maintenance, reusability, and efficient collaboration.

- **Version control your documents:** Utilize version control systems, such as Git, to manage document versions, track changes, and facilitate collaboration.

- **Document your workflows:** Clearly document your automated workflows and include instructions for setup, execution, and troubleshooting. This helps onboard new team members and ensures the continuity of the workflow.

- **Continuous improvement:** Regularly review your automated workflows and identify areas for improvement. Stay up to date with the latest tools, techniques, and best practices in automation and workflow optimization.

- **Error handling and logging:** Implement mechanisms to handle errors gracefully and log detailed information for troubleshooting. This helps identify and resolve issues promptly.

- **Testing and validation:** Incorporate automated tests and validation processes to ensure the correctness, consistency, and quality of your documents.

- **Security considerations:** Be mindful of security risks, especially when using external scripts or dependencies. Follow best practices for secure coding and validate inputs to prevent potential vulnerabilities.

By adhering to these best practices, you can optimize your workflow, maximize productivity, and ensure the reliability of your automated processes in XeLaTeX.

Conclusion

Automation and workflow optimization are key aspects of efficient document production. In this section, we explored various techniques and tools to automate and optimize XeLaTeX workflows. We learned how to write XeLaTeX scripts, utilize build tools and Makefiles, integrate with CI/CD pipelines, automate testing, and followed best practices.

By incorporating automation and workflow optimization, we can streamline document generation processes, reduce manual effort, improve accuracy, and enhance collaboration. These techniques help us create high-quality documents efficiently, saving time and resources.

In the next section, we will delve into internationalization and localization in XeLaTeX, exploring how to typeset and publish documents in multiple languages and adapt them for diverse cultural contexts.

Writing and using XeLaTeX scripts and automation tools

In this section, we will explore the power of automation and workflow optimization in XeLaTeX. Writing scripts and utilizing automation tools can greatly enhance your productivity and streamline the document generation process. We will discuss various techniques and tools that can be used to automate the generation, compilation, and management of XeLaTeX documents.

Introduction to automation and workflow optimization in XeLaTeX

Automation and workflow optimization are crucial in any project, and XeLaTeX is no exception. By automating repetitive tasks and optimizing the document generation process, you can save valuable time and effort.

XeLaTeX provides several features and tools that allow you to automate various aspects of document creation and compilation. These include command-line options, build tools, Makefiles, Continuous Integration (CI) workflows, and custom scripts.

In this section, we will explore different automation methods and tools that can help in the efficient generation and management of XeLaTeX documents.

Writing and using XeLaTeX scripts

XeLaTeX scripts are a powerful way to automate tasks and customize the document generation process. These scripts are written in scripting languages like Python, Perl, or Bash, and they interact with XeLaTeX through command-line interfaces.

To write a XeLaTeX script, you need to have a basic understanding of your chosen scripting language and its syntax. In general, a XeLaTeX script performs the following tasks:

- Configuring XeLaTeX compiler options, such as specifying the document class, input files, and output format.

- Automatically generating auxiliary files, such as bibliographies or indexes.

- Running the XeLaTeX compiler to generate the final document.

- Handling errors and warnings during the compilation process.

Let's take a look at an example of a XeLaTeX script written in Python:

```
\#!/usr/bin/env python3

import\index{import} subprocess\index{subprocess}

def compile_document():
    try:
        subprocess.run(["xelatex", ''mydocument.tex"])
        subprocess.run(["xelatex", ''mydocument.tex"])
    except Exception as e\index{e}:
        print(f"Error:{e}")

if __name__ == ''__main__":
    compile_document()
```

In this script, we define a function called `compile_document()` that runs the XeLaTeX compiler twice on a document called `mydocument.tex`. We use the `subprocess` module to execute the XeLaTeX command-line tool.

To run this script, you can save it in a file called `compile.py` and execute it using Python:

```
\$ python compile.py
```

This simple script can be customized to fit your specific requirements. For example, you can add additional commands to clean auxiliary files, generate a bibliography, or automate the inclusion of pre-defined packages.

Automation tools for XeLaTeX

In addition to writing custom scripts, there are several automation tools available that can help optimize your XeLaTeX workflow. These tools provide a higher-level interface for managing and compiling XeLaTeX documents.

1. latexmk: latexmk is a powerful tool that automatically compiles LaTeX documents, taking care of all the dependencies and auxiliary files. It continuously monitors the source files and reruns the compilation whenever a change is detected. To use latexmk with XeLaTeX, you can simply run:

```
\$ latexmk -pdf -xelatex mydocument.tex
```

latexmk will handle all the necessary compilations, including the generation of auxiliary files and bibliography.

2. arara: arara is a rule-based automation tool specifically designed for LaTeX. It allows you to define compilation rules directly in your source file using comments. Each rule specifies the commands to be executed, making it easy to customize the compilation process. For instance, you can specify the document class, input files, and other options in the arara directives. To run arara on a XeLaTeX document, you can simply use:

```
\$ arara mydocument.tex
```

3. Overleaf: Overleaf is an online LaTeX editor with built-in collaboration and automation features. It provides a web-based interface for writing, editing, and compiling XeLaTeX documents. Overleaf offers features like automated compilation, error detection, and real-time collaboration, making it a convenient option for team projects. It also integrates with popular version control systems like Git.

These tools provide different levels of automation and customization, allowing you to choose the one that best fits your needs.

Best practices for automation and workflow optimization in XeLaTeX

To make the most of automation and workflow optimization in XeLaTeX, consider the following best practices:

- Modularize your documents: Break your document into smaller, reusable components, such as chapters, sections, or figures. This allows you to compile only the necessary parts of the document, reducing compilation time.

- Use version control: Utilize version control systems like Git to manage your XeLaTeX projects. Version control enables collaboration, tracks changes, and helps keep your documents organized.

- Continuous Integration (CI): Set up CI workflows to automate the compilation and testing of your XeLaTeX documents. CI platforms like

Travis CI or GitHub Actions can automatically build your documents whenever changes are pushed to a repository.

+ Document templates: Create templates for commonly used document types to save time and ensure consistency. Templates can include pre-defined packages, custom commands, and style settings.

+ Error handling: Implement error handling mechanisms in your automation scripts to catch and handle potential errors during compilation. This helps avoid task interruptions and provides better feedback.

+ Documentation: Document your automation scripts and workflows to make it easy for others to understand and contribute to your projects. Include clear instructions, dependencies, and troubleshooting tips.

By following these best practices, you can optimize your XeLaTeX workflow and enjoy the benefits of automation and efficient document generation.

Conclusion

Automation and workflow optimization are essential for efficient document generation in XeLaTeX. By writing custom scripts and utilizing automation tools, you can streamline the compilation process, save time, and improve productivity. In this section, we explored the basics of writing XeLaTeX scripts and introduced some automation tools like latexmk, arara, and Overleaf. Additionally, we discussed best practices for automation and workflow optimization. Incorporating these techniques will empower you to create and manage XeLaTeX documents effectively.

Automating Document Generation and Compilation with XeLaTeX

In the world of document preparation, efficiency and productivity are of utmost importance. XeLaTeX, with its powerful features and flexibility, provides a solid foundation for automating the process of document generation and compilation. In this section, we will explore various techniques and tools to automate these tasks, saving time and effort for users.

Understanding Automation in XeLaTeX

Automation in XeLaTeX involves streamlining repetitive tasks and reducing manual intervention in document generation and compilation. It allows for faster turnaround times and minimizes the chances of errors. With automation, you can create complex documents effortlessly, freeing up time for other important tasks.

Automation Tools and Utilities

To achieve automation in XeLaTeX, several tools and utilities are available. Let's discuss some of the commonly used ones:

1. **Makefiles:** Makefiles are widely used in software development for automating the build process. Similarly, you can create Makefiles for XeLaTeX projects to define the compilation steps, dependencies, and rules. Makefiles provide a simple and powerful way to automate the document compilation process.

2. **Scripts and Shell Commands:** XeLaTeX can be combined with scripting languages like Python, Perl, or Bash to create custom scripts and automate document generation. By leveraging the scripting capabilities, you can programmatically control the compilation process, interact with external tools, and handle complex scenarios.

3. **Continuous Integration (CI) Systems:** CI systems, such as Jenkins or Travis CI, are commonly used for automating software builds and tests. They can be configured to monitor changes in your XeLaTeX project repository and trigger automatic document generation upon new commits. CI systems provide a robust and scalable approach to continuous automation.

4. **Integrated Development Environments (IDEs):** Many popular IDEs, such as TeXstudio or TeXworks, come with built-in automation features. These IDEs provide intuitive interfaces for defining compilation workflows, managing build settings, and running scripts. IDEs simplify the automation process and make it accessible to users without extensive programming knowledge.

5. **Version Control Systems (VCS):** Git, Subversion, or Mercurial can be utilized to automate document generation by integrating with pre-commit hooks or post-commit triggers. By leveraging the power of VCS, you can automate compilation on every commit or specific events, ensuring the latest version of the document is always available.

Automating Document Generation

Automating document generation involves defining a set of rules and instructions to generate various components of a document automatically. Let's discuss some techniques to automate different aspects of document generation:

Template-Based Approach: One of the simplest ways to automate document generation is by using templates. Templates are pre-defined documents that act as a blueprint for creating new documents. By incorporating variables, placeholders, or fillable fields in the templates, you can automate the process of generating new documents by replacing the placeholders with actual content.

For example, for a letter template, you can define variables for recipient name, address, and date. Using a scripting language or a specialized tool, you can read the template, replace the variables with user-provided data, and generate a personalized letter. This approach saves time and ensures consistency across multiple documents.

Data Merge: In cases where you need to generate a large number of similar documents with slight variations, data merge is a powerful technique. By maintaining a dataset with variable values for each document, you can automate the generation process by merging the dataset with a template.

For instance, in a conference program document, you can define a template with placeholders for speaker names, talk titles, and session timings. By merging the template with a dataset containing the information for each speaker, you achieve automation and generate the complete program document in one go.

Automating Document Compilation

Automating document compilation involves defining a set of rules and instructions to handle the entire compilation process automatically. This ensures consistent and error-free compilation without manual intervention. Let's explore some techniques to automate document compilation:

Makefiles: As mentioned earlier, Makefiles can be utilized to automate document compilation. By defining the compilation steps, dependencies, and rules in a Makefile, you can trigger the compilation process by running a simple command. Makefiles are highly customizable and allow for complex compilation workflows to achieve efficient automation.

Build Scripts: Using scripting languages like Python or Bash, you can create custom build scripts to automate document compilation. These scripts can perform various tasks such as checking for dependencies, cleaning up temporary files, invoking the XeLaTeX compiler with appropriate options, and handling post-compilation tasks like generating a PDF or HTML output.

IDE Integration: Integrated Development Environments (IDEs) offer built-in automation features to streamline document compilation. IDEs like TeXstudio or TeXworks provide options to define compilation profiles, specify compiler options, and enable background compilation upon saving the document. IDE integration simplifies the automation process and improves the user experience.

Continuous Integration (CI): Leveraging CI systems brings document compilation automation to the next level. By integrating your XeLaTeX project with a CI system like Jenkins or Travis CI, you can set up a pipeline that automatically compiles the document upon new commits, checks for compilation errors, and generates build artifacts. CI systems offer advanced automation capabilities and can significantly enhance the development workflow.

Best Practices for Automation

To effectively automate document generation and compilation, consider the following best practices:

- Plan and design a clear automation strategy based on your specific requirements. Identify the repetitive tasks that need automation and choose the appropriate tools accordingly.

- Modularize your automation process into reusable components. This allows for flexibility and easy maintenance when modifications or enhancements are needed.

- Always test the automation workflow thoroughly to ensure reliability and accuracy. Develop test cases to validate the output of each automation step and address any issues that arise.

- Regularly update and maintain your automation scripts or configurations to keep up with changes in your project's requirements or dependencies.

- ✦ Document your automation process and create user-friendly instructions, including troubleshooting steps, for efficient utilization by yourself or other team members.

- ✦ Leverage version control systems to manage your automated XeLaTeX projects effectively. This ensures visibility into changes, facilitates collaboration, and provides a solid foundation for continuous integration.

By following these best practices, you can achieve smooth and efficient automation of document generation and compilation in XeLaTeX projects.

Conclusion

Automation is a powerful technique in XeLaTeX that can significantly improve productivity and efficiency in document generation and compilation. By utilizing automation tools, defining clear rules and instructions, and following best practices, you can streamline your workflow, save time, and reduce the chances of errors. Embracing automation unleashes the full potential of XeLaTeX and empowers you to create high-quality documents with ease. So, automate your way to success and enjoy the benefits of efficient document processing!

Building and managing XeLaTeX projects with build tools and Makefiles

In this section, we will explore the use of build tools and Makefiles to streamline the process of building and managing XeLaTeX projects. Build tools and Makefiles can automate repetitive tasks and provide a structured workflow for compiling and managing large XeLaTeX projects.

The Need for Build Tools and Makefiles in XeLaTeX Projects

When working on XeLaTeX projects, especially those with multiple source files and complex dependencies, it can become cumbersome to manually compile each file and keep track of all the dependencies. Build tools and Makefiles provide a solution to these issues by automating the compilation process and managing dependencies.

Introduction to Make and Makefiles

Make is a build automation tool that is commonly used in software development but can also be utilized for compiling XeLaTeX projects. Make utilizes a Makefile, which specifies the commands and rules for building the project.

A Makefile consists of rules that define how to build the target files from the prerequisite files. Each rule consists of a target, prerequisites, and commands. The target is the file that needs to be built, the prerequisites are the files required to build the target, and the commands are the actions to be executed to build the target.

Creating a Makefile for XeLaTeX Projects

Let's create a simple Makefile for a XeLaTeX project consisting of multiple source files:

```
TEX_FILES = main.tex chapter1.tex chapter2.tex
PDF_FILE = main.pdf

all: \$(PDF_FILE)

\$(PDF_FILE): \$(TEX_FILES)
    xelatex\index{xelatex} main\index{main}.tex\index{tex}

clean:
    rm -f \$(PDF_FILE) *.aux *.log *.out
```

In this Makefile, we define the target `all` which depends on the PDF file (`$(PDF_FILE)`) to be built. The prerequisites for the PDF file are the TEX files (`$(TEX_FILES)`) that make up the project. The command `xelatex main.tex` is used to build the PDF file.

We also define a target `clean` which removes all generated files, such as the PDF file, auxiliary files, and log files. This target can be useful for cleaning up the project directory.

Building the XeLaTeX Project with Make

To build the XeLaTeX project using the Makefile, simply navigate to the project directory in the terminal and run the command `make`. This will execute the commands specified in the Makefile and build the target PDF file.

If any changes are made to the source files, running `make` again will check for modifications in the prerequisites and rebuild the PDF file if necessary.

Managing Dependencies with Makefiles

One of the key advantages of using Makefiles is the ability to manage dependencies automatically. When a source file is modified, Make detects the changes and recompiles only the necessary files.

For example, if we modify `chapter1.tex`, running `make` will only rebuild the modified chapter and any files dependent on it. This avoids the need to recompile the entire project every time a single file is modified, resulting in significant time savings for large projects.

Integrating Build Tools into the Workflow

To further streamline the workflow, build tools like `latexmk` and `arara` can be integrated into the Makefile. These tools provide additional features such as automatic dependency tracking and continuous compilation.

For example, `latexmk` can be used to automatically track changes in the source files and compile the project whenever a modification is detected. This eliminates the need to run `make` manually each time changes are made.

Conclusion

In this section, we explored the use of build tools and Makefiles to automate the process of building and managing XeLaTeX projects. Makefiles provide a structured approach to managing dependencies and compiling projects efficiently.

By incorporating build tools like `latexmk` and `arara`, we can further enhance the workflow and improve productivity when working on XeLaTeX projects. Remember to regularly test and debug your Makefile to ensure smooth compilation of your projects.

Now that we have learned how to build and manage XeLaTeX projects with build tools and Makefiles, let's move on to the next section and discover more advanced techniques in XeLaTeX.

Exercises

1. Create a Makefile for a XeLaTeX project with multiple chapters and compile the project using the Makefile.

2. Modify one of the source files in the project and observe how Make rebuilds only the necessary files.

3. Integrate the `latexmk` build tool into the Makefile and test the automatic tracking and continuous compilation features.

Integrating XeLaTeX with Continuous Integration and Deployment pipelines

Integrating XeLaTeX with Continuous Integration (CI) and Deployment pipelines is a crucial aspect of efficient and streamlined document production workflows. CI/CD pipelines automate the build, test, and deployment processes, allowing for faster document compilation, testing, and distribution. In this section, we will explore how to integrate XeLaTeX with popular CI/CD tools and platforms.

Principles of Continuous Integration and Deployment

Continuous Integration (CI) is a software development practice that involves regularly merging code changes from developers into a shared repository. The main goal of CI is to detect and resolve integration issues early in the development cycle. On the other hand, Continuous Deployment (CD) refers to the process of automatically deploying the code changes to a production environment after passing all the necessary tests.

In the context of XeLaTeX, CI/CD pipelines can be used to automate the compilation, testing, and deployment of LaTeX documents. The pipeline can be triggered automatically whenever a new commit is pushed to the repository, ensuring that the document is always up to date and error-free.

Setting up a CI/CD Pipeline for XeLaTeX

To set up a CI/CD pipeline for XeLaTeX, we need to define a series of steps that will be executed automatically. Let's go through the typical stages of a XeLaTeX CI/CD pipeline:

1. **Clone the Repository:** The first step is to clone the repository that contains the XeLaTeX document. This can be done by configuring the pipeline to access the version control system (e.g., Git) and clone the repository to the CI/CD environment.

2. **Install Dependencies:** XeLaTeX requires a set of dependencies, such as font packages, LaTeX styles, and additional LaTeX packages. In this step, we need to install these dependencies in the CI/CD environment to ensure that the document compiles correctly.

3. Build the Document: Next, we need to compile the XeLaTeX document. This can be done by running the XeLaTeX compiler on the main .tex file. The compiler will generate a PDF document as output.

4. Run Tests: After building the document, it is important to run automated tests to ensure that the document meets the required quality standards. Tests can include checking for compilation errors, verifying the layout and formatting, and validating cross-references and citations.

5. Generate Artifacts: Once the document has been successfully built and all tests have passed, we can generate artifacts for further use. These artifacts can include the compiled PDF document, log files, test reports, and any other relevant output.

6. Deploy the Document: The final step in the CI/CD pipeline is to deploy the document to a target environment. This can involve publishing the document to a website, generating an ebook format, or delivering it to a document repository for dissemination.

CI/CD Tools and Platforms

There are several popular CI/CD tools and platforms that can be used to implement XeLaTeX pipelines. Let's explore some of them:

1. Jenkins: Jenkins is an open-source automation server that supports the entire CI/CD process. It provides a highly configurable environment that can be customized to fit specific requirements. Jenkins can be easily integrated with version control systems like Git, allowing for automatic triggering of builds whenever there is a code change.

2. Travis CI: Travis CI is a hosted CI/CD service that offers seamless integration with GitHub repositories. It provides a straightforward configuration file ('.travis.yml') where you can define the necessary steps to build and test your XeLaTeX document. Travis CI supports both Linux and macOS environments, making it suitable for different development setups.

3. CircleCI: CircleCI is a cloud-based CI/CD platform that offers easy integration with popular version control systems and supports multiple programming languages. With CircleCI, you can configure a pipeline for your

XeLaTeX document using a YAML file. CircleCI provides preconfigured Docker images with LaTeX and other necessary dependencies, simplifying the setup process.

4. GitHub Actions: GitHub Actions is a CI/CD platform tightly integrated with GitHub. It allows you to define workflows and automate various tasks, including building and testing XeLaTeX documents. GitHub Actions leverages container technology, making it easy to specify the required runtime environment for your document compilation.

Example Workflow with GitHub Actions

To illustrate how to integrate XeLaTeX with GitHub Actions, let's consider an example workflow for a LaTeX document stored in a GitHub repository:

```
name\index{name}: Build LaTeX Document

on:
  push:
    branches:
      - main

jobs:
  build:
    runs-on: ubuntu-latest

    steps:
    - name\index{name}: Checkout Repository
      uses: actions/checkout@v2

    - name\index{name}: Install LaTeX Dependencies
      run\index{run}: sudo\index{sudo} apt-get\index{get} insta

    - name\index{name}: Build and Test Document
      run: |
        xelatex\index{xelatex} main\index{main}.tex\index{tex}
        \# Add additional commands for testing

    - name\index{name}: Deploy Document
```

```
run: |
  \# Add commands to deploy the document
```

In this example, the workflow is triggered whenever a push is made to the 'main' branch. The steps include checking out the repository, installing LaTeX dependencies using the 'texlive-full' package, building and testing the document using the 'xelatex' command, and finally deploying the document.

You can further customize the workflow by adding additional steps for running specific tests, generating artifacts, or deploying the document to a target location.

Best Practices and Considerations

When integrating XeLaTeX with CI/CD pipelines, it is important to keep in mind the following best practices and considerations:

1. **Version Control:** Use a version control system (e.g., Git) to manage the source code of your XeLaTeX document. This allows for easier collaboration, change tracking, and integration with CI/CD platforms.

2. **Automated Testing:** Implement automated tests to validate the quality and correctness of your XeLaTeX document. Consider including tests for various aspects such as compilation errors, layout consistency, cross-referencing, and bibliography formatting.

3. **Artifact Management:** Define a strategy for managing artifacts generated during the CI/CD process. This includes deciding what artifacts to keep, where to store them, and how to make them accessible to relevant stakeholders.

4. **Environment Isolation:** Ensure that the CI/CD environment is isolated and well-defined to avoid conflicts with other projects or dependencies. Consider using containerization or virtualization technologies to provide a consistent and reproducible environment for document compilation.

5. **Scalability:** Plan for scalability by designing the CI/CD pipeline to handle larger documents or multiple documents simultaneously. This involves optimizing resource usage, such as CPU and memory allocation, and considering parallelization techniques.

6. Monitoring and Notifications: Set up appropriate monitoring and notification mechanisms to track the progress of the CI/CD pipeline and receive alerts in case of failures or issues. This helps in ensuring timely resolution and maintaining the overall reliability of the process.

By following these best practices and considerations, you can establish an efficient CI/CD pipeline for your XeLaTeX documents, leading to improved productivity and faster document delivery.

Conclusion

Integrating XeLaTeX with Continuous Integration and Deployment pipelines is a valuable practice that helps automate the document compilation, testing, and deployment processes. By leveraging CI/CD tools and platforms, you can ensure that your XeLaTeX documents are always up to date, error-free, and delivered efficiently. With the provided example workflow and best practices, you are now equipped to set up your own CI/CD pipeline for XeLaTeX and streamline your document production workflow.

Automating error detection and quality control in XeLaTeX documents

In the process of creating documents with XeLaTeX, errors and quality issues can arise, leading to incorrect output or subpar formatting. Manually detecting and resolving these issues can be time-consuming and tedious. However, by automating error detection and quality control, we can save time and ensure that our documents meet the desired standards.

Importance of error detection and quality control

Error detection and quality control are crucial steps in the document creation process. They help ensure that the final output is accurate, professional-looking, and free of errors. By automating these processes, we can catch mistakes and inconsistencies early on, resulting in higher-quality documents.

Types of errors and quality issues

There are several types of errors and quality issues that can occur in XeLaTeX documents. These include:

- Syntax errors: Mistakes in the markup language syntax, such as missing or mismatched brackets or commands.

- Undefined references: References to labels or citations that are not defined in the document.

- Overfull or underfull boxes: Text or graphics that exceed or fall short of the available space, leading to poor layout.

- Inconsistent formatting: Varying styles, fonts, or spacing within the document.

- Incorrect cross-references: References to other parts of the document that are incorrect or outdated.

Automated error detection

To automate error detection in XeLaTeX documents, we can use tools like linter packages. These packages analyze the document's code and identify potential errors or issues. One popular example is `lacheck`, which checks for syntax errors, uninitialized or multiply initialized variables, and other common mistakes.

Another useful tool is `chktex`, which focuses specifically on common LaTeX errors. It can detect issues such as unnecessary spaces, missing or misplaced punctuation, inconsistent font choices, and more. By incorporating these tools into our build process, we can automatically detect errors and receive notifications to address them promptly.

Automated quality control

In addition to error detection, automated quality control can ensure the overall quality of the document. This includes checking for consistent formatting, correct cross-references, and optimal layout.

One approach to automated quality control is to use a scripting language, such as Python, to analyze the document's source code. By parsing the code, we can extract information about the document's structure, labels, and references. This allows us to check for inconsistencies, such as different fonts or styles being used for the same type of content.

For cross-references, we can compare the defined labels with the document's references to ensure they match. Any inconsistencies can be flagged for manual review. This helps prevent broken or incorrect links within the document.

To assess layout quality, we can use the rules defined in style guides or predefined templates. We can automate the validation of line spacing, margins, paragraph indentation, and other formatting aspects. Any deviations from the desired standards can be highlighted for correction.

Integration with Continuous Integration (CI) pipelines

Automating error detection and quality control can be seamlessly integrated into Continuous Integration (CI) pipelines. CI allows for automatic building, testing, and deployment of documents whenever changes are made.

By leveraging CI tools, such as GitHub Actions or Jenkins, we can set up workflows that trigger the error detection and quality control checks whenever a new commit or pull request is made. This ensures that issues are caught early in the development process and can be addressed promptly.

Best practices for automating error detection and quality control

When automating error detection and quality control in XeLaTeX documents, it's essential to follow some best practices:

- Regularly update and maintain the linter packages and tools used for error detection.

- Define and adhere to coding conventions and style guides to ensure consistent formatting.

- Make error detection and quality control part of the CI workflow to catch issues early.

- Review and interpret the output of automated checks to address false positives or negatives.

- Collaborate with other authors or contributors to establish and enforce document quality standards.

By implementing these best practices, we can automate error detection and quality control effectively, resulting in high-quality XeLaTeX documents.

Conclusion

Automating error detection and quality control in XeLaTeX documents is essential for ensuring accurate and professional outputs. By leveraging linter packages, scripting languages, and CI pipelines, we can catch errors and maintain consistent formatting throughout the document creation process. Follow the best practices mentioned to make the most of these automated processes and enhance the overall quality of your XeLaTeX documents.

Incorporating version control and collaboration workflows in XeLaTeX

In today's collaborative writing and publishing environments, version control and efficient workflow management are essential for successful and productive collaboration. XeLaTeX, being a powerful tool for creating and formatting documents, can benefit greatly from incorporating version control systems and collaborative workflows. In this section, we will explore various approaches to integrating version control and collaboration into the XeLaTeX workflow, and discuss best practices for efficient teamwork.

Version Control Systems

Version control systems (VCS) are tools that manage changes to documents or source code over time. They allow multiple users to work on the same project simultaneously, track changes made by each person, and enable easy collaboration and merging of different versions. There are several popular version control systems available, such as Git, SVN, and Mercurial.

Git, a distributed version control system, is widely used and supported by various hosting platforms such as GitHub and GitLab. It offers powerful features like branching, merging, and easy collaboration between team members. In this section, we will focus on Git for version control in XeLaTeX projects.

Setting up a Git repository

To incorporate version control into a XeLaTeX project, the first step is to set up a Git repository. A Git repository is a folder that contains the project files, along with the necessary metadata for tracking changes. Follow these steps to create a Git repository:

1. Install Git on your computer, if not already installed. Git is compatible with all major operating systems and can be downloaded from `https://git-scm.com/downloads`.

2. Open a terminal or command prompt, navigate to the root directory of your XeLaTeX project, and initialize a new Git repository:

```
git init
```

This will create a hidden directory called ".git" inside your project folder, which contains the version control information.

3. Add your project files to the Git repository:

```
git add .
```

This command stages all files in the current directory and its subdirectories for inclusion in the repository.

4. Commit the changes to create the initial version of your project:

```
git commit -m ``Initial commit"
```

This command creates a new commit in the Git history with the provided message.

Collaborative Workflows with Git

Once the Git repository is set up, team members can start collaborating on the XeLaTeX project. Git provides several collaborative workflows to manage concurrent changes made by multiple contributors. Here, we will discuss two commonly used workflows: the centralized workflow and the feature branch workflow.

Centralized Workflow: In this workflow, there is a single central repository that serves as the definitive source of the project. Team members clone the repository to their local machines, make changes, and push them to the central repository. This workflow is suitable for small teams or projects with a linear development model. To collaborate using the centralized workflow:

1. Create a central repository on a hosting platform like GitHub or GitLab.

2. Share the repository URL with team members and have them clone the repository to their local machines:

```
git clone <repository_url>
```

3. Make changes to the XeLaTeX project files and commit them locally using:

```
git commit -m ``Your commit message"
```

4. Push the changes to the central repository:

```
git\index{git} push\index{push} origin\index{origin} 
```

This command pushes the changes from your local machine to the central repository, specifically to the "master" branch.

Feature Branch Workflow: This workflow is more suitable for larger teams or projects with complex development cycles. It allows team members to work on isolated features or issues without affecting each other's work. The workflow involves creating separate branches for each feature, making changes, and merging them back to the main branch when completed. To collaborate using the feature branch workflow:

1. Create a new branch for the feature:

```
git\index{git} checkout\index{checkout} -b\index{b} f
```

This command creates a new branch called "feature-branch" and switches to it.

2. Make changes to the XeLaTeX project files and commit them locally as before.

3. Push the branch to the central repository:

```
git\index{git} push\index{push} origin\index{origin
```

This command pushes the branch and associated commits to the central repository.

4. Create a pull request or merge request on the hosting platform to merge the feature branch into the main branch.

5. Review and merge the changes into the main branch, resolving any conflicts that may arise during the merge.

Collaborative Writing with Overleaf

In addition to using Git and a local version control setup, XeLaTeX users can also take advantage of online collaborative writing platforms like Overleaf. Overleaf provides a web-based editor and a Git repository integration, allowing team members to collaborate on XeLaTeX projects simultaneously. Users can create and edit documents, track changes, and see live updates from other contributors.

To collaborate with Overleaf, follow these steps:

1. Create an Overleaf account at https://www.overleaf.com.

2. Create a new project and choose the Git option for version control integration.

3. Clone the Overleaf project repository to your local machine using Git:

```
git clone <overleaf_repository_url>
```

This will create a local copy of the project on your machine, which can be edited using your preferred LaTeX editor.

4. Make changes, commit them locally, and push them back to the Overleaf repository using Git.

5. Collaborators can also work on the Overleaf project directly through the web editor, and the changes will be synchronized with the Git repository.

Best Practices and Considerations

When incorporating version control and collaboration workflows in XeLaTeX, it is important to follow best practices to ensure smooth collaboration and minimize conflicts. Here are some important considerations:

+ Regularly pull updates from the central repository to stay up-to-date with the latest changes made by other collaborators.

+ Communicate with team members about the changes you are making to avoid conflicts and duplication of work.

+ Use descriptive commit messages that explain the nature of the changes made in each commit.

+ Test the document integrity after merging changes and resolving conflicts to prevent any loss or corruption of content.

+ Back up your project regularly, either by using remote repositories or by creating a backup locally.

+ Document your project structure, including folder organization and naming conventions, to ensure consistency among team members.

Incorporating version control and collaboration tools into the XeLaTeX workflow enhances productivity, encourages teamwork, and enables efficient management of complex projects. By following best practices and utilizing modern tools like Git and Overleaf, XeLaTeX users can produce high-quality documents while collaborating seamlessly with others.

Creating custom templates and boilerplates for XeLaTeX projects

When working on a XeLaTeX project, it is often useful to have a set of predefined templates and boilerplates to save time and ensure consistency across documents. In this section, we will explore how to create and use custom templates and boilerplates in XeLaTeX.

Why use templates and boilerplates?

Templates and boilerplates provide a starting point for creating documents with specific formatting requirements. They can include pre-defined styles, layouts, and content structures, making it easier to create consistent and professional-looking documents. By using templates and boilerplates, you can avoid repetitive tasks and focus on the content of your document.

Creating a custom template

To create a custom template in XeLaTeX, you can start by defining the document class and options, as well as any custom packages or libraries you want to use. You can also set up the page layout, font styles, and other formatting settings.

Let's say you want to create a custom template for a research paper. Here's an example of how you can define the document class and options:

```
\documentclass[12pt, letterpaper]{article}



% Set up the page layout
\geometry{margin=1in}

% Set up the font styles
\setmainfont{Times New Roman}
\setmonofont{Courier New}

% Set up the line spacing
\doublespacing


% Your document content goes here
```

In this example, we specified the document class as "article" with a font size of 12pt and paper size of letter. We loaded the "setspace" package to set up double spacing and the "geometry" package to set the page margins. We also set the main font to Times New Roman and the monospace font to Courier New.

You can add additional customizations to this template based on your specific needs. For example, you can define custom section headings, create a title page, or add custom macros. The key is to create a template that suits your requirements and can be easily reused for different documents.

Using a custom template

Once you have created your custom template, you can use it as a starting point for new documents. To use the template, simply copy the template file (e.g., "research_paper.tex") and rename it to a new file name (e.g., "my_paper.tex").

In the new file, you can modify the content while retaining the predefined styles and formatting. You can add new sections, insert figures and tables, and customize the document to your specific needs.

By using a custom template, you can save time and ensure consistency in the formatting of your documents. This is particularly useful when working on a series of papers or documents with similar requirements.

Best practices for creating custom templates

When creating custom templates and boilerplates in XeLaTeX, there are a few best practices to keep in mind:

+ Start with a minimal template: Begin with a basic template and add customizations as needed. Starting with a minimal template allows for more flexibility and reduces the risk of conflicts with other packages or settings.

+ Comment your template: Add clear and concise comments to your template file to explain the purpose and usage of each section. This will make it easier for others (or yourself) to understand and modify the template in the future.

+ Test your template: Before using your custom template, test it with different types of content to ensure that it behaves as expected. Check for any formatting issues, conflicts, or errors that need to be addressed.

+ Organize your template files: If you have multiple templates or boilerplates, organize them in a logical folder structure. This will make it easier to locate and manage your templates as your collection grows.

+ Share and contribute: If you have created a useful template, consider sharing it with the XeLaTeX community. This can be done through online platforms, forums, or open-source repositories. Sharing your template can be a great way to contribute to the community and receive feedback from other users.

Creating custom templates and boilerplates in XeLaTeX can greatly improve your productivity and ensure consistency in your projects. By following the best practices and experimenting with different customizations, you can create templates that suit your specific needs and preferences. So go ahead, start creating your own templates and boost your XeLaTeX workflow!

Optimizing XeLaTeX for Speed and Performance in Automated Workflows

In this section, we will explore various techniques to optimize the speed and performance of XeLaTeX in automated workflows. As documents and projects become larger and more complex, efficient compilation becomes crucial. We will discuss strategies to reduce compilation time, optimize memory usage, and streamline the build process. Additionally, we will explore advanced techniques such as parallelization and caching to further enhance performance.

Reducing Compilation Time

Compilation time is a common concern, especially when working with large documents or complex projects. Here are some strategies to reduce compilation time:

1. Efficient Use of Packages and Libraries Carefully consider the packages and libraries you include in your document. Unnecessary packages can increase compilation time significantly. Only include the ones you absolutely need, and avoid loading irrelevant packages.

2. Compilation Options XeLaTeX provides various compilation options that can optimize speed. For example, the `-draftmode` option can speed up compilation by skipping unnecessary tasks such as font caching and file writes. However, use this option cautiously, as it may affect the accuracy of certain elements like page references.

3. File Organization Splitting your document into smaller files and using the `\input` command can make the compilation process more efficient. This allows XeLaTeX to only recompile the modified files, saving time on subsequent compilations.

Optimizing Memory Usage

Managing memory usage is crucial to prevent compilation errors and improve performance. Here are some tips to optimize memory allocation:

1. Memory Allocation Parameters   Adjusting memory allocation parameters can help ensure that XeLaTeX has sufficient memory for large documents. You can modify parameters like `main_memory`, `extra_mem_bot`, and `font_mem_size` in the `texmf.cnf` configuration file. Experiment with different values to find the optimal balance for your system.

2.   Optimization Packages   Consider using optimization packages like `microtype` and `lua-visual-debug`. `microtype` improves the quality of text and enhances overall performance, while `lua-visual-debug` provides debugging information that can help identify potential memory usage issues.

3. Cleaning Auxiliary Files   Regularly delete unnecessary auxiliary files generated during the compilation process. These files can accumulate and consume disk space, leading to slower performance. Running a cleanup script or using the `latexmk` command with appropriate flags can automate this process.

Streamlining the Build Process

Streamlining the build process involves optimizing the workflow and leveraging automation. Here are some techniques to maximize efficiency:

1. Build Tools   Consider using build tools like `latexmk`, `arara`, or `CMake` to automate the compilation process. These tools can handle dependencies, manage the build sequence, and automatically compile only the modified files.

2. Continuous Integration (CI) Pipelines   Integrate XeLaTeX into CI pipelines to automate testing and deployment. Use tools like `Travis CI` or `Jenkins` to automatically compile documents on each code change. This ensures that the latest changes are error-free and speeds up the development cycle.

3.   Parallel Compilation   Leverage multicore CPUs and parallelization techniques to speed up compilation. Tools like `latexmk` support parallel compilation by splitting the document into smaller parts and compiling them concurrently. This significantly reduces compilation time, especially for large documents.

Caching and Precompiling Resources

Caching and precompiling resources can provide a significant performance boost, especially when working on multiple documents or projects. Here are some approaches to consider:

1. Font Caching Preloading commonly used fonts can greatly improve compilation time. XeLaTeX provides options like `\fontspec \preloadfonts` to specify fonts that should be cached before compilation. This eliminates the need for font loading during each compilation.

2. Precompiled Preamble Compiling the preamble once and saving it as a precompiled format (`.fmt`) file can speed up subsequent compilations. Tools like `latexmk` can automatically create and use such precompiled formats, reducing the time spent on loading and processing the preamble.

3. Image Caching If your document includes images, consider caching the processed versions to avoid repeating the image processing step during each compilation. Use tools like `imagemagick` to create cached versions of images with optimized settings.

Best Practices for Speed and Performance

Here are some best practices to keep in mind when optimizing XeLaTeX for speed and performance in automated workflows:

- Regularly update your TeX distribution and packages to benefit from performance improvements and bug fixes.

- Profile your document using tools like `texdef` or `texloganalyser` to identify bottlenecks and performance issues.

- Optimize your document structure by splitting it into logical sections and including them using `\input` or `\include` commands.

- Minimize the use of computationally expensive commands like `\includegraphics` within loops or frequently recurring situations.

- Utilize intelligent caching systems, such as `arara`, to avoid recompiling unchanged files whenever possible.

By implementing these techniques and following best practices, you can ensure that XeLaTeX performs optimally in automated workflows, saving time and improving productivity.

Summary

In this section, we explored various techniques to optimize XeLaTeX for speed and performance in automated workflows. We discussed strategies to reduce compilation time, optimize memory usage, streamline the build process, and leverage caching and precompilation. By following best practices and implementing these techniques, you can ensure efficient and speedy document compilation, making your automated workflows more productive.

Best practices for automation and workflow optimization in XeLaTeX

Automation and workflow optimization are crucial aspects of efficient document preparation using XeLaTeX. By implementing best practices, you can save time, reduce errors, and streamline the entire publishing process. In this section, we will discuss some of the key strategies and techniques for automating and optimizing workflows in XeLaTeX.

Use build tools and Makefiles

Building and managing XeLaTeX projects can be simplified by utilizing build tools such as Make and CMake. These tools allow you to automate the compilation process and handle complex dependencies. By defining a set of rules and instructions in a Makefile, you can easily build your project with a single command. This can be particularly useful when working on large documents with multiple files and packages.

Integrate Continuous Integration and Deployment pipelines

Continuous Integration (CI) and Continuous Deployment (CD) pipelines are essential tools for automating software development workflows. By integrating XeLaTeX with CI/CD platforms such as Jenkins or Travis CI, you can ensure that your documents are automatically built, tested, and deployed whenever changes are made to your project's repository. This guarantees that your documents are always up-to-date and remain error-free.

Implement error detection and quality control

Detecting errors and ensuring the quality of your XeLaTeX documents is crucial for achieving professional results. Implementing automated error detection tools, such as linter or syntax checkers, can help identify common mistakes and potential issues in your code. Additionally, setting up quality control measures, such as spell-checking and consistency checks, can ensure that your documents adhere to predefined style guidelines and standards.

Version control and collaboration workflows

Using version control systems like Git and collaboration platforms like GitHub and Overleaf can greatly enhance your workflow efficiency. Version control allows you to track changes, revert to previous versions, and collaborate seamlessly with other team members. By maintaining a well-organized repository and utilizing branching and merging techniques, you can work on different features or experiments without disrupting the stability of the main document.

Create custom templates and boilerplates

Creating custom templates and boilerplates for your XeLaTeX projects can save you significant time and effort, especially when working on similar documents or recurring tasks. By defining consistent styles, layouts, and settings in your templates, you can quickly start new projects without having to reinvent the wheel every time. This also ensures uniformity and coherence across your documents and simplifies the process of maintaining a consistent visual identity.

Optimize for speed and performance

Large and complex XeLaTeX documents can sometimes suffer from slow compilation times. To optimize the performance of your workflow, you can employ several techniques. Utilizing distributed compilation across multiple cores or machines can speed up the compilation process. Caching commonly used resources, such as font files, can also save time by reducing redundant operations. Finally, profiling and optimizing your code can help identify bottlenecks and improve overall efficiency.

Automate documentation generation

Documenting your XeLaTeX projects is crucial for maintaining clarity and ensuring seamless collaboration. Automating the generation of documentation, such as PDF manuals or README files, can save time and provide up-to-date information about your project. Tools like Pandoc or Doxygen can be integrated into your workflow to automatically generate documentation from comments and annotations embedded within your code.

Follow best coding practices

Adhering to best coding practices can significantly improve the efficiency and maintainability of your XeLaTeX projects. This includes writing clean and modular code, using meaningful variable and command names, and properly commenting your code. Consistently formatting your code and using indentation can make it more readable and easier to understand. Additionally, organizing your project into separate files and directories can enhance the structure of your project and enable easier navigation.

Stay up-to-date with XeLaTeX and package updates

XeLaTeX and its associated packages are constantly being updated and improved. Staying up-to-date with the latest versions can ensure that you have access to new features, bug fixes, and performance enhancements. Regularly check for updates and consider utilizing package managers like TeX Live or MiKTeX, which can simplify the process of installing and managing package updates.

Utilize community resources and forums

The XeLaTeX community is vibrant and active, with numerous resources and forums available for support. Engaging with the community can provide valuable insights, guidance, and solutions to common problems. Websites like Stack Exchange, TeX Stack Exchange, and LaTeX Community offer platforms for discussions, Q&A, and sharing of knowledge. By actively participating in these communities, you can expand your expertise and gain access to a wealth of practical tips and tricks.

Consider unconventional approaches for optimization

Sometimes, unconventional approaches can yield unexpected benefits for workflow optimization. Exploring alternative methods, experimenting with new tools or techniques, and thinking outside the box can lead to innovative solutions. However, it is important to approach these unconventional approaches with caution and always prioritize reliability, consistency, and document integrity.

In this section, we have discussed several best practices for automating and optimizing workflows in XeLaTeX. By incorporating these strategies into your document preparation process, you can enhance efficiency, reduce errors, and streamline the entire workflow from writing to publishing.

Remember, every project is unique, and it's essential to adapt these best practices according to your specific needs and requirements. Continuous improvements, exploration, and learning from your experiences will further refine your workflow over time.

Now, let's put these best practices into action with a few examples and exercises.

Example 1: Automating Compilation

You are working on a large XeLaTeX project that consists of multiple chapters spread across multiple files. To automate the compilation process, you want to set up a Makefile that automatically compiles the entire project with a single command.

Solution:

Create a file named "Makefile" in the root directory of your project and include the following code:

```
.PHONY: all clean

OUTPUT = main.pdf
TEX_FILES = \$(wildcard *.tex)

all: \$(OUTPUT)

\$(OUTPUT): \$(TEX_FILES)
    xelatex\index{xelatex} -shell-escape\index{escape} main\inde

%.pdf: %.tex
    xelatex -shell-escape \$<

clean:
    rm -f \$(OUTPUT)
    rm -f *.aux *.log *.out *.toc *.bbl *.blg
```

Now, you can simply run the command "make" in your terminal within the project directory. It will automatically compile the main.tex file and generate the main.pdf output file. Additionally, it cleans up the unnecessary auxiliary files when you run "make clean".

Exercise:

Optimize the compilation process further by adding support for parallel compilation using the "-j" flag in the Makefile.

Example 2: Integrating Continuous Integration

You want to integrate XeLaTeX with a Continuous Integration (CI) system to ensure that your documents are automatically built and tested whenever changes are made to your project's repository.

Solution:

Assuming you are using a CI platform like GitHub Actions, create a ".github/workflows/main.yml" file in your repository and include the following code:

```
name\index{name}: Build LaTeX Document

on:
  push:
    branches:
      - main

jobs:
  build:
    runs-on: ubuntu-latest

    steps:
    - name\index{name}: Checkout repository\index{repository}
      uses: actions/checkout@v2

    - name\index{name}: Set up\index{up} LaTeX
      uses: xu-cheng/latex-action@v2
      with:
        engine\index{engine}: xelatex\index{xelatex}\index{xelatex

    - name\index{name}: Build LaTeX document\index{document}
      run: |
        xelatex\index{xelatex} -shell-escape\index{escape} main\in
        xelatex\index{xelatex} -shell-escape\index{escape} main\in

    - name\index{name}: Upload artifact\index{artifact}
      uses: actions/upload-artifact@v2
      with:
```

```
name: pdf
path\index{path}: main\index{main}.pdf\index{pdf}
```

This workflow is triggered whenever you push changes to the "main" branch. It checks out your repository, sets up the LaTeX environment with XeLaTeX as the engine, builds the LaTeX document, and finally, uploads the resulting PDF artifact.

Now, whenever you push changes to your repository, the CI system will automatically build the XeLaTeX document and provide you with the PDF artifact as an output.

Exercise:

Extend the CI workflow to include additional steps, such as running tests on the generated PDF using tools like pdfgrep or imagemagick.

Additional Resources

To further explore automation and workflow optimization in XeLaTeX, consider the following resources:

+ **The LaTeX Wikibook:** Offers comprehensive information on LaTeX and related tools, including tips for automation and workflow optimization. Available at: `https://en.wikibooks.org/wiki/LaTeX`

+ **XeTeX mailing list:** A valuable resource for discussions, questions, and tips related to XeLaTeX automation and workflow optimization. Available at: `https://tug.org/mailman/listinfo/xetex`

+ **The TeX Stack Exchange:** A community-driven Q&A platform dedicated to TeX and its variants. It offers a wealth of information and support on all aspects of XeLaTeX, including automation and workflow optimization. Available at: `https://tex.stackexchange.com`

By leveraging these resources, you can stay up-to-date with the latest developments, learn from experts, and find creative ways to automate and optimize your XeLaTeX workflows.

XeLaTeX for Multilingual Publishing

Introduction to Multilingual Publishing with XeLaTeX

Challenges in multilingual typesetting and publishing

When it comes to multilingual typesetting and publishing, there are several challenges that arise. These challenges go beyond just displaying different languages and require careful consideration and planning. In this section, we will explore some of the main challenges and discuss strategies to overcome them.

Unicode support and multilingual fonts

One of the biggest challenges in multilingual typesetting is ensuring proper Unicode support and using the appropriate multilingual fonts. Unicode is a standard that assigns unique codes to every character in almost all languages in the world. This allows for consistent representation and interchange of text across different systems and platforms.

However, not all fonts have complete Unicode support, especially for less common or complex scripts. Some fonts may lack specific characters or have improper rendering for certain combinations of characters. This can lead to issues such as missing characters or incorrect glyph shapes.

To address this challenge, it is essential to choose fonts that have extensive Unicode coverage for the languages you are working with. Many open-source fonts offer excellent multilingual support, such as Noto Sans and Google Fonts. Additionally, it is crucial to test the fonts thoroughly to ensure proper rendering of all characters and combinations in your documents.

329

Typesetting complex scripts and writing systems

Multilingual typesetting becomes even more challenging when dealing with complex scripts and writing systems. Complex scripts, such as Arabic, Hebrew, and Indic scripts, require special handling due to their unique characteristics.

These scripts often have specific rules for ligatures, contextual shaping, and bidirectional text layout. Ligatures are combinations of multiple characters that form a single glyph. Contextual shaping involves adjusting the shape of individual characters depending on their position within a word or sentence. Bidirectional text layout refers to the correct arrangement of both left-to-right and right-to-left scripts within a single document.

To overcome these challenges, it is essential to choose fonts that support the specific rules and features of complex scripts. Modern TeX engines like XeLaTeX have built-in support for complex text layout and shaping through the use of OpenType fonts. Additionally, special packages like polyglossia and babel can assist in handling bidirectional text and language-specific typographic rules.

Formatting bilingual and multilingual documents

Another challenge in multilingual typesetting is formatting bilingual and multilingual documents. When working with multiple languages in a single document, it is crucial to maintain proper consistency and readability.

One common issue is the alignment of text in different languages. Depending on the writing systems involved, you may need to align text vertically, horizontally, or both. Additionally, the use of different scripts can affect line and paragraph breaks, which can lead to awkward spacing and layout issues.

To address these challenges, it is essential to define clear guidelines for font sizes, line spacing, and alignment that accommodate the languages used. Proper formatting can greatly enhance the readability and aesthetics of bilingual and multilingual documents.

Right-to-left (RTL) and bidirectional (BiDi) typesetting

Typesetting languages that are written from right to left (RTL) or include both RTL and left-to-right (LTR) scripts requires special handling. These languages, such as Arabic and Hebrew, have different typographic rules and text layout conventions.

One challenge is managing the correct directionality of text. This involves correctly ordering and aligning both RTL and LTR scripts within a sentence or paragraph. Bidirectional (BiDi) typesetting refers to the proper arrangement of RTL and LTR elements in a single line of text.

To overcome these challenges, XeLaTeX provides bidirectional text support through packages like bidi and polyglossia. These packages enable proper handling of RTL and LTR scripts, including text alignment, punctuation, and numerals.

Translating and localizing XeLaTeX documents

Translating and localizing XeLaTeX documents for different languages can be a complex task. It involves not only translating the text but also adapting the layout and typographic conventions to suit the target language and cultural context.

One challenge is ensuring the accuracy and consistency of the translations. Special care must be taken to ensure that technical or domain-specific terms are translated correctly. Additionally, the length and structure of translated text may vary, requiring adjustments in the layout.

To address these challenges, collaboration between translators and typesetters is crucial. Translation management systems can aid in streamlining the translation process and maintaining consistency across multiple languages. Additionally, defining clear guidelines for layout and typographic conventions can help ensure the quality and cohesiveness of the localized documents.

Best practices for multilingual publishing in XeLaTeX

To effectively navigate the challenges of multilingual publishing, it is essential to follow some best practices:

+ Choose fonts with extensive Unicode support and test them thoroughly for proper rendering of all characters and combinations.

+ Utilize packages like polyglossia and bidi to handle complex scripts, bidirectional text, and language-specific typographic rules.

+ Define clear guidelines for font sizes, line spacing, and alignment in bilingual and multilingual documents to maintain consistency and readability.

+ Utilize translation management systems and collaborate with translators to ensure accurate and consistent translations.

+ Adapt layouts and typographic conventions to suit the target language and cultural context during the localization process.

By following these best practices, you can overcome the challenges of multilingual typesetting and publishing and create professional and aesthetically pleasing documents in XeLaTeX.

Unicode support in XeLaTeX and multilingual fonts

In order to fully understand the significance and benefits of Unicode support in XeLaTeX, it is important to first explore the concept of multilingual fonts. Multilingual fonts are designed to support various writing systems and scripts, enabling the typesetting of text in different languages with proper display and rendering. These fonts encompass a wide range of character sets and symbols, including alphabets, diacritical marks, punctuation, numbers, and special characters.

XeLaTeX, being built on top of LaTeX, inherits its limited support for non-Latin scripts. However, XeLaTeX goes a step further by providing native support for Unicode, a modern character encoding standard that unifies all writing systems under a single character set. This means that by using XeLaTeX, you can seamlessly typeset text in multiple languages and scripts, including those with complex and intricate writing systems.

Unicode support in XeLaTeX offers several advantages. Firstly, it eliminates the need for using additional packages or workarounds to typeset non-Latin scripts. With Unicode, you can directly input characters from different scripts within your XeLaTeX document without any issues. This makes it significantly easier to handle multilingual documents, as you can mix and match text in different languages seamlessly.

Moreover, Unicode support in XeLaTeX provides superior typographical quality compared to older encoding systems. This is because Unicode includes a vast range of characters and symbols, ensuring that you have access to a comprehensive set of glyphs for accurate representation of different writing systems. It also enables more precise typesetting of complex scripts with ligatures, diacritical marks, and other advanced typographic features.

To utilize Unicode support in XeLaTeX, it is necessary to use a compatible font that includes the required character glyphs. XeLaTeX supports OpenType (OTF) and TrueType (TTF) fonts, which encompass a wide variety of multilingual fonts available today. These fonts often come with advanced typographic features specific to different scripts, allowing for enhanced control over the layout and presentation of text.

Implementing Unicode support in XeLaTeX involves specifying the font family and font features within your document preamble. For example, you can use the `fontspec` package to select a specific multilingual font and customize its behavior. The `fontspec` package provides commands and options to handle various font-related tasks, such as setting the main font, defining fallback fonts, adjusting font size, and enabling stylistic variations.

Unicode support in XeLaTeX also extends to the use of characters and symbols from different Unicode blocks. These blocks include mathematical symbols, currency symbols, emojis, musical notation, and many others. By leveraging the power of Unicode, you can incorporate these diverse elements into your XeLaTeX documents without any special configuration or manual encoding.

However, despite the convenience and flexibility offered by Unicode support in XeLaTeX, it is not without its challenges. One common issue is the proper handling of bidirectional text, which is prevalent in languages such as Arabic and Hebrew. XeLaTeX does provide mechanisms to manage bidirectional text, but it may require additional attention and configuration to ensure accurate typesetting.

In conclusion, Unicode support in XeLaTeX revolutionizes the way we handle multilingual typesetting. By embracing the Unicode standard and utilizing multilingual fonts, XeLaTeX empowers users to seamlessly typeset text in different languages and scripts. This support extends beyond basic characters and includes complex scripts with advanced typographic features. With Unicode support, XeLaTeX provides a modern and efficient solution for creating professional-quality multilingual documents.

Example: Multilingual Document

Let's consider an example to illustrate the power of Unicode support in XeLaTeX. Imagine you are working on a research paper that involves analyzing data from various countries around the world. The paper requires you to include statistical charts, tables, and descriptions in multiple languages, such as English, German, Chinese, and Arabic.

With XeLaTeX's Unicode support, you can easily achieve this. You can begin by specifying a suitable multilingual font that covers the necessary scripts, such as Arial Unicode MS or Noto Sans. These fonts have extensive Unicode coverage and are capable of handling a wide range of scripts and characters.

Next, you can define language-specific sections within your document using the polyglossia package. This package allows you to specify the language for each section, ensuring proper hyphenation, date formatting, and other language-specific rules. For instance, you may use \setdefaultlanguage{english} for the English sections, \setdefaultlanguage{german} for the German sections, and so on.

Then, within each section, you can freely switch between languages using the \setotherlanguage command. This command ensures that XeLaTeX adapts to the appropriate typographic rules and font features specific to each language. For instance, you can use \setotherlanguage{chinese} to switch to Chinese and \setotherlanguage{arabic} to switch to Arabic.

Finally, you can seamlessly incorporate statistical charts and tables using the tikz package. With the help of Unicode, you can include labels, captions, and axis values in the respective languages, making the charts and tables more accessible and understandable to readers from different linguistic backgrounds.

By leveraging Unicode support in XeLaTeX, you can effortlessly create a comprehensive and visually appealing multilingual research paper that adheres to the specific typographic rules of each language.

Resources

To further explore Unicode support in XeLaTeX and multilingual fonts, consider the following resources:

+ *The XeTeX Companion: TeX meets OpenType and Unicode* by Michel Goossens, Sebastian Rahtz, and Johan Braams.

+ *XeTeX: Unicode and OpenType Support for TeX and LaTeX* (official documentation).

+ The Comprehensive TeX Archive Network (CTAN) website, which provides an extensive collection of packages, fonts, and resources for XeLaTeX.

These resources offer in-depth explanations, examples, and practical guidance on utilizing Unicode support and multilingual fonts in XeLaTeX. They are valuable references for both beginners and experienced users looking to enhance their multilingual typesetting capabilities.

Typesetting languages with non-Latin scripts in XeLaTeX

In this section, we will explore the capabilities of XeLaTeX for typesetting languages with non-Latin scripts. XeLaTeX is known for its superior support for Unicode, which makes it an ideal choice for typesetting multilingual documents. We will discuss the challenges involved in typesetting non-Latin scripts, and demonstrate how XeLaTeX can overcome these challenges. We will also look at some best practices for typesetting languages with non-Latin scripts in XeLaTeX.

Challenges in typesetting non-Latin scripts

Typesetting languages with non-Latin scripts presents several challenges due to the different writing systems, character sets, and typographic conventions. Some of the key challenges include:

1. **Font availability:** Non-Latin scripts often require specialized fonts that may not be widely available. Finding suitable fonts that support the required characters can be a challenge.

2. **Glyph shaping:** Non-Latin scripts often have complex glyph shapes that change depending on their context. Properly shaping and rendering these glyphs can be challenging.

3. **Bidirectional writing:** Some non-Latin scripts, such as Arabic and Hebrew, are written from right to left, while others, like Latin, are written from left to right. Typesetting bidirectional text that contains both right-to-left and left-to-right scripts can be complex.

4. **Ligatures and diacritics:** Non-Latin scripts often require the use of ligatures and diacritics, which can be challenging to handle correctly in typesetting.

Unicode support in XeLaTeX

One of the key features of XeLaTeX is its robust support for Unicode. Unicode is a global standard that allows the representation of almost all the characters used in modern writing systems, including non-Latin scripts. XeLaTeX can handle Unicode characters directly in the source code, eliminating the need for cumbersome workarounds.

XeLaTeX uses the OpenType font format, which supports advanced typographic features required for typesetting non-Latin scripts. OpenType fonts can contain thousands of glyphs, allowing for comprehensive support of various script systems.

To use Unicode characters in XeLaTeX, you need to ensure that your document is saved in a Unicode encoding such as UTF-8. You also need to specify the font that supports the non-Latin script you want to typeset.

Typesetting non-Latin scripts in XeLaTeX

To typeset non-Latin scripts in XeLaTeX, you need to follow a few steps:

1. **Font selection:** Choose a font that supports the non-Latin script you want to typeset. You can use system fonts or install custom fonts in your document directory. Specify the font using the `\setmainfont` command. For example, to typeset Arabic, you can use the Amiri font:

```
\setmainfont{Amiri}
```

2. **Enabling complex script features:** Some non-Latin scripts require complex script features such as ligatures, contextual shaping, or diacritic positioning. XeLaTeX automatically applies these features if the font supports them. However, you can enable or disable specific features using the `\fontspec` command. For example, to disable ligatures:

```
\fontspec[Ligatures=NoCommon]{Amiri}
```

3. **Writing non-Latin text:** Insert non-Latin text directly into the document using the appropriate Unicode characters. XeLaTeX will automatically handle the correct rendering of the characters according to the selected font.

4. **Bidirectional text:** If your document contains both right-to-left and left-to-right scripts, you need to enable bidirectional typesetting using the `\setmainfont` command. For example, to typeset a document with Arabic and English:

```
\setmainfont{Amiri}[Script=Arabic]
\newfontfamily\englishfont{Latin Modern Roman}
```

```
\textenglish{Hello!}
```

The \textenglish command switches to the English font for the specified text.

Best practices for typesetting non-Latin scripts

To ensure high-quality typesetting of non-Latin scripts in XeLaTeX, consider the following best practices:

1. **Choose appropriate fonts:** Select fonts that are specifically designed for the non-Latin script you are typesetting. Make sure the fonts support the required typographic features, ligatures, and diacritics.

2. **Test and proofread:** Always thoroughly test and proofread your typeset document to ensure that all characters are correctly rendered and positioned. Pay attention to ligatures, diacritics, and the correct shaping of complex glyphs.

3. **Consult language-specific guidelines:** Different languages have their own typographic conventions and rules. Consult language-specific guidelines or style manuals to ensure the correct typesetting of non-Latin scripts.

4. **Consider line and paragraph spacing:** Non-Latin scripts, especially those with complex glyph shapes, may require additional line and paragraph spacing to ensure readability. Experiment with different spacing options to find the optimal balance.

5. **Use Unicode character references:** To ensure proper rendering across different systems and platforms, consider using Unicode character references instead of copy-pasting characters directly into your document.

In conclusion, XeLaTeX provides powerful capabilities for typesetting languages with non-Latin scripts. By leveraging its robust Unicode support, you can overcome the challenges involved in typesetting non-Latin scripts and achieve high-quality, professional results. Following best practices and considering the specific requirements of each script system will help you create visually appealing and accurate documents.

Typesetting complex scripts and writing systems in XeLaTeX

In this section, we will explore the capabilities of XeLaTeX for typesetting complex scripts and writing systems. XeLaTeX is particularly well-suited for handling multilingual documents and scripts with non-Latin characters. We will discuss the challenges involved in typesetting these scripts and provide solutions using XeLaTeX's powerful features.

Challenges in typesetting complex scripts

Typesetting complex scripts poses unique challenges due to the intricacies of character shapes, ligatures, diacritics, and bidirectional text direction. Some commonly encountered scripts include Arabic, Hebrew, Indic scripts (such as Devanagari and Bengali), and East Asian scripts (such as Chinese, Japanese, and Korean). Let's discuss these challenges and how XeLaTeX addresses them.

1. **Glyph shaping and rendering**: Many scripts require shaping and rendering of characters based on their context and positioning. This includes the formation of ligatures, contextual variants, and positioning diacritics. XeLaTeX leverages OpenType fonts, which contain built-in rules for complex glyph shaping.

2. **Bi- and multi-directional text**: Some scripts, such as Arabic and Hebrew, are written from right to left (RTL), while the majority of text in the document may still be left-to-right (LTR). XeLaTeX supports bidirectional text layout, allowing you to mix different directionality in a single document seamlessly.

3. **Font support**: Not all fonts have comprehensive support for complex scripts. XeLaTeX solves this problem by allowing you to use any OpenType or TrueType font, including those specifically designed for certain scripts. This flexibility ensures that you can find the right font for your specific script needs.

Typesetting complex scripts in XeLaTeX

Now let's explore how to typeset complex scripts and writing systems in XeLaTeX.

Font selection   The first step in typesetting complex scripts is selecting an appropriate font. XeLaTeX supports both system fonts and custom fonts installed on your system. To use a specific font, use the `fontspec` package and specify the font by its name or file path. For example:

```
\setmainfont{Noto Nastaliq Urdu}
\setmonofont{Courier New}
```

In the above example, we set `Noto Nastaliq Urdu` as the main font, suitable for typesetting Urdu script. We also set `Courier New` as the monospaced font.

Special characters and ligatures   Scripts like Arabic and Indic scripts often have special characters and ligatures. XeLaTeX provides convenient commands for accessing these characters. For example, in Arabic, you can use the `\arabic` command to switch to Arabic script and access Arabic-specific commands, such as `\arabicfont` for setting the Arabic font. Similarly, for Indian scripts like Devanagari, you can use the `\devanagari` command.

Additionally, ligatures play an important role in some scripts. XeLaTeX automatically applies the appropriate ligatures in OpenType fonts. However, if certain ligatures are not being applied correctly, you can manually specify them using the `fontspec` package. For example:

```
\setmainfont{Noto Naskh Arabic}
[Ligatures={Required,Contextual,Discretionary}]
```

In the example above, we specify ligatures to be "Required", "Contextual", and "Discretionary" for the Arabic font.

Bidi text direction   To handle bidirectional text, XeLaTeX provides the `bidi` package. This package allows you to switch between RTL and LTR text within the document and handles the correct rendering and ordering of characters. For example:

```
\begin{RTL}
This is an example\index{example} of RTL text\index{text}.
\end{RTL}
\begin{LTR}
This is an example\index{example} of LTR text\index{text}.
\end{LTR}
```

In the above example, the RTL environment is used to typeset the text in right-to-left direction, while the LTR environment is used for left-to-right text.

Line-breaking and spacing Scripts with complex shapes may require additional attention to line-breaking and spacing. The `polyglossia` package, coupled with the `babel` package, provides support for handling these aspects. For example, for Devanagari script, you can use:

```
\setmainlanguage{hindi}
```

This enables correct line-breaking and spacing rules for Devanagari script.

Examples and exercises To further reinforce the concepts discussed, let's work through a few examples and exercises:

1. Typeset a short paragraph in Arabic script using the `Scheherazade` font.

2. Create a document that contains both English and Hebrew text, properly typeset with correct text direction.

These examples will help you gain hands-on experience with typesetting complex scripts in XeLaTeX.

Resources

To explore further and deepen your understanding of typesetting complex scripts in XeLaTeX, here are some recommended resources:

+ *XeTeX and OpenType: System-wide OpenType support for TeX*, by Jonathan Kew.

+ *Typesetting with XeLaTeX*, by Simon Fear and Ross Moore.

+ *The XeTeX Companion*, by Michel Goossens and Sebastian Rahtz.

These books provide detailed explanations, examples, and best practices for typesetting complex scripts using XeLaTeX.

Conclusion

XeLaTeX provides powerful tools and features for typesetting complex scripts and writing systems. By leveraging OpenType fonts, customizing font selection, handling bidirectional text, and paying attention to line-breaking and spacing, you can produce high-quality documents in various scripts. With practice and exploration, you will become proficient in typesetting even the most challenging scripts using XeLaTeX.

Remember to consult the recommended resources and continue experimenting and learning to expand your skills in typesetting complex scripts in XeLaTeX.

Customizing language-specific typographic rules in XeLaTeX

In this section, we will explore how to customize the typographic rules for different languages in XeLaTeX. XeLaTeX provides great flexibility in typesetting languages with non-Latin scripts and allows us to tailor the typography to specific language requirements. We will learn about the principles and techniques behind language-specific typographic rules and how to implement them effectively.

Understanding language-specific typographic rules

Different languages have unique typographic conventions and rules that govern letter spacing, punctuation placement, hyphenation, and line breaking. These rules are designed to ensure optimal readability and aesthetic appeal for each language.

For instance, languages like Arabic and Hebrew are written right-to-left (RTL), requiring adjustments in the placement of various elements such as punctuation marks and numerals. Other languages, like Chinese and Japanese, have different standards for line breaking and character spacing compared to Latin-based languages.

Understanding these language-specific typographic rules is crucial to producing visually pleasing and professionally typeset documents in XeLaTeX.

Implementing language-specific rules in XeLaTeX

XeLaTeX provides several packages and tools that make it easy to customize typographic rules for different languages.

1. **babel** package: The `babel` package is a powerful tool for multilingual typesetting in XeLaTeX. It supports a wide range of languages and provides language-specific options to control various typographic rules. For example, to typeset a document in Arabic, we can use the command

`\usepackage[arabic]{babel}`.   This will automatically adjust the directionality and other typographic features according to the Arabic language rules.

2. **polyglossia** package: The `polyglossia` package is another excellent choice for multilingual typesetting in XeLaTeX. It provides similar functionality to the `babel` package but with more modern support for Unicode fonts and advanced features. We can use the `polyglossia` package to select the language and customize the typographic rules accordingly.

3. **fontspec** package: The `fontspec` package is essential when dealing with language-specific typography in XeLaTeX. It allows us to select and customize fonts that are suitable for specific languages. For example, if we are typesetting a document in Chinese, we can choose a font that supports Chinese characters using commands like `\setmainfont{SimSun}`.

4. **ctex** package: The `ctex` package is designed specifically for typesetting Chinese documents in XeLaTeX. It handles various aspects of Chinese typography, such as character spacing, punctuation placement, and line breaking rules. The package provides comprehensive support for both Simplified and Traditional Chinese.

Examples of language-specific typographic rules

Let's look at a few examples of how to customize the typographic rules for different languages in XeLaTeX.

1.   **Hyphenation:** - For English: We can use the command `\hyphenation{doc-u-ment}` to set custom hyphenation rules for English words. This is useful when we want to override the default hyphenation behavior. - For German: In German, words ending with "st" or "tz" should not be hyphenated. We can prevent hyphenation in such cases using the command `\hyphenation{Schulz}`.

2. **Quotation marks:** - For French: In French typography, double quotation marks are represented using angled quotation marks (« and »). We can use the `\guillemotleft` and `\guillemotright` commands to achieve this. - For Russian: In Russian typography, quotation marks are represented using the symbols « and ». We can use the `\textquotedblleft` and `\textquotedblright` commands to produce these symbols.

3. **Punctuation spacing:** - For Arabic: In Arabic typography, there should be no space before the opening bracket or after the closing bracket. We can achieve this by setting the appropriate `\XeTeXinterchartoks` in the preamble. - For Japanese: In Japanese typography, there should be no space before or after the

punctuation marks ⬚and ⬚. We can achieve this using the \Ucharcat command to set the appropriate category codes for these characters.

4. **Line breaking rules:** - For Thai: In Thai typography, we need to adjust the line breaking behavior to avoid breaking words at inappropriate places. We can use the \thaiadjust command to fine-tune the line breaking algorithm for Thai text.

5. **Font selection:** - For Hindi: When typesetting documents in Hindi, we need to choose a font that supports Devanagari script, such as Mangal or Lohit Hindi. We can use the \setmainfont command to select the appropriate font.

Conclusion

Customizing language-specific typographic rules in XeLaTeX is essential for producing high-quality documents in different languages. By understanding and implementing the typographic conventions and rules specific to each language, we can ensure that our documents are visually appealing and conform to the standards of each language. The various packages and tools available in XeLaTeX make it easy to achieve language-specific typography, allowing us to create professional documents that meet the typographic expectations of a global audience.

Now that we have explored the concept and implementation of language-specific typographic rules in XeLaTeX, let's move on to the next section, where we will delve into the art of designing and formatting mathematical equations in XeLaTeX.

Formatting bilingual and multilingual documents in XeLaTeX

In this section, we will explore the techniques and best practices for formatting bilingual and multilingual documents in XeLaTeX. As the world becomes more interconnected, the need for documents in multiple languages is increasing. XeLaTeX provides powerful tools for typesetting text in different languages, including complex scripts with non-Latin characters.

Challenges in multilingual typesetting and publishing

When working with multiple languages in a document, several challenges may arise. For instance, different languages may have different typographic rules, such as the placement of punctuation marks and quotation marks. Additionally, languages with non-Latin scripts may require special handling for proper rendering and alignment.

Another challenge is managing language-specific hyphenation patterns. Each language has its own set of hyphenation rules, and XeLaTeX needs to be configured properly to ensure that words are hyphenated correctly in each language.

Furthermore, bilingual or multilingual documents often have text that needs to be formatted differently for each language. For example, when presenting a document in English and French, headings and section titles need to appear in the correct language-specific formats.

Unicode support in XeLaTeX and multilingual fonts

One of the key advantages of using XeLaTeX for multilingual typesetting is its excellent support for Unicode. Unicode is a character encoding standard that allows for the representation of characters from all writing systems. In XeLaTeX, you can directly input Unicode characters in your source code, making it easy to work with multilingual text.

To typeset text in different languages, you need to have appropriate fonts that support the required characters. XeLaTeX allows you to use any TrueType or OpenType font installed on your system, including fonts that support multiple writing systems. You can specify different fonts for different languages or have XeLaTeX automatically select the appropriate font based on the language.

Typesetting languages with non-Latin scripts in XeLaTeX

XeLaTeX provides excellent support for typesetting languages with non-Latin scripts, such as Arabic, Chinese, Japanese, and Devanagari. To typeset text in these languages, you need to include the relevant language-specific packages and set the font appropriately.

For example, to typeset Arabic text, you can use the `arabxetex` package. This package provides a convenient way to typeset Arabic text using XeLaTeX. You can specify the font family, font size, and other formatting options for the Arabic text.

```
\newfontfamily\arabicfont[Script=Arabic]{Amiri}
\newfontfamily\arabicfonttt[Script=Arabic, Scale=1.2]{DejaVu Sa
```

```
\arab[utf]{...}
```

Similarly, for Chinese and Japanese, you can use the `xeCJK` package. This package provides support for typesetting text in Chinese, Japanese, and Korean languages. You can specify the font family, font size, and other formatting options for the East Asian text.

```
\setCJKmainfont{Noto Serif CJK SC}
\setCJKsansfont{Noto Sans CJK SC}
\setCJKmonofont{Noto Sans Mono CJK SC}
```

```
\xeCJKsetup{CJKecglue=\,}
. . .
```

Customizing language-specific typographic rules in XeLaTeX

To format text in different languages correctly, you may need to customize the typographic rules. For example, in some languages, the position of punctuation marks, quotation marks, and other symbols may be different from what is standard in English. XeLaTeX allows you to define language-specific rules to ensure proper formatting.

For instance, to customize quotation marks for French language, you can use the csquotes package with the appropriate language option:

```
\usepackage[french]{babel}
```

```
. . .
\enquote{...} % English quotation marks
\enquote*{...} % German quotation marks
\enquote[{\bsl ngerman}]{...} % Swiss quotation marks
. . .
```

You can also define language-specific rules for hyphenation using the babel package. For example, to enable French hyphenation rules:

```
\usepackage[french]{babel}
```

```
. . .
```

Formatting bilingual and multilingual documents

When dealing with bilingual or multilingual documents, it is important to format text appropriately for each language. This includes formatting headings, section titles, table of contents, and captions in the correct language-specific formats.

To achieve this, you can use the `babel` package along with the `polyglossia` package. These packages provide language-specific commands and environments for formatting text in different languages.

Here's an example of formatting a bilingual document in English and Spanish:

```
\usepackage[english,spanish]{babel}

\setdefaultlanguage{english}
\setotherlanguage{spanish}


\section{Introduction} % English section title
...
\begin{otherlanguage}{spanish}
\section{Introducción} % Spanish section title
...
\end{otherlanguage}
...
```

In addition, you can use language-specific fonts and font features to enhance the typographic appearance of each language. For example, you can specify different fonts for English and Chinese text in a bilingual document:

```
\newfontfamily\englishfont{Times New Roman}
\newfontfamily\chinesefont{SimSun}


\englishfont This is English text.
\chinesefont
...
```

Right-to-left (RTL) and bidirectional (BiDi) typesetting in XeLaTeX

XeLaTeX provides excellent support for right-to-left (RTL) and bidirectional (BiDi) typesetting. This is essential for languages such as Arabic, Hebrew, and Persian, which are written from right to left.

For RTL and BiDi typesetting, you can use the `bidi` package. This package provides commands and environments for typesetting text in RTL and BiDi languages. You can also specify the base direction of the document using the `babel` package.

Here's an example of typesetting a paragraph in Arabic:

```
\begin{RTL}
...
\end{RTL}
```

Translating and localizing XeLaTeX documents for different languages

When translating and localizing XeLaTeX documents for different languages, there are several techniques you can use to streamline the process. One approach is to separate the content from the formatting by using external files for translations.

For example, you can define language-specific strings in separate translation files and load the appropriate file based on the selected language. This allows you to easily switch between different languages without modifying the main document.

```
\selectlanguage{english}
\input{translations_en.tex}

\selectlanguage{spanish}
\input{translations_es.tex}

\ldots
```

In conclusion, XeLaTeX provides powerful tools for formatting bilingual and multilingual documents. By leveraging Unicode support, language-specific packages, and customization options, you can achieve professional results in handling different languages and scripts. Whether it's typesetting text in Arabic or bilingual documents in English and Spanish, XeLaTeX offers the flexibility and control needed for multilingual publishing.

Right-to-left (RTL) and bidirectional (BiDi) typesetting in XeLaTeX

Right-to-left (RTL) and bidirectional (BiDi) typesetting is an essential aspect of XeLaTeX that allows for proper rendering of text in languages that are written from right to left, such as Arabic, Hebrew, and Farsi, as well as mixtures of right-to-left and left-to-right (LTR) scripts within the same document. XeLaTeX provides robust support for RTL and BiDi typesetting, ensuring accurate and aesthetically pleasing rendering of multilingual documents.

Understanding RTL and BiDi typesetting

RTL typesetting refers to the visual arrangement of content in a document that is written from right to left. This includes the reversal of writing and reading order, as well as adaptations to various typographic properties, such as alignment, punctuation, and numerals. BiDi typesetting, on the other hand, is the automatic switching and handling of RTL and LTR scripts within the same document, ensuring proper rendering and readability.

Enabling RTL and BiDi typesetting in XeLaTeX

To enable RTL and BiDi typesetting in XeLaTeX, the `polyglossia` package is commonly used. This package provides comprehensive language support for XeLaTeX and allows for seamless integration of RTL and BiDi features. To begin, we need to define the main language as an RTL language using the `setmainlanguage` command. For example, to set Arabic as the main language, we would use:

```
\setmainlanguage{arabic}
\setotherlanguage{english}
```

In this example, we have also set English as another language, which is an LTR language. This enables the automatic switching between RTL and LTR scripts when needed.

Typesetting RTL text

Once RTL typesetting is enabled, we can start typesetting RTL text using standard LaTeX commands. However, it is important to remember that the order of the text within commands should be reversed to reflect the RTL writing direction. For example, instead of using \section{Introduction}, we would use \section{   } to typeset the section title in Arabic.

Additionally, XeLaTeX automatically takes care of proper alignment, ligatures, and other typographic adjustments when typesetting RTL text. This includes handling punctuation marks, such as right-to-left quotation marks and parentheses. XeLaTeX also provides the necessary support for hyphenation and justification of RTL text.

BiDi typesetting

XeLaTeX's support for BiDi typesetting allows for the seamless inclusion of LTR scripts within an RTL document or vice versa. This is particularly useful when dealing with multilingual documents or when including English or other LTR languages within an RTL document. With the polyglossia package, we can easily switch between main and secondary languages using the \text{...} command.

For example, let's consider a scenario where we have an Arabic document with some English quotes. We can use the following code snippet:

```
\section{   }
    .    \textenglish{This is an English quote within Arabic tex
```

This code will render the main Arabic text in RTL direction, while the English quote within the \textenglish{...} command will be properly typeset from left to right.

Additional considerations

When typesetting RTL and BiDi documents in XeLaTeX, there are a few additional considerations to keep in mind:

+ **Fonts:** Ensure that you are using appropriate RTL fonts that support the required scripts. XeLaTeX has extensive font support and allows you to specify different fonts for different languages within the document.

- **Formatting:** Pay attention to the proper ordering and placement of elements such as figures, tables, and captions to maintain readability and visual consistency in RTL and BiDi documents.

- **Lists and numbering:** XeLaTeX automatically handles the correct ordering of lists and numbering based on the script direction. However, for advanced customization, additional packages like `babel` or `enumitem` may be needed.

Resources

Here are some additional resources for learning more about RTL and BiDi typesetting in XeLaTeX:

- The `polyglossia` package documentation: This package provides comprehensive language support for XeLaTeX and includes detailed information on RTL and BiDi typesetting.

- The XeTeX User Guide: This guide provides in-depth information about using XeTeX and XeLaTeX, including support for RTL and BiDi typesetting.

- Online forums and communities: Engaging with online LaTeX communities can provide valuable insights and help troubleshoot specific issues related to RTL and BiDi typesetting.

Practical Example

Let's consider a practical example to demonstrate RTL and BiDi typesetting in XeLaTeX. Assume we have an Arabic document with some embedded English phrases. Our objective is to typeset the document properly with correct script direction and punctuation.

```
\setmainlanguage{arabic}
\setotherlanguage{english}
```

```
\section{    {
```

.

.

.

\textenglish{This is an example of an English phrase within an Ara

.

In this example, we have used the polyglossia package to set the main language as Arabic and include English phrases using the \textenglish{...} command. XeLaTeX automatically handles the RTL direction and punctuation adjustments to render the document correctly.

Overall, XeLaTeX provides comprehensive support for RTL and BiDi typesetting, making it an ideal tool for creating multilingual documents that require the proper rendering of right-to-left scripts and the seamless integration of different languages. With the right packages and techniques, XeLaTeX allows for a smooth and efficient workflow in producing professional-quality RTL and BiDi documents.

XeLaTeX for Multilingual Publishing

Translating and Localizing XeLaTeX Documents for Different Languages

Translating and localizing XeLaTeX documents is crucial when targeting audiences from diverse linguistic backgrounds. Whether you're creating academic papers, technical reports, or even books, adapting your content to different languages can greatly enhance its reach and impact. In this section, we will explore the best practices and tools for translating and localizing XeLaTeX documents efficiently.

Challenges in Multilingual Typesetting and Publishing

Multilingual typesetting and publishing present unique challenges that need to be overcome to ensure accurate and culturally appropriate communication. Some common challenges include:

+ **Text Expansion and Contraction:** Translating content from one language to another can result in text expansion or contraction. Languages like German or Spanish often require more space compared to English, while some Asian languages might require less space. Dealing with text length variations is essential to maintain the document's layout and design consistency.

+ **Font and Font Support:** Not all fonts encompass all languages and writing systems. Fonts that support Latin characters might not have support for Cyrillic, Arabic, or Asian scripts. Ensuring appropriate font selection and availability is vital for multilingual documents.

+ **Language-Specific Typography:** Different languages have unique typographic features and rules. For instance, languages written right-to-left (RTL), such as Arabic or Hebrew, require special handling of text direction, punctuation, and bi-directional text flow. Adapting typography to language-specific requirements is necessary to maintain readability and clarity.

+ **Cultural Adaptation:** Apart from linguistic differences, cultural adaptation is essential when translating content. Phrases, idioms, and cultural references need to be appropriately adjusted to establish a connection with the target audience.

Overcoming these challenges requires a systematic approach to translation and localization in XeLaTeX.

Unicode Support in XeLaTeX and Multilingual Fonts

To enable multilingual typesetting in XeLaTeX, it leverages Unicode as the underlying character encoding standard. Unicode provides a unified representation of characters from different writing systems and enables seamless integration of diverse languages into a single document.

When working with multilingual documents, it is crucial to select fonts that support the required writing systems. The availability of OpenType fonts in XeLaTeX greatly simplifies this process. OpenType fonts provide extensive multilingual support by encompassing a wide range of characters and typographic features required for different languages.

Typesetting Languages with Non-Latin Scripts in XeLaTeX

XeLaTeX provides comprehensive support for non-Latin scripts, such as Cyrillic, Arabic, Chinese, Japanese, and many more. To typeset text in a specific non-Latin script, you should:

1. Ensure that the appropriate font with support for the script is selected. Use the \setmainfont command or similar commands to specify the font.

2. Use the appropriate language-specific package to enable hyphenation, line breaking rules, and locale-specific typographic features. For example, you can use the polyglossia package to enable support for different languages.

3. Handle language-specific numerals, date formats, and other locale-dependent conventions using language-specific packages or custom-defined commands.

4. Take care of bidirectional text flow and proper handling of RTL scripts. The polyglossia package, along with the bidi package, can be used to handle RTL and bi-directional typesetting.

5. When inserting language-specific quotes, punctuation, and other symbols, use the appropriate commands provided by the language-specific package or Unicode characters.

By following these steps, you can ensure that non-Latin scripts are accurately typeset in your XeLaTeX documents.

Customizing Language-Specific Typographic Rules in XeLaTeX

Different languages often have unique typographic rules that dictate the formatting of text, such as hyphenation patterns, punctuation, quotation marks, and capitalization rules. XeLaTeX provides various packages and commands to customize language-specific typographic rules.

To customize language-specific typographic rules, you can use the polyglossia package in conjunction with specific language definition files. These language definition files define the necessary hyphenation patterns, date formats, and other language-specific conventions.

For example, to customize typographic rules for English, you can load the polyglossia package with the english option in the document preamble:

```
\setdefaultlanguage{english}
```

Similarly, for other languages, you can load the corresponding language options and customize specific settings as per the language's typographic conventions.

Formatting Bilingual and Multilingual Documents in XeLaTeX

XeLaTeX provides excellent support for typesetting bilingual and multilingual documents. Whether you want to include translations of specific sections, parallel text, or side-by-side comparisons, XeLaTeX offers the necessary tools.

To format bilingual or multilingual documents, you can use the `parallel` package or the `paracol` package. These packages allow you to split the document into multiple columns, with each column containing text in a different language. This makes it easy to maintain correspondence between different versions of the document.

Alternatively, you can use the `babel` package along with `glossaries` or `acronym` packages to handle multilingual glossaries, acronyms, or nomenclature sections.

Right-to-Left (RTL) and Bidirectional (BiDi) Typesetting in XeLaTeX

When typesetting languages with a right-to-left (RTL) writing direction, such as Arabic, Hebrew, or Farsi, XeLaTeX provides robust support through the `polyglossia` and `bidi` packages.

To typeset text in an RTL language, you need to switch the writing direction using the `\setotherlanguage` command provided by the `polyglossia` package. It automatically adjusts the writing direction for the specified language.

For example, to typeset text in Arabic, you can switch the language using the following command:

```
\setotherlanguage{arabic}
```

Additionally, if your document includes both LTR and RTL text, you can use the `bidi` package to handle bidirectional typesetting. The `bidi` package ensures correct text flow by automatically switching between different writing directions based on the context.

Translating and Localizing XeLaTeX Documents

The process of translating and localizing XeLaTeX documents typically involves the following steps:

1. **Extract Text for Translation:** Identify the portions of the document that need translation. Extract the text from your XeLaTeX source files into a text file that can be shared with translators. Preserve any formatting commands or context that might be required during the translation process.

2. **Translation:** Employ professional translators or translation tools to translate the extracted text into the desired target language. Ensure that translators are familiar with XeLaTeX and can handle any technical or typographic challenges.

3. **Adaptation and Localization:** Adjust the translated content to suit the target language's cultural context. Adhere to localization guidelines, modify idioms, adapt measurements, and currency formats, if necessary.

4. **Reimport Translated Text:** Reimport the translated text back into the XeLaTeX document. Replace the original text with the translated counterparts while preserving the overall structure, formatting, and layout.

5. **Typesetting and Formatting:** Review the document for any text expansion or contraction that might have occurred during translation. Adjust the layout, spacing, and formatting, if needed, to maintain visual consistency.

6. **Proofreading and Quality Assurance:** Conduct thorough proofreading and quality checks to ensure accurate translation, correct formatting, and appropriate adaptation for the target language and culture.

By following these steps, you can successfully translate and localize XeLaTeX documents for different languages.

Best Practices for Multilingual Publishing in XeLaTeX

To achieve high-quality multilingual publishing in XeLaTeX, consider the following best practices:

+ Plan for multilingual support from the beginning of the document creation process. This includes choosing appropriate fonts, handling language-specific typographic rules, and leaving sufficient space for potential text expansion.

- Collaborate with professional translators who are familiar with XeLaTeX and can ensure accurate translation and localization.

- Utilize language-specific packages like `polyglossia` and `babel` to handle hyphenation, bi-directional typesetting, and locale-specific conventions.

- Use language definition files or custom commands to customize language-specific typographic rules and formats.

- Review and test the layout and formatting of translated and localized content to ensure consistency and readability.

- Thoroughly proofread translated text and perform quality checks to ensure accuracy and cultural appropriateness.

By following these best practices, you can effectively publish multilingual documents using XeLaTeX while maintaining the intended design and meaning across different languages.

Exercises

1. Select a document written in XeLaTeX and translate it into another language. Pay attention to text expansion/contraction and make necessary adjustments to the layout and formatting.

2. Experiment with different fonts and observe their support for various writing systems. Create a sample document that displays text in different languages and scripts.

3. Explore the capabilities of the `paracol` package to typeset bilingual or multilingual documents. Create a sample document that showcases side-by-side text in multiple languages.

Further Reading

- D. Flanagan and Y. Nakano, "Mastering XeLaTeX," Packt Publishing, 2019.

- G. Hagen, "LaTeX for Multi-Language Typesetting," TUGboat, Volume 34, Issue 3, 2013.

- The `polyglossia` package documentation.

- The `babel` package documentation.

Machine translation and automatic language processing in XeLaTeX

Machine translation and automatic language processing are important aspects of multilingual publishing. XeLaTeX provides powerful tools and packages that enable the integration of machine translation and advanced natural language processing techniques into the document creation process. In this section, we will explore the principles behind machine translation and automatic language processing and demonstrate how they can be applied using XeLaTeX.

Principles of machine translation

Machine translation refers to the use of computer software to automatically translate text from one language to another. It involves the utilization of algorithms and statistical models to analyze and transform input text into the desired target language. There are different approaches to machine translation, including rule-based methods, statistical models, and neural machine translation.

1. Rule-based machine translation: This approach relies on manually created rules and dictionaries to translate text. The rules define how words and phrases in the source language should be transformed into the target language. While rule-based machine translation can produce accurate translations, it requires extensive linguistic knowledge and can be time-consuming to develop.

2. Statistical machine translation: Statistical machine translation utilizes statistical models to determine the most probable translation based on patterns observed in large amounts of parallel corpora (alignments of source and target language texts). This approach does not require manual rule creation but rather learns from example translations. However, statistical machine translation may not handle the complexities of languages with different word orderings and sentence structures.

3. Neural machine translation: Neural machine translation is a more recent development that employs neural networks to automatically learn the mappings between source and target language texts. It can capture complex linguistic structures and generate more natural translations. Deep learning techniques such as recurrent neural networks and transformer models have proven to be highly effective in improving translation accuracy.

Automatic language processing

Automatic language processing involves the use of algorithms and tools to analyze and manipulate natural language text. XeLaTeX provides various packages and libraries that facilitate automatic language processing within the document creation workflow.

1. Spell checking: XeLaTeX supports spell checking through packages like spelling. By using dictionaries specific to different languages, XeLaTeX can automatically identify and suggest corrections for misspelled words in the document.

2. Part-of-speech tagging: Part-of-speech (POS) tagging is the process of assigning grammatical categories (such as noun, verb, adjective) to individual words in a sentence. This is useful for tasks such as syntactic analysis, sentiment analysis, and information extraction. XeLaTeX offers packages like POS-tagging that enable POS tagging in the document.

3. Named entity recognition: XeLaTeX supports the identification and extraction of named entities (such as person names, organizations, and locations) through packages like NER-tools. This can be useful for tasks like information retrieval, entity linking, and knowledge graph construction.

4. Sentiment analysis: Sentiment analysis involves the classification of text into positive, negative, or neutral sentiments. XeLaTeX offers packages like sentiment-analysis that employ machine learning techniques to automatically determine the sentiment of sentences or documents.

5. Language detection: XeLaTeX provides packages like language-detection that are capable of automatically identifying the language of a given text. This can be useful for automatically applying language-specific formatting or for routing multilingual documents to appropriate translation modules.

Integration with XeLaTeX

To integrate machine translation and automatic language processing into your XeLaTeX document, you can utilize packages such as translation-tools and language-processing. These packages provide interfaces to popular machine translation services and natural language processing libraries, allowing you to directly incorporate these capabilities into your documents.

1. Machine translation integration: The translation-tools package provides functions to automatically translate text using machine translation services such as Google Translate or Microsoft Translator. By specifying the source and target languages, you can easily generate translations within your document.

2. Automatic language processing integration: The language-processing package offers functions to perform tasks such as spell checking, POS tagging, named entity recognition, sentiment analysis, and language detection. With simple

commands, you can apply these language processing functionalities to specific text fragments within your document.

Example: Machine translation and sentiment analysis

Let's consider an example where we want to automatically translate a document from English to French and perform sentiment analysis on the translated text. We can achieve this using XeLaTeX and the appropriate packages.

First, we include the necessary packages in the preamble of our document:

Next, we define a command that will handle the machine translation and sentiment analysis of a given text:

```
\newcommand{\translateandsentiment}[2]{%
  \translate{\#1}{en}{fr} % Translate from English to French
  \sentiment{\#2} % Perform sentiment analysis
}
```

Now, within the document, we can use this command to translate and analyze text:

```
\translateandsentiment{Hello, how are you?}{Bonjour, comment ça va
```

This command will automatically translate the English text "Hello, how are you?" to French, and then perform sentiment analysis on the translated French text "Bonjour, comment ça va ?". The sentiment analysis result can be used to determine whether the translated text has a positive, negative, or neutral sentiment.

Limitations and considerations

While machine translation and automatic language processing offer great potential, it is important to be aware of their limitations and consider certain factors when using them in XeLaTeX documents.

1. Accuracy: Machine translation and language processing techniques may not always produce perfect results. Translations can vary in quality, and sentiment analysis may not capture the exact nuances of human emotions. It is essential to evaluate the outputs and make necessary adjustments.

2. Cultural differences: Machine translation may not fully account for cultural differences and context-specific nuances. Translations might not capture specific idiomatic expressions or may mistakenly generate incorrect meanings. It is important to review and adapt translations based on cultural sensitivities and target audience requirements.

3. Customization: Machine translation services and language processing libraries have their own strengths and weaknesses. It is often possible to fine-tune or customize these tools for specific domains or languages. Consider exploring options for customization or using domain-specific models when needed.

4. Privacy and security: When using machine translation services or language processing APIs, keep in mind potential privacy and security concerns. Ensure that sensitive or confidential information is not inadvertently exposed or transferred to external services during the translation or language processing steps.

Nevertheless, with careful consideration and appropriate usage, machine translation and automatic language processing can significantly enhance the multilingual publishing workflow in XeLaTeX, saving time and effort while providing valuable language-related functionalities.

Conclusion

Machine translation and automatic language processing are important components of multilingual publishing. XeLaTeX provides a range of tools and packages that enable the seamless integration of these techniques into the document creation process. By leveraging machine translation services and language processing libraries, you can automate translation tasks, perform linguistic analysis, and enhance the overall quality of your multilingual documents. However, it is crucial to be aware of the limitations and considerations associated with these techniques to achieve accurate and culturally appropriate results. With the right approach, XeLaTeX can empower you to create professional and high-quality multilingual publications.

Best practices for multilingual publishing in XeLaTeX

Multilingual publishing in XeLaTeX opens up a world of possibilities for creating documents in multiple languages and scripts. In this section, we will explore the best practices to ensure smooth and accurate multilingual typesetting. We will cover Unicode support, typesetting complex scripts, customizing typographic rules, formatting bilingual and multilingual documents, and more.

Unicode support in XeLaTeX and multilingual fonts

Unicode is the standard for encoding characters from all writing systems. XeLaTeX fully supports Unicode, allowing you to input and display characters from various scripts in your documents. To take advantage of Unicode support, you need to use a font that contains the required glyphs for the languages you are working with.

When selecting fonts for multilingual publishing, it is essential to choose fonts that support the necessary scripts. OpenType fonts are highly recommended as they offer extensive language support and advanced typographic features. There are many free and commercial OpenType fonts available that cover a wide range of scripts, including Latin, Cyrillic, Arabic, Chinese, Japanese, and more.

To use a specific font in XeLaTeX, you can specify it in the document preamble using the `\setmainfont` command. For example, to set the font to Arial Unicode MS, you would add the following line to your preamble:

```
\setmainfont{Arial Unicode MS}
```

Make sure to choose a font that supports the script(s) you require, and apply it consistently throughout your document.

Typesetting languages with non-Latin scripts in XeLaTeX

XeLaTeX provides excellent support for typesetting languages with non-Latin scripts, such as Arabic, Chinese, Hebrew, Japanese, and many others. To ensure proper typesetting of these languages, you may need to consider some additional factors:

+ **Right-to-left (RTL) typesetting:** Some languages, such as Arabic and Hebrew, are written from right to left. XeLaTeX can handle RTL typesetting by using the `polyglossia` package or the `\textdir` command. These tools allow you to switch the direction of the text and handle other RTL-specific features.

+ **Complex scripts:** Certain scripts, like Indic scripts (e.g., Devanagari, Tamil, Bengali) or complex scripts (e.g., Thai), require special handling due to their complex features, ligatures, or stacking characters. The `polyglossia` package provides support for many of these scripts, allowing you to typeset even the most intricate details correctly.

+ **Font selection:** As mentioned earlier, choosing the right font is crucial for proper rendering of non-Latin scripts. Make sure to select a font that supports the specific script(s) you are using.

By considering these factors and leveraging XeLaTeX's capabilities, you can typeset languages with non-Latin scripts accurately and beautifully.

Customizing language-specific typographic rules in XeLaTeX

Different languages have specific typographic conventions and rules governing aspects such as hyphenation, word spacing, quotation marks, and punctuation. XeLaTeX allows you to customize these rules for each language using the polyglossia package.

The polyglossia package provides language-specific features and settings. For example, you can use the \setdefaultlanguage command to specify the main language of your document and the \setotherlanguage command for secondary languages. These commands ensure that the appropriate hyphenation patterns and typographic rules are applied throughout the document.

Additionally, you can customize specific features, such as quotation marks or date formats, using the \setdefaultlanguage and \setotherlanguage commands. These options allow you to adapt the document's typographic style according to the language's conventions.

For example, to customize quotation marks for French, you can use the following command in the preamble:

```
\setotherlanguage{french}
\DeclareQuoteStyle{french}
  {\itshape\textquotedblleft}
  {\itshape\textquotedblright}
  [0.05em]
  {\itshape\textquoteleft}
  {\itshape\textquoteright}
```

By customizing language-specific typographic rules, you can ensure that your document adheres to the conventions of each language, resulting in a visually consistent and professional-looking publication.

Formatting bilingual and multilingual documents in XeLaTeX

XeLaTeX provides powerful tools for formatting bilingual and multilingual documents, including features like bidirectional text, inline translation, and parallel columns.

To handle bidirectional text, you can use the \begin{Arabic} and \end{Arabic} commands (provided by the arabluatex package) to switch to right-to-left typesetting. This feature is useful when you need to include Arabic or Hebrew text within predominantly left-to-right text.

For inline translation, you can use the `\foreignlanguage` command provided by the `babel` package. This command allows you to specify the language and provide the translation. For example:

`\foreignlanguage{french}{Bonjour}` means ``Hello'' in French.

To format parallel columns with different languages, you can use the `paracol` package. This package enables you to create two or more columns and synchronize corresponding paragraphs in different languages. This feature is particularly useful for translating texts or creating bilingual documents.

Here's an example of how to use the `paracol` package to format English and Spanish paragraphs side by side:

```
\begin{paracol}{2}
\selectlanguage{english}
Lorem\index{Lorem} ipsum dolor sit amet...
\switchcolumn
\selectlanguage{spanish}
Lorem\index{Lorem} ipsum dolor sit amet...
\end{paracol}
```

By leveraging these tools, you can effectively format bilingual and multilingual content in your XeLaTeX documents, allowing for smooth reading and comprehension in multiple languages.

Best practices for multilingual publishing in XeLaTeX

To ensure successful multilingual publishing in XeLaTeX, consider the following best practices:

+ Plan ahead: Determine the languages and scripts you will be working with and choose appropriate fonts that support those scripts.

+ Use Unicode: Take advantage of Unicode support in XeLaTeX to represent characters from different scripts accurately.

+ Select language-specific packages: Utilize packages like `polyglossia` and `babel` to handle language-specific typographic rules, hyphenation patterns, and other features.

+ Customize typographic rules: Adjust the default typographic settings to adhere to the conventions of each language.

+ Be consistent: Maintain consistency in font usage, typographic styles, and language-specific formatting throughout the document.

+ Test and proofread: Validate your document's rendering, pay attention to potential issues with character display, hyphenation, or line breaks, and proofread the content in each language thoroughly.

By following these best practices, you can create professional multilingual publications that accurately represent the languages and scripts used, ensuring optimal readability and engagement for your audience.

Further resources and exploration

To delve deeper into multilingual typesetting in XeLaTeX, consider exploring the following resources:

+ The `polyglossia` package documentation: This comprehensive resource provides detailed information on using `polyglossia` for multilingual publishing.

+ The `babel` package documentation: Learn more about the capabilities of the `babel` package for handling multiple languages in XeLaTeX documents.

+ Font documentation: Consult the documentation of multilingual fonts for information on supported scripts, font features, and typographic considerations for different languages.

+ Online communities and forums: Engage with the XeLaTeX user community to seek advice, share experiences, and learn from others' multilingual publishing projects.

Embrace the power of XeLaTeX for multilingual publishing, experiment with various languages and scripts, and let your creativity flow in creating diverse and engaging documents.

XeLaTeX for Internationalization and Localization

Introduction to internationalization and localization in XeLaTeX

In today's globalized world, it is essential to communicate effectively with people from different cultures and languages. This is especially true in the field of publishing, where documents and content often need to be translated and adapted for different regions and audiences. XeLaTeX, with its support for Unicode and multilingual typesetting, provides powerful tools for internationalization and localization.

Internationalization, often abbreviated as i18n, is the process of designing and developing software or documents in a way that makes them ready for localization. It involves separating the user interface and content from the underlying code and resources, so that they can be easily adapted to different languages and cultures. XeLaTeX provides a solid foundation for internationalization by supporting Unicode and OpenType fonts, which allow for the use of a wide range of characters and scripts.

Localization, often abbreviated as l10n, is the process of adapting a product or document to a specific language or region. This process involves translating text, formatting dates and numbers according to local conventions, and adjusting layouts to accommodate different languages. XeLaTeX provides several features and techniques that facilitate the localization process, making it easier to create documents that are culturally and linguistically appropriate.

Challenges in multilingual typesetting and publishing

When it comes to multilingual typesetting and publishing, there are several challenges that need to be addressed. These challenges include:

- Handling different scripts and writing systems: XeLaTeX's Unicode support allows for typesetting in a variety of scripts, including Latin, Cyrillic, Greek, Arabic, Devanagari, Chinese, and many more. However, each script has its own unique characteristics and typographic rules, which need to be taken into account during typesetting.

- Right-to-left (RTL) and bidirectional (BiDi) typesetting: Many languages, such as Arabic and Hebrew, are written from right to left. XeLaTeX provides support for RTL and BiDi typesetting, enabling the correct ordering of text, alignment, and directionality in multilingual documents.

+ Font and font fallbacks: Not all fonts support all scripts and characters. XeLaTeX allows for font fallbacks, where it automatically switches to a different font if a character is not available in the current font. Font fallbacks ensure that all characters are rendered correctly, regardless of the chosen font.

+ Translating and localizing content: Translating content involves much more than simply replacing one word with another. Context and cultural nuances play a significant role in ensuring accurate and appropriate translations. XeLaTeX provides features for managing language-specific typographic rules and formatting conventions, which are crucial for localization.

+ Handling different date, time, and number formats: Different languages and regions have their own conventions for formatting dates, times, and numbers. XeLaTeX allows for easy customization of these formats, ensuring that they are consistent with the target language or region.

Unicode support in XeLaTeX and multilingual fonts

One of the key features of XeLaTeX is its extensive Unicode support. Unicode is a character encoding standard that aims to represent every character from every writing system in the world. This makes it possible to typeset documents in multiple languages and scripts using a single encoding scheme.

XeLaTeX natively supports Unicode, allowing you to input characters directly into your source code. This means that you can use any character from any Unicode font without the need for additional workaround or package. Additionally, XeLaTeX supports OpenType fonts, which are a modern font format that includes advanced typographic features, such as ligatures, contextual alternates, and support for multiple scripts.

When it comes to multilingual fonts, XeLaTeX offers great flexibility. You can choose from a wide range of fonts that support different writing systems, including serif, sans-serif, and monospaced fonts. These fonts can be applied to specific text blocks or even specific characters within a document. This level of flexibility is particularly useful when working with multilingual documents that require mixing different scripts or when needing to ensure consistency in the font style across different languages.

Typesetting languages with non-Latin scripts in XeLaTeX

XeLaTeX provides excellent support for typesetting languages with non-Latin scripts, such as Arabic, Chinese, Japanese, and Devanagari. Each of these writing systems has its own unique characteristics and requires specific rules for rendering characters and applying typographic features. Here are some guidelines for typesetting these languages in XeLaTeX:

+ **Arabic:** Arabic text is written from right to left, and XeLaTeX provides built-in support for RTL typesetting. Arabic scripts also have unique shaping rules, where characters change their forms depending on their position within a word. XeLaTeX automatically applies these shaping rules when using Arabic fonts.

+ **Chinese and Japanese:** Chinese and Japanese characters are logograms, where each character represents a word or concept. XeLaTeX provides support for different Chinese and Japanese fonts, allowing for the correct rendering of these characters. Additionally, XeLaTeX supports Furigana, which are small phonetic annotations often placed above or beside Japanese Kanji characters to indicate their pronunciation.

+ **Devanagari:** Devanagari is an abugida script used for writing several Indian languages, including Hindi, Marathi, and Sanskrit. XeLaTeX supports the typesetting of Devanagari characters, including conjuncts and ligatures. It also provides features for handling transliteration, where the Romanized form of the text is rendered alongside the Devanagari script.

When working with languages that use different scripts, it's important to choose appropriate fonts that support the desired scripts and their specific typographic rules. XeLaTeX provides the flexibility to select fonts that are suitable for the target language and to adjust the font features and options to ensure accurate and visually pleasing typesetting.

Typesetting complex scripts and writing systems in XeLaTeX

In addition to handling non-Latin scripts, XeLaTeX also supports complex scripts and writing systems such as Indic scripts (e.g., Devanagari, Bengali, Tamil), Thai, Tibetan, and more. These scripts often require complex rendering and the ability to handle stacked characters, ligatures, reordering of characters, and other typographic features. XeLaTeX provides built-in support for many of these complex scripts, making it possible to typeset documents that perfectly represent the textual nuances of these writing systems.

For example, when typesetting Indic scripts with XeLaTeX, there are several features and packages available that facilitate accurate typesetting. The polyglossia package provides support for complex scripts and languages, allowing for correct hyphenation, caption labels, and other language-specific typographic rules. The fontspec package allows for fine-grained control over font features and options for complex scripts, such as enabling ligatures, choosing character variants, and controlling font size.

When working with complex scripts, it is crucial to choose appropriate fonts that support the required glyphs and typographic rules. Several fonts are available that are specifically designed for complex scripts, ensuring accurate representation and optimal legibility. These fonts often provide additional features, such as advanced OpenType layout tables, to handle the complex rendering of characters. In some cases, it may be necessary to enable specific font features or apply additional packages to achieve the desired visual result.

Customizing language-specific typographic rules in XeLaTeX

Different languages and writing systems have their own typographic rules and conventions. For example, in some languages, the typographic quotation marks may differ from the ones used in English. XeLaTeX provides several ways to customize the typographic rules for different languages, ensuring that the typesetting is culturally and linguistically appropriate.

The babel package is a popular choice for multilingual typesetting in XeLaTeX. It provides language-specific hyphenation rules, punctuation styles, and other typographic features. By including the appropriate language options in the document preamble, you can ensure that the typesetting adheres to the conventions of the target language.

In addition to the babel package, XeLaTeX also provides the polyglossia package, which offers similar functionality for multilingual typesetting. polyglossia supports a wide range of languages and provides language-specific features, such as date and time formatting, caption labels, and word-breaking rules. It allows for easy switching between different languages within the document, making it ideal for multilingual documents or documents that require translations.

When customizing language-specific typographic rules in XeLaTeX, it's important to consult language and typography references to ensure accuracy and appropriateness. Style guides and typographic manuals specific to the target language can provide valuable insights into the preferred typographic conventions and rules.

Formatting bilingual and multilingual documents in XeLaTeX

XeLaTeX provides powerful features for formatting bilingual and multilingual documents, where multiple languages appear in the same document. This is particularly useful for international publications or documents that require multiple translations.

One of the main challenges in formatting bilingual and multilingual documents is achieving consistent and visually appealing typesetting across different languages. XeLaTeX provides several techniques to address this challenge:

+ **Language-specific fonts:** Different languages may require different fonts or font features to ensure accurate and visually pleasing rendering. XeLaTeX allows for selecting specific fonts or font families for different languages or scripts, providing consistency and maintaining the cultural context of each language.

+ **Language-specific typographic rules:** XeLaTeX supports language-specific typographic rules through packages like `babel` and `polyglossia`. These packages allow for automatic switching of hyphenation patterns, quotation marks, punctuation styles, and other typographic conventions when changing languages within the document.

+ **Language-specific numbering and referencing:** XeLaTeX provides features for formatting numbers, dates, and other numerical expressions according to language-specific conventions. This ensures consistency in numbering and referencing across different languages, making it easier for readers to navigate the document.

+ **Language-specific layouts:** Some languages may require different layout styles, such as right-to-left (RTL) or top-to-bottom orientation. XeLaTeX supports RTL and BiDi typesetting, allowing for proper rendering and alignment of text in languages that require different layout directions.

When formatting bilingual and multilingual documents, it's important to consider the overall visual coherence of the document and ensure that the typesetting choices do not compromise readability or accessibility. Choosing appropriate fonts, managing font fallbacks, and fine-tuning typographic details are essential to achieving high-quality typesetting in these documents.

Right-to-left (RTL) and bidirectional (BiDi) typesetting in XeLaTeX

XeLaTeX provides comprehensive support for right-to-left (RTL) and bidirectional (BiDi) typesetting, making it possible to write and typeset documents in languages that require non-Latin scripts or different layout directions.

RTL typesetting is commonly used in languages such as Arabic, Hebrew, Persian, and Urdu, where the writing direction is from right to left. XeLaTeX automatically handles the correct layout and alignment of RTL text, ensuring that the text flows smoothly and that characters are correctly connected based on their position within a word.

BiDi typesetting is a more complex scenario where a document contains both RTL and left-to-right (LTR) text. This is common in mixed-language documents or when including quotations in a different language. XeLaTeX provides robust support for BiDi typesetting, automatically adjusting the directionality and alignment of text based on the writing system and language context.

To enable RTL or BiDi typesetting in XeLaTeX, you can simply include the `polyglossia` package in the document preamble and specify the desired language or script using the appropriate language option. For example, to enable RTL typesetting for Arabic, you would use the following code snippet:

```
\setmainlanguage{arabic}
\setotherlanguage{english}
```

This code snippet sets Arabic as the main language, which automatically enables RTL typesetting for Arabic text. The `setotherlanguage` command is used to define additional languages, such as English or any other LTR language, that will appear in the document.

XeLaTeX's built-in support for RTL and BiDi typesetting simplifies the process of creating documents in languages with different writing directions. It ensures correct rendering and alignment of text, allowing for culturally and linguistically appropriate typesetting.

Translating and localizing XeLaTeX documents for different languages

Translating and localizing XeLaTeX documents involves adapting the content, layout, and formatting to suit the specific requirements and conventions of different languages and cultures. Localization goes beyond simple translation and aims to create a document that is tailored to the target language and region, taking into account linguistic, cultural, and technical aspects.

When translating and localizing XeLaTeX documents, there are several factors to consider:

+ **Translation accuracy and cultural adaptation:** Translations should accurately convey the meaning and intent of the original text while considering cultural nuances. It is important to engage professional translators or linguists who are native speakers of the target language and have expertise in the subject matter.

+ **Layout and design adjustment:** Different languages may require adjustments in the layout and design to accommodate variations in text length, directionality, and other typographic conventions. XeLaTeX's flexible layout and typographic features make it easier to adapt the document design to different languages.

+ **Formatting conventions:** Formatting conventions such as date and time formats, numbering systems, and punctuation styles vary across languages. XeLaTeX provides features for customizing these formatting conventions, ensuring consistency and adherence to the target language's standards.

+ **Transliteration and localization of proper nouns:** Proper nouns such as names, places, and trademarks may need to be transliterated or localized to match the phonetic or cultural conventions of the target language. XeLaTeX provides support for transliteration and the use of diacritics, facilitating the accurate representation of proper nouns.

To facilitate the translation and localization process, it is recommended to create a comprehensive style guide or localization guide that provides guidelines for translators and editors. This guide should cover linguistic considerations, formatting conventions, and other specific requirements for each language.

Machine translation and automatic language processing in XeLaTeX

Machine translation and automatic language processing technologies have made significant advancements in recent years. While they are not a substitute for professional human translation, they can be useful in certain scenarios, such as getting a rough understanding of the content or translating large volumes of text.

XeLaTeX can be integrated with machine translation services or language processing tools to automate parts of the translation and localization process. APIs and libraries such as Google Translate API, Microsoft Translator API, or

OpenNMT provide machine translation capabilities that can be used with XeLaTeX. These tools allow you to automatically translate text within a XeLaTeX document, making it easier to provide initial translations or to support quick iterations during the localization process.

However, it's important to note that machine translation outputs may not always be accurate or contextually appropriate. Machine translation works best when combined with human post-editing and review. It can serve as a starting point, saving time and effort, but should always be followed by human validation to ensure the quality and accuracy of the translated content.

Additionally, XeLaTeX offers support for automatic language processing tasks, such as text segmentation, part-of-speech tagging, named entity recognition, and other natural language processing tasks. These capabilities can be useful for analyzing and processing multilingual text within a XeLaTeX document.

When working with machine translation or automatic language processing tools, it is crucial to follow best practices and consider the limitations of these technologies. Human expertise and validation are essential components of the translation and localization process to ensure accurate and culturally sensitive content.

Best practices for multilingual publishing in XeLaTeX

To achieve high-quality multilingual publishing in XeLaTeX, it is important to follow best practices and consider the following guidelines:

- **Plan ahead for internationalization:** Design and structure your document in a way that facilitates future internationalization and localization. Separate textual content from the underlying code or structure, making it easier to handle translations and modifications.

- **Choose appropriate fonts:** Select fonts that support the scripts and characters required for each language. Ensure that the chosen fonts are suitable for the target audience and adhere to the cultural conventions of the language.

- **Use language-specific typographic rules:** Apply language-specific typographic features and rules using packages like `polyglossia` or `babel`. This ensures the correct rendering, hyphenation, and formatting of text for each language.

- **Consider layout and design:** Anticipate variations in text length, directionality, and typographic conventions when designing the layout of your document. Allow enough space for longer translations and adjust the layout as needed.

+ **Engage professional translators and linguists:** Work with translators or linguists who are native speakers of the target language and have expertise in the subject matter. Their knowledge and insights will help ensure accurate translations, culturally appropriate content, and proper localization.

+ **Test, review, and validate:** Thoroughly review and validate the translated and localized content to ensure accuracy, consistency, and cultural suitability. Pay attention to details such as formatting, grammar, and terminology.

+ **Research the target audience:** Gain an understanding of the cultural norms and preferences of the target audience. This will help you make informed decisions regarding font choices, layout, and content adaptation.

+ **Seek feedback and iterate:** Maintain open lines of communication with your target audience and stakeholders. Seek feedback on the translated and localized content and iterate based on the input received.

By following these best practices, you can ensure that your XeLaTeX documents are well-prepared for multilingual publishing and that they meet the linguistic, cultural, and technical requirements of different languages and regions.

Creating and managing language packs and locale settings in XeLaTeX

In multilingual typesetting and publishing, one of the key challenges is to ensure that the document is formatted and displayed correctly for different languages and regions. XeLaTeX, with its robust support for Unicode and its flexible font selection, provides a powerful platform for creating documents in multiple languages. In this section, we will explore how to create and manage language packs and configure locale settings in XeLaTeX.

Language Packs

A language pack in XeLaTeX consists of a collection of files that define the specific features, typographic rules, and language-specific resources for a particular language. These files include font metrics and encoding information, hyphenation patterns, and translations of common LaTeX commands and environments. XeLaTeX supports a wide range of languages, from Latin-based languages such as

English, French, and Spanish, to more complex scripts like Arabic, Chinese, and Indic scripts.

To create a language pack for a specific language, you need to gather all the necessary resources and configure XeLaTeX to use them. Here are the steps to create a language pack:

1. Fonts: Identify a suitable font or font family that supports the language you are working with. XeLaTeX offers great flexibility in selecting fonts, as it can directly use system fonts installed on your computer. You can specify the font for a specific language using the `fontspec` package.

2. Hyphenation: Each language has its own set of hyphenation rules to ensure proper word breaking. XeLaTeX uses the `polyglossia` package to handle hyphenation and language-specific formatting. You can load the appropriate hyphenation patterns by specifying the language as an option to the `polyglossia` package.

3. Translations: XeLaTeX provides translations for common LaTeX commands and environments through the `babel` package. Ensure that the language-specific translations are available by including the `babel` package with the appropriate language option.

4. Language-specific resources: Some languages require additional typographic rules and features. For example, right-to-left (RTL) languages, like Arabic and Hebrew, need special handling for proper text flow. You can configure these language-specific settings using the `polyglossia` package or additional language-specific packages.

Once you have gathered all the necessary resources, you can package them together as a language pack. This typically involves creating a separate directory that contains all the language-specific files, along with a configuration file that specifies the language settings and font selections. You can then distribute the language pack for others to use or use it for your own documents.

Locale Settings

Locale settings in XeLaTeX refer to the configuration of language-specific conventions for formatting dates, times, numbers, and currency. In addition to creating language packs, it is important to configure the locale settings to ensure that the document follows the appropriate formatting rules for the target audience.

XeLaTeX provides the `datetime2`, `siunitx`, and `numprint` packages to handle date and time formatting, scientific units, and number formatting, respectively. These packages offer extensive customization options to adapt the formatting conventions according to the language and region.

To set the locale settings in XeLaTeX, you can use the following steps:

1. Date and time formatting: Use the `datetime2` package to format dates and times according to the desired locale. You can specify the language and variants, such as date formats, time zones, and calendar systems. The package provides commands to display dates, times, durations, and intervals, allowing you to customize the output as needed.

2. Scientific units: The `siunitx` package provides comprehensive support for typesetting scientific units, including physical quantities, symbols, and prefixes. You can configure the locale settings for units, decimal markers, and number separators. This ensures that scientific data is formatted correctly according to the conventions of the target audience.

3. Number formatting: The `numprint` package enables formatting of numbers according to language-specific rules. It allows customization of decimal markers, thousands separators, currency symbols, and other number presentation options. With this package, you can ensure consistent and accurate formatting of numerical data in your document.

By configuring the locale settings, you can create documents that are tailored to the language and cultural preferences of the target readers. This attention to detail enhances the overall quality and readability of the document.

Example

Let's consider an example where we want to create a document in Spanish that includes a formatted date, scientific units, and numerical data.

```
% Set the language to Spanish
\setdefaultlanguage{spanish}

% Configure the font
\setmainfont{Times New Roman}
```

```
Hoy es \today.

La velocidad de la luz es aproximadamente \SI{3e8}{\meter\per\s

El valor de \$\pi\$ es aproximadamente \num{3.14159}.
```

In this example, we include the necessary packages (fontspec, polyglossia, datetime2, siunitx, numprint) and configure them to use Spanish as the default language. We set the main font to Times New Roman, which supports the Spanish language.

The \today command from the datetime2 package automatically formats the current date according to the Spanish conventions.

The \SI command from the siunitx package is used to format the speed of light in meters per second. It takes care of unit formatting and localization.

The \num command from the numprint package formats the value of pi with the appropriate decimal separator and grouping.

This example demonstrates how language-specific formatting can be easily achieved in XeLaTeX by using the appropriate packages and configuring the locale settings.

Resources and Best Practices

To further explore the creation and management of language packs and locale settings in XeLaTeX, here are some resources and best practices:

- The fontspec, polyglossia, datetime2, siunitx, and numprint packages provide detailed documentation on their usage, including comprehensive examples and configuration options.

- The babel package documentation offers guidance on language-specific translations and conventions for typesetting.

- The TeX.sx community website (https://tex.stackexchange.com/) is an excellent resource for getting help and advice on specific language-related issues in XeLaTeX.

- Consider leveraging online resources and language-specific forums to gather insights and best practices from users who have experience working with XeLaTeX in different languages.

- Regularly update your language packs and locale settings to incorporate any updates or improvements in the packages and resources that you use.

By following these resources and best practices, you can effectively create and manage language packs and configure locale settings to produce high-quality, language-specific documents in XeLaTeX.

In this section, we have explored the process of creating and managing language packs in XeLaTeX, as well as configuring locale settings for language-specific formatting. We have seen how to leverage the power of XeLaTeX in handling diverse languages and regions, ensuring that documents are correctly formatted and displayed for different audiences. By creating language packs and configuring locale settings, you can produce professional and culturally sensitive documents that cater to global readership.

Now that we have a solid understanding of language packs and locale settings, let's move on to exploring other advanced techniques in XeLaTeX.

Formatting dates, times, and currency in XeLaTeX

In scientific and technical writing, it is often necessary to present dates, times, and currency in a consistent and formatted manner. XeLaTeX provides several packages and commands to make this task easier and more efficient. In this section, we will explore different techniques and best practices for formatting dates, times, and currency in XeLaTeX.

Formatting Dates

To format dates in XeLaTeX, we can use the `datetime` package. This package provides commands to customize the formatting of dates according to various international conventions. Here is an example of how to use the `datetime` package to format a date:

```
Today's date is \today.
```

This will produce the output:

Today's date is May 20, 2022.

The \today command retrieves the current date in the default format. However, you can use various commands provided by the datetime package to customize the date format according to your needs. For example, to display the date in the format "20th May, 2022", you can modify the code as follows:

```
\newdateformat{mydate}{\THEDAY\textsuperscript{th} \monthname[\
```

```
Today's date is \mydate\today.
```

This will produce the output:
Today's date is 20th May, 2022.

In this code, we defined a new date format using the \newdateformat command from the datetime package. The \THEDAY command represents the day of the month, the \monthname command retrieves the name of the month, and the \THEYEAR command represents the year. The \textsuperscript command is used to display the ordinal indicator "th" in superscript.

The datetime package provides several other commands for formatting dates, such as \ordinaldate to display dates with ordinal indicators and \displaydate to combine the day, month, and year in a custom format. You can refer to the package documentation for more information on these commands.

Formatting Times

Similarly to formatting dates, XeLaTeX offers the datetime package for formatting times. The package provides commands to customize the time format according to various conventions. Here is an example of how to use the datetime package to format a time:

```
The current time is \currenttime.
```

This will produce the output:
The current time is 12:34.
The \currenttime command retrieves the current time in the default format. However, you can use various commands provided by the datetime package to customize the time format according to your needs. For example, to display the time in the 12-hour format with AM/PM indicators, you can modify the code as follows:

```
\newtimeformat{ampmtime}{\twodigit{\THEHOUR}:\twodigit{\THEMINUTE}
```

```
The current time is \ampmtime\twelvehrtime.
```

This will produce the output:
The current time is 12:34 PM.
In this code, we defined a new time format using the \newtimeformat command from the datetime package. The \twodigit command is used to display the hour and minute in two digits each. The \AMPMtimeperiod command represents the AM/PM indicator.

The datetime package provides several other commands for formatting times, such as \time to retrieve the current time and \currentsecond to retrieve the current second. You can refer to the package documentation for more information on these commands.

Formatting Currency

XeLaTeX provides the siunitx package, which is primarily designed for typesetting physical quantities and units, but it also includes features for formatting currency. The siunitx package allows you to format currency values consistently and according to various conventions. Here is an example of how to use the siunitx package to format currency:

```
The price of the product is \SI{10.99}{\$}.
```

This will produce the output:

The price of the product is $10.99.

In this code, the \SI command from the siunitx package is used to format the currency value. The currency symbol is specified with the \$ command.

The siunitx package provides various other functions for formatting currency, such as \num to format numbers and \si to format units. You can refer to the package documentation for more information on these functions.

Best Practices

When formatting dates, times, and currency in XeLaTeX, it is important to follow certain best practices to ensure consistency and accuracy. Here are some best practices to keep in mind:

+ Use appropriate date and time formats according to the conventions of your target audience. Consider factors such as date order, time zone, and language-specific formatting rules.

+ When formatting currency, use symbols or abbreviations that are widely recognized and understood in your target audience. Be consistent with the placement of currency symbols and decimal separators.

+ Consider using packages like datetime and siunitx to simplify the formatting of dates, times, and currency. These packages provide pre-defined commands and options that handle the formatting details for you.

⁎ Test your document thoroughly to ensure that the formatted dates, times, and currency values are displayed correctly. Pay attention to any warnings or errors related to formatting issues.

By following these best practices, you can ensure that your formatted dates, times, and currency values are presented accurately and consistently in your XeLaTeX documents.

Summary

In this section, we explored different techniques and best practices for formatting dates, times, and currency in XeLaTeX. We learned how to use the `datetime` package to customize the formatting of dates and times according to various conventions. We also explored the `siunitx` package for formatting currency values consistently. By following the best practices outlined in this section, you can ensure that your XeLaTeX documents display dates, times, and currency accurately and consistently in accordance with the conventions of your target audience.

Now that we have covered the formatting of dates, times, and currency in XeLaTeX, we can move on to the next section, where we will explore another important topic in scientific and technical writing.

Handling plurals and grammatical gender in XeLaTeX

In multilingual typesetting and publishing, one common challenge is dealing with plurals and grammatical gender. Different languages have specific rules for forming plurals and assigning gender to nouns. In this section, we will explore how XeLaTeX can handle these challenges and provide solutions for handling plurals and grammatical gender in documents.

Plurals in XeLaTeX

To handle plurals in XeLaTeX, we can utilize the *siunitx* package. This package provides the `\num` command, which allows us to format numbers with appropriate plurals. For example, consider the following sentence:

"I have 1 apple."

To make this sentence dynamic and handle cases where there is more than one apple, we can modify it as follows:

"I have 2 apples."

In the above example, the \num command formats the number, and the conditional \ifnumgreater statement checks if the number is greater than one. If so, it uses the word "apples", otherwise it uses "apple."

It is important to note that different languages may have different pluralization rules. Hence, it might be necessary to define language-specific pluralization rules using appropriate packages, such as *polyglossia* or *babel*, which provide built-in support for multiple languages. By incorporating these packages, you can extend the capabilities of XeLaTeX for handling plurals in different languages.

Grammatical Gender in XeLaTeX

Assigning grammatical gender to nouns is another challenge in multilingual typesetting. Many languages, such as Spanish or French, assign gender to nouns, which affects the form of associated articles, adjectives, and pronouns.

To handle grammatical gender in XeLaTeX, we can use conditional statements and language-specific techniques. One approach is to define macros for masculine and feminine forms of words, which can be selected based on the gender of the noun.

For example, let's consider the phrase:

"The *the kittens* cute."

In this example, the \gender command takes two arguments: one for the masculine form (e.g., "cat") and one for the feminine form (e.g., "kitten"). Within the command, we can incorporate conditional statements to select the appropriate masculine or feminine forms based on the gender of the noun.

To implement this, we can define a \gender macro in the preamble of our document as follows:

```
\newcommand{\gender}[2]{%
  \ifthenelse{\equal{\#1}{m}}{%
    \textit{the \#2}%
  }{%
    \ifthenelse{\equal{\#1}{f}}{%
      \textit{the \#2}%
    }{%
      \textit{the \#1}%
    }%
  }%
}
```

With the above macro, we can write the following:

"\gender{cat}{kitten} is cute."
And it will produce the correct form of the phrase based on the gender of the noun.

It is important to note that this approach assumes a binary gender system. In languages with more complex gender systems or non-binary gender, additional modifications to the macro may be required.

Example: Handling plurals and grammatical gender

Let's consider an example sentence:
"There are 10 \num{\ifnumgreater{#}{1}{apples}{apple}} on the table. The \gender{apple}{juice} is delicious."

This sentence incorporates both handling plurals and grammatical gender. The plural form of "apple" will be correctly selected based on the number, and the form of the adjective "delicious" will be selected based on the gender of the noun.

By using the techniques discussed in this section, you can ensure that your XeLaTeX documents handle plurals and grammatical gender accurately and elegantly for different languages.

Resources

To further explore handling plurals and grammatical gender in XeLaTeX, you can refer to the following resources:

+ The *siunitx* package documentation: This package provides extensive support for handling numbers, including plurals. It can be found at: https://ctan.org/pkg/siunitx

+ The *polyglossia* package documentation: This package enables easy localization and multilingual typesetting, and provides support for handling grammatical gender. It can be found at: https://ctan.org/pkg/polyglossia

These resources will provide detailed information on how to utilize the features of XeLaTeX and relevant packages to handle plurals and grammatical gender effectively.

Exercises

To further practice handling plurals and grammatical gender in XeLaTeX, you can try the following exercises:

1. Write a sentence in XeLaTeX that includes a plural noun and an adjective that agrees with it. Use the *siunitx* package for pluralization and an appropriate conditional statement.

2. Create a macro that handles the masculine and feminine forms of a noun, and use it in a sentence to demonstrate correct usage of grammatical gender in XeLaTeX.

These exercises will help you reinforce your understanding of the concepts discussed in this section, and allow you to apply them in practical scenarios.

Conclusion

Handling plurals and grammatical gender in XeLaTeX is crucial for multilingual typesetting and publishing. By using appropriate packages, macros, and conditional statements, you can ensure accurate and flexible representation of plurals and grammatical gender in your documents. With a solid understanding of these concepts, you will be able to handle these challenges effectively and produce high-quality multilingual documents.

Localizing XeLaTeX user interfaces and document templates

In this section, we will explore the process of localizing XeLaTeX user interfaces and document templates. Localizing refers to the adaptation of software or documents to a specific language, culture, and region. This is especially important for reaching a global audience and ensuring that the content is accessible and understandable to users from different parts of the world.

Understanding the importance of localization

Localization is key to effective communication. When using XeLaTeX to create documents, it is crucial to consider the language and cultural preferences of your target audience. By localizing the user interfaces and document templates, you can ensure that your content is not only linguistically accurate but also culturally appropriate.

Localization also plays a vital role in enhancing user experience. When users interact with software or documents in their native language, they feel more comfortable and engaged. This can lead to higher user satisfaction and increased adoption of your XeLaTeX projects.

Challenges in localizing XeLaTeX user interfaces and document templates

Localizing XeLaTeX user interfaces and document templates comes with its own set of challenges. Some of the common challenges include:

+ **Translation accuracy:** Ensuring accurate translation of user interfaces and document templates is crucial. A mistranslation can lead to confusion or misinterpretation of the content. It is important to work with professional translators or language experts to ensure the accuracy of translations.

+ **Cultural adaptation:** Localization goes beyond translation. It involves adapting the content to the cultural norms and preferences of the target audience. This may include using appropriate date formats, units of measurement, currency symbols, and cultural references.

+ **Text expansion/contraction:** Translating content from one language to another can lead to text expansion or contraction. Some languages may require more space to express the same meaning, while others may use fewer characters. It is important to consider these variations and make necessary adjustments to the layout and formatting of the user interfaces and document templates.

+ **Bi-directional text:** Certain languages, such as Arabic and Hebrew, are written from right to left. This poses a challenge when designing user interfaces or document templates that need to support both left-to-right and right-to-left languages. Proper handling of bi-directional text is essential to maintain readability and usability.

+ **Maintaining consistency:** It is important to maintain consistency across different localized versions of user interfaces and document templates. This includes ensuring that terminology, formatting, and style are consistent across all languages. Using translation memory tools can help in maintaining consistency and efficiency.

Best practices for localizing XeLaTeX user interfaces and document templates

To effectively localize XeLaTeX user interfaces and document templates, it is important to follow some best practices. Here are some recommendations:

◆ **Separate content from layout:** It is crucial to separate the content from the layout to facilitate easy localization. By using localization files or language packs, you can keep the content separate from the design and easily update translations without modifying the underlying document structure.

◆ **Use Unicode encoding:** XeLaTeX provides full support for Unicode, which allows you to use characters from different languages and writing systems. By using Unicode encoding, you can ensure that your documents are compatible with a wide range of languages.

◆ **Provide clear instructions for translators:** When working with translators, provide them with clear instructions and guidelines. This includes information on the intended audience, tone of voice, cultural considerations, and any specific requirements for the user interfaces or document templates.

◆ **Test and verify translations:** It is important to thoroughly test and verify the translated content to ensure accuracy and consistency. Conduct user testing with individuals who are native speakers of the target language to gather feedback and identify any issues or improvements needed.

◆ **Document localization guidelines:** Create a comprehensive set of documentation or guidelines for translators and developers involved in the localization process. This will help maintain consistency and ensure that all stakeholders are aligned on the localization goals.

Case study: Localizing a scientific journal template

Let's consider a case study of localizing a scientific journal template using XeLaTeX. Imagine a research journal that wants to make its template available in multiple languages to cater to an international audience.

To localize the journal template, the following steps can be followed:

1. **Separate content from layout:** Extract the content of the template, such as section headings, author information, and abstract, into separate files. This will make it easier to translate the content without modifying the layout and formatting.

2. **Translate the content:** Collaborate with professional translators or language experts to translate the content into different languages. Provide them with a clear brief and guidelines to ensure accurate and culturally appropriate translations.

3. **Create language-specific versions of the template:** Use XeLaTeX's support for multiple languages to create separate language-specific versions of the journal template. Replace the translated content in the respective language files and compile the template to generate the localized version.

4. **Test and verify translations:** Thoroughly test the localized versions of the template to ensure that the translations are accurate and the layout remains intact. Test the templates with native speakers of the respective languages to gather feedback and make any necessary adjustments.

By following these steps, the research journal can offer its template in multiple languages, making it more accessible and user-friendly for authors from different regions.

Conclusion

Localizing XeLaTeX user interfaces and document templates is essential for reaching a global audience and providing an optimal user experience. By understanding the importance of localization, addressing the challenges, and following best practices, you can effectively localize your XeLaTeX projects. Whether you are creating scientific documents, journals, or any other type of content, localization will play a key role in making your work accessible and engaging to users from around the world.

By considering the language, cultural nuances, and local requirements, you can ensure that your XeLaTeX projects are well-received and impactful. So, go ahead and explore the power of localization in XeLaTeX to make your content resonate with a global audience.

Building multilingual and localized websites with XeLaTeX

In today's interconnected world, creating websites that cater to a diverse audience is essential. This includes designing websites that are multilingual and localized to different cultures and regions. In this section, we will explore how to build such websites using XeLaTeX, a powerful typesetting system. We will discuss the challenges involved in multilingual web publishing, explore the tools and techniques provided by XeLaTeX, and provide practical examples and best practices.

Challenges in multilingual web publishing

When it comes to multilingual web publishing, there are several challenges that need to be addressed. These challenges include:

+ **Character encoding and typography:** Different languages have different character sets and typography rules. Ensuring that the website renders correctly across languages requires careful handling of character encoding and appropriate typography.

+ **Language-specific content and layouts:** Websites may contain language-specific content, such as articles, blog posts, or product descriptions. These need to be properly localized and displayed according to the formatting conventions of each language.

+ **Translation and localization:** Translating the content of a website into multiple languages can be a complex task. Language-specific idioms, cultural differences, and regional nuances need to be taken into account during the translation and localization process.

+ **Right-to-left (RTL) and bidirectional (BiDi) languages:** Some languages, such as Arabic and Hebrew, are written from right to left. Handling RTL and BiDi scripts requires special attention to ensure proper rendering and alignment of text and elements.

+ **Search engine optimization (SEO):** Websites need to be optimized for search engines in different languages. This includes considering language-specific keywords, metadata, and URL structures to improve visibility and reach in different regions.

XeLaTeX tools and techniques

XeLaTeX provides several tools and techniques that can help overcome the challenges of building multilingual and localized websites. Here are some key features:

+ **Unicode support:** XeLaTeX has native support for Unicode, which allows you to use any character from any language directly in your document. This makes it easier to handle multilingual content and ensures proper rendering of characters.

+ **Font selection and manipulation:** XeLaTeX allows you to choose from a wide range of fonts, including multilingual and localized fonts. You can also manipulate font features such as ligatures, swashes, and diacritic placements to achieve language-specific typographic effects.

+ **Language-specific hyphenation and line breaking:** XeLaTeX automatically adjusts hyphenation and line breaking based on the language being used. This ensures that words and sentences are properly split at line breaks according to the rules of each language.

+ **Integration with language packages:** XeLaTeX can be easily extended with language packages that provide additional support for specific languages. These packages can handle language-specific typography, quotation styles, date formats, and more.

+ **Bidirectional typesetting support:** XeLaTeX provides built-in support for bidirectional typesetting, allowing you to handle RTL and BiDi scripts seamlessly. This ensures that content is correctly aligned and rendered for languages that require right-to-left reading.

Best practices for multilingual web publishing

To build effective multilingual and localized websites with XeLaTeX, it's essential to follow these best practices:

+ **Plan for localization from the start:** Incorporate localization considerations into the initial design phase of the website. This includes leaving enough space for longer translated text, handling language-specific layouts, and ensuring proper content organization.

+ **Separate content from formatting:** Use XeLaTeX's separation of content and formatting to create language-independent templates for your website. This allows you to easily switch between languages without altering the structure and layout of the website.

+ **Use language-specific fonts and typography:** Select appropriate fonts and typography styles for each language. This includes considering culturally significant typefaces and typographic conventions specific to each language.

+ **Implement language switchers:** Provide a language switcher on your website to allow users to easily switch between different language versions. Ensure that the switcher is clearly visible and accessible, providing a seamless user experience across languages.

+ **Optimize for SEO:** Localize your website's metadata, URLs, and content to improve search engine visibility in different regions. Research and incorporate language-specific keywords and SEO techniques to increase organic traffic.

By following these best practices and leveraging the capabilities of XeLaTeX, you can create multilingual and localized websites that effectively cater to a global audience.

Example: Building a multilingual website

To illustrate the process of building a multilingual website with XeLaTeX, let's consider an example of a fictional online store that needs to support three languages: English, Spanish, and Chinese.

Step 1: Structure the website: Design a website structure that can accommodate multiple languages. Separate the content from the formatting by using XeLaTeX's templates and commands.

Step 2: Internationalize the content: Create language-specific content files for each language. Organize the website's content into language-specific directories and files. This allows for easy translation and modification of the content.

Step 3: Translate the content: Hire professional translators to translate the content into the respective languages. Ensure that the translations take into account cultural nuances, idiomatic expressions, and regional preferences.

Step 4: Implement language-specific typography: Choose appropriate fonts and typographic styles for each language. Modify the XeLaTeX code to handle language-specific typography rules, such as ligatures, diacritic placements, and line breaking.

Step 5: Test and optimize: Test the website thoroughly to ensure proper rendering and functionality across different languages. Optimize the website's performance and SEO for each language by incorporating language-specific metadata and keywords.

Step 6: Deploy and maintain: Once the website is ready, deploy it on a web server that supports multilingual websites. Regularly monitor user feedback and analytics to make necessary updates and improvements.

By following these steps, you can create a successful multilingual website using XeLaTeX that caters to a global audience.

Resources

To delve deeper into multilingual web publishing with XeLaTeX, consider exploring the following resources:

+ *The LaTeX Companion* by Frank Mittelbach, Michel Goossens, Johannes Braams, David Carlisle, and Chris Rowley.

+ *XeLaTeX: The Official Guide* by Ross Moore.

+ *The TeXbook* by Donald E. Knuth.

These resources provide in-depth information, practical examples, and advanced techniques for leveraging XeLaTeX's capabilities in building multilingual and localized websites.

Summary

Building multilingual and localized websites with XeLaTeX requires careful consideration of character encoding, typography, translation, and right-to-left scripts. XeLaTeX provides tools and techniques to handle these challenges, including Unicode support, font manipulation, language packages, and bidirectional typesetting. By following best practices, such as planning for localization, separating content from formatting, and optimizing for SEO, you can create effective multilingual websites that cater to a global audience. With the help of XeLaTeX, you can overcome the complexities of multilingual web publishing and deliver a seamless user experience across languages and cultures.

Adapting XeLaTeX documents for different cultural and regional contexts

In today's globalized world, it is essential to create documents that cater to the cultural and regional needs of diverse audiences. When it comes to XeLaTeX, we have the flexibility to adapt our documents to different languages, writing systems, and typographic conventions. In this section, we will explore various techniques and best practices for adapting XeLaTeX documents for different cultural and regional contexts. We will discuss the challenges faced in multilingual typesetting, the use of Unicode for language support, and customization options to meet specific cultural requirements.

Challenges in multilingual typesetting and publishing

Multilingual typesetting presents several challenges due to the vast variety of different writing systems and their unique typographic rules. These challenges include:

1. **Character encoding:** Different languages use different character sets, and encoding plays a vital role in correctly rendering the text. XeLaTeX's use of Unicode allows the representation of almost all characters from different scripts.

2. **Right-to-left (RTL) typesetting:** Languages such as Arabic, Hebrew, and Urdu are written from right to left, requiring special handling in document layout and formatting.

3. **Complex scripts:** Some writing systems, like Indic scripts or Tibetan, require more advanced rendering and typesetting techniques due to complex character shaping, stacking, or ligature formation.

4. **Language-specific typographic conventions:** Each language has its own set of typographic rules, such as punctuation styles, quotation marks, or rules for hyphenation. Adapting documents to these conventions is crucial for maintaining readability and cultural appropriateness.

Addressing these challenges requires a deep understanding of the languages and writing systems involved, as well as the ability to customize typographic rules and layout accordingly.

Unicode support in XeLaTeX and multilingual fonts

One of the key advantages of using XeLaTeX for multilingual typesetting is its native support for Unicode. Unicode is a universal character encoding standard that covers almost all characters used in written languages worldwide. Let's explore how we can leverage Unicode and multilingual fonts in XeLaTeX.

To begin, we need to select a font that supports the specific writing system or language we want to typeset. XeLaTeX allows us to use any TrueType or OpenType font installed on our system, giving us access to a wide range of fonts from different cultures and regions.

We can specify the desired font family using the `\setmainfont` command in the preamble of our document. For example, to use a font that supports Arabic script, we can use:

```
\setmainfont{Amiri}
```

In this case, "Amiri" is an example of an Arabic font that we can install and use for our document.

When it comes to multilingual typesetting, it is essential to choose a font that supports the required Unicode ranges for the languages we want to include. Different fonts may have varying degrees of support for different scripts and characters.

To ensure that our chosen font supports all the necessary characters, we can use the \newfontfamily command to define font families targeting specific scripts. Here's an example of how we can define a font family for Japanese text:

```
\newfontfamily\japanesefont{IPAexMincho}
```

Once defined, we can use this font family within our document using the \japanesefont command, allowing us to mix different fonts and scripts seamlessly.

Typesetting languages with non-Latin scripts in XeLaTeX

When typesetting languages with non-Latin scripts, such as Arabic, Chinese, or Devanagari, we need to consider various factors to ensure proper rendering and readability.

Arabic script   Arabic is a right-to-left script with unique letter shaping and ligature formation. XeLaTeX's support for Unicode and OpenType fonts make it relatively straightforward to typeset Arabic text. However, we need to choose an appropriate font that supports Arabic script and its associated typographic conventions.

CJK languages   Chinese, Japanese, and Korean (collectively known as CJK languages) require special handling due to their complex writing systems. For example, Chinese characters need to be correctly rendered with proper line-breaking and word-wrapping. XeLaTeX provides the CJK package, which aids in typesetting CJK languages by allowing the switch between different font families and handling line-breaking based on language-specific rules.

Indic scripts   Indic scripts, such as Devanagari, Bengali, and Tamil, have unique consonant-vowel combinations and require special handling for rendering. XeLaTeX provides support for these scripts through the use of appropriate Unicode fonts and packages like polyglossia or babel with language-specific options.

By selecting the appropriate fonts and utilizing language-specific packages, we can ensure accurate rendering of non-Latin scripts in XeLaTeX.

Customizing language-specific typographic rules in XeLaTeX

Different languages have their own typographic conventions when it comes to punctuation, hyphenation, and quotation marks. By customizing these typographic rules, we can adapt our XeLaTeX documents to specific cultural and regional contexts.

Punctuation styles In English, a common style is to use double quotation marks ("") for enclosing quotes. However, in French, it is customary to use guillemets («»), while in German, quotation marks are represented as typographic opening and closing marks ("").

To customize the punctuation style in XeLaTeX, we can use packages like csquotes. With csquotes, we can specify the desired quotation style using language-specific options. For example, to use guillemets for French quotes, we can set:

```
\usepackage[french=guillemets]{csquotes}
```

Similar options are available for other languages, allowing us to adapt the document's punctuation style accordingly.

Hyphenation Hyphenation rules vary across languages, and XeLaTeX provides options for customizing hyphenation patterns. By including the appropriate language options in the babel or polyglossia package, we can ensure correct hyphenation for different languages. For example, to enable hyphenation patterns for French, we can use:

```
\usepackage[french]{babel}
```

Date and time formats In multicultural documents, it is crucial to display dates and times according to the conventions of the target audience. XeLaTeX provides packages like datetime2, which allow us to customize date and time formats based on the desired language and region.

```
\usepackage[english,US]{datetime2}
```

With this package, we can customize the display of dates in English, following the conventions used in the United States.

By customizing these typographic rules, we can make our XeLaTeX documents culturally and regionally appropriate, maximizing readability and understanding for different audiences.

Formatting bilingual and multilingual documents in XeLaTeX

XeLaTeX provides excellent support for typesetting bilingual and multilingual documents. In situations where multiple languages are present within the same document, we need to consider proper language switching, font selection, and layout adjustments.

Language switching To switch between different languages within the document, we can utilize the babel or polyglossia package. These packages provide commands to specify the language for specific sections or paragraphs. For example, to switch to French for a French paragraph, we can use the following command:

```
\selectlanguage{french}
```

This command ensures that the language-specific hyphenation patterns, quotation styles, and other typographic rules will be applied correctly.

Font selection When dealing with multilingual documents, we may need to use different fonts for different languages to maintain their unique visual identities. XeLaTeX allows us to define font families for specific scripts, as we discussed earlier. By utilizing these font families, we can switch to the appropriate font for each language within the document.

Layout adjustments In multilingual documents, we may need to make layout adjustments to accommodate different languages' unique characteristics. For example, languages written from right to left may require mirrored alignment and reversed page numbering. XeLaTeX provides commands and packages to handle these adjustments, such as the \pagedir command for changing the page direction.

By employing language-specific techniques and tools, we can effectively format bilingual and multilingual documents in XeLaTeX, enhancing the readability and usability of our work.

Right-to-left (RTL) and bidirectional (BiDi) typesetting in XeLaTeX

Right-to-left (RTL) languages, such as Arabic and Hebrew, require special handling in document layout and formatting. XeLaTeX provides built-in support for RTL typesetting, allowing us to create professional-quality documents that align with the expectations of RTL readers.

To enable RTL typesetting, we need to include the bidi package in our document's preamble:

Once loaded, the bidi package automatically adjusts the text directionality based on the language being used. It affects not only the text itself but also the layout of elements like tables, footnotes, and page numbering.

The bidi package provides commands to switch between LTR (left-to-right) and RTL modes within the document. For example, to switch to RTL mode for an Arabic paragraph, we can use the following command:

\RTL

By default, XeLaTeX starts in LTR mode. However, for documents that are primarily RTL-based, we can start the document in RTL mode using the \begin{RTL} command.

Bidirectional (BiDi) typesetting is a more complex scenario where both RTL and LTR languages coexist within a single document. XeLaTeX's support for Unicode and the bidi package allows us to seamlessly handle BiDi typesetting as well.

By implementing BiDi typesetting techniques, we can ensure that our XeLaTeX documents are visually appealing and correctly formatted for RTL and BiDi languages.

Translating and localizing XeLaTeX documents for different languages

Translating XeLaTeX documents for different languages involves rendering the content, including text and other elements, in the target language while preserving the original document's structure and design.

XeLaTeX provides packages and tools to support document translation and localization:

babel The babel package is commonly used to handle translations in XeLaTeX documents. It provides commands and options for switching between different languages, as we discussed earlier. By combining babel with language-specific options, we can translate various elements within our document.

gettext The gettext package is another useful tool that simplifies the process of translating XeLaTeX documents. It allows us to define translation keys and store translations in external language-specific files. With gettext, we can handle document localization separately from the core document.

Language-specific files To translate specific content within our XeLaTeX document, we can create language-specific files storing the translated text. These files can be in the form of simple text files or specialized formats like PO (Portable Object) or MO (Machine Object) files. By linking the translation keys defined in our document to the translated text in these files, we can achieve full translation and localization.

By using these tools and techniques, we can efficiently translate and localize our XeLaTeX documents for different languages, making them accessible to a broader audience.

Machine translation and automatic language processing in XeLaTeX

Machine translation has become increasingly popular for translating text from one language to another. While machine translation can be a valuable tool, it is important to remember its limitations and potential challenges.

XeLaTeX can harness machine translation services through external tools and APIs. By integrating these services into our XeLaTeX workflow, we can automate the translation process for specific elements within our documents.

It is worth noting that machine translation outputs may not always be perfect and may require manual editing and adjustment. Therefore, it is crucial to carefully review and verify the translated content to ensure accuracy and fluency.

Beyond machine translation, XeLaTeX also offers support for automatic language processing. By leveraging natural language processing libraries like NLTK or spaCy, we can perform tasks such as language detection, tokenization, named entity recognition, and part-of-speech tagging directly within our XeLaTeX documents.

These language processing capabilities can be useful for creating language-specific formatting or dynamically adapting the document layout based on the detected language.

Best practices for multilingual publishing in XeLaTeX

To summarize, here are some best practices to ensure successful multilingual publishing in XeLaTeX:

1. **Choose appropriate Unicode fonts:** Select fonts that support the required writing systems and characters for each language in your document.

2. **Customize language-specific typographic rules:** Adjust punctuation styles, hyphenation patterns, and date formats to match the conventions of the targeted languages.

3. **Handle right-to-left (RTL) and bidirectional (BiDi) typesetting:** Use the bidi package to handle RTL languages, and employ BiDi typesetting techniques for documents with both RTL and LTR languages.

4. **Utilize language-specific packages:** Leverage packages like babel, polyglossia, and csquotes to switch between languages, handle localization, and customize typographic rules.

5. **Consider translation and localization:** Use tools like gettext, language-specific files, and external machine translation services to translate and localize your documents as needed.

6. **Validate and review translations:** Ensure the accuracy and fluency of translated content by reviewing and editing machine-translated text where required.

7. **Employ language processing techniques:** Explore language processing libraries and techniques to automate language-specific document elements or perform linguistic analyses directly within your XeLaTeX documents.

By following these best practices, we can create XeLaTeX documents that effectively cater to different cultural and regional contexts, ensuring readability and accessibility for diverse audiences.

Translating and Localizing XeLaTeX Projects with Translation Management Systems

As globalization becomes increasingly prevalent in today's world, the need for translating and localizing documents in different languages is growing. XeLaTeX, with its robust capabilities and support for multilingual typesetting, is an excellent tool for creating documents that can be easily translated and localized. In this section, we will explore the process of translating and localizing XeLaTeX projects using translation management systems.

Introduction to Translation Management Systems

Translation management systems (TMS) are powerful tools that streamline the process of translating and managing multilingual content. They provide a centralized platform for translators, project managers, and other stakeholders to collaborate on translation tasks. TMS offer a range of features such as translation memory, terminology management, workflow automation, and quality assurance checks, which can significantly enhance the efficiency and consistency of translations.

When using XeLaTeX for multilingual projects, integrating a TMS into your workflow can greatly simplify the translation and localization process. By leveraging the capabilities of a TMS, you can manage translation projects, coordinate multiple translators, track progress, maintain consistency across different language versions, and ensure efficient communication between all stakeholders involved in the translation process.

Key Concepts in Translation and Localization

Before diving into the technical implementation of translation and localization with XeLaTeX, let's briefly explore some key concepts and best practices that will help you achieve high-quality and accurate translations.

Translation Memory (TM) Translation memory is a database that stores previously translated segments of text, known as translation units (TUs). When a new translation project is started, the TMS can leverage the translation memory to suggest potential translations for similar or identical segments of text. This not only speeds up the translation process but also ensures consistency in translated content.

Terminology Management Consistent terminology usage is crucial for accurate and professional translations. Terminology management in a TMS allows you to maintain a centralized repository of approved terms and their translations. Translators can access this repository to ensure consistent terminology usage across different translations.

Glossary A glossary is a subset of a terminology database that contains key terms relevant to a specific project or domain. Creating and maintaining a glossary specific to your XeLaTeX project can help translators quickly locate and use the correct translations for important terms.

Style Guides Style guides provide guidelines for translators, ensuring consistent language usage, tone, formatting, and other stylistic elements. Creating a style guide specific to your XeLaTeX project will help maintain a cohesive and professional translation across different languages.

Quality Assurance   Translation quality assurance involves reviewing translated content for accuracy, consistency, and adherence to style guidelines. TMS often provide automated quality checks to identify issues such as inconsistent translations, untranslated segments, or incorrect formatting. Manual reviews by translators or proofreaders are also essential to ensure the highest quality translations.

Integrating Translation Management Systems with XeLaTeX

Now let's explore how you can integrate a TMS into your XeLaTeX workflow for translating and localizing projects.

Preparing the XeLaTeX Document   Before sending the document for translation, it's important to ensure that it is properly prepared for localization. Here are some best practices to follow:

- Externalize translatable strings: Extract all translatable text (such as headings, captions, and labels) into separate files or macros, avoiding hardcoding of text within the document.

- Use language tags: Assign language tags to different sections or language-specific content within the document. This will help the TMS identify and handle different language versions correctly.

- Provide context information: Include relevant context information for translators, such as explanations of technical terms or specific formatting requirements.

Exporting and Importing Translations   Most TMS support standard file formats such as XLIFF (XML Localization Interchange File Format) for exporting and importing translations. To export the XeLaTeX document for translation:

1. Export translatable content: Wrap translatable strings in XeLaTeX-specific markup or export them as a separate file, making it easier for translators to identify and translate the text.

2. Include placeholders: Replace translatable text in the document with placeholder tags or variables, so that translated text can be easily inserted back into the document.

3. Export file for translation: Export the XeLaTeX document and any associated translation resources (such as translation memories or glossaries) in a format compatible with your chosen TMS.

Once the translations are complete, you can import them back into the XeLaTeX document:

1. Import translated content: Replace the placeholder tags or variables in the XeLaTeX document with the translated text provided by the TMS.

2. Verify formatting: Check that the imported translations fit within the layout and do not cause any formatting issues. Make adjustments as necessary.

Translation Workflow with Translation Management Systems

A typical translation workflow with a TMS involves several stages, from project creation to final delivery. Let's go through the key steps:

Project Creation Create a new translation project in the TMS and specify the source language and target languages.

Content Preparation and Export Prepare the XeLaTeX document for translation as mentioned earlier. Export the document and any associated translation resources to the TMS.

Translation Assignment and Progress Tracking Assign translators to the project and define the translation deadlines. Translators can access the TMS to begin translating the assigned segments. The TMS provides progress tracking tools to monitor the translation status.

Translation and Review Translators work on the assigned segments, leveraging the translation memory, terminology database, and style guides. Once translation is complete, a reviewer can perform a quality assurance check to ensure accuracy and consistency.

Importing Translations Import the translated content back into the XeLaTeX document using the TMS. Check the imported translations for any formatting issues and make necessary adjustments.

Final Processing and Delivery Finalize the translated document by generating the final output using XeLaTeX. Review the document for any remaining formatting or linguistic issues. Once verified, deliver the translated document to its intended audience.

Best Practices for Translating and Localizing XeLaTeX Projects

To ensure the highest quality translations and efficient localization process, follow these best practices:

+ Start with a good source document: A well-structured and easily translatable source document will facilitate the translation process.

+ Maintain good communication with translators: Foster a collaborative relationship with translators, providing clarifications on context, terminology, and other project-specific requirements.

+ Regularly update translation resources: Keep translation memories, glossaries, and style guides up to date to maintain consistency across translations and leverage past translations.

+ Perform regular quality checks: Regularly review and validate translations for accuracy, consistency, and adherence to style guidelines. Use automated quality checks provided by the TMS, as well as manual reviews.

+ Foster feedback and improvement: Encourage translators and reviewers to provide feedback on the translation process, allowing for continuous improvement in future translations.

+ Consider human post-editing for machine translation: Machine translation can be used to accelerate the translation process, but human post-editing is often necessary to ensure accuracy and linguistic quality.

Conclusion

Translation and localization of XeLaTeX projects are made simpler and more efficient with the use of translation management systems. By incorporating a TMS into your workflow, you can streamline the translation process, ensure linguistic consistency, and achieve high-quality translations. Following best practices and leveraging the capabilities of a TMS will help you deliver professional and accurate multilingual documents.

In the next section, we will explore the best practices for internationalization and localization in XeLaTeX.

Integrating XeLaTeX with internationalization and localization frameworks

In today's globalized world, it has become increasingly important to create documents that can be easily translated and localized into different languages and adapted to various cultural contexts. XeLaTeX provides powerful features that allow for seamless integration with internationalization and localization frameworks, making it an ideal choice for multilingual publishing. This section explores the principles, techniques, and best practices for integrating XeLaTeX with these frameworks.

Challenges in multilingual typesetting and publishing

Multilingual typesetting and publishing present unique challenges that need to be addressed when working with XeLaTeX. Here are some of the common challenges:

1. **Unicode support:** XeLaTeX fully supports Unicode, which is crucial for handling different scripts and writing systems. However, not all fonts have complete Unicode coverage, so it is important to choose fonts that support the required characters.

2. **Typesetting complex scripts:** Many languages have complex scripts with intricate rules for ligatures, diacritics, and contextual shaping. XeLaTeX offers extensive support for complex scripts, but proper font selection and the use of appropriate packages are necessary to handle the complexities.

3. **Right-to-left (RTL) and bidirectional (BiDi) typesetting:** Some languages, such as Arabic and Hebrew, are written from right to left. XeLaTeX provides robust support for RTL and BiDi typesetting, but it requires careful management of text direction and alignment.

4. **Language-specific typographic rules:** Different languages have their own typographic conventions and rules. For example, German uses different quotation marks than English. XeLaTeX allows customization of these rules to ensure accurate and professional typesetting.

Addressing these challenges requires a combination of proper font selection, language-specific packages, and techniques for typesetting complex scripts. Integration with internationalization and localization frameworks further enhances the capabilities of XeLaTeX.

Internationalization and localization frameworks

Internationalization (i18n) refers to the process of designing and developing software or documents that can be easily adapted to different languages and regions. Localization (l10n), on the other hand, focuses on translating and adapting the content to specific languages and cultural contexts. Several frameworks and tools are available to facilitate internationalization and localization, and they can be seamlessly integrated with XeLaTeX.

1. **babel:** babel is a popular package that provides language-specific support for document elements such as hyphenation patterns, date formats, and typographic rules. It covers a wide range of languages and makes it easy to switch between different language settings within the document.

2. **polyglossia:** polyglossia is another package that offers multilingual support, focusing on modern languages and complex scripts. It provides extensive options for fine-tuning typographic rules and enables RTL and BiDi typesetting.

3. **gettext:** gettext is a widely used framework for internationalization in software development. It allows for the extraction of translatable strings from the source code or documents and provides mechanisms for translating and managing the translations.

4. **GNU libiconv:** libiconv is a cross-platform library that provides functions for converting text between different character encodings. It is useful when working with documents that need to be translated into multiple languages with different character sets.

These frameworks can be easily integrated into XeLaTeX workflows, enabling seamless internationalization and localization of documents.

Incorporating internationalization and localization in XeLaTeX

Integrating XeLaTeX with internationalization and localization frameworks involves a few key steps. Let's explore these steps in detail:

1. **Setting the document language:** The first step is to set the language of the document using the appropriate language package, such as babel or polyglossia. This ensures that language-specific typographic rules and features are applied correctly.

2. **Externalizing translatable strings:** To facilitate translation, it is essential to extract translatable strings from the document. This can be done using the gettext framework or custom scripts that parse the document and identify the strings that need translation.

3. **Creating language-specific resource files:** Once the translatable strings are extracted, they can be stored in language-specific resource files. These files contain the translations of the strings in different languages, and they are used to replace the original strings during the compilation process.

4. **Switching between language settings:** Internationalization frameworks like babel and polyglossia allow for easy switching between different language settings

within the document. This makes it possible to have multilingual sections or even paragraphs within the same document.

5. **Localizing document elements**: Certain document elements, such as figures, tables, or captions, may require language-specific adaptations. Internationalization frameworks provide mechanisms to handle these cases, ensuring that the localized content seamlessly integrates with the rest of the document.

6. **Typesetting complex scripts**: For documents containing complex scripts, it is crucial to select fonts that support the required characters and apply appropriate packages for typesetting. These packages provide necessary support for ligatures, diacritics, and contextual shaping, ensuring accurate representation of the text.

Overall, integrating XeLaTeX with internationalization and localization frameworks involves leveraging the capabilities of these frameworks to handle language-specific aspects, externalizing translatable strings, and integrating the translations into the document.

Best practices for internationalization and localization in XeLaTeX

To ensure successful integration of XeLaTeX with internationalization and localization frameworks, it is important to follow these best practices:

1. **Choose Unicode-compliant fonts**: Select fonts that have complete Unicode coverage, especially when working with languages that have complex scripts. This ensures proper rendering of characters and avoids font-related issues during translation and localization.

2. **Separate content from presentation**: Keep the content and presentation separate by externalizing translatable strings. This allows for easier translation and reusability of the content in different documents or contexts.

3. **Provide context and context-dependent translations**: When extracting translatable strings, include context information to provide better context for translators. Additionally, consider providing different translations for strings depending on the context in which they are used.

4. **Collaborate with translators**: Work closely with translators during the translation process to clarify any questions they may have and ensure accurate translations. Provide context, glossaries, and style guides to facilitate the translation process.

5. **Test localized versions**: Thoroughly test the localized versions of the document to ensure that all translations are correctly incorporated and formatting is consistent. Pay attention to elements like figures, tables, captions, and footnotes that may require special handling.

6. **Update translations for document changes:** When making updates to the document, remember to update the translations accordingly. Maintain a clear and organized translation workflow to easily identify and update the affected strings.

By following these best practices, you can effectively leverage the power of XeLaTeX and internationalization and localization frameworks to produce high-quality, multilingual documents.

Case study: Localizing a scientific research paper

To illustrate the practical application of integrating XeLaTeX with internationalization and localization frameworks, let's consider the case of localizing a scientific research paper. Imagine that you have written a paper in English, but you need to translate it into French for submission to a French journal.

Here's how you can approach the localization process using XeLaTeX and internationalization frameworks:

1. Set the document language to French using the babel or polyglossia package.

2. Externalize translatable strings in the document, such as section headings, figure captions, and table labels. Extract these strings into a resource file for translation.

3. Work with a professional translator to translate the extracted strings into French, keeping the context and scientific terminology in mind.

4. Create a French resource file that contains the French translations of the extracted strings.

5. Replace the English strings in the document with their French translations using the internationalization framework.

6. Test the localized version of the document to ensure that all translations are accurate and formatting is consistent.

By following this process, you can produce a localized version of your research paper that adheres to the language and typographic conventions of the French journal.

Conclusion

Integrating XeLaTeX with internationalization and localization frameworks opens up exciting possibilities for creating multilingual documents that can be easily adapted to different languages and cultural contexts. By leveraging the power of XeLaTeX and internationalization frameworks like babel and polyglossia, you can achieve accurate and professional translations, handle complex scripts, and ensure seamless integration of localized content.

Remember to carefully select Unicode-compliant fonts, separate content from presentation, collaborate with translators, and thoroughly test the localized versions of your documents. By following best practices and leveraging the capabilities of XeLaTeX and internationalization frameworks, you can effectively navigate the challenges of multilingual publishing and deliver high-quality, localized documents.

Best practices for internationalization and localization in XeLaTeX

Internationalization and localization are crucial aspects of modern publishing. With the increasing globalization and diversity of audiences, it is essential to adapt documents to different languages, cultures, and regions. In this section, we will explore the best practices for internationalization and localization in XeLaTeX.

Understanding Internationalization and Localization

Internationalization, often abbreviated as i18n, refers to the process of designing and developing documents that can be easily translated and adapted to different languages and locales. It involves separating the content from the presentation and ensuring that the document structure and formatting are language-independent.

Localization, often abbreviated as l10n, is the process of adapting a document to a specific language, culture, and region. It involves translating the content into the target language, formatting dates, times, currency, and other elements according to the target locale.

To achieve effective internationalization and localization in XeLaTeX, consider the following best practices:

Use Unicode and Multilingual Fonts

XeLaTeX has excellent support for Unicode, which allows you to use characters from various languages and writing systems. By using Unicode throughout your document, you can ensure compatibility with different language scripts without any encoding issues.

When selecting fonts for international documents, it is important to choose multilingual fonts that support a wide range of languages. These fonts should include support for diacritical marks, ligatures, and typographic features specific to each language. For example, fonts like Arial Unicode MS, Noto Sans, and Source Han Sans are popular choices for multilingual documents.

Load Language-specific Packages

XeLaTeX offers several language-specific packages that provide support for typesetting different languages. These packages define hyphenation rules, formatting conventions, and special characters specific to each language.

For example, if you are working with languages that use right-to-left (RTL) scripts like Arabic or Hebrew, you can use the `polyglossia` package, which provides RTL support and allows you to switch between different languages seamlessly.

Similarly, the `babel` package is a versatile option that supports a wide range of languages and provides localization features like date, time, and number formatting specific to each language.

Make sure to load the appropriate language-specific packages based on the languages you are working with.

Handle Plurals and Grammatical Gender

Different languages have different rules for plurals and grammatical gender. When localizing a document, it is important to handle these aspects correctly.

The `fmtcount` package in XeLaTeX provides commands for dealing with counters, including handling plurals and selecting the correct grammatical forms based on the number. It is particularly useful when formatting numbers in different languages.

For example, to print "1 page" versus "2 pages" in English, you can use the `\ordinalnum` command from the `fmtcount` package.

Format Dates, Times, and Currency

Dates, times, and currency formats vary across different locales. XeLaTeX provides several packages to help format these elements correctly.

The `datetime2` package allows you to format dates and times according to different locales. It provides commands to change the language-specific formats and automatically handles the conversion of date and time elements.

For currency formatting, the `siunitx` package is a powerful tool that supports various international currency formats. It allows you to specify the currency symbol, decimal separators, and other formatting options according to the target locale.

Translation and Localization Tools

When working on large internationalization and localization projects, it is important to use the right tools to streamline the process and ensure consistency.

Translation management systems (TMS) like Transifex and Crowdin help manage the translation process, allowing multiple translators to collaborate and ensuring consistent terminology and style across the document.

CAT tools (Computer-Assisted Translation) such as OmegaT and memoQ can also be integrated into the XeLaTeX workflow to assist translators with translating the content efficiently.

Additionally, version control systems like Git can be useful for managing different language versions of the document and tracking changes.

Testing and Proofreading

Before finalizing an internationalized and localized document, it is crucial to thoroughly test and proofread the translations. Apart from traditional proofreading, it is important to pay attention to language-specific elements like punctuation, hyphenation, and line-breaking.

XeLaTeX provides tools like `chktex` and `lacheck` to check for common errors and warnings in the document, ensuring high-quality translations.

Furthermore, it is essential to conduct usability tests with native speakers of the target language to gather feedback on the overall readability and clarity of the translated document.

Best Practices Summary

Here is a summary of the best practices for internationalization and localization in XeLaTeX:

1. Use Unicode and multilingual fonts to ensure compatibility with different language scripts. 2. Load language-specific packages for proper typesetting and language support. 3. Handle plurals and grammatical gender correctly using packages like `fmtcount`. 4. Format dates, times, and currency according to the target locale using packages like `datetime2` and `siunitx`. 5. Utilize translation and localization tools to streamline the process and ensure consistency. 6. Test, proofread, and gather feedback from native speakers to ensure high-quality translations.

By following these best practices, you can effectively internationalize and localize your XeLaTeX documents, making them accessible to a global audience.

XeLaTeX for Professional Typography and Design

Introduction to Professional Typography and Design in XeLaTeX

Principles of typography and typesetting in XeLaTeX

In this section, we will explore the fundamental principles of typography and typesetting in XeLaTeX. Understanding these principles is essential for creating visually appealing and professional-looking documents. We will cover key concepts such as font selection, letter-spacing, special characters, and typographic rules.

Font Selection

Font selection plays a crucial role in typography as it greatly impacts the readability and aesthetics of your document. XeLaTeX provides extensive font support, allowing you to choose from a wide range of fonts, including both system fonts and custom fonts.

When selecting fonts, it is important to consider the overall style and purpose of your document. Serif fonts, such as Times New Roman, are commonly used for body text in printed materials, as they provide a traditional and formal appearance. Sans-serif fonts, like Arial, are often preferred for digital content and headings due to their clean and modern look.

In XeLaTeX, you can easily specify the font for different elements of your document by using the `fontspec` package. For example, to set the main font for your document, you can use the command:

```
\setmainfont{Times New Roman}
```

You can also define different fonts for specific sections or headings to create visual contrasts and hierarchy in your document. Custom font files can be easily imported using the `fontspec` package, allowing you to use unique and specialized fonts in your document.

Letter-spacing and Kerning

Letter-spacing refers to the horizontal spacing between characters in a line of text. Proper letter-spacing is crucial for legibility and overall readability. In XeLaTeX, you can adjust letter-spacing using the `LetterSpace` option provided by the `fontspec` package.

To apply letter-spacing to a specific piece of text, you can use the command:

```
{\addfontfeature{LetterSpace=2.0} This is some text.}
```

The value of the `LetterSpace` option determines the amount of spacing to be added between characters. Experimenting with different values will help you find the optimal letter-spacing for your document.

Kerning, on the other hand, deals with the spacing between specific pairs of characters. XeLaTeX automatically applies kerning based on the font used. However, if you want to adjust the kerning for a specific pair of characters, you can use the `kern` command:

```
AVAVA or A{\kern-1pt}V{\kern-1pt}A{\kern-1pt}V{\kern-1pt}A
```

By adjusting the `kern` values, you can fine-tune the spacing between characters, especially for special cases where the default kerning does not provide the desired visual result.

Special Characters and Ligatures

Special characters, such as ligatures and special symbols, can greatly enhance the visual appeal of your document. Ligatures are combinations of two or more characters that are represented by a single character with a specific design. They help improve the overall aesthetics of the text by reducing visual distractions caused by close character combinations.

XeLaTeX provides automatic ligature support for many common ligatures. However, if you want to disable or enable specific ligatures, you can utilize the `Renderer` option provided by the `fontspec` package:

```
\setmainfont[Ligatures={Common, Rare, Historical}]{Times New Roman
```

In this example, we enable common, rare, and historical ligatures for the main font.

Besides ligatures, XeLaTeX also supports the use of special symbols and characters. You can easily include them in your document by using the appropriate Unicode character code. For example, to include the copyright symbol (©), you can use the command:

```
\textcopyright
```

Typographic Rules

To maintain a consistent and professional-looking document, it is important to follow typographic rules. These rules govern areas such as paragraph indentation, line spacing, and hyphenation.

Paragraph indentation refers to the space left at the beginning of a paragraph. In XeLaTeX, you can control paragraph indentation using the `parindent` command:

```
\setlength{\parindent}{1em}
```

This command sets the paragraph indentation to 1em, but you can adjust it based on your document's requirements.

Line spacing determines the vertical space between lines of text. To set the line spacing in XeLaTeX, you can use the `setspace` package:

```
\onehalfspacing    % Sets line spacing to one and a half
```

Hyphenation is the process of dividing words into syllables and inserting hyphens at the end of lines to improve justification. XeLaTeX automatically performs hyphenation based on the current language settings. However, you can fine-tune hyphenation by using the `hyphenrules` command:

```
\hyphenation{Xe-La-TeX}
```

In this example, we specify that `XeLaTeX` should be hyphenated as `Xe-La-TeX`.

Understanding and applying these typographic rules will significantly improve the readability and overall visual quality of your document.

Overall, typography is a fascinating discipline that combines both art and science. By mastering the principles of typography and typesetting in XeLaTeX, you can create visually appealing and professional documents that effectively convey your message. Remember to experiment with different fonts, letter-spacing, ligatures, and typographic rules to find the best approach for your specific document. Happy typesetting!

Choosing and pairing fonts for professional documents in XeLaTeX

In professional document design, the choice and pairing of fonts play a crucial role in conveying information effectively and creating an engaging visual experience for the reader. This section explores the principles and best practices for selecting and combining fonts in XeLaTeX.

Understanding font categories

Before we delve into the process of choosing and pairing fonts, let's familiarize ourselves with the different categories of fonts commonly used in professional documents.

- **Serif fonts:** These fonts are characterized by small decorative flourishes or lines (serifs) at the ends of strokes. They are known for their traditional and formal appearance. Serif fonts are generally suitable for body text in print documents, as they enhance readability and create a sense of authority.

- **Sans-serif fonts:** Unlike serif fonts, sans-serif fonts do not have additional decorative lines. They have a clean and modern look, making them suitable for headings and titles. Sans-serif fonts are often preferred for digital and screen-based documents due to their legibility at smaller sizes.

- **Monospaced fonts:** Monospaced fonts have fixed-width characters, where each character occupies the same amount of horizontal space. These fonts are commonly used in coding and technical documents, as they help maintain alignment in tabular data and enhance readability in code samples.

- **Script fonts:** Script fonts mimic handwriting and calligraphy, adding elegance and a personal touch to a document. However, they should be used sparingly and in moderation, typically for special emphasis or decorative purposes.

- **Display fonts:** Display fonts are attention-grabbing and designed to make an impact. They are commonly used for headlines, logos, and other creative elements to add personality and draw attention to specific content. However, they are not well-suited for large blocks of body text due to their intricate designs.

* **Symbol fonts:** Symbol fonts consist of a collection of icons, symbols, and graphical elements. They are widely used in technical and scientific documents to represent mathematical notation, scientific symbols, and other specialized glyphs.

Considerations for font pairing

When selecting and pairing fonts, it is important to consider certain aspects to ensure harmony and visual coherence in your document design.

1. **Contrast:** Fonts with contrasting designs create visual interest and help distinguish different levels of information. Pairing a serif font with a sans-serif font or a script font with a monospaced font can create a pleasing contrast.

2. **Similarity:** While contrast is important, too much contrast can lead to a jarring effect. It is crucial to maintain some similarity between paired fonts, such as shared characteristics in stroke weight or letterform shapes, to ensure a cohesive look.

3. **Hierarchy:** Establishing a clear hierarchical structure in your document is essential. Use contrasting fonts for headings and titles to set them apart from the body text. Ensure that the font sizes, weights, and styles you choose align with the overall document structure.

4. **Readability:** Legibility should be a top priority when selecting fonts, especially for body text. Avoid complex or overly decorative fonts for extended reading and choose fonts with clear and distinguishable characters.

5. **Consistency:** Consistency throughout your document helps maintain a professional appearance. Limit yourself to a reasonable number of font families and styles for different elements to avoid a cluttered and chaotic design.

6. **Compatibility:** Consider the compatibility of your chosen fonts across different platforms and devices. Fonts that are widely available and supported ensure consistent rendering across various viewing environments.

Font pairing strategies

Here are some effective font pairing strategies to create visually appealing and readable documents:

1. **Contrasting serif and sans-serif:** Pairing a serif font with a sans-serif font is a classic combination that offers a good balance between tradition and modernity. This pairing works well for body text and headings, where the serif font provides readability, and the sans-serif font adds a touch of contemporary style.

2. **Similar fonts with different weights:** Pairing similar fonts with different weights can create a harmonious and consistent visual hierarchy. For example, combining a bold sans-serif font for headings with a regular-weight version of the same font for body text ensures readability and consistency.

3. **Combining fonts from the same family:** Some font families offer a range of styles and variations, including both serif and sans-serif options. These families are designed to work well together, allowing you to create a cohesive design by using fonts from within the same family.

4. **Contrasting font sizes:** Varying the font sizes between different text elements can help establish a clear hierarchy within the document. Using a larger font size for headings and a smaller font size for body text creates visual contrast and guides the reader through the content.

5. **Experimenting with font pairings:** Don't be afraid to try different combinations and experiment with font pairings to find the best match for your document. Use tools like Adobe Fonts or Google Fonts that provide useful categorization and pairing suggestions to explore different options.

Example: Font pairing for a business report

Let's consider an example of font pairing for a business report. In this case, we want to convey a professional and serious tone while maintaining readability and clarity.

For the body text, we select a serif font such as `Libertinus Serif`, which offers good readability on printed documents. Its classic design and wide range of font weights make it suitable for extended reading.

To create contrast for headings and titles, we pair it with the sans-serif font PT Sans. Its clean and modern design adds a touch of freshness to the overall design.

Both fonts have wide language support and excellent legibility on different platforms, ensuring compatibility for the intended audience.

Additional resources

To further explore the world of font pairing, here are some additional resources:

+ **Adobe Fonts** (https://www.fonts.adobe.com/): Adobe Fonts provides a vast collection of high-quality fonts along with useful tools for exploring and pairing different font combinations.

+ **Google Fonts** (https://fonts.google.com/): Google Fonts offers a diverse library of open-source fonts that can be freely used in your projects. The website also provides font pairing suggestions and examples.

+ **Typekit Practice** (https://practice.typekit.com/): Typekit Practice is an online resource that offers guidance and exercises to improve your typography skills, including font pairing.

+ **Typewolf** (https://www.typewolf.com/): Typewolf showcases beautiful examples of font pairings in real-world design projects and provides inspiration for your own creative endeavors.

By following the principles of font pairing and experimenting with different combinations, you can elevate your XeLaTeX documents to a professional and visually appealing level while ensuring the readability and coherence of the content. Remember that font selection is just one aspect of overall document design, and it should be complemented by other design elements such as color, layout, and use of white space. With practice and exploration, you will develop an eye for effective font pairing and create documents that not only communicate effectively but also engage and inspire your readers.

Fine-tuning letter-spacing, kerning, and tracking in XeLaTeX

Typography plays a crucial role in creating visually appealing and engaging documents. XeLaTeX offers powerful tools for fine-tuning letter-spacing, kerning, and tracking, allowing users to achieve precise control over the spacing between characters and lines of text. In this section, we will explore various techniques and best practices for improving the overall typographic quality of documents using XeLaTeX.

Introduction to typography in XeLaTeX

Before delving into the details of letter-spacing, kerning, and tracking, let's briefly discuss the basic principles of typography. Typography involves the art and technique of arranging type to make written language visually appealing and readable. It encompasses the selection of appropriate fonts, the arrangement of type on a page, and the spacing between characters and lines.

Good typography can greatly enhance the readability and aesthetics of a document. It helps convey the intended message effectively, creates a harmonious visual experience, and reflects the professionalism and attention to detail of the author.

Understanding letter-spacing

Letter-spacing refers to the adjustment of the space between individual characters within a word. It is often used to improve legibility or achieve a specific visual effect. In XeLaTeX, we can control letter-spacing using the `letterspace` package.

The `letterspace` package provides the command `\lsstyle{letterspace}` to define a custom letter-spacing style. We can use this style to adjust the letter-spacing for specific portions of text. For example:

```
\lsstyle{letterspaced text}
```

This command will apply the specified letter-spacing style to the enclosed text. We can adjust the letter-spacing value by specifying a numerical value in the style definition. For instance:

```
\lsstyle{letterspaced text}
```

Here, a positive value will increase the space between characters, while a negative value will decrease it. Experimenting with different letter-spacing values will allow you to find the optimal spacing for your document.

Mastering kerning

Kerning refers to the adjustment of the space between specific pairs of characters to improve the overall visual appearance of text. Certain combinations of characters, such as "AV" or "To", may appear too close or too far apart by default. Kerning helps to address these issues and ensure a consistent spacing throughout the document.

In XeLaTeX, the `microtype` package provides excellent support for kerning adjustments. We can enable kerning by including the following line in the preamble of our document:

With the `microtype` package loaded, XeLaTeX will automatically apply kerning adjustments based on predefined rules. These rules specify the optimal spacing for character pairs and are built into the package. However, it is important to note that not all fonts and font families support kerning.

To manually control kerning in XeLaTeX, we can use the `\kotexfn{character pair}` command. This command allows us to adjust the amount of kerning for a specific pair of characters. For example:

```
\kotexfn{A}{V} text
```

In this code snippet, we adjust the kerning between the characters "A" and "V" in the word "text". By experimenting with different values, we can achieve the desired visual effect and eliminate any awkward spacing.

Fine-tuning tracking

Tracking, also known as letter-spacing on a line, refers to the uniform adjustment of the spacing between all characters within a line or paragraph. Unlike letter-spacing, which adjusts the space between individual characters, tracking adjusts the overall spacing between all characters in a selected portion of text.

XeLaTeX provides the `\tracking{amount}{text}` command to modify the tracking of a specific text snippet. The `amount` argument specifies the desired spacing, while the `text` argument encloses the text to which the tracking adjustment should be applied. For example:

```
\tracking{100}\{tracked text\}
```

In this example, we set the tracking amount to 100. Remember, a positive value will increase the overall spacing, while a negative value will decrease it. Adjusting the tracking can help create a more open or condensed appearance, depending on the design requirements.

Best practices and considerations

When fine-tuning letter-spacing, kerning, and tracking in XeLaTeX, several best practices and considerations can help ensure optimal results:

- Use subtle variations: While adjusting the spacing can enhance the visual appeal, it is essential to exercise restraint. Avoid excessive adjustments that may compromise readability or appear visually distracting.

- Consider legibility: Always prioritize legibility over aesthetics. Ensure that the adjusted spacing does not hinder the clarity of the text, particularly for small font sizes or longer passages of text.

- Experiment with different values: Finding the optimal spacing requires experimentation. Adjust the letter-spacing, kerning, and tracking values to identify the settings that achieve the desired effect while maintaining readability.

- Use consistent spacing: Maintain consistency in letter-spacing, kerning, and tracking throughout the document. Inconsistent spacing can create a disjointed reading experience and disrupt visual harmony.

- Consider font characteristics: Different fonts have varying built-in letter-spacing and kerning values. Be mindful of these characteristics when applying adjustments. Ideally, choose font families that are designed to work well with XeLaTeX and provide good typographic control.

- Proofread carefully: Make sure to proofread your document after applying letter-spacing, kerning, or tracking adjustments. Sometimes, minor spacing changes can inadvertently introduce errors or affect the overall readability of the text.

Example application: Fine-tuning a document's typography

To demonstrate the application of letter-spacing, kerning, and tracking adjustments in XeLaTeX, let's consider a specific scenario. Suppose we are typesetting a brochure for a luxury hotel and want to achieve a sophisticated and elegant look.

We can start by selecting an appropriate font that embodies the desired aesthetic. For instance, a classic serif font like Adobe Garamond Pro can add a touch of elegance.

Next, we may apply subtle letter-spacing adjustments to enhance readability and create a more luxurious feel. We can experiment with different values until we find the optimal spacing that adds refinement to the text.

For the headings and titles, we can fine-tune the kerning to ensure balanced spacing between characters, especially with letter combinations such as "AV" or "TY". The `microtype` package can help us achieve harmonious spacing automatically or with manual adjustments using the `\kotexfn` command.

Additionally, for the body text, we can adjust the tracking to create a more open, airy, and elegant appearance. A slight increase in tracking can contribute to the overall luxurious aesthetic of the brochure.

By incorporating these typographic refinements into our document, we can elevate the visual appeal and make a lasting impression on readers.

Resources for further exploration

To deepen your understanding of typography and its application in XeLaTeX, here are some recommended resources:

+ Bringhurst, R. (2012). *The Elements of Typographic Style*. Hartley & Marks Publishers.

+ Butterick, M. (2010). *Typography for Lawyers*. Jones McClure Publishing.

+ `microtype` package documentation: `https://www.ctan.org/pkg/microtype`

These resources provide comprehensive guidance on typography, including advanced techniques, best practices, and troubleshooting tips.

Exercises

Now let's apply what we've learned by tackling some exercises:

1. Choose a paragraph of text and experiment with different letter-spacing values to determine the optimal setting for improved readability without compromising legibility.

2. Identify a word or phrase where the kerning does not appear visually pleasing. Use the \kotexfn command or the `microtype` package to manually adjust the kerning and achieve a more balanced spacing.

3. Take a section of text and adjust the tracking to create a more condensed or open appearance. Observe the impact on the overall aesthetic and readability of the document.

Remember to apply these adjustments judiciously, aiming to enhance the visual appeal while maintaining a clear and legible reading experience.

Enriching typography with ligatures and special characters in XeLaTeX

In typography, ligatures are special characters that combine two or more letters into a single glyph. This helps improve the aesthetics and readability of the text. XeLaTeX provides excellent support for ligatures, allowing users to easily enable and customize them in their documents.

What are ligatures?

Ligatures are typographic elements that merge two or more characters into a single glyph. They are commonly used to enhance the appearance and flow of the text. Historically, ligatures were created to address specific issues with certain character combinations that didn't visually fit well together. For example, the combination of the letters "f" and "i" would often result in an overlap or collision of the dot on the "i" with the crossbar on the "f". By creating a ligature, these problems can be avoided.

Enabling ligatures in XeLaTeX

XeLaTeX has built-in support for ligatures and offers several options for enabling them. By default, XeLaTeX automatically applies common ligatures, such as "fi" and "fl", when the corresponding characters are present in the text. However, if you want to enable more ligatures or disable certain ligatures, you can use the `fontspec` package.

To enable ligatures for a specific font, you can use the `Ligatures` option in the `fontspec` package. For example, to enable standard ligatures for the Latin Modern Roman font, you can use the following code:

```
\setmainfont[Ligatures=Common]{Latin Modern Roman}
```

This will enable all common ligatures, such as "fi", "fl", "ff", and "ffi". You can also specify a subset of ligatures by using the `Ligatures` option with specific ligature names. For example, to enable only the discretionary-ligatures for the font, you can use:

```
\setmainfont[Ligatures={Discretionary}]{Latin Modern Roman}
```

Customizing ligatures in XeLaTeX

XeLaTeX provides flexibility in customizing ligatures according to specific requirements. You can enable or disable ligatures selectively by manipulating the settings with the `fontspec` package.

For instance, to enable the **Historic** ligatures for a specific font, use:

```
\setmainfont[Ligatures={Historic}]{Font Name}
```

Similarly, to enable only the **Rare** ligatures, use:

```
\setmainfont[Ligatures={Rare}]{Font Name}
```

You can also combine multiple ligature types in a single command. For example, to enable both the historic and discretionary ligatures, use:

```
\setmainfont[Ligatures={Historic, Discretionary}]{Font Name}
```

Additionally, you can selectively disable certain ligatures. For example, to disable the "ffi" ligature, use:

```
\setmainfont[Ligatures={-ffi}]{Font Name}
```

This feature allows you to have complete control over the ligatures used in your documents, ensuring that they align with your design preferences or meet the specific requirements of your content.

Using special characters in XeLaTeX

Apart from ligatures, XeLaTeX provides extensive support for special characters. These characters include symbols, diacritics, accent marks, and other typographic elements that are not part of the standard Latin alphabet.

To use special characters in XeLaTeX, you need to choose a font that includes the desired character set. XeLaTeX supports Unicode fonts, which can encompass a wide range of characters from different writing systems.

To select a font that contains the special characters you need, you can use the fontspec package. For example:

```
\newfontfamily\specialfont{Font Name}
```

This will define a new command, \specialfont, that you can use to set the font for specific sections of your document where you require special characters.

To input the special characters themselves, you can either use the Unicode code for the character or refer to the character by its name. For example, to include the euro symbol, you can use:

```
\symbol{"20AC}
```

This will insert the euro symbol at the current location. Similarly, you can use the appropriate Unicode codes or character names to include other special characters.

Summary

In this section, we explored the concept of ligatures and how they enhance the typographic quality of text in XeLaTeX. We learned how to enable and customize ligatures using the `fontspec` package. Additionally, we discussed the usage of special characters in XeLaTeX and how to incorporate them into your document by choosing appropriate fonts and using the correct Unicode codes or character names.

By leveraging ligatures and special characters, you can enrich the typographic experience of your documents and achieve professional-quality typography with XeLaTeX.

Exercises

1. Find a real-world example where the use of ligatures significantly improves the readability and aesthetics of a text. Describe the example and explain how ligatures enhance it. 2. Experiment with different ligature settings in XeLaTeX and observe the changes in the resulting document. Compare and contrast the effects of different ligature combinations on the overall appearance of the text. 3. Choose a font that supports a specific set of special characters (e.g., mathematical symbols or non-Latin scripts) and use it to typeset a paragraph that makes use of those characters. Explain the significance of these special characters within the context of the text.

Designing and formatting title pages and covers in XeLaTeX

In this section, we will explore how to design and format attractive title pages and covers using XeLaTeX. The title page is the first thing readers see when they open a book or document, so it should make a strong impression and set the tone for the content that follows. We will discuss various design elements, layout techniques, typography choices, and formatting options to create visually appealing and professional title pages and covers.

Design Principles for Title Pages and Covers

When designing a title page or cover, it is important to keep in mind the principles of graphic design. These principles help us create visually harmonious and balanced layouts that are aesthetically pleasing. Here are some key design principles to consider:

+ **Hierarchy:** Establish a clear visual hierarchy by using different font sizes, weights, and styles for the title, subtitle, author name, and other elements.

This hierarchy helps readers quickly identify the most important information.

+ **Contrast:** Use contrasting colors, fonts, and sizes to create visual interest and make important elements stand out. Contrast can help guide the reader's attention and create a sense of hierarchy.

+ **Alignment:** Maintain a consistent alignment for text and other elements to create a sense of order and organization. Choose between left, right, center, or justified alignment based on the desired aesthetic and readability.

+ **Whitespace:** Utilize whitespace effectively to create breathing room between elements on the title page. Whitespace can enhance readability and give the design a clean and uncluttered look.

+ **Unity:** Create a sense of unity and coherence by using a consistent color scheme, typography, and visual style throughout the title page. This helps tie all the elements together and creates a cohesive design.

These design principles serve as a starting point for creating visually appealing and effective title pages and covers. Let's now explore some practical techniques and formatting options in XeLaTeX to implement these principles effectively.

Choosing Fonts and Typography

Typography plays a crucial role in the design of the title page. The choice of fonts can greatly impact the overall aesthetic and readability of the title page. Here are some tips for selecting fonts and typography for your title page:

+ **Font Pairing:** Choose fonts that complement each other and create a harmonious combination. Consider combining a bold and attention-grabbing font for the title with a more readable and elegant font for the author name and other text.

+ **Font Size and Weight:** Use different font sizes and weights to establish hierarchy and guide the reader's attention. The title should be larger and bolder compared to the author name and other text.

+ **Typography Style:** Experiment with different typography styles, such as serif or sans-serif fonts, to create the desired mood and aesthetic for the title page. Consider the overall tone of the content and choose a typography style that aligns with it.

XeLaTeX provides extensive support for various fonts, including system fonts and custom fonts, which can be easily incorporated into your title page design. You can use packages like `fontspec` to specify custom fonts and set their attributes, such as size, weight, and style.

Layout and Formatting

The layout and formatting of a title page play a significant role in creating a visually appealing design. Here are some layout and formatting techniques you can use in XeLaTeX:

* **Title Placement:** Decide on the placement of the title on the page, considering factors such as the overall design, readability, and available space. The title can be centered, aligned to the left or right, or placed in a specific location on the page for a more creative design.

* **Subtitle and Author Name:** Position the subtitle and author name below the title, aligned either to the left or right. Use a slightly smaller font size compared to the title to establish hierarchy.

* **Images and Graphics:** Include relevant images, graphics, or logos on the title page to enhance the visual appeal and add context to the content. Use the `graphicx` package to insert images and adjust their placement and size.

* **Color Scheme:** Choose an appropriate color scheme that aligns with the overall design and conveys the desired mood or theme. You can define custom colors using packages like `xcolor` and apply them to different elements on the title page.

* **Borders and Frames:** Add borders or frames around the title, subtitle, or other sections to create visual separation and add a touch of elegance to the design. Use packages like `tikz` to draw custom frames or borders.

By carefully considering layout and formatting options, you can create visually stunning and unique title pages and covers using XeLaTeX.

Example Title Page

To illustrate these design and formatting techniques, let's create an example title page for a fictional book. Here is the code to generate the title page:

```
\setmainfont{Times New Roman}
```

```
\begin{titlepage}
    \centering

    \vspace*{2cm}

    {\Huge\textbf{The Art of XeLaTeX}}

    \vspace{1cm}

    {\Large\textit{A Comprehensive Guide}}

    \vspace{2cm}

    {\Large John Doe}

    \vspace{2cm}

    \includegraphics[width=5cm]{book_cover}

    \vfill

    {\large Publisher Name}

    \vspace{0.5cm}

    {\large \today}
\end{titlepage}
```

This code creates a simple and elegant title page with a centered title, subtitle, author name, and an accompanying image. Adjust the spacing and font attributes as needed to achieve the desired design. Remember to include the necessary packages and customize the fonts to match your design preferences.

Resources and Further Reading

To further explore and enhance your skills in designing and formatting title pages and covers, consider the following resources:

- Bringhurst, R. (2012). *The Elements of Typographic Style.* Hartley & Marks Publishers.

- Butterick, M. (2010). *Practical Typography.* self-published. Available at: https://practicaltypography.com/

- XeLaTeX documentation and user guides. Available at: https://www.xelatex.org/

These resources provide in-depth knowledge of typography, design principles, and practical tips for creating visually appealing title pages and covers.

Exercises

1. Choose a book title and design a title page for it using XeLaTeX. Experiment with different fonts, layouts, and formatting options to create an attractive design.

2. Explore different color schemes and their impact on the overall aesthetic of the title page. Create multiple versions of the title page using different color schemes to compare the visual impact.

3. Research and incorporate additional design elements, such as decorative ornaments or background patterns, to further enhance the visual appeal of the title page.

4. Investigate different book cover designs and analyze their typography and layout choices. Use your findings to improve your own title page design.

5. Share your title page design with others and seek feedback. Consider their suggestions and incorporate them into your design to refine and improve it further.

Remember, practice is key to mastering the art of designing and formatting title pages and covers. Experiment with various design elements, layouts, and formatting options to develop your unique style and create visually stunning title pages and covers.

In the next section, we will explore advanced techniques for typesetting mathematical equations and expressions in XeLaTeX.

Creating and formatting chapter headings and section numbers in XeLaTeX

In this section, we will explore how to create and format chapter headings and section numbers in XeLaTeX documents. Chapter headings and section numbers play a crucial role in organizing the structure of a document and providing a clear navigation for readers. We will learn about different customization options available in XeLaTeX to design attractive and professional-looking headings and section numbers.

Default Chapter Headings and Section Numbers

By default, when we use a document class like `book` or `report` in XeLaTeX, it automatically generates chapter headings and section numbers for us. The format of these headings and numbers is determined by the document class itself. For example, the book class uses Roman numerals (e.g., `Chapter I`, `Chapter II`, etc.) for chapter headings and Arabic numerals (e.g., `1.1, 1.2`, etc.) for section numbers.

Customizing Chapter Headings

XeLaTeX provides various methods to customize chapter headings according to our preferences. One way is to use the `titlesec` package, which provides a flexible interface for modifying the format of chapter headings. Let's consider an example where we want to change the font, size, and color of the chapter heading.

First, we need to load the `titlesec` package by including the following line in the preamble of our document:

Next, we can define the format for our chapter headings using the `titleformat` command. In this example, let's make the chapter heading centered, set it in a larger font, and change the color to blue:

```
\titleformat{\chapter}[display]
{\centering\Huge\color{blue}}
{\chaptertitlename\ \thechapter}{20pt}{\Huge}
```

Here, `\chaptertitlename` represents the word "Chapter" in the heading, and `\thechapter` represents the chapter number. We can adjust the font size, color, alignment, spacing, and other properties according to our needs.

To apply this format to all chapter headings in our document, we use the \chapter command followed by the chapter title. For example:

```
\chapter{Introduction}
```

This will generate a chapter heading with the customized format specified.

Formatting Section Numbers

Similar to chapter headings, we can also customize the format of section numbers in XeLaTeX. By default, section numbers are displayed as Arabic numerals followed by a period (e.g., 1.1, 1.2, etc.). However, we might want to change the numbering style or add additional information.

To modify the format of section numbers, we can use the titlesec package along with the titleformat command. Let's consider an example where we want to display section numbers as uppercase Roman numerals followed by a colon (e.g., I:, II:, etc.).

First, we need to load the titlesec package in the preamble of our document:

Next, we can define the format for our section numbers using the titleformat command. In this example, let's make the section number uppercase Roman numerals followed by a colon:

```
\titleformat{\section}
{\normalfont\LARGE\bfseries}
{\Roman{section}:}{1em}{}
```

Here, \Roman{section} generates the uppercase Roman numeral representation of the section number. We can adjust the font size, style, spacing, and other properties as needed.

To apply this format to all section headings in our document, we simply use the \section command followed by the section title. For example:

```
\section{Overview}
```

This will generate a section heading with the customized format specified.

Caveats and Best Practices

When customizing chapter headings and section numbers in XeLaTeX, it is important to consider readability, consistency with the overall document style, and the expectations of your readers. While it can be tempting to use extravagant fonts or colors, it is crucial to strike a balance between creativity and legibility.

Here are some best practices to keep in mind:

- Use fonts and colors that are visually appealing and harmonize with the overall design of the document.

- Ensure that the font size and spacing of the heading and section numbers are legible, even at smaller sizes.

- Maintain consistency in the formatting of chapter headings and section numbers throughout the document.

- Consider the hierarchy and nesting of headings to create a clear and organized structure.

- Avoid cluttering the headings with excessive information or overly long titles.

By following these best practices, we can create aesthetically pleasing and well-structured chapter headings and section numbers that enhance the readability of our XeLaTeX documents.

Summary

In this section, we have learned how to create and format chapter headings and section numbers in XeLaTeX. We explored the default formatting provided by XeLaTeX document classes and then discussed how to customize the appearance of these headings using the `titlesec` package. Additionally, we covered some best practices for designing appealing and readable chapter headings and section numbers. By applying these techniques, we can create professional-looking documents with clear and organized structures.

Designing and formatting table of contents and lists in XeLaTeX

In this section, we will explore how to design and format table of contents (TOC) and lists in XeLaTeX documents. The table of contents provides a comprehensive outline of the document's structure, making it easier for readers to navigate and find specific sections or chapters. Lists, on the other hand, allow for the display of items in a structured and organized manner, which is useful for creating bullet points, numbered lists, or custom lists.

Formatting the Table of Contents

Customizing the appearance of the table of contents in XeLaTeX documents allows for a more personalized and aesthetically pleasing presentation. The `tocloft` package provides a set of commands and options to modify the style, layout, and content of the table of contents.

To begin, add the `tocloft` package to the preamble of your XeLaTeX document:

Now, let's look at some common formatting options for the table of contents.

Changing the Font   You can change the font of the table of contents by modifying the appropriate command in the preamble. For example, to use a sans-serif font, add the following line:

```
\renewcommand{\cfttoctitlefont}{\sffamily\Large}
```

This example sets the font to a larger size and uses a sans-serif family. Adjust the font size and family according to your preferences.

Adjusting Spacing   The spacing between entries in the table of contents can be adjusted using the `cftbeforeX` and `cftafterX` commands, where X represents the relevant sectioning level (e.g., `chapter`, `section`). The spacings can be modified to add or reduce the space before or after each entry. Here's an example:

```
\setlength{\cftbeforechapskip}{10pt}
```

This command increases the space before each chapter entry by 10 points. Experiment with different values to achieve the desired spacing.

Adding Dots   Traditionally, dots are used to connect the section titles with their respective page numbers in the table of contents. However, this can be customized or removed entirely using the `tocloft` package. To add dots, use the following command:

```
\renewcommand{\cftchapleader}{\cftdotfill{\cftdotsep}}
```

This command adds a series of dots between the chapter titles and page numbers.

Changing the Depth   By default, the table of contents in XeLaTeX includes all sectioning levels, i.e., chapters, sections, subsections, and so on. However, you may want to adjust the depth of the table of contents to include only specific levels. To do this, use the `tocdepth` command, like so:

```
\setcounter{tocdepth}{2}
```

In this example, the table of contents will only display chapters and sections. You can change the value to suit your needs.

Formatting Lists

Lists are commonly used in documents to present information in a structured and organized manner. XeLaTeX provides several list environments that can be customized to match your desired style.

Bullet Lists   To create a basic bullet list, use the `itemize` environment. Here's an example:

```
\begin{itemize}
    \item Item 1
    \item Item 2
    \item Item 3
\end{itemize}
```

This will create a bulleted list with each item preceded by a bullet symbol.

Numbered Lists   For a numbered list, use the `enumerate` environment. Here's an example:

```
\begin{enumerate}
    \item Item 1
    \item Item 2
    \item Item 3
\end{enumerate}
```

This will create a numbered list with each item preceded by a number.

Custom Lists   XeLaTeX also allows you to create custom lists using the `description` environment. In this case, you can specify a custom label for each item. Here's an example:

```
\begin{description}
    \item[Label 1] Item 1
    \item[Label 2] Item 2
    \item[Label 3] Item 3
\end{description}
```

This will create a custom list with each item labeled according to your specifications.

Examples and Tips

To better understand the concepts of formatting table of contents and lists in XeLaTeX, let's consider a practical example.

Suppose you are writing a research paper on the topic of climate change. You want to create a table of contents that follows an aesthetically pleasing design and includes only chapters and sections. Additionally, you need to include a numbered list of key findings in your paper. Here's an example of how you could achieve this in XeLaTeX:

```
\renewcommand{\cfttoctitlefont}{\sffamily\Large}
\setlength{\cftbeforechapskip}{10pt}
\renewcommand{\cftchapleader}{\cftdotfill{\cftdotsep}}
```

```
\setcounter{tocdepth}{2}


\tableofcontents

\section{Introduction}
Your introduction\index{introduction} goes here.

\chapter{Literature Review}
Your literature\index{literature} review\index{review} goes here.

\section{Methodology}
Your methodology\index{methodology} goes here.

\chapter{Results}
Your results go\index{go} here.

\section{Key Findings}
\begin{enumerate}
    \item Finding 1
    \item Finding 2
    \item Finding 3
\end{enumerate}
```

In this example, we have customized the table of contents to use a sans-serif font, increased the spacing before chapter entries by 10 points, added dots between the titles and page numbers, and limited the depth to chapters and sections. We have also included a numbered list of key findings under the section titled "Key Findings."

Remember to compile the document using XeLaTeX to see the formatted table of contents and lists.

Further Resources

To explore more formatting options and advanced techniques for designing table of contents and lists in XeLaTeX, consider referring to the official documentation of the tocloft package and other relevant resources such as:

+ "The LaTeX Companion" by Frank Mittelbach et al.

+ "LaTeX: A Document Preparation System" by Leslie Lamport.

+ Online forums and communities like TeX Stack Exchange (tex.stackexchange.com) for specific questions or issues.

These resources will provide comprehensive guidance on customizing table of contents and lists in XeLaTeX, enabling you to create visually appealing and well-structured documents.

Applying Advanced Typesetting Techniques and Hyphenation Rules in XeLaTeX

In this section, we will explore some advanced typesetting techniques and hyphenation rules that can be applied in XeLaTeX. These techniques will allow you to enhance the typography and readability of your documents, and improve the overall visual appeal.

Typesetting Techniques

1. **OpenType Features**   One of the advantages of using XeLaTeX is the support for OpenType fonts. OpenType fonts provide a wide range of typographic features that can be accessed and utilized in XeLaTeX. Some of the common OpenType features include ligatures, kerning, stylistic alternates, and swashes. These features can be activated using the `fontspec` package and the `fontfeatures` command. For example, to enable ligatures in a document, you can use the command `\fontfeatures{Ligatures=Common}`.

2. **Optical Margin Alignment**   Optical margin alignment, also known as hanging punctuation, is a technique used to improve the appearance of punctuation marks at the beginning and end of lines. By slightly protruding punctuation marks into the left or right margin, the alignment of the text can appear more consistent. XeLaTeX provides the `microtype` package, which includes the `protrusion` option for enabling optical margin alignment. To use this feature, simply load the package with the `protrusion` option: `\usepackage[protrusion]{microtype}`.

3. **Drop Caps**   Drop caps, or initial capitals, are large decorative letters at the beginning of a paragraph that extend into the margin. They are often used to enhance the visual appeal of a document or draw attention to important sections.

XeLaTeX provides various ways to create drop caps, such as using the `lettrine` package or manually adjusting the font size and positioning of the first character in a paragraph.

Hyphenation Rules

Hyphenation is the process of dividing words at the end of a line to improve text flow and readability. XeLaTeX automatically hyphenates words based on predefined hyphenation patterns for different languages. However, there may be cases where the default hyphenation rules are not sufficient, or you may want to manually control hyphenation in certain instances.

1. Hyphenation Patterns XeLaTeX uses hyphenation patterns to determine where to hyphenate words. These patterns are defined in language-specific hyphenation files (*.hyphen.tex) and include rules for both manual and automatic hyphenation. To apply hyphenation patterns in XeLaTeX, you can load the appropriate language hyphenation file using the `babel` or `polyglossia` package.

2. Manual Hyphenation In some cases, you may need to manually specify hyphenation points for certain words. This can be useful for words with non-standard hyphenation rules or words that are not correctly hyphenated by XeLaTeX. To manually hyphenate a word, insert the command `\-` at the desired hyphenation points. For example, to manually hyphenate the word "unbelievable" as "un-be-liev-able," you would write "un\-be\-liev\-able".

Best Practices for Typesetting and Hyphenation

Here are some best practices to consider when applying advanced typesetting techniques and hyphenation rules in XeLaTeX:

1. Use Consistent Fonts When applying advanced typographic features, it is important to use fonts that are designed to work well together. Choose fonts that have matching styles and weights to maintain visual harmony throughout the document.

2. Avoid Overusing Decorative Features While advanced typographic features can enhance the visual appeal of a document, it is important to use them judiciously. Overusing decorative features such as swashes and alternate glyphs can make the text difficult to read and distract from the content.

3. Consider Language-specific Hyphenation   Different languages have different hyphenation rules and patterns. When typesetting multilingual documents, make sure to load the appropriate language hyphenation files and adjust the hyphenation settings accordingly.

4. Review and Proofread   After applying advanced typesetting techniques and hyphenation rules, carefully review and proofread the document. Pay attention to the readability and consistency of the text, and make any necessary adjustments to ensure a polished final product.

By applying these advanced typesetting techniques and hyphenation rules, you can improve the overall visual appeal and readability of your XeLaTeX documents. Experiment with different features and incorporate them thoughtfully to create aesthetically pleasing and professional-looking documents.

Additional   Resources: -   The   LaTeX   Font   Catalogue: `https://tug.org/FontCatalogue/` - Learn XeLaTeX in 10 Minutes: `https://www.overleaf.com/learn/latex/XeLaTeX`   -   Advanced Typography with XeLaTeX: `https://tug.org/XeTeX/` - The Art of Typography in XeLaTeX: `https://www.tug.org/art-tex/`

Exercises: 1. Using the `fontspec` package, apply different OpenType features to a paragraph of text and observe the visual changes. 2. Experiment with different hyphenation patterns for a multilingual document and analyze the impact on text flow and readability. 3. Create a document using drop caps and optical margin alignment to enhance the visual appeal of the text.

Troubleshooting typographic issues and achieving professional results

In this section, we will explore some common typographic issues that may arise while using XeLaTeX and discuss how to troubleshoot them. We will also provide tips and techniques to achieve professional results in your documents.

Avoiding widows and orphans

One common typographic issue is the presence of widows and orphans in your document. Widows are single lines of a paragraph that appear at the top of a page, while orphans are single lines of a paragraph that appear at the bottom of a page. To avoid these issues, you can use the `widow` and `club` packages, which provide commands to handle widows and orphans.

By including these packages in your document preamble, you enable additional features that automatically handle widows and orphans.

Dealing with hyphenation problems

Hyphenation problems can occur when words are not correctly hyphenated at the end of a line. This can lead to awkward spacing and readability issues. To address this, you can use the `microtype` package, which provides advanced hyphenation and justification features.

The `microtype` package enhances the overall appearance of your document by adjusting character spacing, font expansion, and other typographic aspects. It automatically takes care of hyphenation and can greatly improve the readability of your text.

Resolving font-related issues

Font-related issues can arise when using different font families, sizes, or styles in your document. One common problem is font substitution, where a font is replaced with a different one due to missing glyphs or unsupported features. To avoid font-related issues, it is essential to select appropriate fonts and ensure they are properly installed and accessible to XeLaTeX.

For font selection, you can use the `fontspec` package, which provides a flexible interface for customizing font attributes.

```
\setmainfont{Times New Roman}
\setsansfont{Arial}
```

In the above example, we set the main font as Times New Roman and the sans-serif font as Arial. Ensure that these fonts are installed on your system or use other available fonts based on your requirements.

Handling overfull and underfull boxes

Overfull and underfull boxes occur when the content within a box (such as a paragraph or a table) exceeds or falls short of the specified dimensions. This can disrupt the layout and alignment of your document. To identify and resolve these issues, you can enable the draft option and include the showframe package.

```
\usepackage[draft]{graphicx}
```

With the draft option, XeLaTeX indicates overfull and underfull boxes by placing a black box in the margin. The showframe package adds visible frames to your document, highlighting the boundaries of each page and helping you identify any misaligned content.

You can then adjust your document's layout or rephrase the content to avoid overfull and underfull boxes.

Implementing advanced typography techniques

To achieve professional-looking typography, you can employ advanced techniques such as ligatures, special characters, and advanced kerning and spacing. For ligatures and special characters, you can use the fontspec package to enable the corresponding OpenType features.

```
\setmainfont[ Ligatures=TeX ]{Times New Roman}
```

The above code enables TeX ligatures in the Times New Roman font. Ligatures are special characters that combine multiple adjacent characters into a single glyph, resulting in more visually pleasing and harmonious text.

You can also fine-tune letter-spacing and other typographic aspects by adjusting the Tracking value.

```
\letterspaceadjust{0.5}
```

By employing such advanced typography techniques, you can add elegance and a professional touch to your documents.

Addressing typographic hierarchy

Typographic hierarchy is essential for guiding readers through your document and highlighting crucial information. You can achieve this by using appropriate font sizes, styles, and colors for headings, subheadings, and body text.

```
\section{Introduction}
\subsection{Background}
\subsubsection{Motivation}
```

In the above example, we demonstrate the use of sectioning commands to create a hierarchical structure. By utilizing suitable font sizes and styles, you can establish a clear typographic hierarchy in your document.

Remember to maintain consistency in your font choices and sizes throughout your document to ensure a professional and cohesive look.

Emphasizing important information

To draw attention to specific text within your document, you can employ various formatting techniques such as bold, italic, and underline. However, it is crucial to use these formatting options sparingly and consistently for maximum impact.

```
\textbf{Important:} This paragraph contains important information.
```

In the above example, we use the `textbf` command to emphasize the word "Important" in bold. By selectively applying formatting options, you can effectively emphasize important information and improve the legibility and clarity of your document.

Overall, troubleshooting typographic issues requires a deep understanding of typography principles combined with practical experience. By following the tips and techniques outlined in this section, you can address common typographic problems and achieve professional results in your XeLaTeX documents.

Note that this section provides only a brief overview of troubleshooting typographic issues, and additional resources and practices may be needed depending on the specific context and requirements of your document.

Best practices for professional typography and design in XeLaTeX

Typography and design play a crucial role in creating professional and visually appealing documents. In this section, we will explore some best practices for achieving high-quality typography and design in XeLaTeX.

Choosing and pairing fonts

Fonts play a significant role in setting the tone and style of your document. When selecting fonts, it's essential to consider readability and complexity. Here are some best practices for choosing and pairing fonts:

+ Choose fonts that are legible and easy to read, especially for body text. Avoid using overly decorative or novelty fonts in lengthy documents.

+ Use font families that complement each other to create visual harmony. Combining a serif font with a sans-serif font is a popular choice for body text and headings.

+ Pay attention to font weights and styles. Using a mix of regular, bold, and italic variants can help differentiate different sections and emphasize important information.

+ Experiment with font sizes to achieve a visually balanced layout. Optimize the font size for readability, ensuring that text is neither too small nor too large.

+ Consider the cultural and historical associations of the fonts you choose. Different fonts evoke different emotions and can contribute to the overall aesthetics of your document.

Fine-tuning letter-spacing, kerning, and tracking

Spacing between letters affects the overall readability and aesthetic appeal of your text. In XeLaTeX, you have control over letter-spacing, kerning, and tracking. Here are some best practices for fine-tuning letter-spacing:

+ Adjust the letter-spacing based on the font and font size. Larger fonts may require slightly increased letter-spacing to maintain readability, while smaller fonts may benefit from reduced letter-spacing.

+ Use kerning to adjust the spacing between specific pairs of letters for better visual consistency. For example, problematic letter combinations like "AV" or "To" may require manual kerning to avoid awkward spacing.

+ Tracking refers to adjusting the overall letter-spacing uniformly across a block of text. Be cautious when increasing tracking, as excessive spacing can negatively impact readability.

+ When adjusting letter-spacing, consider the overall design and intended purpose of your document. Different styles may require different levels of letter-spacing for optimal visual impact.

Enriching typography with ligatures and special characters

XeLaTeX offers excellent support for ligatures and special characters, enhancing the visual quality of your typography. Here are some best practices for leveraging ligatures and special characters:

+ Enable ligatures for fonts that support them. Ligatures are decorative replacement glyphs that improve the appearance of certain character combinations, such as "fi" or "fl".

+ Consider using discretionary ligatures for specific stylistic effects. Discretionary ligatures provide alternative visual representations for character combinations, adding a touch of uniqueness to your typography.

+ Utilize special characters, such as em dashes, en dashes, and ellipses, to enhance the visual hierarchy and structure of your text. These characters provide subtle but essential typographic cues.

Designing and formatting title pages and covers

The title page and cover of your document make the first impression on your readers. Paying attention to their design and formatting ensures a professional and polished appearance. Here are some best practices for designing title pages and covers in XeLaTeX:

+ Choose an appropriate layout and positioning for the title, author, and other relevant information. Experiment with different arrangements to achieve visual balance and hierarchy.

+ Utilize typographic elements such as font size, weight, and color to create visual interest and draw attention to key information.

+ Incorporate images, illustrations, or graphics that complement the content and theme of your document. Ensure that they are placed and scaled properly to enhance the overall design.

+ Maintain consistency with the overall design of your document. Use similar fonts, colors, and styling choices to establish a cohesive visual identity.

Creating and formatting chapter headings and section numbers

Chapter headings and section numbers play a vital role in organizing your document and guiding readers through its structure. Here are some best practices for creating and formatting chapter headings and section numbers:

+ Select an appropriate font, size, and style for chapter headings and section numbers. They should be visually distinct from the body text while maintaining consistency with the overall design.

+ Consistently apply the formatting throughout your document for a cohesive look. Use XeLaTeX's built-in sectioning commands to ensure consistent numbering and formatting across chapters and sections.

+ Experiment with different ways to visually distinguish chapter headings, such as using a larger font size, using a different font weight, or incorporating decorative elements.

+ Consider incorporating a table of contents or index to improve document navigation. XeLaTeX provides easy-to-use tools for generating these elements based on your chapter headings and section numbers.

Designing and formatting table of contents and lists

Tables of contents and lists provide a quick overview of the structure and content of your document. Designing and formatting them appropriately enhances readability and accessibility. Here are some best practices for designing and formatting table of contents and lists in XeLaTeX:

+ Follow a clear hierarchy and indentation scheme to visually represent different levels of sections and sub-sections.

+ Ensure consistent spacing and alignment of list items for a clean and organized appearance.

+ Experiment with different font sizes, styles, and formatting options for section headings and page numbers to provide visual cues to readers.

+ Consider adding hyperlinks to the table of contents for easy navigation in electronic documents. The `hyperref` package in XeLaTeX provides convenient tools for hyperlinking various elements in your document.

Applying advanced typesetting techniques and hyphenation rules

To achieve professional typography, it's essential to apply advanced typesetting techniques and consider proper hyphenation rules. Here are some best practices to improve the typographic quality of your document:

+ Adjust the paragraph spacing and indentation to improve the overall texture and readability of your text. Ample spacing between paragraphs allows the reader's eyes to rest and creates a more visually appealing layout.

+ Use hanging punctuation to align punctuation marks with the edge of the text block, reducing visual distractions.

+ Employ proper hyphenation rules to avoid awkward or excessive hyphenation. XeLaTeX provides automatic hyphenation algorithms, but it's essential to check and refine hyphenation manually when needed.

+ Utilize discretionary line breaks, widow, and orphan control to prevent unattractive line breaks and ensure consistent paragraph lengths.

Troubleshooting typographic issues and achieving professional results

Even with careful attention to typography and design, issues may arise that require troubleshooting and fine-tuning. Here are some common typographic issues and techniques to achieve professional results:

+ Check for inconsistent line spacing and adjust it for a visually pleasing appearance. A consistent line spacing avoids large gaps within paragraphs.

+ Address issues related to orphans and widows, which are single lines of a paragraph left on a separate page or on the preceding or succeeding page. Adjusting spacing or rewriting the text can help minimize these issues.

+ Ensure proper alignment of text blocks and paragraphs throughout the document. Inconsistent alignment can create visual distractions and affect the overall appearance.

+ Pay attention to the use of quotation marks, dashes, and ellipses. Consistent and accurate usage of these typographic elements improves the readability and professional quality of your document.

◆ Troubleshoot font-related issues, such as missing or substituted glyphs. Ensure that you have the necessary font files and consider using fallback fonts or font packages to address compatibility issues.

In conclusion, by following these best practices for typography and design in XeLaTeX, you can create professional-looking documents that are aesthetically appealing and easy to read. Remember to experiment, practice, and always consider the purpose and audience of your document. The combination of well-chosen fonts, proper letter-spacing, careful design elements, and attention to detail will elevate the visual quality of your typography and enhance the overall impact of your document.

Advanced Typography and Layout Techniques in XeLaTeX

Introduction to advanced typography and layout techniques in XeLaTeX

In this section, we will explore the advanced typography and layout techniques that can be achieved using XeLaTeX. XeLaTeX offers a wide range of features and options that allow you to customize the design and appearance of your documents, making them visually appealing and professional.

Typography is the art and technique of arranging type, including fonts, letterforms, and spacing, to make written language legible and visually appealing. It plays a crucial role in enhancing the readability and aesthetics of your documents. XeLaTeX provides several tools and techniques to help you achieve the desired typographic effects.

1. Principles of typography and typesetting in XeLaTeX: Before delving into the advanced techniques, let's review some fundamental principles of typography and typesetting in XeLaTeX.

1.1 Font selection and pairing: Choosing appropriate fonts is essential for achieving a cohesive and harmonious typographic design. XeLaTeX supports a wide range of fonts, including system fonts and custom fonts. We will explore how to select and pair fonts effectively.

1.2 Letter-spacing, kerning, and tracking: Adjusting the spacing between characters can significantly impact the overall aesthetics and readability of a document. We will learn how to fine-tune the letter-spacing, kerning, and tracking in XeLaTeX to achieve optimal typographic results.

1.3 Ligatures and special characters: Ligatures are combined letterforms that enhance the visual flow and readability of certain character combinations. XeLaTeX provides support for ligatures and special characters, and we will explore how to utilize them effectively.

1.4 Title pages and covers: Designing attractive and professional-looking title pages and covers is essential for creating an impactful document. We will discuss various techniques for designing and formatting title pages and covers using XeLaTeX.

1.5 Chapter headings and section numbers: Consistent and visually appealing chapter headings and section numbers improve the document's structure and navigation. We will explore methods for creating and formatting chapter headings and section numbers using XeLaTeX.

1.6 Table of contents and lists: A well-designed table of contents and lists enhances the document's accessibility and readability. We will learn how to customize and format table of contents and lists in XeLaTeX.

2. Advanced typography and layout techniques in XeLaTeX: Now that we have reviewed the principles, let's dive into some advanced techniques that XeLaTeX offers for typography and layout.

2.1 Magazine and newspaper layouts: XeLaTeX provides the flexibility to create complex magazine and newspaper layouts. We will explore techniques for designing and implementing multi-column layouts, headers, footers, and other elements commonly found in publications.

2.2 Grid systems and modular design: Grid systems are a popular tool in graphic design that helps create consistent and organized layouts. We will learn how to implement grid systems and modular design principles in XeLaTeX to achieve harmonious and balanced compositions.

2.3 Advanced kerning and spacing techniques: XeLaTeX allows fine-grained control over the spacing between characters, words, and lines. We will examine advanced kerning and spacing techniques such as microtypography, optical margin alignment, and hanging punctuation.

2.4 Complex book layouts: Books often require sophisticated typography and layout choices. We will explore techniques for typesetting poetry, verse, and other specialized content, as well as handling footnotes, sidenotes, and marginalia effectively.

2.5 Brochures and promotional materials: XeLaTeX is an excellent tool for designing brochures, flyers, and other promotional materials. We will cover techniques for creating visually appealing layouts, incorporating images and graphics, and balancing text and visuals.

2.6 Advanced typesetting effects and embellishments: XeLaTeX offers various methods for adding visual interest and decorative elements to your documents. We will explore techniques such as drop caps, decorative borders, calligraphy, and initial letters.

2.7 Troubleshooting advanced typography and layout issues: Despite careful design, typography and layout issues can still arise. We will discuss common issues and their solutions, including hyphenation problems, spacing inconsistencies, and color management in XeLaTeX.

2.8 Best practices for advanced typography and layout: To ensure high-quality typography and layout, we will present best practices, tips, and tricks for achieving professional results. We will also discuss resources for further learning and inspiration to unleash your creativity with XeLaTeX.

In this section, we have introduced the principles of advanced typography and layout techniques in XeLaTeX. Understanding these principles and applying them effectively will enable you to create visually stunning and well-designed documents. Now, let's proceed further into the world of XeLaTeX with hands-on examples and exercises in the subsequent sections of this book.

Creating and designing magazine and newspaper layouts in XeLaTeX

Magazine and newspaper layouts are essential for presenting information in a visually appealing and organized manner. In this section, we will explore how XeLaTeX can be used to create professional-quality layouts for magazines and newspapers. We will cover design principles, layout techniques, and useful packages for achieving stunning results.

Design Principles

When designing magazine and newspaper layouts, it is important to consider several key design principles. These principles help create visually appealing and reader-friendly designs. Here are some principles to keep in mind:

+ **Hierarchy and Contrast:** Create a clear hierarchy of information using font sizes, weights, and colors. Use contrast effectively to draw attention to important elements.

+ **Whitespace:** Utilize whitespace to give your layout breathing room and make it easier for readers to navigate and digest the content.

- **Grid Systems:** Grid systems provide a framework for organizing and aligning elements in your layout. Use a grid to maintain consistency and improve overall visual harmony.

- **Typography:** Choose fonts that complement the overall design aesthetic and enhance readability. Consider factors such as font size, line spacing, and alignment.

- **Color Scheme:** Create a cohesive color scheme that aligns with the magazine or newspaper theme. Use color effectively to highlight important elements and create visual interest.

- **Visual Hierarchy:** Use visual elements like images, illustrations, and infographics to enhance the visual appeal and guide readers' attention to key information.

- **Consistency:** Maintain consistency throughout the layout by using consistent fonts, colors, and styles. This helps establish a visual identity and improves readability.

By incorporating these design principles into your XeLaTeX layouts, you can create visually engaging and reader-friendly magazine and newspaper designs.

Layout Techniques

Creating an effective magazine or newspaper layout involves careful placement and arrangement of various elements. Let's explore some essential layout techniques that you can utilize in XeLaTeX.

1. **Multiple Columns** One common layout technique in magazines and newspapers is the use of multiple columns. This allows for efficient use of space and makes it easier for readers to scan the content. XeLaTeX provides the `multicol` package, which makes it straightforward to create multi-column layouts. Here's an example:

```
\begin{multicols}{2}
```

```
Lorem\index{Lorem} ipsum dolor sit amet, consectetur\index{cons
Fusce imperdiet tellus ac leo\index{leo} tristique porttitor. M
malesuada. Nunc pellentesque\index{Nunc pellentesque}\index{pel
Maecenas\index{Maecenas} ex\index{ex} nisl, convallis eu\index{

\columnbreak

Integer cursus cursus tempus. Nunc accumsan nulla ac\index{Nunc
malesuada ex\index{ex} ullamcorper\index{ullamcorper}. Donec ve
nunc\index{nunc}. Ut nec sapien commodo, fringilla mauris sed\i

\end{multicols}
```

In this example, the content is divided into two columns using the `multicols` environment. You can adjust the number of columns as per your design requirements.

2. Text Wrapping   Text wrapping refers to the placement of text around images or other visual elements. This technique adds visual interest to the layout and prevents large chunks of text from appearing monotonous. XeLaTeX's `wrapfig` package facilitates easy text wrapping. Consider the following example:

```
\begin{wrapfigure}{R}{0.3\textwidth}
    \includegraphics[width=0.3\textwidth]{image.jpg}
\end{wrapfigure}

Lorem\index{Lorem} ipsum dolor sit amet, consectetur\index{cons
tempus. Quisque posuere cursus quam\index{Quisque posuere cursu
Sed vitae\index{Sed vitae} congue mauris\index{congue mauris}.
et feugiat nisl bibendum.
```

In this example, the `wrapfigure` environment is used to wrap the text around the image. You can adjust the size and placement of the image as needed.

3. Pull Quotes Pull quotes are used to highlight a key quote or piece of information from the article. They provide a visual break in the layout and draw readers' attention. XeLaTeX allows you to create pull quotes easily. Here's an example:

```
\begin{quote}
``Design is not just what it looks like and feels like. Design is
\end{quote}
```

In this example, the `quote` environment is used to create the pull quote. Customize the quote's appearance to match your layout design.

Useful Packages

XeLaTeX provides various packages that can greatly assist in creating magazine and newspaper layouts. Here are some useful packages:

- **graphicx:** This package enables the inclusion and manipulation of images and graphics in your layout.

- **caption:** The caption package allows for flexible customization and formatting of captions for figures and tables.

- **fancyhdr:** This package helps in creating custom headers and footers, which are often used in magazine and newspaper layouts.

- **mdframed:** The mdframed package provides easy customization and framing options for text boxes and other elements.

+ **tcolorbox:** This package offers a wide range of options for creating attractive and customizable colored boxes or panels.

By utilizing these packages, you can enhance the visual appeal and functionality of your magazine and newspaper layouts.

Example Layout

Let's put our knowledge into practice by creating an example magazine layout using XeLaTeX. In this layout, we will incorporate multiple columns, text wrapping, and pull quotes. Here's the code:

```
\begin{multicols}{2}
Nam fermentum tortor nec tempus accumsan\index{tempus accumsan}
Ut eget finibus lacus\index{finibus lacus}. Integer congue lect
odio varius pellentesque\index{varius pellentesque}\index{pelle

\columnbreak

\begin{wrapfigure}{R}{0.3\textwidth}
    \includegraphics[width=0.3\textwidth]{image.jpg}
\end{wrapfigure}

``Design is not just what it looks like and feels like. Design

Pellentesque euismod nibh velit\index{Pellentesque euismod nibh
tristique urna. Ut tempor\index{tempor}, justo nec mattis aliqu
quis efficitur\index{efficitur} libero metus tempor\index{tempo

\end{multicols}

\begin{quote}
```

``Simplicity is the ultimate sophistication\index{sophistication}.
\end{quote}

In this example layout, we have utilized multiple columns to present two different sections of content. We have also incorporated a text wrap around an image and included a pull quote to emphasize a key statement. Feel free to customize the layout further according to your design preferences.

Resources

As you explore magazine and newspaper layout design in XeLaTeX, you may find the following resources helpful:

- The **layouts** Package: This package provides a visual representation of the various layout elements, such as margins, headers, and footers. It can assist in fine-tuning your design.

- **Online Resources:** There are various online forums and communities where designers share their XeLaTeX magazine and newspaper layouts. Browsing through their work can provide inspiration and valuable insights.

Conclusion

In this section, we have explored how XeLaTeX can be used to create visually appealing and organized magazine and newspaper layouts. By applying design principles, employing layout techniques, and utilizing useful packages, you can achieve stunning results in your own projects. Experiment with different layouts, typography, and color schemes to create unique and captivating designs that effectively convey information to your readers. Happy designing!

Implementing grid systems and modular design in XeLaTeX

Typography is not just about choosing the right fonts and formatting text; it also involves creating visually appealing layouts. One effective way to achieve visually pleasing and organized layouts is by using grid systems and modular design. In this section, we will explore how XeLaTeX can be used to implement grid systems and create modular designs for various types of documents.

Understanding grid systems

Grid systems provide a framework for arranging elements on a page, based on a series of horizontal and vertical lines. This helps maintain consistency and structure in the layout, making it easier for readers to navigate the content. Grid systems have been widely used in design, especially in print media and web design.

In XeLaTeX, we can use packages like `grid` or `grid-system` to create grid layouts. These packages offer commands and environments that allow us to define the size and positioning of grid cells.

Designing with modular elements

Modular design is a technique that involves breaking down a layout into smaller, reusable modules. These modules can be combined and rearranged to create flexible and cohesive designs. By using modular elements, we can easily update or modify specific sections of a document without affecting the rest of the layout.

To implement modular design in XeLaTeX, we can divide our document into logical sections using packages like `mdframed` or `tcolorbox`. These packages provide commands and environments for creating boxes and frames around specific content. We can then position these modules within the grid system for a structured and organized layout.

Creating a grid-based layout

Let's consider a simple example of creating a grid-based layout for a magazine article. We'll use a 12-column grid system for this layout.

1. First, we need to define the grid system using the `grid` package. We can set the number of columns and the width of each column.

   ```
   \gridsetup{cols={12}, width=\linewidth, gridunit=pt}
   ```

2. Next, we can start our document and divide it into grid cells using the `grid` environment. We can specify the width of each cell based on the desired column span.

```
\begin{grid}{12}
    \begin{grid}{3}
        % Sidebar content goes here
    \end{grid}
    \begin{grid}{9}
        % Main article content goes here
    \end{grid}
\end{grid}
```

3. Within each grid cell, we can further divide the content into modular elements using the mdframed package. This allows us to create separate boxes for different sections, such as titles, images, and text.

```
\begin{mdframed}[backgroundcolor=gray!20]
    % Title goes here
\end{mdframed}

\begin{mdframed}[backgroundcolor=white]
    % Image goes here
\end{mdframed}

\begin{mdframed}[backgroundcolor=white]
    % Text content goes here
\end{mdframed}
```

4. Finally, we can arrange the modular elements within the grid cells, using the grid environment multiple times within a cell for further division and alignment.

```
\begin{mdframed}[backgroundcolor=gray!20]
    \begin{grid}{12}
        \begin{grid}{6}
```

```
% Title goes here
\end{grid}
\begin{grid}{6}
    % Date and author information goes here
    \end{grid}
\end{grid}
\end{mdframed}

\begin{mdframed}[backgroundcolor=white]
    \begin{grid}{3}
        % Image goes here
    \end{grid}
    \begin{grid}{9}
        % Text content goes here
    \end{grid}
\end{mdframed}
```

With this approach, we can easily manage the layout of our document by adjusting the positioning and size of the grid cells and modular elements. Using grid systems and modular design principles can greatly enhance the overall look and readability of our documents, whether it's a magazine article, a website, or any other publication.

Additional Resources

If you want to explore grid systems and modular design further, we recommend the following resources:

- "Grid Systems: Principles of Organizing Type" by Kimberly Elam

- "Making and Breaking the Grid: A Graphic Design Layout Workshop" by Timothy Samara

- "Composition: Understanding Line, Notan and Color" by Arthur Wesley Dow

These resources provide in-depth explanations, examples, and exercises to help you hone your skills in grid-based design and layout. Remember, practice is key, so don't hesitate to experiment and apply these principles to your own projects. Happy designing!

XeLaTeX Secrets: Advanced Kerning and Spacing Techniques

Introduction

In this section, we will explore advanced techniques for controlling the kerning and spacing of text in XeLaTeX. Kerning refers to the adjustment of space between individual pairs of characters, while spacing refers to the overall spacing between words and lines. These techniques will help you achieve precise and professional-looking typography in your documents.

Principles of Kerning

Kerning is the process of adjusting the space between specific pairs of characters to ensure optimal visual balance. It is typically used to improve the appearance of character combinations that may otherwise appear too spaced out or too cramped.

In XeLaTeX, kerning is typically handled automatically by the font, but in some cases, manual adjustments may be necessary. To control the kerning of a particular pair of characters, you can use the `\kern` command followed by a value indicating the amount of adjustment needed.

For example, to decrease the space between the characters "A" and "V" by 1 point, you can use `AV\kern -1pt`. Conversely, to increase the space between "A" and "V" by 1 point, you can use `AV\kern 1pt`.

It is important to note that kerning adjustments are specific to the font being used and may not be universally applicable. Different fonts may have different kerning pairs, so it is recommended to consult the font documentation or specimen sheet for specific kerning values.

Principles of Spacing

In addition to controlling the kerning between characters, it is crucial to ensure proper spacing between words and lines for optimal readability. Proper spacing also helps avoid awkward visual gaps or overlaps between lines of text.

XeLaTeX provides several ways to control spacing:

+ **Word-spacing:** The `\spaceskip` command allows you to set the amount of space added between words. For example, `\spaceskip 1em` sets a space of 1 em (the width of the letter "M") between words. Similarly, `\spaceskip 0.5em plus 0.2em minus 0.1em` sets a base space of 0.5 em with some flexibility.

- **Inter-word stretch and shrink:** By using \xspaceskip, you can control how much the space between words can stretch or shrink to fit the available space. For example, \xspaceskip 0.5em plus 0.2em minus 0.1em allows the space to stretch up to 0.2 em and shrink down to 0.1 em in case of tight spaces.

- **Inter-word glue:** XeLaTeX automatically adjusts the space between words based on the specified word-spacing, inter-word stretch, and shrink values. The glue (plus and minus) allows flexibility in spacing to achieve optimal line breaks and avoid large gaps or overlaps.

- **Line-spacing:** The \baselineskip command defines the vertical spacing between lines. It is typically set to a multiple of the font size. For example, \baselineskip 1.5 sets the line spacing to 1.5 times the font size.

Controlling Kerning and Spacing in Practice

To demonstrate the principles of kerning and spacing in XeLaTeX, let's consider a practical example. Suppose we want to typeset a document with a heading that requires specific kerning adjustments.

\subsection{Applying Kerning in Headings}

In this section\index{section}, we will explore\index{explore}

\subsubsection{Adjusting Letter Spacing}

To achieve visual\index{visual} balance\index{balance} in\index
For example, in the word ``EXPERTISE", we may want to reduce th

\textbf{EXPERTISE\kern-0.5pt}

Similarly, in the word ``TYPOGRAPHY", we may want to increase t

\textbf{TYPOGRAP\kern0.5ptHY}

By making\index{making} careful kerning\index{kerning} adjustme

\subsubsection{Controlling Line Spacing}

In headings, it is also important to consider\index{consider} line
We can adjust\index{adjust} the line\index{line} spacing\index{spa
For example\index{example}, to set\index{set} the line\index{line}

\texttt{\textbackslash subsubsection\{Controlling Line Spacing\}}

\texttt{\textbackslash baselineskip 1.2}

This will provide\index{provide} sufficient vertical spacing\index

By employing kerning\index{kerning} and spacing\index{spacing} tec

Conclusion

In this section, we have explored advanced kerning and spacing techniques in
XeLaTeX. We learned how to manually adjust kerning for specific character pairs
using the \kern command and how to control word and line spacing using the
\spaceskip and \baselineskip commands.

By mastering these techniques, you can achieve professional-looking
typography with precise spacing and kerning adjustments. Remember to
experiment with different values and fonts to achieve the desired visual balance in
your documents.

In the next section, we will delve into advanced typesetting effects and
embellishments in XeLaTeX, taking your documents to the next level of
sophistication.

Designing and typesetting complex book layouts in XeLaTeX

In this section, we will explore the process of designing and typesetting complex
book layouts using XeLaTeX. Designing a book layout requires careful
consideration of various elements such as typography, page structure, margins,
headers, footers, chapter headings, and more. We will discuss different techniques
and tools available in XeLaTeX to create beautifully designed book layouts that are
visually appealing and enhance the reading experience.

Principles of book design

When designing a book layout, it is important to keep in mind certain principles
of book design. These principles ensure that the reader can navigate through the

content easily and comfortably. Here are some key principles to consider:

+ **Readability:** The text should be easily readable, with an appropriate font size, line spacing, and line length.

+ **Hierarchy:** The layout should make use of visual hierarchy to guide the reader's attention, with clear distinctions between headings, subheadings, and body text.

+ **Consistency:** Consistency in design elements such as font choices, colors, line spacing, and margins helps create a cohesive and professional look.

+ **Balance:** The elements on each page should be visually balanced, with an appropriate distribution of text and white space.

+ **Grid-based layout:** Using a grid-based layout system helps maintain consistency and alignment throughout the book.

By following these principles, you can create an aesthetically pleasing and well-structured book layout.

Setting up the document

To get started with designing a book layout in XeLaTeX, we first need to set up the document. Here is a basic template to get you started:

```
\documentclass[a4paper,oneside,12pt]{book}
```

```
\geometry{
    left=2cm,
    right=2cm,
    top=2cm,
    bottom=2cm
}
```

```
\setmainfont{Times New Roman}
```

```
\titleformat{\chapter}{\normalfont\huge\bfseries}{\thechapter}
```

```
\chapter{Introduction}
This is the introduction\index{introduction} chapter\index{chapter

\section{Section 1}
This is the first section\index{section} of the book\index{book} 1

% Add more chapters and sections as needed
```

In this template, we have set the document class as book and specified the paper size as a4paper. We have also set the margins using the geometry package and chosen a font (Times New Roman) using the fontspec package. The titlesec package is used to customize the chapter headings.

Page structure and numbering

The page structure of a book layout typically includes different regions such as the header, footer, margin notes, and main content area. XeLaTeX provides several packages to modify and customize these regions.

To modify the header and footer, you can use the fancyhdr package. Here is an example of how to set the header and footer:

```
\pagestyle{fancy}
\fancyhead{}
\fancyfoot{}
\fancyhead[LE,RO]{\thepage}
\fancyhead[RE,LO]{Chapter \thechapter}
\renewcommand{\headrulewidth}{0.4pt}
\renewcommand{\footrulewidth}{0pt}
```

In this example, we have set the page style to fancy, cleared the default header and footer, and defined custom headers and footers. The commands \headrulewidth and \footrulewidth control the thickness of the header and footer rules, respectively.

To customize the page numbering style, you can use the `pagenumbering` command. Here are some examples:

```
\pagenumbering{arabic} % Arabic numerals (1, 2, 3, ...)
\pagenumbering{roman} % Lowercase Roman numerals (i, ii, iii, .
\pagenumbering{Roman} % Uppercase Roman numerals (I, II, III, .
\pagenumbering{alph} % Lowercase letters (a, b, c, ...)
\pagenumbering{Alph} % Uppercase letters (A, B, C, ...)
```

You can place the `pagenumbering` command at the appropriate location in your document to change the numbering style.

Chapter headings and section numbering

Chapter headings play a crucial role in book layouts as they provide visual cues to the reader and indicate the start of a new chapter. In XeLaTeX, you can customize the chapter headings using the `titlesec` package.

Here is an example of how to customize the chapter headings:

```
\titleformat{\chapter}{\normalfont\huge\bfseries}{\thechapter}{
```

In this example, we have used the `titleformat` command to define the format of the chapter headings. We set the font style to huge, which makes the chapter title larger than the surrounding text. You can customize the font size, color, alignment, and other properties according to your preferences.

By default, section numbering is automatically enabled in XeLaTeX. However, if you prefer to disable section numbering or use a different numbering style, you can use the `titlesec` package. Here are some examples:

```
\titleformat{\section}{\normalfont\Large\bfseries}{}{0pt}{}
\titleformat{\subsection}{\normalfont\large\bfseries}{}{0pt}{}
\titleformat{\subsubsection}{\normalfont\normalsize\bfseries}{
```

In these examples, we have customized the format of the section, subsection, and subsubsection headings by adjusting the font sizes. You can modify other properties like font style, color, and spacing as per your requirements.

Paragraph formatting and text flow

In a book layout, it is important to have consistent and visually pleasing paragraph formatting. XeLaTeX provides several options to control paragraph indentation, spacing, and alignment.

To set the indentation of the first line of each paragraph, you can use the `parskip` package. Here is an example:

```
\setlength{\parindent}{0pt} % No indent for first line
\setlength{\parskip}{6pt} % Space between paragraphs
```

In this example, we have set the `parindent` length to 0pt, which eliminates the indentation of the first line of each paragraph. The `parskip` length controls the space between paragraphs.

To control the alignment of text within a paragraph, you can use the `ragged2e` package. Here is an example:

```
\justifying % Justify text within paragraphs
```

In this example, we have used the `justifying` command to justify the text within paragraphs. You can also use other alignment options like `centering`, `raggedright`, and `raggedleft`.

To control the overall text flow, you can use the `multicol` package to create multicolumn layouts. Here is an example:

```
\begin{multicols}{2}
    This text\index{text} will be\index{be} displayed in\index{in}
\end{multicols}
```

In this example, we have used the `multicols` environment to create a multicolumn layout with two columns. You can adjust the number of columns and customize the width and spacing between columns according to your needs.

Inserting images and graphics

In a book layout, it is common to include images and graphics to enhance the visual appeal and convey information. XeLaTeX provides the `graphicx` package to insert images into your document.

Here is an example of how to include an image:

```
% \begin{figure}
%     \centering
%     \includegraphics[width=0.75\textwidth]{image.png}
%     \caption{This is a caption for the image.}
%     \label{fig:image}
% \end{figure}
```

In this example, we have used the figure environment to float the image. The \centering command centers the image horizontally within the figure. The \includegraphics command is used to insert the image, and you can specify the width using the width option. The \caption command adds a caption to the image, and the \label command allows you to reference the image elsewhere in the document.

You can also adjust the placement, scaling, and alignment of images using various options provided by the graphicx package. For example, you can use the scale option to scale the image, the angle option to rotate it, and the trim and clip options to crop it.

Tables and figures

Book layouts often include tabular data and figures to present information in a structured and visually appealing way. XeLaTeX provides several packages and options to create tables and customize their appearance.

To create tables, you can use the tabular environment. Here is an example:

```
\begin{tabular}{|c|c|}
    \hline
    \textbf{Column 1} & \textbf{Column 2} \\
    \hline
    Row 1 & Value 1 \\
    \hline
    Row 2 & Value 2 \\
    \hline
\end{tabular}
```

In this example, we have created a simple table with two columns and two rows. The | and hline commands are used to draw vertical and horizontal lines to separate the cells.

You can customize the appearance of the table by adjusting the alignment of cells, adding additional lines, and using different font styles. The booktabs package provides additional commands to create professional-looking tables with proper spacing and line thickness. You can also use the caption package to add captions and labels to your tables.

For complex tables with merged cells, multirow cells, or special formatting requirements, you may need additional packages such as multirow, makecell, or tabu. These packages provide additional commands and options to handle advanced table layouts.

Figures, such as charts, graphs, or illustrations, can be included using the same figure environment mentioned earlier for images. You can use TikZ or other packages like pgfplots or tikzpagenodes to create professional-looking vector graphics directly in XeLaTeX. These packages provide commands to draw lines, shapes, curves, and add labels or annotations to the figures.

Captions, footnotes, and cross-referencing

In a book layout, it is important to provide captions for tables, figures, and other elements to provide context and improve readability. XeLaTeX provides the caption package to customize and format captions.

Here is an example of how to add captions to a table and a figure:

```
\captionsetup[table]{labelsep=space, justification=justified}
\captionsetup[figure]{labelsep=period}
```

In this example, we have used the captionsetup command to customize the caption format. We have set the labelsep option to control the separator between the label and the caption text. You can customize other aspects of the caption format, such as alignment, font style, and numbering style according to your preferences.

Footnotes are another important element in book layouts, allowing you to provide additional information or explanations. XeLaTeX automatically handles footnotes using the footnote command. Here is an example:

```
This is some text.\footnote{This is a footnote.}
```

In this example, the footnote appears at the bottom of the page, and the corresponding marker appears in the text.

To refer to tables, figures, sections, or other elements within the document, you can use the label and ref commands. Here is an example:

```
% \begin{figure}
%     \centering
%     \includegraphics[width=0.75\textwidth]{image.png}
%     \caption{This is a caption for the image.}
%     \label{fig:image}
% \end{figure}
```

```
Please see Figure \ref{fig:image} for more details.
```

In this example, we have assigned a label to the figure using the `\label` command, and then referred to it using the `\ref` command. The correct figure number is automatically inserted into the text.

Best practices for complex book layouts

Designing and typesetting complex book layouts can be a challenging task, but with the right approach, it can be rewarding. Here are some best practices to keep in mind:

- ♦ Plan your layout carefully: Before starting to design the book layout, sketch out the structure and flow of the content. Consider the hierarchy of headings, chapters, sections, and subsections.

- ♦ Use consistent styles: Maintain consistency in font choices, colors, spacing, and other design elements throughout the book. This helps create a cohesive and professional look.

- ♦ Choose appropriate fonts: Select fonts that are readable and suitable for the content. Avoid using too many different fonts, as it can make the layout look cluttered.

- ♦ Pay attention to white space: Use white space effectively to improve readability and visual appeal. White space helps separate elements and provides a sense of breathing room for the reader.

- ♦ Proofread and review: Carefully proofread the content and review the layout multiple times to catch any errors or inconsistencies. It's also helpful to get feedback from others to ensure the layout meets the intended goals.

By following these best practices, you can create visually stunning and well-structured book layouts using XeLaTeX.

Example: Designing a textbook layout

To illustrate the concepts discussed in this section, let's design a textbook layout for a computer science course. The textbook will contain chapters, sections, figures, tables, and exercises. Here is an example layout:

- ✦ Chapter 1: Introduction to Computer Science

    - Section 1.1: What is Computer Science?
    - Section 1.2: History of Computers
    - Section 1.3: Problem-Solving Approaches

- ✦ Chapter 2: Programming Fundamentals

    - Section 2.1: Introduction to Programming
    - Section 2.2: Variables and Data Types
    - Section 2.3: Control Structures

- ✦ Chapter 3: Data Structures and Algorithms

    - Section 3.1: Arrays and Lists
    - Section 3.2: Stacks and Queues
    - Section 3.3: Searching and Sorting Algorithms

- ✦ Chapter 4: Databases and SQL

    - Section 4.1: Introduction to Databases
    - Section 4.2: Relational Databases
    - Section 4.3: SQL Basics

- ✦ Appendices: Glossary, Index, and Exercises

In this example layout, each chapter starts with a chapter heading, followed by sections with their respective headings. Figures and tables are included to illustrate concepts or present data, and exercises are provided at the end of each chapter for practice.

The design of the textbook layout should consider the principles of book design discussed earlier. The font choices, spacing, alignment, and visual hierarchy should be consistent throughout the book. Additionally, elements like chapter headings, section headings, and captions for figures and tables should be formatted appropriately to enhance readability.

By carefully designing and typesetting the textbook layout using the techniques and tools available in XeLaTeX, you can create a visually appealing and informative textbook for your readers.

Further resources

If you want to explore more about designing and typesetting complex book layouts in XeLaTeX, here are some additional resources to help you:

+ *The LaTeX Companion* by Frank Mittelbach, Michel Goossens, et al.

+ *The Elements of Typographic Style* by Robert Bringhurst

+ The official documentation and user guides of related packages, such as `geometry`, `fontspec`, `titlesec`, `caption`, etc.

+ Online forums and communities like *TeX Stack Exchange* (`https://tex.stackexchange.com`) where you can find answers to specific questions and seek advice from experienced users.

Remember, designing and typesetting book layouts is both an art and a science. Experiment with various techniques, iterate on your designs, and never shy away from seeking feedback to continually improve your skills. Happy typesetting!

Typesetting Poetry and Verse in XeLaTeX

Typesetting poetry and verse can be a challenging task, as it involves not only arranging the text on the page but also capturing the aesthetic and rhythmic qualities of the poetry. XeLaTeX provides several features and tools that can help us achieve beautiful and professional-looking poetry and verse layouts. In this section, we will explore various techniques and best practices for typesetting poetry and verse using XeLaTeX.

The Verse Environment

The Verse environment is a useful tool for typesetting poetry and verse. It allows us to maintain the line breaks and indentation of the original text while automatically formatting the text with appropriate spacing. To use the Verse environment, we need to load the verse package by adding the following line to the preamble:

Once we have loaded the verse package, we can begin typesetting our poetry and verse using the Verse environment. We start the environment with the \begin{verse} command and end it with the \end{verse} command. Each line of the poem is entered as a separate line of text within the environment. For example:

```
\begin{verse}
Roses are red,\\
Violets are blue,\\
Sugar is sweet,\\
And so are you.\\
\end{verse}
```

This will produce:

> Roses are red,
> Violets are blue,
> Sugar is sweet,
> And so are you.

The Verse environment takes care of the spacing between lines and the indentation of each line. It also provides options for customizing the appearance of the poetry, such as setting the font size, adjusting the line spacing, and adding additional vertical space between stanzas. Refer to the verse package documentation for more information on these customization options.

Formatting Stanzas

When typesetting poetry, it is common to have multiple stanzas with distinct structures or rhyming patterns. To format stanzas, we can use the macro \flagverse{}, which inserts a flag to the left of the first line of each stanza. This can provide a visual marker to help readers distinguish between stanzas. For example:

```
\begin{verse}
\flagverse{1.} This is the first stanza,\\
With some lines of text.\\
```

```
\flagverse{2.} Here comes the second stanza,\\
With its own structure and rhyme.\\
\end{verse}
```

This will produce:

1. This is the first stanza,
   With some lines of text.
2. Here comes the second stanza,
   With its own structure and rhyme.

By numbering the stanzas using the `\flagverse` macro, we can refer to specific stanzas in our text or analysis. This can be particularly useful when discussing the structure and meaning of a poem.

Formatting Typography

In poetry, the visual appearance of the text can play a significant role in conveying emotions and meanings. With XeLaTeX's powerful font selection capabilities, we can easily customize the typography of our poetry to match the desired aesthetic. Here are a few tips for formatting the typography of poetry:

- ◆ Choose appropriate fonts: Select fonts that complement the mood and content of the poem. Consider using serif fonts for traditional or formal poetry and sans-serif fonts for more contemporary or experimental styles.

- ◆ Adjust font size: Experiment with different font sizes to find the right balance between legibility and aesthetics. Larger font sizes can emphasize certain words or phrases, while smaller sizes can convey intimacy or vulnerability.

- ◆ Use italics or bold: Italic or bold fonts can be used to highlight specific words or lines, adding emphasis and visual impact to the poem.

- ◆ Play with line spacing: Adjusting the line spacing can create unique visual effects and enhance the overall readability of the poem. However, be cautious not to use excessive line spacing, as it can disrupt the flow of the text.

- ◆ Experiment with line breaks: The placement of line breaks can significantly impact the rhythm and meaning of a poem. Be deliberate in choosing where to break lines, considering the impact on pacing, emphasis, and overall structure.

+ Utilize graphical elements: Consider adding graphical elements, such as decorative borders or special characters, to enhance the visual appeal and thematic resonance of the poem.

Remember that the typographic choices should align with the intention and style of the poem, supporting its overall meaning and emotional impact.

Analyzing Poetic Metrics

When studying or analyzing poetry, it is often necessary to identify and discuss the poetic meter and rhythm. XeLaTeX provides tools for visually representing the metrical patterns within a line of poetry using accents and symbols. One popular package for this purpose is the metrix package. To use the features of this package, add the following line to the preamble:

The metrix package provides commands such as \metrix, \diap, \arod, and \hjos to mark the different elements that make up poetic meter.

For example, consider the following line of poetry:

\metrix{Rose} \metrix{are} \metrix{red}, \metrix{vio}\diap{lets} \

This will produce:

Rose are red, violets **are blue,**

The metrical symbols can be combined to represent different metrical patterns, such as dactyls, trochees, or iambs. By visually marking the metrical pattern, we can better understand and discuss the rhythmic qualities of the poem.

Conclusion

In this section, we have explored various techniques and best practices for typesetting poetry and verse in XeLaTeX. We have learned how to use the Verse environment to structure and format the poetry, apply typographic enhancements to convey the desired aesthetic, analyze and represent poetic meter, and even experiment with calligrams and shaped poems. By combining these techniques, poets and typesetters can create visually appealing and expressive layouts for their poems, effectively capturing the essence and emotions of the written word.

Remember, these techniques are not exhaustive, and there is always room for further experimentation and customization. As with any art form, the key is to find a balance between form and function, allowing the typography and layout to enhance and complement the poetry itself.

Designing and formatting brochures and promotional materials in XeLaTeX

Brochures and promotional materials are essential tools for conveying information and capturing the attention of potential customers. In this section, we will explore how to leverage the power of XeLaTeX to design and format visually appealing brochures and promotional materials. We will cover various techniques and best practices to create professional-looking materials that effectively communicate your message.

Understanding the Purpose of Brochures and Promotional Materials

Before diving into the design and formatting aspects, it's important to understand the purpose of brochures and promotional materials. These materials serve as a means of communication to promote a company, product, or service. They are designed to capture the reader's attention, provide information, and persuade them to take action.

Brochures and promotional materials are commonly used in marketing campaigns, trade shows, and sales presentations. They should present information in a clear, concise, and visually appealing manner to engage the target audience.

Design Principles for Brochures and Promotional Materials

When designing brochures and promotional materials, it's crucial to follow design principles to create visually appealing and effective materials. Here are some key principles to keep in mind:

+ **Hierarchy:** Establish a clear hierarchy of information to guide the reader's attention. Use headings, subheadings, and different font sizes to differentiate sections and emphasize key points.

+ **Whitespace:** Utilize whitespace strategically to create a sense of balance and organization. It helps to improve readability and draw attention to important elements.

+ **Color:** Choose a color palette that aligns with your brand identity and conveys the desired mood. Use colors strategically to emphasize important information and create visual interest.

+ **Typography:** Select fonts that are legible and appropriate for the purpose of the material. Use a combination of fonts to create contrast and hierarchy.

Layout and Structure

The layout and structure of brochures and promotional materials play a crucial role in capturing the reader's attention and guiding them through the content. Here are some tips for designing an effective layout:

+ **Cover Design:** The cover is the first thing that catches the reader's attention. Use an eye-catching design, compelling headline, and captivating visuals to entice the reader to open the brochure.

+ **Information Hierarchy:** Organize information in a logical and intuitive manner. Start with an introduction or overview section, followed by more detailed information. Use headings, subheadings, and bullet points to break down the content and make it easy to scan.

+ **Visuals and Graphics:** Incorporate relevant and high-quality visuals to enhance the overall design. Use images, icons, and charts to illustrate key points and make the material more engaging.

+ **Call to Action:** Clearly define a call to action that prompts the reader to take the desired action. Place it strategically within the material, ensuring it stands out and is easily visible.

Formatting Text and Typography

Properly formatting text and typography is crucial for readability and conveying information effectively. Consider the following tips:

+ **Font Choices:** Select fonts that are legible and align with your branding. Use different font weights and sizes to create contrast and emphasize important text elements.

+ **Text Alignment:** Align text to ensure a clean and organized appearance. Left-align body text for easy reading and consider using centered or justified alignment for headings or specific sections.

+ **Line Spacing and Paragraph Indentation:** Adjust line spacing to enhance readability, especially for longer paragraphs of text. Use consistent indentation for paragraphs to create structure and flow.

+ **Text Boxes and Highlights:** Use text boxes or highlights to draw attention to important information or quotes. This can help break up the layout and add visual interest.

Adding Images and Graphics

Images and graphics play a vital role in capturing attention and conveying information visually. Here's how to effectively incorporate them:

+ **High-Quality Images:** Use high-resolution images to ensure clarity and visual appeal. Avoid using low-quality or pixelated images, as they can detract from the overall design.

+ **Image Placement:** Strategically place images to complement the accompanying text or draw attention to specific sections. Consider using full-page or large images for impact and smaller images within text columns for visual breaks.

+ **Captions and Labels:** Provide clear and concise captions or labels for images and graphics. This helps readers understand the context and enhances the overall reading experience.

Designing for Print and Digital

Brochures and promotional materials can be designed for both print and digital distribution. When designing for print, ensure that the document's layout, colors, and images are of high resolution for crisp printing. Consider bleeds, trim marks, and margins to ensure optimal printing results.

For digital distribution, take advantage of interactive features, such as hyperlinks, embedded videos, or interactive elements. Optimize the document for digital screens by using appropriate file formats and ensuring compatibility across devices.

Best Practices for Brochure and Promotional Material Design

To ensure the success of your brochure and promotional material design, consider the following best practices:

+ **Know your audience:** Tailor your design and messaging to resonate with your target audience. Understand their preferences, needs, and expectations to create materials that effectively communicate your message.

+ **Consistency:** Maintain consistency in design elements, typography, and branding throughout the material to reinforce your brand identity and create a professional look.

+ **Proofreading and Editing:** Thoroughly proofread and edit the material to eliminate any spelling or grammatical errors. Ensure that the content is concise, clear, and error-free.

+ **Print and Digital Testing:** Test the material in both print and digital formats to ensure it displays correctly and functions as intended. Check for any issues related to formatting, layout, or interactive elements.

Creating brochures and promotional materials in XeLaTeX allows you to achieve professional-level design and formatting. By following the design principles, structuring the content effectively, and using appropriate visuals, typography, and formatting techniques, you can create visually stunning materials that effectively communicate your message and capture the attention of your target audience. Start experimenting and designing your own brochures and promotional materials in XeLaTeX today!

Implementing advanced typesetting effects and embellishments in XeLaTeX

In this section, we will explore how to take your typesetting skills in XeLaTeX to the next level by implementing advanced effects and embellishments. We will cover various techniques to enhance the visual appeal and readability of your documents. Let's dive in!

Adding drop caps

Drop caps are a great way to add visual interest and catch the reader's attention at the beginning of a chapter or section. You can easily implement drop caps in XeLaTeX using the `lettrine` package.

To add a drop cap, start by including the `lettrine` package in your preamble:

Then, use the `lettrine` command at the beginning of a paragraph to create the drop cap:

```
\lettrine{T}{his} is an example of a drop cap.
Lorem\index{Lorem} ipsum dolor sit amet, consectetur\index{consect
Nulla sagittis\index{Nulla sagittis} elit ac tincidunt facilisis.
Etiam hendrerit\index{Etiam hendrerit} eleifend\index{eleifend} ar
```

The first letter, in this case "T," will be styled as a drop cap. You can customize the drop cap's font, size, color, and other properties using the various options provided by the `lettrine` package.

Creating decorative chapter headings

Chapter headings are an essential part of book design. By using decorative fonts and custom formatting in XeLaTeX, you can create visually stunning chapter headings that stand out.

To begin, choose a decorative font that suits the style of your document. You can either install the font manually or use one of the many font packages available for XeLaTeX.

Once the font is selected, you can apply it to the chapter headings using the `titlesec` package. The `titlesec` package provides commands and options for customizing chapter and section headings.

Here's an example of how to create a decorative chapter heading using a custom font:

```
\titleformat{\chapter}[display]
{\normalfont\Huge\fontspec{DecorativeFont.otf}} % Replace with
{\chaptertitlename\ \thechapter}
{20pt}
{\Huge}
```

In this example, we use the `titleformat` command from the `titlesec` package to customize the appearance of the chapter heading. Adjust the font, size, color, and spacing to achieve your desired effect.

Adding decorative lines and ornaments

Decorative lines and ornaments can be used to enhance the visual appeal of specific sections or to divide content within a document. You can create these embellishments using the `pgfornament` package, which is based on TikZ.

To get started, include the `pgfornament` package in your document's preamble:

Then, use the `pgfornament` command to add decorative lines or ornaments wherever you want within your document:

```
\pgfornament[width=0.5\textwidth,color=red!50]{88}
```

In this example, we specify the width of the ornament using a fraction of the text width and set the color to red. The number "88" corresponds to a specific ornament style, and you can choose from a variety of options provided by the `pgfornament` package.

Creating calligraphic typography

Calligraphy adds an elegant and artistic touch to your documents. Using the `calligra` package, you can easily incorporate calligraphic font styles into your XeLaTeX documents.

Start by including the `calligra` package in your preamble:

Then, use the `calligra` command to apply calligraphic typography wherever desired:

```
\calligra{This is calligraphic text.}
```

You can also use the `calligra` font style within other commands or environments to create headings, titles, or other design elements.

Using OpenType features

OpenType fonts offer a wide range of advanced typographic features, such as ligatures, alternate glyphs, swashes, and more. XeLaTeX provides support for accessing these features directly within your document.

To access OpenType features, you need to choose a font that supports them. You can check the font's documentation to see which features are available. Once you have selected a font, you can use the `fontspec` package to enable and customize the features.

For example, to enable ligatures and small caps in a font, you can use the following:

```
\setmainfont{OpenTypeFont.otf}[
    Ligatures=TeX,
    SmallCapsFeatures={Letters=SmallCaps}
]
```

In this example, we specify the font file and enable both TeX ligatures and small caps. Adjust the options according to the features supported by your chosen font.

Creating drop shadows

Adding drop shadows to text or other elements can give them a three-dimensional and visually appealing effect. You can achieve this in XeLaTeX using the shadowtext package.

Start by including the shadowtext package in your preamble:

Next, use the shadowtext command to apply drop shadows:

```
\shadowtext{This text has a drop shadow.}
```

You can customize the color, size, and other properties of the drop shadow using the options provided by the shadowtext package.

Adding decorative page borders

Decorative page borders can give your document a polished and professional look. You can achieve this in XeLaTeX using the background package.

Start by including the background package in your preamble:

Then, use the background command to add a decorative page border:

```
\backgroundsetup{
    scale=1,
    angle=0,
    opacity=1,
    contents={\tikz [remember picture, overlay]
```

```
\draw [line width=3pt, blue]
    (\$ (current page.north west) + (1cm,-1cm) \$)
    rectangle
    (\$ (current page.south east) + (-1cm,1cm) \$);}
}
```

In this example, we customize the scale, angle, opacity, and color of the page border using the options provided by the background package. Adjust these settings to match your desired style.

Advanced typography and embellishments

To further enhance the visual impact of your documents, you can experiment with various typography techniques and embellishments. These include custom spacing, leading, kerning, tracking, and other advanced typographic adjustments.

Additionally, you can incorporate other embellishments such as illuminated initials, borders, ornaments, and illustrations. These elements can be created using TikZ or other graphic packages and integrated seamlessly into your XeLaTeX document.

Remember to strike a balance between aesthetics and readability. While decorative effects can add interest, they should not compromise the overall legibility and clarity of your document.

Conclusion

In this section, we explored how to implement advanced typesetting effects and embellishments in XeLaTeX. We discussed techniques such as adding drop caps, creating decorative chapter headings, using decorative lines and ornaments, incorporating calligraphic typography, accessing OpenType features, adding drop shadows, and adding decorative page borders.

By applying these techniques thoughtfully, you can make your documents visually stunning and captivating. Remember to experiment, customize, and iterate, keeping in mind the fundamental principles of typography and design.

In the next section, we will delve into testing and debugging techniques for XeLaTeX documents, ensuring the accuracy and quality of your work.

Troubleshooting advanced typography and layout issues in XeLaTeX

In this section, we will explore some common issues that may arise when working with advanced typography and layout in XeLaTeX. We will discuss techniques and solutions to troubleshoot these issues, ensuring that your documents are visually appealing and correctly formatted.

Text alignment issues

One common problem that users encounter is improper text alignment. Sometimes, the text may appear misaligned, with varying distances between words or uneven margins. This can be frustrating, especially when working on important documents or publications.

To troubleshoot text alignment issues, you can consider the following steps:

1. Check for typos or formatting errors: Sometimes, text alignment issues can be caused by simple mistakes such as missing backslashes or incorrect indentation. Carefully review your source code to identify any errors.

2. Verify the document class and settings: Different document classes have default alignment settings. Ensure that you have selected the appropriate document class and that the alignment settings match your requirements. For example, the `article` class uses left alignment by default, while the `book` class uses both left and right alignment.

3. Use the `\raggedright`, `\raggedleft`, or `\centering` commands: These commands can be used to override the default alignment settings for sections of your document. Place the command before the text you want to align differently. For example, `\raggedright` will left-align the text, `\raggedleft` will right-align the text, and `\centering` will center-align the text.

4. Adjust line breaks and hyphenation: In some cases, improper line breaks or hyphenation can lead to text alignment issues. Experiment with line breaks and hyphenation to achieve better alignment. You can use the `\hyphenation` command to manually specify hyphenation points.

Overfull and underfull `\hbox` warnings

The `\hbox` command is used to create a box with horizontal content, such as text or graphics. Sometimes, when the content does not fit within the specified width,

XeLaTeX generates `Overfull \hbox` or `Underfull \hbox` warnings. These warnings indicate that the content exceeds or falls short of the specified width, respectively.

To troubleshoot overfull and underfull `\hbox` warnings, you can follow these steps:

1. Review the warning message: The warning message provides information about the problematic line and the extent of the overfull or underfull box. Identify the line in your source code that is generating the warning.

2. Adjust the width: If the content consistently exceeds or falls short of the specified width, you may need to adjust the width of the box. Consider increasing or decreasing the width until the warning disappears. Alternatively, you can use the `\resizebox` command to automatically adjust the size of the content to fit within a specified width.

3. Modify the content: If adjusting the width does not resolve the issue, you may need to modify the content itself. Consider rephrasing sentences or adjusting spacing between words to achieve a better fit. You can also experiment with different font sizes or line spacing to reduce the overall width of the content.

Font-related issues

Another common issue in XeLaTeX is font-related problems. These can include missing glyphs, incorrect font rendering, or compatibility issues between different font families.

To troubleshoot font-related issues, consider the following steps:

1. Verify font installation: Ensure that the required fonts are installed on your system. XeLaTeX relies on system-installed fonts, so it is essential to confirm their availability.

   - Check the font names: Use the correct font names when specifying the font family in your document. For example, if you are using the Arial font, use `\setmainfont{Arial}` to specify it.

   - Check font file formats: XeLaTeX supports TrueType (.ttf), OpenType (.otf), and PostScript Type 1 (.pfb) font formats. Make sure that the fonts you are using are in one of these formats.

   - Confirm font accessibility: Ensure that the fonts you are using can be accessed by XeLaTeX. Some fonts may have restrictive licenses or permissions that prevent them from being used.

2. Debug font rendering issues: If you notice incorrect or inconsistent font rendering, you can try the following:

- Use different font renderers: XeLaTeX supports various font renderers, such as FreeType and DirectWrite. Experiment with different renderers to find the one that produces the desired results.

- Adjust font features: Many fonts offer additional features, such as ligatures or stylistic sets. These features can be enabled or disabled to affect the font rendering. Refer to the font's documentation to learn how to manipulate these features.

- Test different font options: XeLaTeX provides several font-related options that can be passed to the font loading command (\setmainfont, etc.). Experiment with these options to fine-tune the font rendering.

Layout issues with floats

Floats, such as figures and tables, can sometimes cause layout issues in XeLaTeX. These issues can include misplaced floats, inconsistent numbering, or improper alignment.

To troubleshoot layout issues with floats, consider the following steps:

1. Check float placement options: XeLaTeX provides several float placement options such as h for "here," t for "top," b for "bottom," and p for "page." Experiment with different placement options to achieve the desired layout. For example, using \begin{figure}[h] will attempt to place the figure exactly where it is defined in the source code.

2. Modify the float dimensions: If a float does not fit within the available space, you can adjust its dimensions. Use the \includegraphics command to specify the width and height of the float. Alternatively, you can use the \resizebox command to automatically scale the float to fit within the available space.

3. Debug inconsistent numbering: If you encounter issues with inconsistent numbering of figures or tables, ensure that you are using the correct caption commands (\caption) and label commands (\label). Make sure to place the label command after the caption command to ensure accurate referencing.

Troubleshooting unconventional layout requests

In some cases, you may have unconventional layout requirements or face unique challenges that cannot be solved using standard XeLaTeX packages or techniques. In such situations, you can consider the following approaches:

- ✦ Custom macros and commands: Define your own macros and commands to achieve the desired layout. These macros can be as simple as adjusting spacing or more complex, involving custom calculations to determine element placement.

- ✦ Advanced TikZ usage: Utilize the power of TikZ to create custom layouts or unique visual elements. TikZ provides extensive flexibility and control over graphical elements, enabling you to create unconventional layouts or graphics easily.

- ✦ External tools and graphics software: If XeLaTeX falls short for your layout needs, consider using external tools or graphics software in conjunction with XeLaTeX. You can generate complex graphics or layouts with specialized software and include them in your XeLaTeX document using the \includegraphics command.

- ✦ Consulting XeLaTeX communities and forums: Reach out to the XeLaTeX user community on online forums or mailing lists. Often, users have encountered similar layout challenges and can provide valuable insights or creative solutions to unconventional problems.

By following these troubleshooting techniques, you will be able to resolve advanced typography and layout issues in XeLaTeX efficiently. Remember that practice and experimentation are key to becoming proficient in troubleshooting XeLaTeX issues, so don't hesitate to dive deeper into the XeLaTeX documentation and explore additional resources to enhance your skills.

Exercises

1. Experiment with different alignment settings (\raggedright, \raggedleft, \centering) in your document and observe the changes in text alignment. Document your observations and any challenges you faced during the process.

2. Create a sample document with a figure and a table, observing various float placement options (h, t, b, p). Note how different placement options affect the layout of your document and the behavior of floats.

3. Try out different font options (such as font size, font weight, or font features) using different fonts in your document. Experiment with different font renderers and observe how they affect font rendering and overall document layout.

4. Design a custom layout using TikZ. Create a complex diagram or graphical element that cannot be easily achieved using standard XeLaTeX techniques. Include it in your document and describe the steps you took to create it.

Resources

+ *The LaTeX Font Catalogue* (https://tug.org/FontCatalogue/) provides an extensive collection of fonts compatible with XeLaTeX, along with examples and instructions on how to use them.

+ The   TikZ   &   PGF   *Manual* (https://texdoc.org/serve/tikzpgf/manual/tikzpgf.pdf/0) is a comprehensive guide to using TikZ for creating graphics and diagrams in XeLaTeX.

+ *tex.stackexchange.com* is an active online community where you can find answers to specific XeLaTeX troubleshooting questions. It is a great resource for learning from other users' experiences.

Now that we have covered troubleshooting techniques for advanced typography and layout issues, you are well-equipped to tackle any challenges that may arise in your XeLaTeX projects. Remember to experiment, be persistent, and seek help when needed. Happy typesetting!

Best practices for advanced typography and layout in XeLaTeX

In this section, we will explore some best practices for achieving professional typography and layout design in XeLaTeX. Typography is the art and technique of arranging type to make written language readable and visually appealing. Good typography is crucial to ensure that the content of your document is easily readable, engaging, and aesthetically pleasing. Layout design, on the other hand, involves the arrangement of elements on a page to create a visually harmonious and well-structured composition.

1. Choosing and pairing fonts

Fonts play a vital role in determining the overall look and feel of your document. When selecting fonts, consider their readability, appropriateness for the content, and the desired impression you want to convey. XeLaTeX provides a wide range of font options, including system fonts, TrueType, OpenType, and even custom fonts. To choose a font, consider the following principles:

+ Readability: Choose a font that is easy to read in various sizes and styles. Avoid fonts with intricate or decorative elements that may hinder legibility.

+ Hierarchy: Use different fonts or font styles (e.g., bold, italic, etc.) to create a visual hierarchy that emphasizes important elements such as headings or captions.

+ Contrast: Pair fonts with contrasting characteristics (e.g., a serif font with a sans-serif font) to add visual interest and make important information stand out.

+ Consistency: Maintain consistency in font usage throughout your document to create a cohesive and professional look.

In XeLaTeX, you can easily set global font options using the \setmainfont and \setmonofont commands. For example, to set a serif font as the main font, you can use:

```
\setmainfont{Times New Roman}
```

To set a monospace font for code snippets, you can use:

```
\setmonofont{Courier New}
```

Remember to choose fonts that are legally licensed and suitable for your project.

2. Fine-tuning letter-spacing, kerning, and tracking

Letter-spacing, kerning, and tracking refer to the adjustments made to the spacing between characters in a line of text. These adjustments can greatly impact the overall readability and appearance of your document.

In XeLaTeX, you can fine-tune letter-spacing using the \addfontfeature command. For example, to increase the letter-spacing by 1 point, you can use:

```
\addfontfeature{LetterSpace=1.0}
```

Kerning refers to the adjustment of the spacing between specific pairs of characters to improve their visual harmony. XeLaTeX automatically applies kerning information from the font, but you can adjust it manually using the \kern command. For example, to increase the kerning between the letters "T" and "A", you can use:

```
T\kern0.5pt A
```

Tracking refers to the adjustment of the overall spacing between characters in a line of text. It can be used to improve the legibility and visual balance of the text. XeLaTeX provides the \textls command from the microtype package to adjust the tracking. For example, to increase the tracking of a paragraph by 20%, you can use:

```
\textls[20]{Paragraph text}
```

However, be cautious when adjusting letter-spacing, kerning, and tracking, as excessive changes can negatively affect readability.

3. Enriching typography with ligatures and special characters

Ligatures are special characters that combine two or more characters together for better visual integration. They enhance typography and make it more aesthetically pleasing by eliminating awkward character combinations. XeLaTeX has built-in support for ligatures of various types, including common ligatures, discretionary ligatures, and historical ligatures.

To enable ligatures, you can use the \addfontfeature command along with the Ligatures option. For example, to enable common ligatures, you can use:

```
\addfontfeature{Ligatures=Common}
```

In addition to ligatures, XeLaTeX allows you to use special characters and symbols from the selected font. You can access these characters using the \symbol command. For example, to insert the registered trademark symbol, you can use:

```
\symbol{"00AE}
```

4. Designing and formatting title pages and covers

Title pages and covers are essential components of a professional document. They serve as the first impression and set the tone for the entire document. When designing title pages and covers, consider the following tips:

+ Simplicity: Keep the design clean and uncluttered to focus attention on the title and other important information.

+ Hierarchy: Use font sizes, styles, and positioning to create a clear hierarchy of information, with the title standing out prominently.

+ Alignment: Pay attention to the alignment of elements to create a visually balanced composition. Use grids or guides to maintain consistency.

+ White space: Utilize white space effectively to create breathing room and enhance readability. Avoid overcrowding elements.

+ Branding: Incorporate the appropriate logos, graphics, or visual elements that represent the brand or theme of the document.

To create a title page, you can use the titlepage environment provided by the document class. Customize the layout, fonts, and positioning of each element to align with your desired design.

5. Creating and formatting chapter headings and section numbers

Chapter headings and section numbers play a crucial role in guiding readers through your document. Well-designed headings and section numbers improve readability and make it easier for readers to navigate the content. Consider the following tips when creating and formatting chapter headings and section numbers:

+ Consistency: Maintain a consistent style for headings throughout your document. Choose a font, size, and weight that align with the overall design.

+ Hierarchy: Use a clear visual hierarchy to differentiate between different levels of headings. For example, use larger font sizes or bold formatting for chapter headings and smaller font sizes or italics for section headings.

+ Alignment: Align headings and section numbers with the text to create a cohesive visual flow. Pay attention to vertical spacing and indentation.

+ Styling: Experiment with different styles to make headings stand out, such as using different font colors or background shading.

In XeLaTeX, you can customize chapter headings and section numbers by defining custom commands or using packages like `titlesec`.

6. Designing and formatting table of contents and lists

Table of contents and lists provide an overview of the document's structure and help readers navigate through its content. When designing and formatting these elements, follow these guidelines:

+ Clarity: Ensure that the table of contents and lists provide a clear and concise overview of the document's structure. Use meaningful titles and organize the information hierarchically.

+ Formatting: Use consistent formatting for entries in the table of contents and lists. Align section numbers, use appropriate indentation, and maintain a consistent font style.

+ Hyperlinks: If your document will be viewed digitally, consider adding hyperlinks to the entries in the table of contents and lists, allowing readers to directly navigate to each section.

In XeLaTeX, you can generate the table of contents and lists automatically using the \tableofcontents and \listoftables commands. Customize the appearance and formatting using packages like `titletoc` or `tocloft`.

7. Applying advanced typesetting techniques and hyphenation rules

To achieve sophisticated typesetting and improve the overall readability of your document, consider applying advanced techniques and hyphenation rules. Here are some tips:

+ Hyphenation: Use proper hyphenation rules to prevent excessive hyphenation and ensure that the text flows naturally. You can specify custom hyphenation rules using the `babel` package.

+ Orphans and widows: Avoid single lines at the beginning or end of a paragraph (orphans) and single lines at the bottom of a page (widows). Adjust the text, line spacing, or page layout to prevent these types of formatting issues.

+ Hanging punctuation: For aesthetically pleasing text, consider using hanging punctuation, where punctuation marks extend into the margin instead of intruding into the main text area. The `microtype` package provides options for enabling hanging punctuation.

Experiment with different techniques and packages available in XeLaTeX to achieve the desired typographic effects and improve the overall readability of your document.

8. Troubleshooting advanced typography and layout issues

Advanced typography and layout design can sometimes introduce complex issues. Here are some common problems you may encounter and their solutions:

+ Overfull or underfull lines: Adjust line spacing, hyphenation settings, or justify the text to resolve issues with lines that are too long (overfull) or too short (underfull).

+ Inconsistent spacing: Ensure consistent spacing between elements by adjusting line heights, paragraph indents, or margins.

+ Font or glyph rendering issues: Verify that the chosen fonts are properly installed and include all necessary glyphs. Consider using font fallbacks or alternative fonts to handle missing glyphs.

+ Overlapping elements: Check for overlapping text or graphical elements and adjust their positioning or size to resolve the issue.

In complex cases, consult relevant documentation and forums, and experiment with different combinations of font settings, packages, and layout adjustments to troubleshoot the issues.

9. Resources and further reading

To deepen your understanding and improve your skills in advanced typography and layout design, consider exploring the following resources:

+ *The Elements of Typographic Style* by Robert Bringhurst is a comprehensive guide to typography principles and techniques.

+ Websites such as *Typewolf, Fonts In Use*, and *I Love Typography* provide inspiration and showcase exemplary typography and layout designs.

+ The documentation and user guides for XeLaTeX, LaTeX, and relevant packages such as microtype, titlesec, and fontspec offer detailed information on specific features and functions.

+ Online forums and communities like *TeX Stack Exchange* allow you to ask questions, seek advice, and learn from experienced users.

Continue practicing and experimenting with different typographic and layout techniques to refine your skills and create compelling documents.

10. Exercise

To practice advanced typography and layout design in XeLaTeX, create a one-page document that showcases different heading styles, font combinations, and layout elements. Experiment with font sizes, weights, and alignments to create a visually appealing and well-structured composition. Use appropriate spacing, indentations, and hyphenation to ensure readability.

XeLaTeX Testing and Debugging Techniques

Introduction to Testing and Debugging in XeLaTeX

Importance of testing and debugging in XeLaTeX

Testing and debugging are crucial processes in any software development, and XeLaTeX is no exception. In fact, due to its complex nature and the wide range of functionalities it offers, XeLaTeX projects are prone to various errors and bugs. Proper testing and debugging practices help ensure the correctness, reliability, and efficiency of XeLaTeX documents and applications. This section explores the importance of testing and debugging in XeLaTeX and provides strategies and techniques to effectively identify and resolve issues that arise during development.

Ensuring Correctness and Reliability

One of the main reasons to test and debug XeLaTeX projects is to ensure their correctness and reliability. A minor error in a document can lead to incorrect formatting, invalid equations, or missing or misplaced content. This can result in misunderstandings or even misinformation in scientific or technical documents, which is unacceptable.

By thoroughly testing the document, we can identify and fix errors such as syntax issues, missing or incorrect package dependencies, or problems with font handling. Additionally, debugging allows us to trace and correct logical errors in custom commands, macros, or complex document structures. This ensures that the document outputs the desired content and behaves as expected.

Identifying and Resolving Performance Issues

Testing and debugging are also important for identifying and resolving performance issues in XeLaTeX projects. These issues can arise from inefficient code, excessive memory usage, or suboptimal resource utilization. In large documents or complex layouts, performance problems can significantly slow down the compilation process or even lead to compilation failures.

Profiling tools can help identify bottlenecks and resource-intensive operations in XeLaTeX code. By carefully analyzing the profiling results, we can optimize the document structure, reduce unnecessary computations, or implement caching mechanisms to improve performance. Through testing and debugging, we can ensure that the XeLaTeX project performs efficiently even with large datasets or complex designs.

Detecting and Fixing Cross-platform Compatibility Issues

XeLaTeX projects are often developed on one platform and then shared or deployed on different operating systems or devices. This can introduce cross-platform compatibility issues, where the document may behave differently or fail to compile on certain platforms. It is important to test and debug the document on various platforms to ensure its portability and compatibility.

By testing the document on different operating systems, like Windows, macOS, and Linux, we can identify any platform-specific behavior and address it. Additionally, testing on different devices, such as desktop computers, laptops, tablets, and smartphones, allows us to verify that the document is responsive and displays correctly on different screen sizes and resolutions. Testing and debugging ensure that the XeLaTeX project can be seamlessly used and shared across various platforms and devices.

Effective Testing and Debugging Strategies

To effectively test and debug XeLaTeX projects, it is essential to follow a systematic approach. Here are some strategies and techniques that can help during the testing and debugging process:

+ **Unit Testing:** Divide the document into smaller functional units and test each unit independently. This allows for targeted testing and identification of specific errors or issues.

+ **Regression Testing:** Maintain a suite of tests that cover different aspects of the document and run these tests regularly. This helps to identify any regressions that may occur when modifications or new features are added.

+ **Error Logging and Tracing:** Implement error logging and tracing mechanisms to capture and record errors or issues that occur during the compilation process. This provides valuable information for debugging and troubleshooting.

+ **Code Reviews:** Conduct code reviews with other developers or experts to identify potential issues or areas of improvement in the XeLaTeX project. A fresh pair of eyes can often catch errors or suggest optimizations that may have been overlooked.

+ **Documentation and Issue Tracking:** Maintain comprehensive documentation and track issues and resolutions. This helps in maintaining a record of identified issues and their solutions, which can be referenced in future testing and debugging efforts.

By following these strategies and techniques, developers can streamline the testing and debugging process, reduce the time taken to identify and resolve issues, and improve the overall quality of the XeLaTeX project.

Summary

Testing and debugging play a critical role in ensuring the correctness, reliability, and performance of XeLaTeX projects. By conducting thorough testing, identifying and resolving errors and performance issues, and ensuring cross-platform compatibility, developers can create high-quality XeLaTeX documents and applications. With effective testing and debugging strategies, developers can produce reliable and efficient documents that meet the requirements and expectations of modern audiences.

Exercises

1. Write a XeLaTeX document with a custom command for converting temperature from Celsius to Fahrenheit. Test the command with different input values and verify the correctness of the output.

2. Identify a XeLaTeX package that you frequently use in your projects and review its code for potential bugs or improvements. Discuss your findings with a colleague or on an online forum dedicated to XeLaTeX development.

3. Develop a unit test suite for a XeLaTeX document that involves complex mathematical equations. Test the equations with different input values and document any unexpected behavior or errors.

4. Debug a XeLaTeX document that fails to compile on multiple platforms. Identify the platform-specific issue and propose a solution to make the document compatible across different operating systems.

Resources

1. The Art of Debugging with XeLaTeX by John Doe: This book provides comprehensive techniques and strategies for debugging XeLaTeX projects, along with practical examples and case studies.

2. Overleaf Documentation: The Overleaf platform provides extensive documentation on testing and debugging in XeLaTeX, offering guidelines and tutorials for common testing and debugging scenarios.

3. Stack Exchange: The XeLaTeX tag on Stack Exchange is a valuable resource for seeking help or discussing specific testing and debugging issues. Many experienced XeLaTeX developers frequent these forums and can provide insights and solutions.

4. XeLaTeX Debugging Tools: This GitHub repository contains a collection of debugging tools and extensions for XeLaTeX development. It includes profiling tools, error log analyzers, and other utilities to aid in the testing and debugging process.

Remember, testing and debugging are ongoing processes that should be integrated into the development workflow. Regularly test and update your XeLaTeX projects to ensure their correctness, reliability, and efficiency.

Testing and Verifying Document Validity and Syntax in XeLaTeX

In this section, we will discuss the importance of testing and verifying the validity and syntax of documents in XeLaTeX. As with any programming language, it is crucial to ensure that the code is correct and error-free before compiling. This section will provide you with the knowledge and tools necessary to validate and verify your XeLaTeX documents, ensuring their accuracy and reliability.

The Importance of Document Validation

Document validation is the process of verifying that a document adheres to the rules and syntax defined by the XeLaTeX language. Validating your documents is essential for several reasons:

+ **Error detection:** Validating your document helps identify errors, such as typos, missing commands, or incorrect syntax, before compiling. This saves time and effort by preventing unnecessary compilation errors.

+ **Consistency:** By validating your document, you ensure that it follows a consistent structure and format, improving its readability and maintainability.

+ **Compatibility:** Validating your document helps ensure compatibility with different versions of XeLaTeX and prevents issues that may arise from using deprecated or incompatible commands or packages.

+ **Accessibility and standards compliance:** Document validation is vital for ensuring accessibility and compliance with industry standards, such as those for publishing, academia, or governmental institutions.

Now let's discuss various techniques and tools for testing and validating document validity and syntax in XeLaTeX.

Syntax Checking Techniques

There are multiple techniques you can use to perform syntax checking on your XeLaTeX documents. These techniques help identify common syntax errors and ensure that your document follows the correct structure.

1. **Manual Inspection:** Manual inspection involves carefully reviewing your document line by line, checking for typos, missing or misplaced commands, and incorrect syntax. This technique is time-consuming but effective for small documents or when you want to gain an in-depth understanding of your code.

2. **Compiler Error Messages:** XeLaTeX provides detailed error messages that can help pinpoint syntax errors in your document. When a compilation error occurs, the error message will show the line number and a description of the error. By analyzing these messages, you can identify and correct the syntax errors.

3. **Syntax Highlighting Editors:** Using a syntax highlighting editor tailored for XeLaTeX can significantly help in identifying syntax errors. These editors highlight different elements of your code, making it easier to spot mistakes. They provide real-time feedback, making the identification of errors faster and more efficient.

4. **Linting Tools:** Linting tools analyze your XeLaTeX code and provide warnings or error messages for potential syntax errors or bad practices. These tools can catch errors such as unmatched brackets, missing commands, or deprecated packages. Running a linter on your document helps ensure that it adheres to best practices and standards.

Using the XeLaTeX linter

The XeLaTeX linter is a powerful tool for analyzing your document and identifying syntax errors, deprecated commands, or potential compatibility issues. It performs a thorough analysis of your code, providing feedback and suggestions for improvement.

To use the XeLaTeX linter, follow these steps:

1. Install the XeLaTeX linter package, which is available for most LaTeX editors.

2. Open your document in your preferred editor and enable the linter plugin.

3. Run the linter on your document. The linter will analyze your code and display any syntax errors or warnings.

4. Review the linter output, which will include information about the location, type, and description of each error or warning.

5. Correct the errors and warnings in your code.

By using the XeLaTeX linter, you can automate the process of checking for syntax errors in your document, saving time and effort. It is an essential tool for maintaining a clean and error-free codebase.

Best Practices

Here are some best practices to consider when testing and verifying document validity and syntax in XeLaTeX:

+ Use a version control system (e.g., Git) to track changes to your document and easily revert back to a known working state if needed.

+ Break your document into smaller, modular files for easier management and testing.

+ Regularly compile and test your document as you make changes to catch errors early.

+ Verify that the required packages and libraries are installed and up to date.

+ Familiarize yourself with the XeLaTeX command reference and consult it when in doubt about correct syntax or usage.

✦ Keep your code clean and organized by following consistent indentation, commenting, and formatting standards.

Remember, document validation and syntax checking are ongoing processes. It's essential to perform these checks regularly, especially when making significant changes to your document.

Conclusion

Testing and verifying the validity and syntax of your XeLaTeX documents is a crucial step in ensuring their accuracy, reliability, and compatibility. By following the techniques and best practices discussed in this section, you can catch errors early and produce high-quality documents. Incorporate these practices into your workflow to create reliable and well-structured XeLaTeX documents.

Now that we have covered document validation and syntax checking, we will move on to the next section, where we will discuss debugging techniques for XeLaTeX.

Debugging and fixing common errors and warnings in XeLaTeX

Debugging and fixing errors and warnings are essential skills for any XeLaTeX user. In this section, we will explore common issues that arise during the compilation of XeLaTeX documents and learn effective strategies for identifying and resolving them.

Understanding XeLaTeX Error Messages

When XeLaTeX encounters an error, it provides an error message that describes the nature of the problem. Understanding these error messages is the first step in debugging your document.

Error messages usually consist of three parts: the error type, the line number where the error occurred, and a description of the error. For example:

```
! Undefined control\index{control} sequence\index{sequence}.
<recently read> \mycommand
\maketitle

l.10 \maketitle

?
```

In this example, the error type is "Undefined control sequence," indicating that a command (\mycommand) was used, but it hasn't been defined. The line number where the error occurred is 10, and the description of the error suggests that the command \maketitle is involved.

It's important to carefully read the entire error message to understand the cause of the error.

Common Errors and Their Solutions

Let's now explore some common errors encountered when using XeLaTeX and their solutions:

1. **Undefined control sequence:** This error occurs when a command is used that hasn't been defined. To fix this error, check if the command is spelled correctly and if it should be included in your document. If the command is a custom command, make sure it is defined properly.

2. **File not found:** This error occurs when a required file cannot be located. Double-check the file path and ensure that the file exists in the specified location. Also, verify that the file name and extension are correct.

3. **Package not found:** This error occurs when a required package is missing. Make sure the package is installed on your system, and if not, install it using the package manager. If the package is already installed, ensure that the package name is spelled correctly and that it is loaded in the document using the \usepackage command.

4. **Overfull hbox or vbox:** These warnings indicate that a line or page in your document is too long, causing text or elements to extend beyond the margins. To fix this warning, consider adjusting the layout, breaking the text into smaller paragraphs, or using manual line breaks.

5. **Missing \begin{document}:** This error occurs when the document starts without the required \begin{document} command. Check that you have included this command at the beginning of your document.

Debugging Tips and Tricks

Debugging XeLaTeX errors can sometimes be challenging, especially when the error message is not clear or when the error is hard to identify. Here are some additional tips and tricks to help you in the debugging process:

1. **Comment out problematic sections:** If you suspect that a specific section of your document is causing the error, temporarily comment it out using the % symbol. This will help you isolate the issue and narrow down the problematic code.

2. **Divide and conquer:** If you have a large document, it can be helpful to split it into smaller parts and compile each part separately. By identifying the part that causes the error, you can focus your debugging efforts on that specific section.

3. **Check for missing brackets and braces:** Unclosed or mismatched brackets and braces can lead to errors in your document. Make sure that every opening bracket or brace is properly closed.

4. **Review recent changes:** If you recently made modifications to your document and the error appeared afterward, carefully review the changes you made. Undoing those changes or revising them may resolve the error.

5. **Consult online resources and forums:** If you are unable to identify the cause of the error, don't hesitate to seek help from online resources and forums. The LaTeX community is vast, and chances are someone has encountered a similar problem and can provide guidance.

Exercises

Now, let's apply what we have learned by solving these exercises:

Exercise 1: You encounter an error "Undefined control sequence: \mycommand" in your document. How would you fix this error?

Exercise 2: You receive a warning "Overfull hbox" when compiling your document. What are some possible solutions for resolving this warning?

Exercise 3: Your document fails to compile, and the error message indicates a missing package. How would you resolve this error?

Resources and Further Reading

To enhance your understanding of debugging and troubleshooting in XeLaTeX, you can refer to the following resources:

* *The LaTeX Companion* by Frank Mittelbach, Michel Goossens, Johannes Braams, David Carlisle, and Chris Rowley.

* *TeX Stack Exchange* (https://tex.stackexchange.com/): An online community for asking and answering LaTeX-related questions.

* *LaTeX Wikibook* (https://en.wikibooks.org/wiki/LaTeX): An open-content LaTeX textbook that covers various topics, including debugging and error handling.

Conclusion

In this section, we explored the process of debugging and fixing common errors and warnings in XeLaTeX. By understanding the error messages, being familiar with common mistakes, and applying effective debugging strategies, you'll be able to troubleshoot and resolve issues with your XeLaTeX documents. Remember to practice regularly and seek help when needed to improve your debugging skills.

Profiling and optimizing XeLaTeX code for performance and efficiency

In this section, we will explore techniques for profiling and optimizing XeLaTeX code to improve its performance and efficiency. As XeLaTeX is a powerful tool for typesetting, it is essential to ensure that our document compiles and renders quickly without excessive resource usage. We will discuss various profiling tools and optimization strategies to achieve optimal performance.

Profiling XeLaTeX Code

Profiling allows us to identify bottlenecks and inefficiencies in our XeLaTeX code. It helps us understand which parts of our code are taking the most time or using excessive resources. By identifying these areas, we can focus on optimizing them for better performance. Here are some profiling techniques for XeLaTeX code:

1. **Compilation Time Profiling:** Measure the time it takes for XeLaTeX to process your document. This can be done using the `timing` package. By analyzing the time taken by each component of the compilation process, we can identify areas that need optimization.

2. **Heap Profiling:** Use memory profiling tools, such as `memprof`, to identify memory usage patterns in your XeLaTeX code. This helps in detecting memory leaks and excessive memory consumption. By reducing unnecessary memory usage, we can improve the efficiency of our code.

3. **Performance Monitoring:** Monitor the performance of your XeLaTeX code using tools like `perf`. This helps in identifying CPU utilization, cache misses, and other performance-related metrics. By analyzing the performance data, we can pinpoint areas that need optimization.

Optimizing XeLaTeX Code

Once we have identified the bottlenecks through profiling, we can focus on optimizing our XeLaTeX code for better performance and efficiency. Here are some optimization strategies:

1. **Minimize Package Usage:** Only load the packages that are necessary for your document. Unnecessary packages consume memory and add to the compilation time. By loading only the required packages, we can reduce the overhead and improve performance.

2. **Use Efficient Fonts:** Different fonts have different rendering complexities. Choose fonts that are optimized for speed and efficiency, especially when using custom fonts. Simplify complex fonts or use subsets of fonts to reduce rendering time and memory usage.

3. **Avoid Excessive Macros:** Macros can be powerful, but excessive use of macros can impact performance. Avoid using overly complex or nested macros that require significant processing time. Instead, opt for simpler and more efficient alternatives.

4. **Optimize Graphics and Images:** Graphics and images can impact compilation time and document size. Optimize graphics by using appropriate image formats (e.g., JPEG for photographs, PNG for line art), reducing image resolution when possible, and compressing images without sacrificing quality.

5. **Cache Intermediate Results:** If your document contains computationally expensive calculations or repetitive tasks, consider caching intermediate results. This helps avoid redundant computations and speeds up the compilation process.

6. **Parallelize Compilation:** XeLaTeX can take advantage of multiple CPU cores through parallelization. Use compilation flags or build tools like `xelatexmk` to parallelize the compilation process, reducing the overall compilation time.

These are just a few optimization strategies for XeLaTeX code. Experiment with different techniques and measure their impact on performance. Keep in mind that optimization should not come at the expense of code readability and maintainability.

Example: Optimizing Graphics

Let's consider an example where we have a document with multiple high-resolution images that slow down the compilation time and increase the file size. We can optimize the graphics in the following ways:

+ Convert images to appropriate formats based on their content (JPEG for photographs, PNG for line art).

+ Compress images using tools like `imagemagick` to reduce file size without sacrificing quality.

+ Downscale images to a resolution suitable for the intended output. High-resolution images are often unnecessary for print or screen display.

+ Use vector graphics (e.g., PDF, SVG) instead of raster images whenever possible. Vector graphics are scalable and usually result in smaller file sizes.

With these optimizations, we can significantly reduce the compilation time and final document size.

Resources and Best Practices

To further explore profiling and optimizing techniques in XeLaTeX, consider the following resources:

+ The `timing`, `memprof`, and `perf` packages for profiling XeLaTeX code.

+ The official XeLaTeX documentation for performance optimization tips and best practices.

+ Online forums and communities dedicated to XeLaTeX, where you can find discussions and advice on optimizing code for specific use cases.

In addition to these resources, it is essential to follow best practices such as keeping your code clean and organized, minimizing unnecessary computations, and using efficient algorithms.

Conclusion

Profiling and optimizing XeLaTeX code for performance and efficiency is crucial to ensure smooth compilation and rendering of documents. By profiling our code, we can identify bottlenecks and areas that require improvement. Through optimization, we can reduce compilation time, conserve memory resources, and create more efficient documents. By following best practices and utilizing the available resources, we can achieve optimal performance in our XeLaTeX projects.

Remember to test and measure the impact of your optimizations to ensure they provide the desired improvements. Optimization is an iterative process, and continuous evaluation and refinement are key to achieving optimal performance.

Testing and validating cross-platform compatibility in XeLaTeX

In the world of document preparation, it's crucial to ensure that your documents are compatible across different platforms. This includes testing and validating your XeLaTeX documents to ensure they render correctly on various operating systems, web browsers, and devices. In this section, we will explore the techniques and best practices for testing and validating cross-platform compatibility in XeLaTeX.

Importance of cross-platform compatibility testing

With the increasing diversity of platforms and devices that people use to access documents, it is important to make sure that your XeLaTeX documents are optimized for cross-platform compatibility. Testing and validating cross-platform compatibility helps to ensure that your documents render correctly and consistently across different operating systems, web browsers, and devices.

By conducting cross-platform compatibility testing, you can identify and address any issues related to font rendering, layout, and functionality. This ensures that your documents are accessible to a wider audience and maintain their intended design and functionality, regardless of the platform or device being used.

Testing methods for cross-platform compatibility

To test the cross-platform compatibility of your XeLaTeX documents, you can employ various methods and tools. Here are some commonly used testing methods:

1. **Manual Testing:** The simplest method is manual testing, where you manually open and view your XeLaTeX documents on different platforms

and devices. This allows you to visually inspect the rendering and layout of your documents. However, it is a time-consuming process and may not catch all issues.

2. **Cross-browser Testing:** To ensure compatibility across different web browsers, you can use online services such as BrowserStack or LambdaTest. These services allow you to test your XeLaTeX documents on various web browsers and operating systems without the need to install them locally.

3. **Virtual Machines:** Another approach is to use virtual machines (VMs) to simulate different operating systems and environments. Tools like VirtualBox or VMware allow you to set up VMs running different operating systems, which can be used to test the compatibility of your XeLaTeX documents.

4. **Online Platforms:** Several online platforms, such as Overleaf or ShareLaTeX, provide real-time collaboration and rendering. You can use these platforms to share your XeLaTeX documents with others and test their rendering on different platforms and devices.

5. **Continuous Integration (CI) Testing:** By integrating your XeLaTeX documents with a CI service like Travis CI or GitHub Actions, you can automate the testing process. CI testing allows you to automatically build and test your XeLaTeX documents on different platforms, making it easier to catch compatibility issues early on.

Validating cross-platform compatibility

Apart from testing, it is also important to validate the cross-platform compatibility of your XeLaTeX documents. This involves ensuring that your documents adhere to best practices and standards. Here are some ways to validate the cross-platform compatibility:

1. **Validate LaTeX markup:** Use tools like the `lacheck` or `chktex` command-line utilities to validate your LaTeX markup. These tools can detect common syntax errors and potential compatibility issues.

2. **Check font compatibility:** While using custom fonts in XeLaTeX can enhance your document's aesthetics, it is important to ensure that the chosen fonts are compatible with different platforms and devices. Use web-safe fonts or embed the necessary font files to maintain consistent rendering across platforms.

3. **Validate accessibility:** Ensure that your XeLaTeX documents are accessible to users with disabilities. Use tools like the `accsupp` package to provide alternative text for images and tables. Test the accessibility of your documents using screen readers and other assistive technologies.

4. **Test hyperlinks:** Check that hyperlinks within your XeLaTeX documents work correctly across different platforms and devices. Verify that clicking on hyperlinks takes the user to the intended destination.

5. **Document metadata:** Make sure that your XeLaTeX documents include accurate and complete metadata, such as titles, authors, and keywords. This metadata is essential for search engine optimization and proper indexing on different platforms.

Best practices for cross-platform compatibility

To maximize cross-platform compatibility when using XeLaTeX, consider the following best practices:

+ Stick to standard document classes and packages: While it's exciting to experiment with different document classes and packages, using standard ones ensures greater compatibility across platforms.

+ Use scalable vector graphics (SVG): When including graphics in your XeLaTeX documents, prefer using scalable vector graphics (SVG) instead of bitmap images like JPEG or PNG. SVG graphics can scale seamlessly without losing quality.

+ Test with multiple fonts and font sizes: Test your XeLaTeX documents with different fonts and font sizes to ensure that the layout remains intact. Some fonts may have different metrics, causing layout issues.

+ Avoid hard-coded sizes and positions: Instead of hard-coding sizes and positions, use relative units like `em` or `ex` to ensure consistent rendering across platforms with different display resolutions.

+ Regularly update packages and distributions: Keep your XeLaTeX packages and distributions up to date to benefit from bug fixes, compatibility improvements, and new features.

+ Consult platform-specific guidelines: If you are targeting specific platforms or devices, it is beneficial to consult their documentation or guidelines for any specific requirements or recommendations.

Conclusion

Testing and validating cross-platform compatibility in XeLaTeX is essential to ensure that your documents can be accessed and rendered correctly across different operating systems, web browsers, and devices. By employing testing methods and following best practices, you can catch compatibility issues early on and deliver consistent experiences to your audience. Regularly updating packages, adhering to standards, and consulting platform-specific guidelines will further enhance the compatibility of your XeLaTeX documents.

Debugging and resolving font-related issues in XeLaTeX

Font-related issues can arise when using XeLaTeX, especially when working with non-standard or special fonts. These issues can cause errors or inconsistencies in the document output. In this section, we will explore common font-related problems and learn how to debug and resolve them in XeLaTeX.

Understanding Fonts in XeLaTeX

Before we dive into debugging font-related issues, let's briefly understand how fonts work in XeLaTeX. XeLaTeX natively supports TrueType (TTF) and OpenType (OTF) fonts, which provide various typographic features like ligatures, small caps, and stylistic alternates.

Fonts in XeLaTeX are managed using fontspec package, which provides a simple and intuitive interface for selecting and loading fonts. The fontspec package allows you to specify fonts for various text elements, such as the main font, sans-serif font, and monospaced font.

To load a font, you can use the \setmainfont command, followed by the font name enclosed in curly braces. For example, to set the main font to "Arial", you would use the following command:

```
\setmainfont{Arial}
```

By default, XeLaTeX uses Latin Modern fonts, so you don't need to explicitly specify a font unless you want to use a different one.

Common Font-related Issues and Solutions

Now let's explore some common font-related issues that you may encounter when working with XeLaTeX and how to resolve them.

Font Not Found Error   One of the most common font-related issues is the "Font not found" error. This error occurs when XeLaTeX cannot locate the specified font file on your system. To resolve this issue, make sure that the font file is installed and accessible to XeLaTeX.

You can check the system font directories to verify if the font file is present. On Unix-based systems, you can usually find the fonts in the `/usr/share/fonts` directory, while on Windows, they are typically located in the `C:\Windows\Fonts` directory.

If the font file is not present, you can either install it manually or use a different font. Alternatively, you can specify the full path to the font file when loading the font using the `Path` option in fontspec.

Missing Glyphs or Incorrect Glyph Rendering   Another common issue is missing glyphs or incorrect glyph rendering. This can happen when the font you are using does not have certain characters or does not support the specific language or writing system you are working with.

To resolve this issue, you can try using a different font that supports the required characters. You can also check the font documentation or the Unicode Standard to ensure that the characters you are using are supported by the font.

If the font supports the required characters but they are not rendering correctly, it might be due to font rendering settings or system configurations. You can experiment with different font rendering options or consult the documentation of your operating system to adjust the font rendering settings.

Inconsistent Font Sizes   Sometimes, when using different fonts or font styles, you may notice inconsistent font sizes within your document. This can be caused by variations in font metrics, especially when mixing fonts from different font families.

To address this issue, you can use the `Scale` option provided by fontspec to adjust the font size manually. The `Scale` option allows you to scale the font to a specific size relative to its original design size. For example, you can use `\setmainfont[Scale=0.9]{Arial}` to scale down the Arial font by 10%.

Additionally, you can experiment with different fonts that have similar metrics to ensure consistent font sizes throughout your document.

Best Practices for Debugging Font-related Issues

When debugging font-related issues in XeLaTeX, it's important to follow some best practices to ensure smooth and error-free document compilation:

- Verify that the font files are properly installed and accessible by XeLaTeX.

- Use font files that are specifically designed for use with XeLaTeX and have proper Unicode support.

- Check the font documentation for any restrictions or known issues with certain characters or features.

- Experiment with different fonts and font families to find the one that best suits your document's requirements.

- Keep the font selection consistent throughout the document to maintain a professional and cohesive look.

- Regularly update your TeX distribution and any font packages to ensure compatibility and access to the latest features and bug fixes.

- When encountering complex font-related issues, consult the XeLaTeX community forums or mailing lists for assistance.

By following these best practices, you can minimize font-related issues and ensure a smooth and hassle-free experience with XeLaTeX.

Summary

In this section, we explored common font-related issues in XeLaTeX and learned how to debug and resolve them. We discussed the importance of understanding fonts in XeLaTeX and how to load and configure them using the fontspec package. We also addressed common font-related problems such as font not found errors, missing or incorrectly rendered glyphs, and inconsistent font sizes. Following best practices for debugging font-related issues can help you create professional-looking documents with XeLaTeX.

Troubleshooting package conflicts and incompatibilities in XeLaTeX

One of the great advantages of using XeLaTeX is the wide variety of packages and libraries available for customizing and enhancing document layouts. However, sometimes these packages can conflict with each other or with the core functionality of XeLaTeX. In this section, we will explore some common issues related to package conflicts and incompatibilities in XeLaTeX and provide troubleshooting techniques to resolve them.

Identifying package conflicts

When encountering issues related to package conflicts or incompatibilities in XeLaTeX, the first step is to identify the conflicting packages. This can be done by following these steps:

1. Check for error messages: XeLaTeX often provides error messages that indicate which package is causing the conflict. These messages can be found in the log file generated during the compilation process. Look for any error messages related to package names or conflicts.

2. Comment out packages: If the error message does not explicitly identify the conflicting package, you can try commenting out packages one by one to isolate the issue. By selectively commenting out packages in your document's preamble, you can determine which package is causing the conflict.

3. Consult package documentation: If you are unsure which packages are conflicting, consult the documentation of the packages you are using. Many package documentation includes information about incompatibilities with other packages.

Once you have identified the conflicting packages, you can proceed with resolving the conflict.

Resolving package conflicts

There are several approaches you can take to resolve package conflicts in XeLaTeX:

1. Reorder package loading: In some cases, the order in which packages are loaded can affect whether conflicts arise. Experiment with changing the order of package loading in your document's preamble. Sometimes simply reversing the order in which conflicting packages are loaded can resolve the conflict.

2. Use etoolbox package: The etoolbox package provides tools for manipulating package loading and can help resolve conflicts. You can use commands like \AtBeginDocument and \AfterEndPreamble to control the order in which packages are loaded. Refer to the etoolbox documentation for more information on how to use these commands.

3. Use alternative packages: If two packages are incompatible and you cannot resolve the conflict, consider using alternative packages that provide similar functionality. There are often multiple packages available for achieving the same purpose, so explore the options and choose packages that work well together.

4. Consult package authors: If you have exhausted all other options and are still unable to resolve the conflict, consider reaching out to the authors of the conflicting

packages. They may be able to provide insights or suggestions on how to resolve the conflict.

Preventing package conflicts

While resolving package conflicts is important, it is equally important to prevent them from occurring in the first place. Here are some best practices to help prevent package conflicts in XeLaTeX:

1. Keep packages up to date: Make sure to regularly update the packages you use to the latest versions. Updated packages often include bug fixes and compatibility improvements that can help prevent conflicts.

2. Limit package usage: Avoid using unnecessary packages or loading too many packages. Only load the packages that are essential for your document. This can reduce the chances of conflicts and improve compilation speed.

3. Read package documentation: Before using a package, thoroughly read its documentation. Pay attention to any compatibility notes or known issues mentioned in the documentation. Being aware of potential conflicts beforehand can help you choose compatible packages.

4. Test new packages: Whenever you introduce a new package into your document, test it thoroughly to ensure it does not conflict with existing packages. Create a minimal working example that includes both the new package and the existing packages to check for any conflicts.

By following these best practices and utilizing the troubleshooting techniques mentioned earlier, you can minimize the occurrence of package conflicts and ensure smooth compilation of your XeLaTeX documents.

Example: Package conflict with graphics

Let's consider a common scenario where a document needs both the graphicx package and the svg package, both of which provide functionality for including graphics. However, these two packages can sometimes conflict due to their different approaches to handling images.

To identify the conflict, we compile the document and encounter an error message indicating that the conflict is between the graphicx and svg packages. We can see this by examining the log file.

To resolve this conflict, we can try reordering the package loading in the preamble by putting the svg package before the graphicx package. After making this change, we compile the document again, and the conflict is resolved.

Alternatively, we can consider using an alternative package for one of the functionalities. In this case, we could use the epstopdf package instead of the svg package if vector graphics are not required.

It's important to note that this is just one example of a package conflict, and the specific conflicts and resolutions will vary depending on the packages and their functionalities used in your document.

By following the troubleshooting steps and techniques outlined in this section, you will be better equipped to handle package conflicts and incompatibilities in XeLaTeX and ensure smooth compilation of your documents. Remember to consult package documentation, experiment with package ordering, and seek help from package authors when needed.

Testing and debugging complex mathematical and scientific equations in XeLaTeX

In scientific and technical writing, it is crucial to ensure the accuracy and reliability of mathematical equations and scientific notations. XeLaTeX provides a powerful toolset for typesetting complex mathematical expressions, but it is equally important to test and debug these equations to avoid any errors or inconsistencies. In this section, we will explore some techniques for testing and debugging complex mathematical and scientific equations in XeLaTeX.

Understanding the principles of mathematical typesetting

Before we dive into testing and debugging, it is essential to have a solid understanding of the principles of mathematical typesetting. XeLaTeX uses the amsmath package, which provides a comprehensive set of functions and symbols for typesetting mathematical equations. Familiarize yourself with the syntax and usage of these commands, as they will form the foundation of our testing and debugging efforts.

When typesetting mathematical equations, it is important to:

+ Use the correct symbols and notation for each mathematical concept.

+ Maintain consistency in font styles and sizes.

+ Ensure proper alignment and spacing between symbols and elements.

+ Use appropriate delimiters such as parentheses, brackets, and braces.

By adhering to these principles, you can create visually appealing and mathematically accurate equations in your documents.

Testing mathematical expressions

Testing mathematical expressions involves verifying their correctness by comparing the output against expected results. In XeLaTeX, you can perform this testing using the `assert` package, which provides a framework for creating unit tests.

To illustrate testing, let's consider a simple mathematical expression:

$$f(x) = x^2 + 2x + 1$$

We can write a test case to verify that the equation is correctly typeset in XeLaTeX:

```
\assert[f(x)]{f(x) = x^2 + 2x + 1}
```

By running this document through XeLaTeX and compiling it, the `assert` package will compare the expected result of the equation with the actual output. If they match, the test passes; otherwise, it will raise an error indicating that the equation is not correctly typeset.

Additionally, you can extend your testing to cover a range of input values and edge cases to ensure that the equations are valid and produce the expected results in all scenarios.

Debugging mathematical equations

Debugging complex mathematical equations can be challenging, especially when errors occur due to syntax issues, incorrect symbols, or improper formatting. Thankfully, XeLaTeX provides robust error messages that can guide us in identifying and fixing these issues.

When a mathematical equation encounters an error during compilation, XeLaTeX displays an error message that points to the location of the problem. Examine the error message carefully to identify the specific cause of the issue.

To aid in debugging, you can enable verbose error messages in XeLaTeX by adding the `-interaction=errorstopmode` flag to the compilation command. This setting stops the compilation process at the first encountered error, allowing you to address it immediately.

In addition to verbose error messages, you can use the `logreq` package to generate a log file that provides detailed information about the compilation process. This log file can help identify any warnings, errors, or other issues that occurred during the compilation. You can then analyze the log file to track down and resolve the problem.

Example: Debugging a complex scientific equation

Let's consider an example of debugging a complex scientific equation:

$$E = mc^2$$

Suppose we have mistakenly typed the equation as:

$$E = mc2$$

When we compile the document, XeLaTeX will generate an error message indicating that the syntax is incorrect. By carefully examining the error message and comparing it to the equation, we can quickly identify and correct the issue.

To prevent such errors, it is good practice to break complex equations into smaller, manageable parts and test each part individually. By verifying the correctness of each component, you can be confident that the entire equation will be error-free.

Resources for testing and debugging

When it comes to testing and debugging mathematical equations in XeLaTeX, the following resources can be valuable references:

+ The `amsmath` package documentation provides detailed information on typesetting mathematical equations and using various mathematical symbols and notations.

+ The `assert` package documentation offers guidance on creating unit tests for mathematical expressions in XeLaTeX.

+ The XeLaTeX user community is an excellent resource for troubleshooting issues and seeking assistance in testing and debugging mathematical equations.

Exercises

To practice testing and debugging complex mathematical equations in XeLaTeX, consider the following exercises:

1. Write a test case to verify the correctness of the quadratic formula in XeLaTeX.

2. Debug the equation $\int_a^b f(x)\,dx = F(b) - F(a)$ by identifying and fixing any syntax or formatting errors.

3. Test the equation $\sum_{i=1}^n i = \frac{n(n+1)}{2}$ for a range of integer values of n to ensure accurate results.

By completing these exercises, you will become more proficient in testing and debugging mathematical equations in XeLaTeX.

In conclusion, testing and debugging complex mathematical and scientific equations in XeLaTeX require a solid understanding of mathematical typesetting principles, careful testing of equations using tools like the `assert` package, and thorough error analysis using verbose error messages and log files. By following these techniques and utilizing available resources, you can create accurate and reliable mathematical content in your XeLaTeX documents.

Remember to practice regularly and learn from real-world examples to enhance your skills in testing and debugging mathematical equations.

Automated testing and continuous integration for XeLaTeX projects

In the process of developing XeLaTeX projects, it is important to have a reliable and efficient way to test and validate the documents. This ensures that the final output meets the desired requirements and minimizes the possibility of errors or inconsistencies. This section focuses on automated testing and continuous integration techniques that can be used in XeLaTeX projects.

Importance of automated testing

Automated testing plays a crucial role in the software development life cycle, and XeLaTeX projects are no exception. It allows developers to verify the correctness of their code and catch potential issues early on. By automating the testing process, developers can ensure consistent and reliable results, decrease the likelihood of human error, and save time and effort.

In the context of XeLaTeX projects, automated testing involves checking the correctness of the generated output, detecting any unexpected behaviors or inconsistencies, and validating the code against predefined criteria. This can include various aspects such as document structure, typography, page layout, font usage, cross-referencing, and bibliography formatting.

Continuous integration for XeLaTeX projects

Continuous integration (CI) is a development practice that involves regularly merging code changes from multiple developers into a shared repository. This process triggers an automated build and test procedure to ensure that the changes do not introduce any conflicts or regressions. CI enables teams to quickly identify and resolve issues and maintain a stable and reliable codebase.

To implement CI in XeLaTeX projects, a suitable CI system needs to be set up. Popular choices include Jenkins, Travis CI, and GitLab CI/CD. These tools integrate with version control systems like Git and can be configured to automatically build and test XeLaTeX documents whenever changes are pushed to the repository.

The CI process for XeLaTeX projects typically involves the following steps:

1. **Build setup:** Define the necessary build environment, including specific TeX distributions, packages, and fonts required for the project. This ensures consistent and reproducible builds across different machines.

2. **Build process:** Configure the CI system to execute the necessary commands to compile the XeLaTeX documents. This may involve running multiple passes to resolve cross-references, generate bibliographies, and update table of contents.

3. **Testing:** Define the tests to be performed on the generated output. This can include checking for the presence of expected elements, verifying the correctness of the typography and formatting, and comparing the output with predefined baselines.

4. **Reporting:** Generate reports that summarize the results of the tests. This can include detailed information about failed tests, warnings, or errors encountered during the build process. These reports help developers identify and address issues quickly.

5. **Integration with other tools:** Integrate the CI system with other tools commonly used in the development process, such as version control systems,

issue trackers, or project management tools. This ensures seamless collaboration and efficient handling of code changes and issue tracking.

Benefits and challenges of automated testing and CI in XeLaTeX projects

Automated testing and CI bring several benefits to XeLaTeX projects:

+ **Early detection of errors**: Automated tests can identify issues early in the development cycle, allowing developers to fix them before they become more difficult and costly to resolve.

+ **Consistent and reliable results**: By defining and automating tests, developers can ensure that the output of their XeLaTeX projects meets the desired requirements consistently.

+ **Efficient collaboration**: CI systems facilitate collaboration among team members by providing a centralized environment for code changes, testing, and issue tracking. This leads to faster development cycles and better overall project coordination.

+ **Increased productivity**: Automated testing and CI save time and effort by performing repetitive tasks automatically. This allows developers to focus on more critical aspects of their XeLaTeX projects, such as content creation and fine-tuning.

+ **Improved code quality**: CI encourages good development practices by enforcing code reviews, test coverage, and documentation. This leads to higher code quality and maintainability.

However, there are also some challenges associated with automated testing and CI in XeLaTeX projects:

+ **Complexity of test setup**: Setting up and configuring the testing environment for XeLaTeX projects can be complex, especially when dealing with different operating systems, font packages, and language-specific requirements.

+ **Test coverage**: Ensuring comprehensive test coverage for XeLaTeX projects can be challenging due to the wide range of potential document structures, fonts, and typographical elements. It is important to prioritize critical components and focus on meaningful tests.

+ **Test maintenance:** Automated tests need to be updated and maintained as the XeLaTeX project evolves. This includes adapting tests to accommodate changes in the document structure, layout, or software dependencies.

+ **Evaluating test results:** Interpreting the results of automated tests can be complex, especially when dealing with output files that require visual inspection. Developing clear guidelines and criteria for test evaluation is important to ensure consistent and reliable results.

Conclusion

Automated testing and continuous integration are crucial aspects of developing reliable and high-quality XeLaTeX projects. By implementing suitable testing processes and integrating them into the development workflow, developers can ensure the correctness, consistency, and robustness of their projects. While there are challenges in setting up and maintaining automated tests, the benefits in terms of increased productivity, code quality, and collaboration make it a worthwhile investment.

In the next section, we will explore techniques for performance optimization and scalability in XeLaTeX projects.

Best practices for testing and debugging in XeLaTeX

As with any software development process, testing and debugging play a crucial role in ensuring the quality and reliability of your XeLaTeX documents. In this section, we will explore some best practices that can help you effectively test and debug your XeLaTeX projects.

1. Developing a testing strategy

Before diving into testing and debugging, it is important to develop a testing strategy that outlines your goals and objectives. This strategy should define the scope of testing, identify the types of tests to be conducted, and establish the resources and tools needed for testing.

The testing strategy should include the following:

+ **Unit testing:** This involves testing individual components and functions of your XeLaTeX document to ensure they work as intended. Unit tests should cover basic functionality and edge cases.

+ **Integration testing:** Integration tests check how well different components of your XeLaTeX document work together. This ensures that all parts of your document interact correctly and produce the desired output.

+ **System testing:** System tests evaluate the overall behavior and functionality of your XeLaTeX document. This includes testing different document layouts, fonts, and styles, as well as checking for compatibility with various XeLaTeX packages and libraries.

+ **Regression testing:** Regression tests are performed to ensure that recent changes or fixes in your XeLaTeX document do not introduce new errors or break existing functionality.

+ **Performance testing:** Performance tests measure the speed, efficiency, and resource usage of your XeLaTeX document. This helps identify potential bottlenecks and optimize the performance of your document.

+ **User acceptance testing:** User acceptance tests involve getting feedback from end users or clients to validate that your XeLaTeX document meets their requirements and expectations.

By following a well-defined testing strategy, you can identify and fix issues early in the development process, resulting in a more stable and reliable XeLaTeX document.

2. Use a version control system

Using a version control system, such as Git, is essential for effective testing and debugging. Version control allows you to track changes made to your XeLaTeX document, revert to earlier versions if necessary, and collaborate with other developers.

Here are some best practices for using version control in XeLaTeX:

+ **Commit frequently:** Make frequent commits to capture smaller, logical changes in your XeLaTeX document. This makes it easier to track the progression of your document and isolate issues.

+ **Branching and merging:** Use branches to work on new features or fixes without affecting the main codebase. When a feature or fix is complete, merge it back into the main branch.

+ **Tagging releases:** Tagging releases in your version control system allows you to easily revert to a specific stable version of your XeLaTeX document if needed.

+ **Collaboration:** If you are working on a XeLaTeX project with multiple collaborators, ensure that everyone follows the same version control workflow and communicates any changes or issues effectively.

Version control not only helps with tracking changes but also provides a safety net for testing and debugging, allowing you to try different approaches and easily revert back if necessary.

3. Debugging techniques

When issues or errors arise in your XeLaTeX document, effective debugging techniques can help identify the root cause and find a solution. Here are some techniques to consider:

+ **Read error messages:** XeLaTeX is known for producing detailed error messages, which can provide valuable information about what went wrong. Always take the time to carefully read and understand error messages to pinpoint the problem.

+ **Print statements:** Adding print statements throughout your XeLaTeX document can help track the flow of execution and identify problematic areas. Use the \message command to print messages to the output or log file.

+ **Comment out sections:** If you suspect a specific part of your XeLaTeX document is causing an issue, try commenting out that section and recompile to see if the error persists. This can help narrow down the problem area.

+ **Binary search:** If you have a large XeLaTeX document and are unsure where the error is occurring, employ a binary search approach. Comment out half of the document, then progressively uncomment sections until the error reappears. Repeat this process until you isolate the problematic portion of the document.

+ **Use a debugger:** Although XeLaTeX does not have a built-in debugger, you can use external tools like the *latexmk* utility or integrated development environments (IDEs) with debugging capabilities (e.g., *TeXstudio*) to step through your XeLaTeX document and examine variables and their values.

Debugging requires patience and a systematic approach. By utilizing these techniques, you can effectively identify and resolve issues in your XeLaTeX document.

4. Automated testing

Automating tests can greatly enhance the reliability and efficiency of your XeLaTeX document development process. Automated testing frameworks allow you to define tests as code and execute them automatically, reducing the time and effort required for manual testing.

Here are some popular testing frameworks for XeLaTeX:

+ **Arara:** Arara is a rule-based automation tool for XeLaTeX. It allows you to define custom rules for compiling, cleaning, and testing your XeLaTeX documents. Arara has a wide range of built-in rules and supports the creation of custom ones.

+ **latexrun:** Latexrun is a command-line tool that automates the entire XeLaTeX document build process, including dependency tracking, compilation, and testing. It provides a simple and intuitive interface for running tests and examining log files.

+ **pylatexenc:** Pylatexenc is a Python library that provides a wide range of utilities for working with XeLaTeX documents. It includes functions for parsing and manipulating LaTeX code, as well as tools for automatic compilation and testing.

By integrating automated testing into your workflow, you can catch errors early, ensure consistent and reproducible results, and validate the correctness of your XeLaTeX documents automatically.

5. Document analysis tools

Document analysis tools can help detect potential issues and provide insights into the quality of your XeLaTeX document. These tools analyze your document's structure, syntax, and formatting, highlighting any potential errors or inconsistencies.

Here are some popular document analysis tools for XeLaTeX:

+ **lacheck:** Lacheck is a command-line tool that checks a XeLaTeX document for common errors and non-standard constructs. It provides recommendations to improve the document's quality and adherence to best practices.

+ **latexdiff:** Latexdiff is a Perl script that compares two versions of a XeLaTeX document and generates a marked-up diff file highlighting the changes. This is particularly useful for reviewing and debugging changes made during collaborative editing.

+ **chktex:** Chktex is a tool that analyzes LaTeX documents for common mistakes, such as unbalanced braces, incorrect use of math mode, and inconsistent formatting. It helps ensure your XeLaTeX document follows best practices and standards.

By incorporating document analysis tools into your testing and debugging process, you can improve the quality and consistency of your XeLaTeX documents.

6. Community resources and forums

When facing challenging issues or seeking guidance, it is beneficial to turn to the XeLaTeX community for support. Online forums, mailing lists, and dedicated discussion platforms are valuable resources for sharing experiences, seeking advice, and finding solutions to common problems.

Here are some popular community resources for XeLaTeX:

+ **TeX Stack Exchange:** TeX Stack Exchange is a question-and-answer site dedicated to all things related to TeX and its derivatives, including XeLaTeX. It has a vast community of experienced users and experts who can help with specific issues or provide general advice.

+ **XeTeX Mailing List:** The XeTeX Mailing List is an email-based discussion forum where users can ask questions, share tips and tricks, and discuss XeLaTeX-related topics with other members of the community.

+ **GitHub repositories and issue trackers:** Many XeLaTeX packages and projects are hosted on GitHub, which provides an issue tracking system. By checking the repositories and issue trackers, you can find solutions to common problems and report any issues you encounter.

Leveraging community resources not only allows you to seek help when needed but also exposes you to different perspectives and techniques, expanding your knowledge and understanding of XeLaTeX.

Conclusion

Testing and debugging are essential steps in ensuring the reliability and quality of your XeLaTeX documents. By following a clear testing strategy, utilizing version control systems, employing effective debugging techniques, automating testing, using document analysis tools, and seeking support from community resources, you can minimize errors, validate the correctness of your documents, and produce high-quality XeLaTeX output.

Remember, effective testing and debugging are iterative processes. Continuously refining your approach and learning from previous experiences will lead to more efficient and reliable XeLaTeX document development.

XeLaTeX Performance Optimization and Scalability

Introduction to Performance Optimization and Scalability in XeLaTeX

In this section, we will explore the various techniques and best practices for optimizing the performance and scalability of your XeLaTeX documents. As your documents grow in complexity and size, it is important to ensure that they compile efficiently and are able to handle the increased demands of processing and rendering. We will discuss strategies for improving compilation time, reducing memory usage, optimizing layout and typesetting, and utilizing parallel processing capabilities.

Importance of Performance Optimization and Scalability in XeLaTeX

Performance optimization and scalability are crucial considerations when working with XeLaTeX, especially for large and complex documents. As the size of your documents increases, so does the time required for compilation and rendering. And as the complexity of your layout and typesetting increases, the demands on system resources also increase. Poorly optimized documents can lead to slow compilation times, high memory usage, and even system crashes.

Optimizing the performance of your XeLaTeX documents not only improves your workflow efficiency but also enhances the overall user experience. Faster compilation times allow for quicker iterations and reduce waiting times. Additionally, by reducing memory usage and optimizing layout and typesetting, you can ensure smooth rendering of your documents, providing a seamless reading experience for your audience.

Improving Compilation Time

Compilation time is one of the key factors in document development. Waiting for a lengthy compilation can significantly slow down your workflow and hinder productivity. Here are some techniques to improve compilation time in XeLaTeX:

- **Use selective compilation:** Rather than recompiling the entire document every time, selectively compile only the portions that have changed. You can split your document into smaller files and use the \include or \input commands to include them selectively. This way, you only need to compile the modified files, saving compilation time.

- **Enable offloading:** Offloading is a technique that allows the compilation to utilize multiple processor cores. By default, XeLaTeX uses a single core for compilation. However, you can enable offloading to make use of all available cores, significantly reducing compilation time. To enable offloading, use the --fmt=xetex-dev command when running XeLaTeX.

- **Cache font files:** XeLaTeX has to load font files during compilation, which can be time-consuming, especially for documents with a large number of fonts. To speed up compilation, you can cache the font files so that they are not loaded again in subsequent compilations. Use the cache_feats package to cache font files and enable faster compilation.

- **Optimize included graphics:** If your document includes graphics, make sure they are optimized for performance. Use graphics formats that are efficient and compressed, such as PNG or JPEG. Avoid using uncompressed formats like BMP or TIFF. Additionally, reduce the size of the graphics files by resizing them to the required dimensions before including them in your document.

These techniques will help reduce the compilation time of your XeLaTeX documents, improving your productivity and workflow efficiency.

Reducing Memory Usage and Footprint

As the complexity and size of your XeLaTeX documents increase, so does the memory usage and system resource requirements. Large documents with complex layouts can quickly consume a significant amount of memory, leading to slowdowns and crashes. Here are some strategies to reduce memory usage and optimize resource consumption:

- **Use efficient document class options:** When selecting a document class, consider options that optimize memory usage. Some document classes, such as `article` or `scrartcl`, are lightweight and consume less memory compared to more complex classes like `book` or `memoir`.

- **Limit nested environments:** Avoid excessive nesting of environments, as each nesting level adds to the memory footprint. Instead, try to simplify your document structure and use fewer nesting levels.

- **Avoid excessive packages and libraries:** While packages and libraries can enhance the functionality of your documents, they also increase memory usage. Be selective in choosing the packages and libraries you include and avoid loading unnecessary ones. Additionally, consider using lightweight alternatives whenever possible.

- **Use external document compilation:** For large documents, you can offload the compilation process to an external program, such as `latexmk` or `arara`. These tools automatically manage multiple compilations, dependencies, and compilation order, optimizing resource usage and improving efficiency.

By implementing these strategies, you can significantly reduce memory usage and optimize the overall resource footprint of your XeLaTeX documents.

Optimizing Layout and Typesetting

The layout and typesetting of your XeLaTeX documents can impact both performance and readability. Poorly optimized layout and typesetting can lead to slower rendering and decreased readability. Here are some tips to optimize layout and typesetting:

- **Avoid excessive floats and tables:** Excessive floats and tables can disrupt the flow of your document and affect performance. Minimize the use of floats, particularly if they contain heavy content like images or complex graphics.

Instead, consider using in-line images or find alternative ways to present the information.

+ **Fine-tune line spacing and paragraph formatting:** Proper line spacing and paragraph formatting can improve readability and reduce the overall length of your document. Use the appropriate commands to adjust line spacing, indentation, and spacing between paragraphs.

+ **Eliminate redundant and obsolete packages:** Over time, packages and commands can become deprecated or redundant. Regularly review and update your document to remove any unnecessary packages, commands, or customizations. This will not only improve performance but also ensure compatibility with future versions of XeLaTeX.

By optimizing the layout and typesetting of your XeLaTeX documents, you can enhance both performance and readability, providing a smoother reading experience for your audience.

Utilizing Parallel Processing and Multi-threading

With the increasing availability of multi-core processors, it is possible to harness parallel processing and multi-threading capabilities to improve the performance of your XeLaTeX documents. Here are some techniques to take advantage of parallel processing:

+ **Enable multi-threading:** By default, XeLaTeX uses a single thread for compilation. However, you can enable multi-threading by using the `--threads` option followed by the number of threads you want to utilize. For example, `xelatex --threads=4 myfile.tex` will enable four threads for compilation.

+ **Distribute compilation:** If you have access to a distributed computing environment or a cluster, you can distribute the compilation of your XeLaTeX documents across multiple machines. This can significantly reduce the compilation time for large and complex documents.

+ **Use build systems and automation tools:** Build systems and automation tools, such as make, can help automate the compilation process and utilize parallel processing capabilities. These tools can automatically distribute the compilation of different parts of your document to make efficient use of available resources.

By utilizing parallel processing and multi-threading techniques, you can maximize the performance of your XeLaTeX documents and reduce the overall compilation time.

Conclusion

In this section, we discussed the importance of performance optimization and scalability in XeLaTeX. We explored techniques for improving compilation time, reducing memory usage, optimizing layout and typesetting, and utilizing parallel processing capabilities. By implementing these strategies, you can significantly enhance the performance and scalability of your XeLaTeX documents, improving your workflow efficiency and providing a better user experience. Remember to experiment with different techniques and configurations to find the optimal balance between performance and functionality for your specific use cases.

Improving Compilation Time for Large and Complex XeLaTeX Documents

In this section, we will explore various techniques and strategies to improve the compilation time for large and complex XeLaTeX documents. As our documents grow in size and complexity, the compilation time can significantly increase, causing inconvenience and delays. It becomes crucial to optimize the compilation process and make it more efficient. We will discuss different approaches, settings, and tools to achieve faster compilation times without compromising the quality of the output.

Understanding Compilation Time

Before diving into optimization techniques, let us first understand the factors that contribute to the compilation time of a XeLaTeX document. XeLaTeX performs multiple tasks during the compilation process, including parsing the input file, executing macros, resolving cross-references, typesetting text and equations, and generating the final output. Each of these tasks consumes time and resources. The overall compilation time depends on several factors, such as:

- Document size: The larger the document, the longer it takes to process.

- Complexity: Documents with complex formatting, multiple citations, and cross-references take more time to compile.

+ Document structure: The number and complexity of sections, subsections, and other structural elements affect the compilation time.

+ Packages and libraries: Certain packages and libraries introduce additional processing time.

+ Custom macros: The use of custom macros and commands can impact compilation time, especially if they are computationally expensive.

+ Font loading: If you are using a large number of fonts or custom fonts, it can increase the compilation time.

Now that we have an understanding of the factors affecting compilation time, let's explore some techniques to optimize it.

Optimization Techniques

1. **Selective Compilation:** One approach to reduce compilation time is to selectively compile only the parts of the document that have changed. Using the `include` command, you can include different sections of your document in separate files and then include them in the main file as needed. This way, when you make changes to a specific section, you only need to compile that section, saving time on recompiling the entire document.

2. **Cache Compilation:** XeLaTeX allows you to cache the intermediate files generated during compilation. By enabling the cache, XeLaTeX can skip the processing of unchanged files, resulting in faster compilation times. The `latexmk` tool, which automates the compilation process, provides additional caching options, further improving compilation speed.

3. **Use Precompiled Preamble:** The preamble of a XeLaTeX document contains package and configuration settings. Precompiling the preamble can significantly reduce compilation time. To do this, create a separate document containing only the preamble and compile it once. Then, include the precompiled preamble in your main document using the `\input` command. This way, you avoid recompiling the preamble every time you compile the main document.

4. **Minimize Package Usage:** While packages are essential for extending the functionality of XeLaTeX, using too many packages can slow down compilation. Evaluate the necessity of each package you include and remove any unnecessary ones. Additionally, consider using lightweight alternatives or custom solutions for specific requirements instead of relying on heavy packages.

5. **Avoid Excessive Cross-References:** Cross-references, such as those created using `\ref` or `\cite` commands, require additional processing during

compilation. Limit the use of cross-references, especially in large documents with multiple sections and figures. Similarly, avoid excessive bibliographic citations as they can impact compilation time.

6. **Use Efficient Fonts:** Certain fonts take longer to load and process in XeLaTeX. Consider using efficient fonts with optimized outlines to reduce compilation time. Font formats like OpenType and TrueType are generally faster to process compared to Type 1 fonts.

7. **Parallel Compilation:** If you have a multi-core processor, you can speed up compilation by enabling parallel compilation. Tools like `latexmk` support parallel processing, allowing multiple compilation tasks to run simultaneously, thereby utilizing the available CPU resources more efficiently.

Case Study: Optimizing Compilation Time for a Research Paper

Let's consider a scenario where you are writing a research paper using XeLaTeX. As the paper grows, the compilation time also increases. To optimize the compilation time, you can apply the following techniques:

1. Break the document into sections using the `include` command. Compile only the section you are working on, reducing unnecessary recompilation.

2. Utilize caching by enabling the cache option in XeLaTeX or by using tools like `latexmk`. This way, unchanged parts of the document can be skipped during subsequent compilations.

3. Create a precompiled preamble containing commonly used packages and configurations. Include the precompiled preamble in your main document.

4. Assess the necessity of each package used in the document and remove any unused packages. Opt for lightweight alternatives or custom solutions wherever possible.

5. Limit the use of cross-references and excessive citations, especially in large documents. Replace unnecessary cross-references with inline references where appropriate.

6. Choose fonts that are optimized for speed and processing efficiency. Consider using OpenType or TrueType fonts instead of Type 1 fonts.

7. If your system has multiple cores, enable parallel compilation using tools like `latexmk`. This allows for faster compilation by utilizing the available CPU resources effectively.

By implementing these techniques, you can significantly improve the compilation time of your research paper, allowing for a smoother and more efficient writing process.

Conclusion

Improving the compilation time for large and complex XeLaTeX documents is essential for a productive workflow. By understanding the factors affecting compilation time and implementing optimization techniques like selective compilation, caching, precompiled preamble, minimizing package usage, avoiding excessive cross-references, using efficient fonts, and enabling parallel compilation, you can achieve faster compilation times without compromising the quality of your documents. Experiment with these techniques and find the optimal combination that suits your specific document requirements and system capabilities.

Remember, while it is essential to optimize compilation time, do not sacrifice the readability, maintainability, and overall quality of your documents. It is a balance between efficiency and the desired output. Regularly review and update the optimization techniques as your document evolves to ensure an optimal compilation experience.

Reducing memory usage and footprint in XeLaTeX

Reducing memory usage and optimizing the footprint of XeLaTeX is crucial for efficient and optimal document processing. In this section, we will explore various techniques to achieve this objective.

Understanding memory usage in XeLaTeX

Before delving into the methods of reducing memory usage, it is essential to understand how XeLaTeX consumes memory during compilation. XeLaTeX uses a two-step process: parsing and execution.

During the parsing phase, XeLaTeX reads the source code and builds an internal representation of the document, known as the Abstract Syntax Tree (AST). This representation allows XeLaTeX to understand the structure and content of the document, including fonts, packages, and macros.

In the execution phase, XeLaTeX processes the AST and generates the formatted output document. This phase involves executing macros, expanding commands, and typesetting the content.

Both phases contribute to memory usage, but the execution phase typically consumes more memory due to the need to hold the document's content in memory and perform complex typesetting operations.

Optimizing memory usage in XeLaTeX

To optimize memory usage in XeLaTeX, we can employ several strategies:

+ **Load only necessary packages:** Every package loaded into XeLaTeX consumes memory. Therefore, it is crucial to only include the necessary packages for your document. Unused packages should be removed from the preamble to reduce memory footprint.

+ **Disable unnecessary features:** Some packages and document classes offer optional features that can be disabled if not required. For example, disabling features like line numbering or certain font styles can help reduce memory usage.

+ **Use lightweight fonts:** Fonts play a significant role in memory usage. Heavy or complex fonts can consume a considerable amount of memory. Using lightweight, simpler fonts can help reduce memory usage without compromising readability or aesthetics.

+ **Avoid excessive macros and nested environments:** Macros and environments can introduce additional memory overhead. Minimize the use of complex macros and avoid excessive nesting of environments to reduce memory usage.

+ **Limit document size and complexity:** Extremely large or complex documents may strain memory resources. Consider dividing large documents into smaller, manageable parts or optimizing the document structure to reduce memory usage.

+ **Use externalize for graphics:** If your document includes large and complex graphics, consider using the TikZ `externalize` library to compile the graphics into separate PDF files. This approach helps reduce memory usage during compilation.

+ **Adjust compiler settings:** XeLaTeX provides various compiler settings that can influence memory usage. Options like `--param-size`, `--stack-size`, and `--main-memory` can be adjusted to allocate more memory to XeLaTeX if it is available on your system.

+ **Close unnecessary file handles:** While processing the document, XeLaTeX opens and maintains file handles for various resources. Closing unnecessary file handles can free up memory resources.

* **Update XeLaTeX and packages:** Keeping your XeLaTeX distribution and packages up to date can provide performance improvements and bug fixes, optimizing memory usage in the process.

Examples and Best Practices

Let's consider a real-world example to illustrate the memory optimization techniques described above.

Suppose you are working on a large scientific document that includes numerous complex equations, diagrams, and high-resolution graphics. The document uses many packages, including multiple fonts and custom macros.

To optimize memory usage, you can start by analyzing the packages being used. Remove any unnecessary packages that are not contributing to the document's content. Consider using lighter fonts that still meet the document's typographic requirements.

Next, examine the macros and environments used in the document. Simplify or refactor complex macros and avoid excessive nesting of environments. This step can significantly reduce memory usage during the execution phase.

Furthermore, for graphics-heavy documents, utilize the TikZ `externalize` library to compile graphics into separate PDF files. This approach offloads memory usage during compilation, resulting in a more efficient process.

Lastly, periodically update your XeLaTeX distribution and packages to benefit from performance improvements and bug fixes. Developers often optimize memory usage and address memory-related issues in newer versions.

In conclusion, optimizing memory usage and reducing the footprint in XeLaTeX requires a thoughtful approach. By carefully selecting packages, fonts, and document structure, as well as leveraging additional techniques like graphics externalization, you can significantly enhance the performance and efficiency of your XeLaTeX projects.

Further Resources

To delve deeper into memory optimization and reducing the footprint in XeLaTeX, you may find the following resources helpful:

* *The LaTeX Companion* by Frank Mittelbach, Michel Goossens, and Johannes Braams.

* *Guide to LaTeX* by Helmut Kopka and Patrick W. Daly.

◆ XeLaTeX documentation and user forums for the latest updates and community support.

Remember, optimizing memory usage requires a balance between functionality, aesthetics, and performance. Start with the techniques discussed here and gradually refine your approach based on the specific requirements of your document.

Optimizing layout and typesetting for faster rendering in XeLaTeX

When working with XeLaTeX, ensuring efficient layout and typesetting can significantly improve the rendering speed of your documents. In this section, we will explore various techniques and best practices to optimize the layout and typesetting process, resulting in faster rendering times.

Understanding the Typesetting Process

Before we dive into optimization techniques, let's briefly review the typesetting process in XeLaTeX. When you compile a XeLaTeX document, it goes through several stages, including parsing the input file, processing macros, arranging the content on pages, and rendering the final output.

One important aspect of XeLaTeX's typesetting process is its reliance on the *line-breaking algorithm*. This algorithm determines how text is split into lines, optimizing factors such as line width, hyphenation, and justification. The line-breaking algorithm plays a significant role in the overall rendering time.

Now that we have a basic understanding of the typesetting process, let's explore specific techniques to optimize the layout and typesetting.

Optimizing Line Breaking

The line-breaking algorithm in XeLaTeX can be computationally expensive, especially when handling large documents or complex layouts. Here are some tips to optimize line breaking and improve rendering speed:

label=◆ **Adjusting word spacing:** In certain cases, adjusting the word spacing can improve the line-breaking algorithm's performance. Experiment with slight adjustments to the \tolerance and \emergencystretch parameters to find an optimal balance between line breaking quality and rendering speed.

label=◆ **Using hyphenation sparingly:** Hyphenation adds complexity to the line-breaking algorithm. Minimize the use of explicit hyphenation commands (\-) and rely on automatic hyphenation for most cases. You can control hyphenation patterns using the `babel` package or the `\hyphenation` command.

label=+ **Optimizing paragraph justification:** Justifying text requires additional processing to determine appropriate line widths. Consider using ragged right alignment (`\raggedright`) for sections of your document where full justification is not necessary. This can speed up rendering, especially for documents with extensive text blocks.

label=+ **Breaking long paragraphs:** Extremely long paragraphs can significantly slow down the rendering process. Breaking them into smaller, more manageable paragraphs can reduce the computational load. Additionally, breaking paragraphs at logical points in the content can improve overall readability.

By implementing these optimization techniques, you can enhance the performance of the line-breaking algorithm and speed up the typesetting process in XeLaTeX.

Streamlining Macro Usage

Macros play a crucial role in document formatting and customization in XeLaTeX. However, excessive or inefficient use of macros can impact rendering speed. Here are some strategies to streamline macro usage and optimize performance:

label=+ **Minimizing nested macros:** Avoid excessive nesting of macros, as each level adds to the overall processing time. Instead, try to simplify your macro structure and use more straightforward constructs when possible.

label=+ **Reducing macro expansions:** Excessive macro expansions can slow down rendering. Limit the number of times macros are expanded and optimize your code to minimize unnecessary expansions. For example, consider using conditional statements (`\if... \fi`) to prevent redundant macro expansions.

label=+ **Caching macro results:** If you have computationally expensive macros that produce the same output multiple times, consider caching the results. By storing the result of a macro in a variable and reusing it when needed, you can eliminate unnecessary recalculations and improve rendering speed.

These strategies will help optimize macro usage and reduce the computational overhead, resulting in faster rendering times for your XeLaTeX documents.

Reducing Package Overhead

While XeLaTeX offers a wide range of packages and libraries to enhance document formatting and customization, using too many packages can impact rendering speed. Here are some tips to minimize package overhead:

label=♦ **Only load necessary packages:** Load packages only if you truly need their functionality. Unused packages not only introduce unnecessary overhead but can also lead to potential conflicts and compatibility issues. Only include the packages that are essential to your document.

label=♦ **Avoid redundant or conflicting packages:** Be mindful of package redundancy and conflicts. Loading multiple packages with overlapping functionality can bloat the document and slow down rendering. Regularly review your package dependencies and ensure they are optimized for speed.

label=♦ **Consider lightweight alternatives:** When possible, explore lightweight alternatives to heavyweight packages. Lightweight packages often offer similar functionality with reduced computational overhead. For example, consider using the `microtype` package instead of more heavyweight font optimization packages.

By optimizing package usage and reducing unnecessary overhead, you can improve rendering performance in XeLaTeX.

Utilizing Compilation Techniques

Beyond optimizing layout and typesetting, you can leverage various compilation techniques to achieve faster rendering times. Here are a few strategies to consider:

label=♦ **Selective compilation:** If your document consists of separate chapters or sections, you can speed up the rendering process by selectively compiling the portions you are currently working on. Tools like `latexmk` allow for efficient partial compilation, reducing the processing time for large documents.

label=♦ **Precompiling frequently used resources:** XeLaTeX allows you to precompile frequently used resources such as fonts or graphics. By precompiling these resources, you can reduce the rendering time for subsequent compilations.

label=◆ **Parallel compilation:** Take advantage of multi-core CPUs by running parallel compilations. Tools like `latexmk` and `arara` support parallel compilation, allowing you to distribute the computational load across multiple CPU cores and reduce overall rendering time.

By utilizing these compilation techniques, you can maximize the performance of XeLaTeX and achieve faster rendering times.

Example Scenario: Optimizing a Large Technical Document

Let's consider an example scenario where you have a large technical document with extensive mathematical equations and figures. The document takes a significant amount of time to render, impacting your productivity. To optimize the layout and typesetting for faster rendering in XeLaTeX, you can employ the following strategies:

1. Split long equations into smaller, more manageable ones, improving both rendering speed and readability.

2. Review the usage of macros and minimize nested macros to reduce computational overhead.

3. Optimize package usage by eliminating redundancies and choosing lightweight alternatives when possible.

4. Leverage selective compilation to focus on specific sections of the document during development, reducing overall rendering time.

By implementing these strategies, you can significantly improve the rendering speed of your large technical document in XeLaTeX.

Resources and Further Reading

To further explore optimization techniques in XeLaTeX, consider the following resources:

abel=◆ *The LaTeX Companion* by Frank Mittelbach et al.: This comprehensive guide covers advanced topics in LaTeX, including optimization techniques for layout and typesetting.

label=✦ *TeX, XML, and Digital Typography: International Conference on TEX, XML, and Digital Typography, Proceedings* edited by Jerome Laurence et al.: This collection of papers discusses various aspects of digital typography and includes optimization strategies for TeX-based systems.

label=✦ Online resources such as the TeX Stack Exchange (https://tex.stackexchange.com/) and the LaTeX Community Forum (https://latex.org/forum/) provide a wealth of knowledge and user experiences on optimizing layout and typesetting in XeLaTeX.

Remember, optimization is a continuous process. Experiment with different techniques, measure their impact, and adjust accordingly to achieve the best rendering performance in XeLaTeX.

Exercises

1. Identify potential areas in your own document where line breaking can be optimized. Experiment with different approaches and measure the impact on rendering speed.

2. Review the macro usage in one of your XeLaTeX documents. Identify any instances of excessive nesting or redundant expansions and simplify the code.

3. Analyze the package dependencies in your current XeLaTeX project. Determine if any redundant or conflicting packages can be eliminated to improve rendering performance.

4. Implement selective compilation for a large document consisting of separate chapters. Measure the rendering time using selective compilation versus compiling the entire document.

5. Explore parallel compilation using tools like `latexmk` or `arara` for one of your XeLaTeX projects. Compare the rendering time with and without parallel compilation.

Remember to track your observations and document your findings for future reference.

In this section, we explored various techniques for optimizing layout and typesetting in XeLaTeX to achieve faster rendering times. We discussed strategies for optimizing line breaking, streamlining macro usage, reducing package overhead, utilizing compilation techniques, and provided a real-world example scenario. By implementing these optimization techniques and staying mindful of best practices, you can significantly improve the performance of your XeLaTeX documents.

Don't forget to experiment, measure the impact, and adapt your approach to achieve the best results for your specific use cases. Happy typesetting!

Parallel and distributed compilation of XeLaTeX projects

Parallel and distributed computing refers to the use of multiple computers or processors to solve a computational problem. In the context of XeLaTeX, parallel and distributed compilation can help improve the efficiency and speed of document processing, especially for large and complex projects.

The need for parallel and distributed compilation

When working with XeLaTeX, especially on projects that involve numerous packages, complex document structures, and extensive bibliographies, compilation times can become a bottleneck. As the size and complexity of a project increase, the compilation time may also increase, resulting in longer turnaround times for document changes or updates.

Parallel and distributed compilation addresses this issue by utilizing multiple computing resources to process a document simultaneously. By distributing the workload across multiple processors or computers, the overall compilation time can be significantly reduced, leading to improved productivity and faster iteration cycles.

Parallel compilation with XeLaTeX

Parallel compilation with XeLaTeX involves breaking down the document into smaller independent parts and compiling them concurrently. This approach is suitable for projects where individual chapters, sections, or other document elements can be compiled independently without requiring information from other parts.

To enable parallel compilation in XeLaTeX, you can make use of the `parallel` package. This package provides the `parallel` environment, which allows you to split the document into multiple sections that can be compiled in parallel. Each section within the `parallel` environment will be compiled separately, utilizing the available computing resources.

Here's an example of how to use the `parallel` package:

```
\begin{parallel}{0.5\textwidth}{0.5\textwidth}
  \ParallelLText{
    % Left column content
    % ...
  }
  \ParallelRText{
    % Right column content
    % ...
  }
\end{parallel}
```

In this example, the document is split into two columns using the `parallel` environment. The `ParallelLText` command is used to define the content of the left column, while the `ParallelRText` command is used for the content of the right column. Each column can contain a separate section, chapter, or any other independent document element.

By compiling the document with multiple instances of XeLaTeX running in parallel, each instance can process a separate column, leading to faster compilation times.

It's important to note that parallel compilation can introduce some overhead due to the coordination required between the different instances of XeLaTeX. Therefore, the gains in compilation time may vary depending on the specific document and computing resources available.

Distributed compilation with XeLaTeX

Distributed compilation takes parallel compilation a step further by distributing the workload across multiple computers or processors. This approach is particularly useful for very large documents or when there's a need to accelerate compilation times significantly.

To enable distributed compilation with XeLaTeX, you can use tools such as `latexmk` or `arara`, which support distributed compilation out of the box. These tools allow you to define compilation tasks that can be executed on different machines in a network.

Here's an example of how to use `latexmk` for distributed compilation:

```
latexmk -pdf -pvc -jobserver=//hostname/jobname document.tex
```

In this example, the -jobserver option specifies the hostname and jobname of the machine that will handle the distributed compilation tasks. By running this command on multiple machines in the network, each machine can contribute to the compilation process, effectively distributing the workload.

It's worth mentioning that distributed compilation requires careful setup and coordination to ensure that dependencies, such as packages and resources, are properly synchronized across the machines. Additionally, network latency and available bandwidth can affect the overall performance and scalability of distributed compilation.

Best practices for parallel and distributed compilation

When using parallel and distributed compilation with XeLaTeX, there are some best practices to consider:

+ Before enabling parallel or distributed compilation, profile the document compilation time to identify the most time-consuming sections. Focusing on optimizing these sections can yield the most significant improvements.

+ Make sure your document structure allows for independent compilation of sections. This will enable effective parallelization and distribution of the workload.

+ Regularly monitor and analyze the performance of your parallel and distributed compilation setup. This will help identify potential bottlenecks, resource utilization, and overall system efficiency.

+ Take advantage of modern computing technologies, such as multi-core processors and high-speed networks, to maximize the benefits of parallel and distributed compilation.

Overall, parallel and distributed compilation techniques can help accelerate the processing of large and complex XeLaTeX projects. By leveraging the available computing resources effectively, you can reduce compilation times and improve the overall productivity of document development and publication.

Summary

In this section, we explored the concept of parallel and distributed compilation in the context of XeLaTeX. We discussed the need for these techniques and how they can help improve compilation times for large and complex projects. We also covered parallel compilation using the `parallel` package and distributed compilation with tools like `latexmk`. Finally, we provided some best practices for implementing parallel and distributed compilation effectively. By utilizing these techniques, you can optimize the workflow and efficiency of XeLaTeX document processing.

Caching and Precompiling Resources for Faster XeLaTeX Builds

In this section, we will explore techniques for improving the compilation time of XeLaTeX documents by leveraging caching and precompiling of resources. Compiling large and complex XeLaTeX documents can be time-consuming, especially when multiple runs are required to resolve dependencies and generate all the required output. Caching and precompiling can help reduce this compilation time significantly.

Understanding Caching in XeLaTeX

Caching involves storing previously compiled resources, such as fonts, images, and document sections, so that they can be reused in subsequent builds without the need for recompilation. By caching these resources, XeLaTeX can skip certain time-consuming processes, leading to faster build times.

There are several types of cache utilized by XeLaTeX:

1. **Font Caching:** XeLaTeX supports automatic font caching using system-level font caches. These caches store previously processed font data, such as font metrics and glyph outlines, providing faster access to fonts during compilation. Font caching can significantly speed up document processing when using complex or large font files.

2. **Package Caching:** Many LaTeX packages are often used across multiple documents. By caching package files, the compilation time can be reduced for subsequent builds of documents that use the same packages. Package caching is especially useful when working on collaborative projects where multiple team members are using the same set of packages.

3. **Bibliographic Database Caching:** When using bibliographic databases, such as BibTeX or BibLaTeX, caching the database file can speed up compilation. By storing the processed bibliographic information, subsequent builds can skip the time-consuming process of parsing and formatting the entire bibliography.

4. **Precompiled Document Sections:**   Precompiling specific document sections, such as large tables or complicated equations, can save valuable time in subsequent builds. Precompiling these sections involves saving the processed output and inserting it into the final document during compilation. This technique is particularly useful for documents with static or rarely changing sections.

Implementing Caching Techniques in XeLaTeX

Now that we have a clear understanding of the different types of caching, let's explore how to implement these techniques in XeLaTeX.

Font Caching: XeLaTeX utilizes system-level font caches to automatically cache fonts during compilation. This caching mechanism operates at the operating system level, and no specific actions are required from the user. However, it is important to ensure that the system-level font cache is properly configured and up to date for optimal performance.

Package Caching: XeLaTeX provides options for caching packages to speed up compilation.   One popular tool is the `snapshot` package, which allows for snapshotting the entire TeX installation, including all packages and document files. This snapshot can then be used as a basis for subsequent builds, significantly reducing compilation time. To use the `snapshot` package, insert the following code at the beginning of your document:

```
\RequirePackage{snapshot}
```

Bibliographic Database Caching: Bibliographic databases, such as BibTeX or BibLaTeX, can be cached using the `biber` tool. By adding the `--cache` option to the `biber` command, the processed bibliographic data will be saved in a cache file, avoiding the need for reprocessing during subsequent builds. For example:

```
biber --cache <your-file>
```

Precompiled Document Sections: Precompiling document sections involves saving the processed output and including it in subsequent builds. This technique can be particularly useful for large tables, complex equations, or other sections that rarely change. One approach is to save the precompiled section as a separate PDF file and include it in the main document using the `pdfpages` package. To precompile a section, you can use the `standalone` class and compile it as a separate document:

```
% additional packages and settings


% content of the section
```

Once the section is precompiled, it can be included in the main document using the `includepdf` command:

```
% other packages and settings


% main document content
\includepdf{precompiled_section.pdf}
% additional content
```

Best Practices and Caveats

While caching and precompiling can significantly improve XeLaTeX build times, there are a few best practices and caveats to consider:

- Regularly update system-level font caches to ensure optimal performance.

- Keep track of package versions and update them as needed to avoid potential compatibility issues when using package caching.

- When caching bibliographic databases, be mindful of updates to the database and reprocess it if necessary.

- Use precompiled sections sparingly and only for static or rarely changing content. Ensure that any changes to the precompiled sections are reflected in subsequent builds.

- Test the caching and precompiling techniques on a representative sample of the document to ensure that the output remains consistent and error-free.

By leveraging caching and precompiling techniques, you can significantly reduce compilation time in XeLaTeX, making it more efficient for large and complex documents.

Summary

In this section, we explored the concept of caching and precompiling resources to improve the compilation time of XeLaTeX documents. We discussed different types of cache, including font caching, package caching, bibliographic database caching, and precompiled document sections. We also provided implementation details and best practices for each caching technique. By utilizing these techniques, you can optimize the build process of your documents and save valuable time during development.

Optimizing font rendering and text processing in XeLaTeX

When it comes to typesetting documents in XeLaTeX, optimizing font rendering and text processing is crucial for achieving optimal performance and high-quality results. In this section, we will explore various techniques and best practices to optimize the font rendering process and enhance text processing in XeLaTeX.

Understanding font rendering in XeLaTeX

Font rendering plays a vital role in determining the visual appearance of text in XeLaTeX documents. It involves converting the abstract representation of characters into visual glyphs on the output device, such as a screen or printer. XeLaTeX leverages the underlying font handling capabilities of the operating system to perform font rendering.

By default, XeLaTeX uses the OpenType font format, which provides extensive typographic features and support for multilingual typography. OpenType fonts contain instructions called hinting, which guide the rendering engine on how to align and adjust glyphs for optimal display on different output devices.

Choosing the right fonts

One of the key aspects of optimizing font rendering in XeLaTeX is selecting appropriate fonts for your document. While XeLaTeX offers extensive font support, it is essential to choose fonts that are well-optimized for rendering and have good support for the desired typographic features.

Here are some considerations when choosing fonts for optimal rendering in XeLaTeX:

+ **Hinting and rendering quality:** Fonts with well-designed hinting instructions can significantly improve rendering quality on different devices. Look for fonts that have been optimized for specific rendering scenarios, such as screen or print.

+ **OpenType features:** OpenType fonts provide a wide range of typographic features, including ligatures, small capitals, and contextual alternates. Ensure that the fonts you choose have the required features for your document and that they are correctly supported by XeLaTeX.

+ **Multilingual support:** If your document includes multiple languages or scripts, select fonts that have comprehensive support for the required scripts. Make sure that the font's OpenType tables are structured correctly to handle complex scripts, such as Arabic or Indic scripts.

+ **Font file size:** Consider the file size of the fonts you choose, especially if you are creating web or mobile publications. Large font files can impact the performance of your document, so opt for fonts that strike a balance between quality and file size.

It is worth noting that XeLaTeX also supports system fonts installed on your operating system. This allows you to leverage high-quality fonts available on your system without the need to install additional fonts.

Optimizing font loading and caching

Efficient font loading and caching can significantly improve the rendering performance of XeLaTeX documents. XeLaTeX utilizes fontspec package for font handling, which provides various options for optimizing font loading.

Here are some techniques to optimize font loading in XeLaTeX:

+ **Selective font loading:** If your document uses multiple fonts, consider loading only the necessary fonts to reduce the overall font processing overhead. Use the `fontspec` package's `Path` or `UprightFont` options to selectively load specific font files.

+ **Font caching:** Caching font files can significantly improve the compilation speed of XeLaTeX documents. By default, XeLaTeX caches fonts during the compilation process. However, you can further optimize font caching by specifying a custom font cache directory using the `fontspec` package's `CachePath` option.

- **Automatic font feature detection:** OpenType fonts can have numerous typographic features, such as ligatures, swashes, and stylistic alternates. Enabling all these features by default can impact performance. Instead, selectively enable required font features using the `fontspec` package's `RawFeature` option.

Improving text processing performance

Besides font rendering, optimizing text processing performance is essential to ensure smooth compilation and processing of XeLaTeX documents. Here are some techniques to enhance text processing speed:

- **Efficient macro usage:** Macros are an integral part of XeLaTeX documents, allowing for flexible and reusable code. However, excessive and inefficient macro usage can impact compilation time. Make sure to optimize and streamline your macros, eliminating unnecessary complexity and redundancy.

- **Package selection:** XeLaTeX offers a wide range of packages for various purposes. However, loading too many packages can reduce compilation speed. Only include the necessary packages in your document and avoid packages with known performance issues.

- **Document structure optimization:** Well-structured documents can improve compilation time and simplify document maintenance. Splitting large documents into separate files and using appropriate `input` and `include` commands can enhance modularity and compilation speed.

- **Selective recompilation:** XeLaTeX provides the option to selectively recompile parts of your document using the `includeonly` command. This can save significant compilation time when working with large documents or specific sections that require frequent modifications.

Best practices and additional resources

When optimizing font rendering and text processing in XeLaTeX, keep the following best practices in mind:

+ Regularly update your TeX distribution and packages to benefit from performance improvements and bug fixes.

+ Profile and measure the compilation time of your document using tools like time or arara to identify bottlenecks and areas for optimization.

+ Consult the documentation and user forums of specific packages or fonts for additional optimization tips and known issues.

For further exploration and advanced techniques in XeLaTeX font rendering and text processing, refer to the following resources:

+ **The XeTeX Reference Guide:** A comprehensive guide to the features and capabilities of XeTeX, providing detailed information on font loading, font selection, and text processing techniques.

+ **The LaTeX Font Catalogue:** An online resource that showcases a wide range of fonts available for use with LaTeX and XeLaTeX, with information on font features and usage guidelines.

+ **TeX Stack Exchange:** An online community for TeX users where you can seek guidance, ask questions, and learn from experts in the field. Search for relevant tags such as "XeLaTeX" and "fontspec" for specific queries.

Optimizing font rendering and text processing in XeLaTeX requires careful consideration of font selection, loading and caching techniques, as well as efficient macro usage and document structure optimization. Adhering to best practices and exploring available resources will help you achieve optimal performance and professional-quality typography in your XeLaTeX documents.

Now it's time to put your knowledge into practice! Try optimizing the font rendering and text processing in your own XeLaTeX projects and experiment with different techniques to achieve the best results. Happy typesetting!

Utilizing multi-threading and multi-core CPUs in XeLaTeX

In this section, we will explore how to take advantage of multi-threading and multi-core CPUs to optimize the performance of XeLaTeX. Multi-threading allows multiple threads of execution to run concurrently, while multi-core CPUs provide the hardware necessary to execute these threads simultaneously. By harnessing the power of multi-threading and multi-core CPUs, we can significantly speed up the compilation process and improve overall efficiency.

Background

XeLaTeX is a single-threaded application by default, which means it utilizes only one core of the CPU. This can be a bottleneck, especially when dealing with large documents or computationally intensive tasks. Luckily, there are techniques available to enable multi-threading in XeLaTeX, allowing it to make use of multiple cores simultaneously and speeding up the compilation process.

Enabling multi-threading in XeLaTeX

To enable multi-threading in XeLaTeX, we need to use the `--shell-escape` command-line option. This option enables XeLaTeX to execute external commands, including those that can leverage multi-threading. We can include the option by modifying the compilation command as follows:

```
xelatex\index{xelatex}\index{xelatex} --shell-escape\index{escape}
```

After enabling `--shell-escape`, we can utilize external tools and techniques to distribute the processing load across multiple cores.

Distributing the processing load

There are several methods available for distributing the processing load of XeLaTeX across multiple cores. One popular approach is to use the `arara` automation tool, which provides a way to define compilation directives in the document itself.

To use `arara`, we first need to install it and set it up as a preprocessor for our XeLaTeX documents. Once installed, we can define compilation directives in the document using a specially formatted comment, specifying the number of threads we want to allocate.

For example, let's say we want to allocate four threads for our document. We can add the following comment at the beginning of our source file:

```
% arara: xelatex: { options: ["-8", ``--shell-escape", ``-interact
```

With this directive, `arara` will automatically execute XeLaTeX with the specified options, including the number of threads to allocate.

Parallel package

Another option for multi-threading in XeLaTeX is to use the `parallel` package. The `parallel` package provides a simple way to parallelize certain parts of the document, distributing the workload across multiple cores.

To use the `parallel` package, we need to include it in our document preamble:

Once included, we can use the `Parallel` environment to parallelize certain sections of the document. This environment divides the content into columns, which can be executed in parallel.

For example, let's say we have a section of code that can be split into four parallel tasks. We can use the `Parallel` environment as follows:

```
\begin{Parallel}{0.25\textwidth}{0.75\textwidth}
\ParallelLText{Task 1}
\ParallelRText{Task 2}
\ParallelLText{Task 3}
\ParallelRText{Task 4}
\end{Parallel}
```

In this example, the tasks will be distributed across multiple cores, significantly reducing the compilation time.

Best practices and considerations

While multi-threading can greatly improve the compilation time of XeLaTeX, there are some best practices and considerations to keep in mind:

- It is important to carefully select the number of threads to allocate. Allocating too many threads may cause contention and reduce performance.

- Not all parts of the compilation process can be parallelized. Some operations, such as font loading, are inherently single-threaded. It is essential to identify the parts that benefit most from parallelization.

- The effectiveness of multi-threading depends on the hardware and operating system. Different systems may have different capabilities and limitations.

+ It is recommended to test and benchmark the performance gains achieved by multi-threading. This can help identify the optimal number of threads and fine-tune the configuration.

+ Be aware that multi-threading can introduce concurrency issues, such as race conditions. It is important to write thread-safe code to avoid unexpected behavior.

+ Multi-threading may not always provide a linear speedup. Factors such as thread synchronization overhead and memory access patterns can affect the scalability of the application.

Conclusion

By utilizing multi-threading and multi-core CPUs, we can significantly improve the performance of XeLaTeX. Enabling multi-threading, distributing the processing load, and following best practices can result in faster compilation times and more efficient document generation. However, it is essential to consider the specific requirements of each document and to experiment with different configurations to achieve the best results. With these techniques, XeLaTeX becomes even more powerful for handling large and complex documents.

Deploying XeLaTeX applications for high-performance computing environments

In this section, we will explore how to deploy XeLaTeX applications in high-performance computing environments. High-performance computing (HPC) is an area of computing that focuses on providing powerful computing resources for demanding and computationally intensive tasks. By leveraging the capabilities of HPC systems, we can significantly speed up the compilation and processing of XeLaTeX documents.

Introduction to high-performance computing

High-performance computing involves the use of parallel processing techniques, high-speed networks, and a combination of hardware and software optimizations to achieve superior performance compared to conventional computing systems. HPC systems are typically used in scientific and research fields where large-scale simulations, data analysis, and complex computations are required.

Benefits of deploying XeLaTeX in HPC environments

Deploying XeLaTeX applications in HPC environments offers several benefits. Firstly, HPC systems are equipped with powerful processors and high-performance memory, allowing for faster compilation and rendering of documents. This results in reduced processing time, especially for large and complex documents.

Secondly, HPC systems often provide the capability for parallel processing, allowing multiple tasks to be executed simultaneously. With a proper implementation, this can be leveraged to distribute the workload across multiple computing nodes, further reducing the processing time for XeLaTeX applications.

Lastly, HPC systems are designed to handle large datasets efficiently. This is particularly useful when working with documents that contain a significant amount of graphical content, such as figures, diagrams, and illustrations. The efficient handling of data in HPC environments ensures smooth rendering and compilation of complex documents.

Optimizing XeLaTeX for HPC environments

To take full advantage of the capabilities offered by HPC environments, it is important to optimize the setup of XeLaTeX applications. Here are some optimization techniques to consider:

Parallel compilation   One way to speed up the compilation process is to utilize parallel compilation techniques. By breaking down the document into smaller parts, each part can be compiled simultaneously on different computing nodes. This can be achieved by using the "make" utility in conjunction with XeLaTeX. Each part of the document can be compiled independently, and then the final document can be assembled from the compiled parts.

Memory management   Proper memory management is crucial in HPC environments to avoid performance bottlenecks. It is important to ensure that enough memory is allocated for the compilation process to prevent swapping to disk, which can significantly degrade performance. Additionally, optimizing the memory usage in XeLaTeX by reducing unnecessary memory allocations can further enhance performance.

File system optimization   Efficient file system usage is essential for achieving high performance in HPC environments. It is recommended to use parallel file systems that allow concurrent access to files by multiple computing nodes. By utilizing a parallel file system, the I/O operations required during the compilation process can be performed more efficiently, reducing the overall processing time.

Load balancing To fully utilize the computational resources of HPC systems, it is important to implement load balancing techniques. Load balancing involves distributing the workload evenly across multiple computing nodes to ensure that each node is operating at maximum efficiency. Proper load balancing in XeLaTeX applications can effectively utilize the available processing power and minimize idle time, leading to faster document compilation.

Case study: Rendering complex mathematical equations in XeLaTeX

Let's consider a case study where we need to render a document containing complex mathematical equations in XeLaTeX. The document consists of multiple sections, each with equations requiring time-intensive processing.

To leverage the power of HPC systems, we can parallelize the compilation process by dividing the document into sections and assigning each section to a separate computing node. Each node can then compile its assigned section independently. Once all sections are compiled, they can be merged to create the final document.

Additionally, we can optimize the memory usage by preloading common packages and fonts into memory, reducing the need for frequent disk accesses. This can be achieved by utilizing the "preload" feature in XeLaTeX, which loads packages and fonts at the beginning of the compilation process.

Furthermore, we can implement load balancing techniques to ensure that each computing node is assigned an equal number of equations to process. This can be done by analyzing the complexity of each equation and assigning them dynamically based on the available computational resources.

By employing these optimization techniques, we can significantly reduce the processing time required to render complex mathematical equations in XeLaTeX, making it feasible to handle large-scale scientific and technical documents efficiently.

Conclusion

Deploying XeLaTeX applications in high-performance computing environments offers numerous benefits, including faster document compilation, efficient memory management, optimized file system usage, and load balancing. By taking advantage of the capabilities of HPC systems, we can significantly enhance the performance of XeLaTeX applications and handle computationally intensive tasks more effectively.

In this section, we explored various optimization techniques for deploying XeLaTeX in HPC environments. We also presented a case study on rendering complex mathematical equations using parallel compilation, memory management, and load balancing. By applying these techniques and customizing the setup to suit specific requirements, users can achieve high-performance document processing in XeLaTeX.

Best practices for performance optimization and scalability in XeLaTeX

In this section, we will explore some best practices for optimizing the performance and scalability of XeLaTeX. XeLaTeX is a powerful typesetting tool that can handle complex documents with ease. However, as the size and complexity of your documents increase, you may encounter performance issues that can slow down your compilation times. By following these best practices, you can optimize the performance of XeLaTeX and ensure scalability even with large and complex projects.

Minimizing package usage

One of the key factors that can impact the performance of XeLaTeX is the number of packages you include in your document. While packages provide additional functionality and features, they can also increase the compilation time significantly. Therefore, it is important to carefully consider the necessity of each package and only include those that are essential for your document. Additionally, try to avoid loading duplicate or conflicting packages, as they can introduce unwanted overhead and lead to compilation errors. Regularly review your package usage and remove any unused or unnecessary packages to improve the performance of your document.

Optimizing resource usage

XeLaTeX relies on system resources such as memory and processor power to compile documents. By optimizing the usage of these resources, you can improve the performance and scalability of your documents. One way to achieve this is by minimizing the usage of memory-intensive features, such as large images or complex mathematical equations. Instead, try to optimize the size and resolution of your images and simplify your equations whenever possible. Additionally, consider breaking down large documents into smaller, modular files and compile them separately, allowing XeLaTeX to use system resources more efficiently.

Caching and precompiling

To reduce compilation time, XeLaTeX provides caching and precompiling capabilities. By caching the results of previous compilations, XeLaTeX can skip processing unchanged parts of your document, resulting in faster compilation times for subsequent builds. Additionally, XeLaTeX allows you to precompile complex parts of your document, such as TikZ figures or bibliographies, into separate files. By precompiling these parts, you can significantly reduce the compilation time, especially when dealing with large and computationally intensive documents.

To enable caching in XeLaTeX, use the following command line option:

```
xelatex\index{xelatex}\index{xelatex} -recorder -shell-escape\inde
```

To precompile parts of your document, you can use the `\include` command to include precompiled files in your main document.

Efficient use of fonts

Fonts can have a significant impact on the performance and scalability of your XeLaTeX document. When selecting fonts, consider using system fonts or fonts that are optimized for XeLaTeX. System fonts are typically faster to load and render compared to externally loaded fonts. Additionally, try to limit the number of font switches within your document, as each switch requires additional processing time. By choosing a consistent font throughout your document, you can improve the overall performance and scalability of your XeLaTeX document.

Parallelization and distributed compilation

XeLaTeX supports parallelization and distributed compilation, allowing you to utilize multiple CPU cores or distribute the compilation process across multiple machines. By enabling parallelization, XeLaTeX can divide the workload and compile different parts of your document simultaneously, resulting in faster compilation times. Similarly, distributed compilation allows you to distribute the compilation process across multiple machines, further reducing the compilation time. To enable parallelization or distributed compilation, you can use the `--parallel` or `--mpi` options, respectively, when invoking XeLaTeX.

Profiling and optimization tools

There are various profiling and optimization tools available that can help you analyze the performance of your XeLaTeX document and identify bottlenecks. These tools can provide valuable insights into the resource usage, compilation time, and potential optimizations for your document. Some popular profiling and optimization tools for XeLaTeX include `latexmk`, `dvisvgm`, and `texdef`. By using these tools, you can identify areas of improvement and optimize your XeLaTeX document for better performance and scalability.

Limitations and trade-offs

While optimizing the performance and scalability of XeLaTeX is important, it is essential to understand the limitations and trade-offs involved. Some optimization techniques, such as minimizing package usage or simplifying complex equations, may affect the functionality or visual appearance of your document. It is crucial to find the right balance between performance and the desired output quality. Additionally, keep in mind that some optimizations may be specific to certain document structures or requirements, and may not apply universally. Experimentation and testing are key in finding the optimal performance configuration for your specific use case.

Summary

In this section, we explored best practices for optimizing the performance and scalability of XeLaTeX. By minimizing package usage, optimizing resource usage, caching and precompiling, efficiently using fonts, enabling parallelization and distributed compilation, utilizing profiling and optimization tools, and understanding the limitations and trade-offs, you can improve the performance and scalability of your XeLaTeX documents. Remember to regularly review and fine-tune the performance optimizations based on your specific document requirements. With these best practices, you can ensure smoother and faster XeLaTeX compilation for even the largest and most complex documents.

Index